ETHICAL EXPLORATIONS

Ethical Explorations

JOHN SKORUPSKI

OXFORD

UNIVERSITY PRESS

OXFORD

UNIVERSITY PRESS

Great Clarendon Street, Oxford OX2 6DP

Oxford University Press is a department of the University of Oxford.
It furthers the University's objective of excellence in research, scholarship,
and education by publishing worldwide in

Oxford New York

Athens Auckland Bangkok Bogotá Buenos Aires Calcutta
Cape Town Chennai Dar es Salaam Delhi Florence Hong Kong Istanbul
Karachi Kuala Lumpur Madrid Melbourne Mexico City Mumbai
Nairobi Paris São Paulo Singapore Taipei Tokyo Toronto Warsaw

and associated companies in Berlin Ibadan

Oxford is a registered trade mark of Oxford University Press
in the UK and certain other countries

Published in the United States
by Oxford University Press Inc., New York

British Library Cataloguing in Publication Data

Data available

Library of Congress Cataloging in Publication Data
Skorupski, John, 1946– .
Ethical explorations / John Skorupski.
Includes bibliographical references.
1. Ethics. 2. Liberalism—Moral and ethical aspects. I. Title.
BJ1012.S515 1999 170—dc21 99–32395
ISBN 0-19-823830-4

1 3 5 7 9 10 8 6 4 2

Typeset by Hope Services (Abingdon) Ltd.
Printed in Great Britain
on acid-free paper by
Biddles Ltd.
Guildford and King's Lynn

To Barbara, Julia, and Katie

*Freiheit zu geben durch Freiheit ist das
Grundgesetz dieses Reichs.*

*To bestow freedom by means of freedom
is the fundamental law of this kingdom.*

*(Friedrich Schiller, Twenty-Seventh Letter On the
Aesthetic Education of Man, §9)*

CONTENTS

Introduction

The outlines of ethics are neither clear nor distinct. Still, a comprehensive ethics could be expected to include an inquiry into ends of life and ideals of character and activity, and presumably an affirmation of some ends and ideals as the right or the better ones. At least this has always been a main incentive for ethical reflection. Morality must also be a main topic (including its connections to law). It is the most solid and definite shape within the ethical, even though it melts at the edges into the ends and ideals within which it is immersed. Yet, going by the ethical tradition, affirmation of specific moral duties and proposal of laws belongs more to moralists, jurists, and politicians than to moral philosophy. Since before Socrates moral philosophers have theorized about morality and law; they have also engaged in reflective criticism, often from the standpoint of some doctrine of ends or ideals. However, even those who think that morality could in principle be derived from some such doctrine, or from some other philosophical starting point, have in fact not usually engaged in extensive purported deductions of its detailed content.

This pattern is not surprising if one accepts that morality and law are not themselves a part of philosophy or continuous with it, in the way that ethical reflection undoubtedly is, but are more primitively and distinctly rooted systems, an object of study for philosophy rather than one of its products. Such an assumption is obviously not neutral. For example it rules out *strongly* rationalistic views of morality and law which would turn moral philosophy into a set of a priori deductions. Kantian ethics is the most ambitious and instructive effort in that direction. But even assuming such strongly rationalistic views are false, many questions still remain about the respective role of reason and the emotions in ethical life. Ends of life—the ultimately desirable, ideals—the ultimately admirable, and morality/law—that whose infraction is blameworthy, are the subject matter of ethics. The interpretation of those powerful, universally shaping forces in human life, *admiration*, *blame*, and *desire*, are thus inevitable topics for it; but there is still the question of how practical reason interacts with, or alternatively, issues from them. Do normative claims within the domain of ethics always or sometimes come from the emotions or is there something called 'pure practical reason' from which they can also independently come? How do they stand comparison, for example in respect of 'objectivity', to normative claims outside the ethical domain? Such questions lead into moral psychology and then very quickly into the general epistemology and metaphysics of the normative.

A collection of essays is not a systematic treatise. These essays do however range in various ways over the territory that has just been indicated, I hope with some decent amount of system and coherence of view. Roughly speaking, their sequence moves from the more abstract to the more concrete. Essays I–IV deal with questions about the logic, phenomenology, epistemology and metaphysics of normative claims, that is, of claims about reasons to think, feel, or do something. After this discussion of *reasons*, Essays V and VI turn to questions about the *good*. They consider the idea of impartially conceived good and its possible distributive structures, and the idea that the good, well-being, has higher and lower qualities as well as greater or lesser quantities or amounts. Then follow two essays, VII and VIII, on *morality*—what it is, how it is connected to freedom, and how its central category, that of blame, involves the human phenomena of recognition, expulsion, and atonement. The second of these, 'Freedom, Morality, and Recognition', makes a transition to the final four essays, IX–XII. These enter the domain of ideals. They are a mixture of analysis, advocacy, and social theory; variously defending, and exploring the historical and present condition, of the ethical ideal which in these essays I call 'classical liberalism'. I have in mind the form of philosophical liberalism which first developed in Europe in the decades around 1800. Many sources of liberal individualism are of course older, dating back to the early modern period and even earlier. But the origins of this particular humanistic ideal of the individual lie in the romantic hellenism of those revolutionary years. Its characteristic dialectic of enthusiasm and disenchantment is fundamental to the ethics of the modern West. Its vulgarization, or loss or failure (according to one's point of view), must be acknowledged as one of the most significant issues for moral philosophy today—irrespective of whether one would like to regenerate it or supply some inspiring alternative to it.

A few more words, then, about this sequence.

The epistemology which informs the essays takes, one may say, a cognitivist but not realist position about normative claims. That is, (i) it holds that such claims assert propositions, true or false judgeable contents, about what there is reason to think, feel or do; (ii) it assumes that the distinction between normative and factual claims must be characterized in a philosophically uniform way across all these domains—the epistemic, evaluative, and practical; and finally (iii) it holds that nothing in the world *makes* fundamental normative propositions, in any of the domains, true or false. The epistemology of the normative is thus discursive or dialogical— the epistemology of reflection and discussion rather than the 'tracking' epistemology proper to factual knowledge. In its conception of the normative this is neither an expressivist or constructivist view on the one hand, nor a realist view on the other. Normative judgement is inherent in all cognition, including cognition of facts, but is not itself judgement about some domain of fact. Facts give us reason to believe, do, or feel: that they do so is not itself a further fact in any sector of reality, natural or non-natural. No proposition which solely pictures a state of affairs is normative. All cognition thus involves a philosophically fundamental dualism of factual and normative judgement, or in terms adopted in some of these essays, of receptivity and spontaneity.

It almost goes without saying that each of the three claims in the last paragraph is highly debatable. To set out their extensive implications and defend them fully could easily take a book in itself. However the primary focus of these essays is ethical not epistemological, so, though I sketch out the essential arguments by which I believe the claims can be supported (in Essay I, Essay II, Section 7, and again Essay IV, Section 4), epistemology features here only as a framework for the discussion of ethical issues, including the issues in social philosophy considered in the final essays.[1]

As to the theory of the good—the conception advanced in these essays is perhaps most easily set out by comparing it with the classical utilitarianism of Mill. It rejects two outstanding theses of classical utilitarianism: hedonism and the aggregative conception of general good. On the other hand it also has some important similarities to classical utilitarianism. It gives the good philosophical (not necessarily political) primacy over the right, it takes the good to consist in the well-being, impartially assessed, of all beings which are capable of well-being, and it takes well-being to consist not in the satisfaction of preferences but in the attainment of objective ends which a being has reason to pursue. (So, in some current parlance, it is neither deontological, nor perfectionist, nor preference-based utilitarian.) These common characteristics define a generic position which in Essays III and V I call 'philosophical utilitarianism'.[2] Classical utilitarianism is a species of this genus, distinguished by its doctrine concerning the distributive structure and content of the good.

---

[1] The ontology of this view is spelt out somewhat further in Skorupski (1999).

[2] I have borrowed the phrase from Scanlon (1982). Scanlon's view of the connection between philosophical and classical utilitarianism is discussed in Essay V, Sect. 2.

The distributive aspect of this contrast, together with the notion of impartiality, is most fully explored in Essay V, in which I reject classical utilitarianism's aggregative principle of distribution in favour of one which I call 'threshold justice'. On the other hand these essays contain no explicit discussion of what is wrong with hedonism;[3] they simply allow throughout that human well-being may comprise categorial ends other than happiness—knowledge and reflective insight, for example, or perhaps at-one-ness with important others, community, or world.

A third difference between the philosophical utilitarianism of these essays and classical utilitarianism should be pointed out. The former like the latter gives the good philosophical authority over the right, but it does not argue, like the latter, that morality can be *derived* from, as against *corrected* by, a theory of the good. According to the standpoint adopted here, criticism of existing morality and law is a proper task of moral philosophy, derivation of an ideal morality and law from a theory of the good is a completely utopian project and a dangerous one at that. In a sense, Mill recognized this; it was a lesson he drew from his 'Germano-Coleridgean' sources (and spelled out in his pair of essays, 'Bentham' and 'Coleridge'). As pointed out at the beginning, morality has more primitive roots than philosophy and is historically shaped by forces other than philosophy. Certainly Mill could have agreed with that. He recognized that the moral is conceptually distinct from the ethical—that is, from what he calls 'teleology', or 'practical reason' (see Essay VII). And his feeling for the historicity of human nature and society made him a vehement opponent of the social constructivism to which the rational utopias of the enlightened could lead. Yet he still agreed with the *epistemological* base of that utopianism. While he recognized that morality may come from sources other than practical reason, and that new-modelling from the foundations is a dangerous enterprise, he still held that practical reason combined with the human sciences could *in principle* give it a deductive foundation. Against that the argument of these essays (II, VII, and VIII) is that morality's reasons, like many other practical reasons, do not and could not even in principle derive from pure ethical reflection, or what one might call pure practical reason. They are reasons of the heart, grounded in the hermeneutics of the emotions. Ethical reflection can correct them but not generate them.

In this respect Mill did not go far enough in learning from his German sources. For this point, about the relationship between the received moral

[3] I attempted a criticism of what seems to me the most persuasive version of hedonism in philosophy, Mill's, in Skorupski (1989: ch. 10, sects. 1–7). As to the preference-satisfaction conception of well-being, see Essay VI, Sect. 3.

tradition and pure ethical reflection, is one of Hegel's most fundamental insights—in the form of his celebrated distinction between *Moralität* and *Sittlichkeit* and his criticism of the pretensions of the former. Thus Essay VIII turns to Hegel's treatment of morality and his critique of Kant. However this is not the only reason for turning to Kant and Hegel. Those two philosophers provide the deepest modern exploration of the relations between freedom, morality, and recognition, while Hegel fills that out with a profound account of transgression, punishment, and atonement: the phenomenology of the fully free moral agent. In doing so he lays bare the roots of one of classical liberalism's central ideas, that of moral freedom.

The idea of moral freedom appears in Mill, as one would expect from the greatest exponent of the classical-liberal ideal. Yet while Mill applies it gloriously in his social and political thought, he does not give it the pro-found (and ambivalent) ethical scrutiny which Hegel gives it. On the other hand, to the other main idea of the liberal ideal—the culture of developed spontaneity of feeling, *Bildung*—Mill gives much explicit attention. At the level of ethical theory he registers it in his famous distinction between higher and lower pleasure. Essay VI defends this distinction, stripped of its hedonistic, but not its philosophical-utilitarian, context.

The final essays, which are essays in social philosophy or theory, draw on all these themes: the dialogical epistemology of the normative, the framework of philosophical utilitarianism, acknowledgement of the higher in the life of a person and a culture, the conception of moral free-dom inherent in our institutions of blame and respect. Essays IX–XI con-sider in this light various aspects of the liberal ethic and its current predicament. Essay XII extends the discussion to a more explicit consid-eration of the role rational legitimation has played in the modern world and of what brings about the 'disenchantment' that accompanies it.

These are issues which can only be grasped historically, yet amnesia is becoming the chronic disease of political philosophy. One has to keep say-ing that it is simply not possible to assess the current health of the liberal and democratic outlooks, and their relative influence on each other, with-out considering their long development, its direction, and shape. When this is done, it becomes evident that current liberal theory, with its con-tractualism and its preoccupation with strong doctrines of justice and the ethical neutrality of the State, is a very marked departure from the ethos of classical liberalism. In fact, it replaces that ethos by a strategy of epis-temological detachment (Essay XI). Many political philosophers today would argue that in doing so it represents an advance which this century has made over the last; but I myself believe that it represents nothing much more than a concession wrung out of liberalism by populism, a diminution of the liberal in the face of the demotic ethical spirit, from which one can hope for no compensating gain.

This at any rate is the argument of Essays IX–XI, while Essay XII takes the opportunity offered by Ernest Gellner's discussion of post-modernism, Islamic fundamentalism and what he called 'enlightenment fundamentalism' to broaden the historical canvas. Let me add two other introductory remarks about these final four essays.

First, any great ideal has its own immanent corruptions and illusions. The more it 'actually exists'—becomes embodied in real institutions and activities—the more obvious these become. They can then be criticized from the outside; but they can also be criticized from within, from the standpoint of the ideal. The criticisms of contemporary liberalism made in these essays are criticisms from within, from the standpoint of the liberal ideal. Such criticism is not necessarily 'idealistic' in the derogatory sense, that is, unrealistic. To adapt Hegel's saying about the State, the actu-ally-existing liberal State is not a work of art. It is full of pretences, illu-sions, and imperfections, some of which oil its operations and some of which do not. My criticisms, however, are not at that level, the level of statecraft. They are philosophical criticisms directed at positions in the political philosophy of liberalism, both popular and academic. The posi-tions I criticize have become increasingly entrenched and influential in this century and they make an immense difference to the intellectual and ethi-cal climate within which liberal statecraft can work.

Second, to criticize is not to reconstruct. The essays on liberalism in this book do not venture to propose how the ethic of liberalism should develop and regenerate. And, since their criticisms of contemporary liberalism fre-quently rely on comparisons with nineteenth-century ideas, there may be an impression that I am suggesting a 'return' to the ethics of the nineteenth century. Let me say, then, that even though I think the ethical insight of the nineteenth century to be among the most powerful and impressive qualities of its philosophy, its literature, and its music I am not in any way saying that such a 'return' is either possible or desirable. What liberals need (liberals in the sense developed in these essays—I would like to say 'liberals in the true sense', but that would lay too much claim on a word which perhaps no longer *has* a 'true' sense)—is a powerfully regenerated ideal, showing the organic continuity with ancestral forms which charac-terizes a genuine tradition. There is scope to contribute to that in a philo-sophical mode, and it would be pleasing and worth while indeed to do so, but that is not attempted here.

Now let me turn to some acknowledgements, which are as always far from adequate to the debt. And first (if acknowledgement is the right word):

Mill, Kant, and Hegel repeatedly figure in these pages, with some supporting presence from Nietzsche, Sidgwick, and Green, and somewhat more distant signals, so to speak, from Schiller and Matthew Arnold. The amount of attention the first three in particular get does not overestimate their influence on me. It seems to me that I keep on gaining from going back to them.

Let me also take this opportunity to mention the general encouragement, and continuing influence over the years, of three people: Bernard Williams, Robin Horton, and Ernest Gellner. Bernard Williams was my doctoral supervisor; I owe him a considerable debt from those times, particularly for showing neither too little nor too much patience. And I have gone on being influenced by his work ever since, in the way that one can be very influenced by people who strike one as thoroughly and healthily right about what is important and worth discussing, and penetrating in what they have to say about it—even when one finds it impossible, in the end, to follow in the direction they want to go. Horton and Gellner are philosopher-anthropologists rather than moral philosophers. Again my debt to them began when I was writing my dissertation, which was a philosophical study of theories in anthropology about magic and traditional religion. At that time they gave me very crucial encouragement. Again, however, I think I learned something lasting from them. I could label it an 'anthropological attitude' to human phenomena; not just to magic and religion but morality, status, ideals, etc. It would not be easy to explain how this perspective influenced the essays collected here (the influence is opposite to Kant's and parallel to Hegel's) but it certainly did. The last essay is a tribute to the late Ernest Gellner and I hope it testifies to the kind of influence on me that he had. As to Robin Horton's work, it always shows the lucid and hard-headed humanism that should be the basis of anthropology, and could give so much to ethics if it was.

The essays in this volume were presented in various forms to a variety of colloquia, conferences, and lecture series—I am most grateful to the organizers for giving me an opportunity to try out my ideas. The result is that they have assuredly been influenced by the comments of many people. Those to whom I remember a specific debt are acknowledged at the beginning of each essay. Here I would also like to thank Peter Momtchiloff and Oxford University Press's readers, who gave encouragement and sound advice.

All the essays republished here have been revised to a greater or lesser degree. 'Freedom, Morality, and Recognition' is first published here, while 'Neutral and Relative' is effectively a new paper, though partly based on two previously published notes. I would like to thank the original publishers for permission to republish. The previous place of publication is shown at the beginning of each essay.

PART I

Reasons

I

Objectivity and Convergence

1. Kant says,

truth depends upon agreement with the object, and in respect of it the judgements of each and every understanding must therefore be in agreement with each other (*consentientia uni tertio, consentiunt inter se*). The touchstone whereby we decide whether our holding a thing to be true is conviction or mere persuasion is therefore external, namely, the possibility of communicating it and of finding it to be valid for all human reason. For there is then at least a presumption that the ground of the agreement of all judgements with each other, notwithstanding the differing characters of individuals, rests upon the common ground, namely, upon the object, and that it is for this reason that they are all in agreement with the object—the truth of the judgement being thereby proved.[1]

Kant recognizes the importance played by the spontaneous agreement of others in cementing my confidence in the judgements I make. He takes it that this agreement *signals* the rightness of the judgement. It is, he says, a 'touchstone'. If individuals with 'differing characters' converge on the same judgement, the judgement is so much the less likely to be explained by the quirks, obsessions, or partialities of an individual temperament. My confidence that it 'rests upon the common ground', that it corresponds to the 'object', is rightly raised.

I try out on others the considerations which seem to me to warrant a belief, and I discover that they too accept them as warranting the belief. The fact that the agreement is a spontaneous consensus of separate and distinct acts of acceptance is important: convergence derives its authenticating authority from the fact that each individual independently recognizes the rational connection between the judgement and its grounds.

So long . . . as the subject views the judgement merely as an appearance of his mind, persuasion cannot be subjectively distinguished from conviction. The experiment, however, whereby we test upon the understanding of others whether

First published in *Proceedings of the Aristotelian Society*, 86 (1985–6: 235–50).

[1] Kant, *Critique of Pure Reason*, A821 B849 (1968: 645). The passage is quoted by Ian Hacking (1983: 98–9).

those grounds of the judgement which are valid for us have the same effect on the reason of others as on our own, is a means, although only a subjective means, not indeed of producing conviction, but of detecting any merely private validity in the judgement.[2]

A divergence between what I accept as reasons warranting a judgement, and what others accept, may evidence some distortion or unreliability in my reasoning, or judgement-making, propensities, but does not on its own identify it. It does not give me the objective perspective which would explain the distortion and put me in a position to measure the discrepancy between my judgement-making propensities and the facts, allowing me to correct it. It may, equally, indicate that something is wrong with their dispositions to judge rather than with mine. It may arise from a distortion to which they are subject but I am not. And of course it is also true that, even where there is an agreement of judgements, that may itself result from some systematic distortion, illusion, or mystification to which all are subject.

The touchstone of convergence alone gives us no means of judging among these possibilities. To do so we must take the 'objective' view of our reasoning propensities. Considering ourselves as beings within the world about which we reason, we have to ask ourselves whether our best conception of our interactions with that world justifies us in accounting the particular judging disposition whose reliability is in question as suitably sensitive to its subject matter—or whether, on the contrary, it leads us to discount it, as stemming from causes which are 'subjective' because they lack the appropriate sensitivity to subject matter. Thus, Kant goes on,

If, in addition, we can specify the subjective *causes* of the judgement, which we have taken as being its objective *grounds*, and can thus explain the deceptive judgement as an event in our mind, and can do so without having to take account of the character of the object, we expose the illusion and are no longer deceived by it, although always still in some degree liable to come under its influence, in so far as the subjective cause of the illusion is inherent in our nature.[3]

2. We have, then, the idea that stable and spontaneous agreement indicates the objective validity of our judgement-making dispositions, by signalling that we are tracking the same, judgement-independent, states of affairs. Convergence of our judgements betokens that they correspond to,

---

[2] Kant, *Critique of Pure Reason* Kant distinguishes persuasion from conviction as follows: If the judgement is valid for everyone, provided only he is in possession of reason, its ground is objectively sufficient, and the holding of it to be true is entitled *conviction*. If it has its ground only in the special character of the subject, it is entitled *persuasion*.

[3] Ibid. 646.

or that we co-respond to, a fact.[4] Only by using our judgement-making dispositions, it is true, do we get to the picture of ourselves in the world which shows us to what extent, and how, our dispositions track the facts. But this can be a virtuous, not a vicious circle. We may find, and in fact we have found, that our perceptual and cognitive capacities lead us to successively more sophisticated theoretical conceptions of the world, in which we ourselves, together with our perceptual and cognitive capacities, figure, and within which we find their general or normal reliability confirmed.

All of this is common sense. But there is a further, subtly distinct and distinctively philosophical step which one may be tempted to make. It introduces a picture of objectivity in which a judgement or a principle of reasoning—anything which can be said to be correct or incorrect—is so just in virtue of its correspondence or failure to correspond with facts. The picture I have in mind is more than a 'disquotational' truism, for two reasons. First: it takes the acceptably non-metaphysical account of correspondence in terms of co-respondence, of interaction between knowing subjects and known object, and applies it completely generally, to all objective judgements—all judgements which can be said to be correct or incorrect. An immediate consequence is that objectivism and realism cannot be split apart. We cannot take an objectivist view of a domain of discourse without also taking a realist view of it. Second: it modulates, in the course of this generalizing process, into a metaphysical notion of correspondence. Later (in Section 5) I shall try to indicate what is involved in this metaphysical notion. But the two points are not, in the end, distinct. The metaphysical notion and the idea that objectivity *necessarily* involves a subject–object interaction—that objectivism and realism *must* coincide—support each other. I shall call the philosophical thesis which results from taking them together *the correspondence picture of objectivity*. It holds that objectivity is constituted by correspondence.

Against it we can set the idea that objectivity is constituted by an ideally undistorted consensus, surviving critical dialogue. On this view the possibility of communicating my reasons for a judgement and finding them to be acceptable to other reasoners is of the essence. Nothing underwrites the correctness of a judgement beyond the fact that it would survive criticism and be retained in an ideal consensus of rational inquirers. This I shall call *the ideal consensus picture of objectivity*.

The two pictures are incompatible. But do they both incorporate some truth? We have noted that the correspondence picture takes its starting point from indisputable common sense but goes beyond it in presenting a

---

[4] '[W]hether or not true beliefs *correspond with* the facts, true believers must certainly *respond to* the facts' (Blackburn 1984: 246).

distinctive philosophical thesis. What is true in the ideal consensus picture can be put negatively, as the rejection of that thesis: there is a sense, perfectly compatible with common sense, in which nothing vouchsafes the correctness of a judgement beyond its retention in an ideal consensus; so that a 'merely private validity', just because it is incommunicable to others, could not be any kind of validity at all. The mistake comes when one tries to put this in a positive form, by saying such things as that what *makes* a judgement or a principle of reasoning valid is the potential for convergence on it.

To bring out what is right about the negative form and wrong about the positive form we shall have to distinguish between judgements about the world, and norms of reason by which we arrive at such judgements, or at requirements on action. In the domain of reasons, objectivity and realism have to be split apart. There is a connection between the validity of a reason and its acceptance in an ideal consensus: if we cease to be persuaded that agreement on its rational force could ideally be secured, we cease to accept its authority as a reason. But acceptance in an ideal consensus is not what *makes* it valid. It is less misleading to say that nothing at all *makes* it valid. There is, that is to say, no fact in the world *in virtue* of which the consideration constitutes a reason, theoretical or practical; and that holds, in particular, of the fact that it would be recognized as a reason in an ideal consensus of human reasoners. Nor is it that the two statements— that the consideration is a sound reason, and that its force would be accepted in an ideally undistorted consensus of human reasoners—have the same assertion conditions. When we respond to reasons, we have our eye on the reasons, not on the other respondents. The first statement is not based on *evidence*, whereas the second statement requires evidence. But what we accept as a reason (as in the first statement) shapes what evidence we count as appropriate for particular judgements about the world.

In the case of judgements about the world, on the other hand, it is of course a tautology that what makes them true is a fact in the world. The non-metaphysical notion of correspondence applies. We can think of a judgement as a judgement about the world just to the extent that we can conceive of it as causally responsive to something in the world. But the second element in the correspondence picture, the metaphysical notion of correspondence, still fails to apply. I shall try however to pin down what makes it tempting.

3. The correspondence picture of objectivity has powerful philosophical consequences. They stand out clearly in the case of moral discourse, or practical reasoning in general.

We naturally take it that many questions about moral principle or about human ends—most abstractly, about the ultimate principles which determine what considerations count as reasons for acting—have a right answer, and we sometimes argue about what the right answer is. Questions of this kind may not arise all that often; pressingly practical questions bulk larger most of the time, and are related in no simple way to the abstracting and generalizing kind of questions. Nor can one say, of course, that when the questions do arise, they are always or often debated in a way that approximates closely to the model of dialogue: that is, to rational discussion among parties whose contributions are motivated by no 'sinister interest', in Bentham's phrase.

Yet, to the extent that we do engage in moral dialogue about questions of principle—as against moral manipulation, propaganda, bullying, well-poisoning, image-building, special pleading, and so forth—our common pursuit is regulated by the idea that there is a sound conclusion to be arrived at, a right answer at stake, one on which a sufficiently rational and uncurtailed dialogue would converge. The confidence that there is a right answer is precisely measured by the confidence that such a dialogue would find it. Our actual dialogue, curtailed and falling short of rationality, takes place under the ideal of rational convergence. That is what gives it its status as authentic dialogue.

These expectations are evidenced by the way in which we explain a failure to achieve agreement. When the expectations are present, we explain the failure by reference to limitations of time or rationality among one or more participants in the discussion. (Failure of rationality is not a simple matter, of course. It would cover in this case such things as inability to see the question in a certain point of view, or the relevance of certain facts of human experience to it, unwillingness to make relevant distinctions or insistence on making irrelevant ones, and so on.)

Where we become convinced that the best-intentioned, dispassionate, perceptive reasoners cannot, *just in virtue of exercising those qualities*—just through pure responsiveness to the constraints of rationality, as one might say—be expected to agree, we no longer think there is a right answer. Suppose, for example, that I became convinced that agreement of this ideal kind could not be expected in the case of competing principles of distributive justice. Disinterested reasoners might all agree, in the long run, in rejecting many principles as defective (in respect of impartiality, or of some other quality that they might agree on)—but they would still be left with a shortlist. There is then a paradox in holding both that ideal agreement within this shortlist would never be reached in however long a run, and also holding that one of them is nevertheless determinately right.

It is not a contradiction, because rightness is not *defined* by ideal consensus. But it falls short of reflective equilibrium no less surely than if it were.

The more or less explicit recognition of this point serves as the basis for a very common kind of scepticism, or anti-objectivism, about practical rationality. It assumes that there is no norm of practical reason about which we could ever be justified in thinking that rational people are fated to agree, just in virtue of being rational people. There is always a temptation to flop safely onto that sceptical assumption, or to display it as a piece of higher wisdom. But I am not concerned with its plausibility here. I note only that it is a separate assumption. The sound point, that where the expectation of rational convergence is out of place, so too is the belief that there is a right answer, does not by itself escalate into a global scepticism about practical rationality as such. It remains possible that there are indeterminacies within practical reasoning, issues on which dialogue is fated to be inconclusive, but that there are also objective, rational constraints on it. That might be just what one would expect on any realistic view of the interplay between reason, sympathy, and individual temperament in moral matters.

What would undermine this mixed standpoint is the application to practical reasoning of the correspondence picture of objectivity. For it would then immediately follow that we must either give up on the objectivity of moral judgements or move to some sophisticated position of moral realism. We would either have to withdraw the view that convergence is a rationally appropriate ideal for moral dialogue, or we would have to hold that it betokens correspondence with some judgement-independent reality.

But moral realism is certainly not a natural position to hold. However sophisticated it may be, so long as it is genuine realism—so long, in other words, as it measures up to the first element in the correspondence picture—it encounters a devastating objection. No explanation of our dispositions to make practical judgements which we would ever take seriously as a ground-level explanation could portray them as mechanisms by which we reliably track, via moral intuitions, the same moral facts. When this point is combined with the correspondence picture of objectivity it completely upstages the *pragmatic* sceptical argument from disagreement. It makes it irrelevant whether convergence is or is not likely to occur— because even if it occurs it will no longer be a touchstone of objective validity. The point is clearly put by Bernard Williams:

The basic idea behind the distinction between the scientific and the ethical, expressed in terms of convergence, is very simple. In a scientific inquiry there should ideally be convergence on an answer, where the best explanation of the convergence involves the idea that the answer represents how things are; in the area of the ethical, at least at a high level of generality, there is no such coherent hope. The distinction does not turn on any difference in whether convergence will actually occur, and it is important that this is not what the argument is about. It might well turn out that there will be convergence in ethical outlook, at least among human beings. The point of the contrast is that, even if this happens, it will not be correct to think it has come about because convergence has been guided by how things actually are, whereas convergence in the sciences might be explained in that way if it does happen.[5]

One might call this the argument from explanatory redundancy. But suppose I explain the general agreement that causing pain for one's own pleasure is wrong, by pointing out that everyone *sees* that it is wrong, because it *is* wrong. In what way, or in what sense, have I failed to give an explanation which can be taken seriously?

At one level the explanation is perfectly in order—the hermeneutic level at which we understand each other as rationally autonomous, and enter into dialogue. But there is another level—call it the naturalistic level—at which the explanation would be completely out of place. No explanation of our moral convictions which we could ever come to at this level would have the statement that causing pain for one's own pleasure is wrong occurring assertorically in the *explanans*. Nor would it contain an account of human perceptual faculties by the exercise of which we perceive that causing pain for one's pleasure is wrong. Williams is right to see this as undermining moral *realism*, because there is a crucial sense in which the naturalistic level has to be accepted as ground level: it is in terms of what our best explanations at the naturalistic level commit us to that we determine what there really is in the world. That follows from the fact that realism about a domain involves the idea of an interaction between it and the knowing subject, and that the only sense we can make of the notion of interaction is a causal one.

4. The argument from explanatory redundancy forces us to reject moral realism; but it undermines the objectivity of moral reasoning only if we combine it with the correspondence picture of objectivity. But if we do so combine it, then we have forged a weapon which applies quite generally to reasoning as such, and not just to moral reasoning.

In thinking of ourselves at the hermeneutic, or interpretative level, we understand our moral reasoning as guided by something which objectively constrains it. That applies to all our reasoning—it is an inherent feature of

[5] Bernard Williams (1985: 136).

our conception of ourselves as rationally autonomous believers and agents. The Kantian insight that true autonomy consists in the ability to recognize and respond to objectively valid reasons is the central notion in our hermeneutic self-understanding. If there is a clash between our hermeneutic and our naturalistic self-understanding, between our image of ourselves as autonomous reasoners and our image of ourselves as natural objects, then it applies quite generally. There is no basis here for a conclusion which restricts itself to subjectivism or scepticism about moral or practical reasoning alone.

This point may be disputed. Principles of theoretical reason, canons of inductive reasoning (I use the term 'inductive' in the widest possible sense), may be more or less successful. They may lead us to a stable fabric of belief about the world, and to predictively adequate habits of inference about it—or they may not. Nothing comparable can be said about principles of practical reasoning. Theoretical principles can be self-vindicating, in a way that practical principles cannot be.

This is true, and important. We can inductively raise our confidence in inductive processes. Just because they can be self-undermining, they can also be self-vindicating. The point has been rightly stressed by naturalistically minded philosophers from Mill onwards. But (as Mill did not dispute) the whole process presupposes that some inductive rules have some initial authority. The pragmatic or internal appeal to the actual success of a particular set of rules of reasoning can rationally raise a person's confidence in those rules of reasoning, only if he is justified in attaching some positive degree of confidence to some inductive norms in the first place.

It is vital to appreciate this point in the present context. We *accept* certain fundamental norms of induction. They are not in any usably intelligible sense 'analytic' or 'true by definition'. But nor is our acceptance of them a posteriori: we are justified in accepting them so long as no natural history of the inductive process has undermined them. We accept them as objectively valid: we do not 'choose' them, but find ourselves constrained by them. So if objectivity requires correspondence, we shall need a platonic realm of inductive norms, and the argument from explanatory redundancy will spell disaster, just as in the ethical case.

The authority of norms of theoretical or practical reasoning is bound up with our common recognition of them as requirements of reason. The essential misconception here is to impose a relational model of awareness onto this notion of recognizing the applicability of a norm of reason: to treat it as a form of (necessarily non-causal) access to a domain of pure, self-interpreting objects. This is not the place to consider what happens when the misconception is removed—how, from the materials that remain, one gets to the conception of rationally autonomous agents responding to objectively given requirements of reason. My point is that there are no special grounds here for an asymmetrical scepticism or subjectivism about practical reason. Practical and theoretical norms, given equal degrees of convergence, are on the same footing. In neither case does convergence betoken correspondence with a platonic realm of self-interpreting, self-legitimating, imperatives. Realism is inappropriate—just because the idea that 'the answer represents how things are' could not in principle constitute an explanation of our convergence, when convergence occurs. But that does not impugn the objectivity of the norms on which we converge.

5. It does not follow that no explanation of how consensus about a norm of reasoning arises could undermine our confidence in the validity of that norm. Far from it. It will help to consider very briefly some examples of how this might happen.

If I interpret morality as an ideological device for shackling the strong, or oppressing the weak, I give a functional explanation of it. I claim that we accept certain moral principles just because our accepting them fulfils that function. But if I am convinced of that I can no longer feel at ease with those principles. I am forced to raise the question whether it is a *good thing* that the strong be shackled, and prevented from fully exploiting their strength, or that the weak be reconciled to their inferior social position and discouraged from combining to change it. And I cannot of course answer that question, about whether the end-state is a good or a bad one, by referring back to those of our moral convictions which I have explained as tracking that end.

The same point applies to the theory which sees morality as a 'device' for producing cooperation. Suppose we find ourselves in a prisoners' dilemma (and suppose we both have reason to think that we shall not find ourselves in it together again). We are both moved by a principle of fairness, according to which I should not take advantage of you so long as you are not planning to take advantage of me; and each of us has grounds for thinking that the other is so moved. We will then converge on the strategy which makes us both better off. But suppose I become convinced that our commitment to the principle of fairness can be explained functionally: we have it just because there is an advantage to general utility if every agent has it. I shall then ask myself whether there is reason to be fair. And so long as I am convinced that my commitment to fairness is fully explicable in these functional terms, I cannot appeal to it in answering my question. I must get myself a deeper model of what I should do. If that model contains the principle that promoting general utility is a reason for action, well and good. But if it contains only prudential rationality, then I shall find no reason for following the principle of fairness in the prisoners' dilemma.

So two things are needed to make these functional explanations subversive: first, the explanation must present certain dispositions of reasoning as tracking an end-state; second, there must be the reflective conviction that the end-state is in one way or another in conflict with our original acceptance of the authority of those dispositions.

Let us pursue this theme, of how functional explanations of our reasoning propensities or beliefs can acquire a subversive impact, in the context of theoretical reasoning. We may think of the set of general beliefs with which we confront our environment as a theory describing the world and explaining its observed features. The criteria by which we judge the truth of the explanation are its predictive adequacy—that is, its accuracy and comprehensiveness—and its internal simplicity and economy. We may also think of our general beliefs as a system of habits of inference. We prefer habits of inference according to their predictive adequacy and their simplicity. Now consider a possible evolutionary explanation of these preferences. Creatures with correct expectations about their environment have a greater chance of surviving and propagating than creatures with incorrect ones. And creatures with more cost-effective systems of generating correct expectations have the same comparative advantage over those with less cost-effective systems. And now we appear to be able to explain the preference for simplicity—in a way which does not invoke the *truth* of the simpler theory at all. We go for the theory which is simplest relative to our information-processing capacities. Creatures with the same capacities who preferred theories which were complicated relative to those capacities would take longer to process information and would be at a relative disadvantage. Whether the world is complicated or simple, this explanation of our preference for simplicity would remain.

Again the functional explanation forces us up to a new reflective level. But at first sight there seems to be an important difference. In the practical case there is no God's-eye perspective in which we can see what is really rational, and contrast it with our natural reasoning propensities. There can, in principle, be no court of appeal other than our natural propensities. But in the theoretical case, is there not a further court of appeal—the facts of the matter, the way the world actually is? Those reasoning propensities are objectively valid which are prone to get us believing that p, if p. The only trouble is that the explanation of our preference for simplicity gives us no reason to think that that particular preference passes this test. But we seem to have a clear conception of what the test is—we know how, if we but had the God's-eye perspective, we could apply it. In principle, at least, our natural reasoning propensities are not the last court of appeal. And this leads us to instrumentalism: we break the inference from convergence to correspondence, because we have an explanation of convergence which requires us to postulate no correspondence.

The essential mistake, in the theoretical as in the practical case, lies in the idea of a God's-eye perspective, a perspective from which it makes sense to ask whether our reasoning propensities, taken as a whole, lead us to truth. But we can reject the idea that it makes sense to ask that question only if we adopt an epistemic conception of what it is to understand a language.[6] Understanding a sentence is having the ability to recognize circumstances which, against a context of background beliefs, warrant its assertion. That means that the acceptance of certain rules of evidence and reasoning is part of the very process of acquiring mastery of the language.

This is not idealism—it involves no assertibilist definition of (or even epistemic constraint on) truth.[7] But it does require one to reject what I referred to in Section 2 as the second element in the correspondence picture of objectivity, the metaphysical notion of correspondence. This notion comes down to the idea that a language-user can understand sentences, and thus attain a grasp of their truth-conditions, independently of a mastery of norms of evidence—that he can first grasp what it is for a sentence to be true and then consider, *as a separate question*, what norms of evidence might in principle bear on it. In rejecting this idea we precisely deny that any sense can be made of the question whether our norms of evidence (those on which we would in the long run ideally converge) taken as a whole, track facts. And we also come to see how our mastery of the norms of evidence can be, in a certain sense, 'a priori' even though it is not analytic.

6. We are left with the first element in the correspondence picture. We have concluded that it is not an essential feature of the general concept of objectivity. But it gives content to the notion of a judgement of fact, a judgement which is about the world. Fundamental to this latter notion is

---

[6] I no longer think this is true, since, as it seems to me now, one has to distinguish sharply between linguistic rules and epistemic norms. Possession of a concept is constituted by grasp of epistemic norms, while understanding the terms of a language is understanding what concepts they express. So what I should have said is that we can reject the intelligibility of the question only if we accept an epistemic conception of *concepts* (a conception of them as patterns of epistemic norms). For further discussion of these matters see Skorupski (1997*a* and *b*).

[7] Again I explain and defend this further, from the perspective of an epistemic conception of concepts, in Skorupski (1997*a*).

the idea that the knower's judgements characteristically track something ontologically independent of his judgements: the domain which he judges *about*. The attitude of realism is appropriate only where that idea has application. Can we therefore conclude that in the case of judgements about the world, at least, convergence signifies exclusively as a touchstone of correspondence?

It is not clear that we can. To see the puzzle, consider the idea that there may be a plurality of best explanations—that theory is underdetermined by data. On a classical view, one which incorporates the metaphysical notion of correspondence, the very possibility that evidence underdetermines theory seems to lead inescapably to scepticism, or to an instrumentalist view of theoretical inference. But we must be careful to consider the underdetermination thesis against the background of an epistemic conception of language mastery.[8] In that context it is not clear that the thesis has a definite content at all. On the epistemic conception, the statement that a plurality of theories could optimally explain the data—all possible data—is assertible only if a situation could occur which would justify us in saying that a plurality of optimal theories actually exists. But if we ask ourselves what is meant by an optimal theory, we may well begin to wonder whether any such situation could occur. Optimal theories would differ among themselves non-trivially and yet would be of equal overall explanatory power, as judged by all the criteria of good explanation which we could be brought to recognize. But that is not all. It would have to be the case that, as proponents of the respective theories tried to improve them, the theories neither converged, nor fell into a stable rank order, nor came to be superseded by a new theory which non-trivially differed from all of them. If we had no grounds for thinking that that would continue to be the case indefinitely, we would not be in a position to assert the underdetermination thesis.

It is tempting to be sceptical about whether we could ever have such grounds, and sceptical therefore about whether the underdetermination thesis has any genuine sense. But this scepticism is perhaps a little too easy. Imagine a long history of theoretical debate in which every attempt by one theoretical tradition to trump or assimilate another, quite distinct one, was always matched by an effective reply, without any sign of convergence setting in. At some stage of this process, a meta-induction would make the conclusion that no such attempt would ever be successful, that convergence would never set in, increasingly plausible. We can recognize that as the kind of situation which, as it continues, makes the underdetermination

---

[8] Or as I would now say, an epistemic conception of concept possession.

thesis ever more plausible, and that is enough to show that the thesis has sense.

How would we react if it occurred? Would we take a relativist view? There is no obvious inconsistency in that response. Each cognitive tradition could represent its particular judgements, within its own framework, as correctly tracking the facts. So consensus among subscribers to that cognitive tradition could—internally speaking—be explained by correspondence. Within each tradition, 'the answer represents how things are' would be seen as constituting the best explanation of convergence.

But I do not myself believe that that would be our response. We would, rather, lose conviction in either alternative even though our judgements within each of them could be represented as reliably, though not infallibly, sensitive to their subject matter. We would increasingly retreat to an instrumentalist view.

Why should we retreat? After all each cognitive tradition can, by hypothesis, apply the correspondence notion with full cogency—internally. And the internal notion of correspondence is the only notion we have made sense of. Rejection of any other notion is the essence of the epistemic conception of language mastery.[9] A tendency to retreat seems to betray us as 'metaphysical realists' after all. For if we succeeded in exorcizing the classical conception of language mastery completely would we not, by that very fact, eliminate the retreating reaction and become good relativists? There is a great deal of force in this reply. Yet I find myself unconvinced by it. It seems to me that the ground level of analysis is not a particular philosophical conception of language mastery, but the ideal of convergence itself. Our attachment to the ideal is primitive. It explains the appeal of the classical conception, of 'metaphysical realism', rather than the other way round. If that is so, then our adherence to the ideal is *not* fully explicable by the belief that consensus signals correspondence. The only sense we have made of correspondence is an internal sense: but that is consistent with the possibility of underdetermination. We believe something more: that truth, externally and not just internally speaking, is one. That belief simply expresses a primitive attachment to the ideal of convergence. It is something that we expect the world to live up to, rather than something that we learn from it.

---

[9] Or of concept possession.

APPENDIX
Metaphysical Realism

In the last paragraph of 'Objectivity and Convergence' I sought to explain the appeal of metaphysical realism by our attachment to a regulative ideal of inquiry—that 'truth, externally and not just internally speaking, is one'. I still think we are attached to that, and that some of the appeal of metaphysical realism can be explained in terms of it, but I think I did not distinguish it sufficiently from 'the ideal of convergence itself'.

In Essays II (Section 7) and IV (Section 4) I give an argument for what I call the *convergence thesis*, viz., that when I judge that p (for any judgeable content p) I enter a commitment that inquirers whose rationality and evidence could not be faulted would agree that p. This convergence thesis does not as such yield the regulative ideal mentioned above. For suppose we found ourselves faced by conflicting, highly successful cognitive traditions as envisaged in Section 6 of 'Objectivity and Convergence'. As there suggested, the longer this conflict went on without resolution the more we would come to be warranted in accepting a strong thesis of global underdetermination: the thesis that there is more than one optimal comprehensive theory of the world, taking into account *all* reasonable requirements on a good theory.

That conclusion would, of course, always remain defeasible. It would always remain possible that new evidence, or further reflection on existing evidence, would undermine one or both of the theories. And the regulative ideal would encourage us to expect that and search for it, and discourage us from accepting the conclusion. Nevertheless, to say that a conclusion is defeasible is not to say that it is unwarranted, and it seems to me that in a long run of unsuccessful attempts to resolve or supersede the conflict it could eventually become reasonable to accept that there is indeed more than one optimal comprehensive theory of the world. To the extent that became reasonable, the role of the regulative ideal would be exhausted; for that ideal effectively tells us to work on the assumption that such a conclusion is incorrect. No doubt the ideal would still have a strong appeal to us, but equally its status as no more than an ideal would become increasingly clear.

There might still be a reason to believe, available from within the stalemated optimal theories themselves, that the irresolvable stand-off between them arose purely from physical limitations on our inquiring capacities or our equipment. In that case we would legitimately hold that not more than one of them could be correct—since we could envisage a definite acid test which would decide between them, even though we could not carry it out. But this is not the only possible situation. The notion of a 'definite acid test' is vague—shading off gradually; nevertheless it is certainly possible to imagine a theoretical stand-off in which no such test could be specified because only holistic comparisons of the theories' virtues were possible. In this case there would be no definite inquiry, possible or impossible to us, that would decide between the theories—there would simply be balance sheets for both of them, which contained different debits and credits, but added up to the same optimal bottom line (and had done for decades or centuries).

Metaphysical realism comes down to the view that even then we would have to hold that *at most* one of these optimal theories could be correct—not as an expression of a healthy inquiring attitude, but as an insight into the metaphysical nature of reality. That means that metaphysical realism is stronger than the combination of the convergence thesis and the regulative ideal. I would now say that 'the correspondence picture of objectivity' involves (i) *unequivocal* realism about all propositions, whether normative or factual and (ii) *metaphysical* realism about the domain of the factual—and that both these kinds of realism should be rejected.

II

Reasons and Reason

1. We have reasons to believe, to act, to feel. We deal in reasons at every turn—for example I have reason to believe you covered for me in an emergency, reason to feel grateful and so reason to thank you in some more or less substantial way. What we make of a person turns on how that person responds or fails to respond to reasons in one or other of these three domains—belief, feeling, and action. Personality is the manner of one's responsiveness to reasons. A testy person is more easily annoyed than he has reason to be. A credulous person believes when there is insufficient reason to believe. A precipitate person acts when there is insufficient reason to act.

How are these various kinds of reason connected with Reason? And where does morality fit in?

2. Let us call a proposition which is about reasons, or from which a proposition about reasons is analytically deducible, a normative proposition. (Some normative propositions will include a factual content.) Such propositions are about *reason* relations, as one may call them: relations which hold between facts on the one hand and beliefs, actions, or feelings on the other. In the case of belief we have *epistemic* normative propositions, which are or analytically imply propositions about reasons to believe. Example: the fact that the freezer has been left open is a reason for thinking, gives one reason to think, that its contents will melt. I take it to be the fact that rationalizes the belief; if the freezer has not been left open, although you think it has, then there is no reason for you to believe that the food will melt—unless some other fact, such as that the fuse is blown, gives you a reason to believe it. You are indeed right to infer that there is reason to believe the food will melt from your belief that the freezer is open; but your premiss is false and thus your belief that there is reason to believe the food will melt may also be false.

First published in Garrett Cullity and Berys Gaut (eds.), *Morality and Practical Reasoning*, Oxford: Oxford University Press, 1997. I am grateful to the editors for their detailed and helpful comments.

So the reason relation holds in the epistemic case between facts, persons and beliefs. We should also leave a place for time as a term of the relation,[1] and the relation comes in degrees. Its general form in the epistemic case is therefore something like: *the fact that p gives x reason of degree d at time t to believe that q.*

What about reasons for feelings and actions? *Practical* normative propositions are about reasons to act: *the fact that p gives x reason of degree d at time t to* α, where α ranges over action-types as *q* ranges over belief-types. For example the fact that the building is about to explode gives you very good reason to get out right now. *Evaluative* normative propositions are about reasons to feel: *the fact that p gives x reason of degree d at time t to feel* ϕ, where 'ϕ' ranges over types of feeling (i.e. emotions, moods, and desires). The fact that Katie broke the record gives her reason to feel proud. In general the reason relation relates facts, persons, times, a degree of magnitude and a belief, action, or feeling type. *All* thought involves the reason relation: sometimes in the form of explicit normative beliefs but at minimum in the form of primitive normative responses as to what is in context legitimate, justified, reasonable, correct.

3. The view I want to consider is that moral propositions are evaluative normative propositions; propositions about what there is reason to *feel*—specifically, to disapprove, to respond to with blame or guilt. Let us call evaluative normative judgements 'evaluations' for short; so the view is that moral judgements are evaluations in this specific sense.

It should be distinguished from 'expressivist' or 'non-cognitivist' meta-ethical views, such as were advanced earlier this century by emotivists and conventionalists and more recently, with great subtlety, by Simon Blackburn and Alan Gibbard.[2] An expressivist could well adopt it; however one can adopt it and still hold that moral propositions are genuine contents of judgement. In what follows I shall take it that that is what they are. To judge of evaluative reasons—of what there is reason to blame, admire, despise, be frightened, bored, amused, or irritated by—is still to judge. That view seems to me right in general, of all normative claims in all domains of belief, action, and feeling: they are genuine assertions which convey propositional contents assessable as correct or incorrect, rather than being, as an expressivist about any subclass of them holds, expressions of a feeling or a choice or an act of will. On the other hand, it does not (I believe) follow from this general view that there must be, as well

---

[1] The fact that Paula has a meeting at noon gives her at noon a reason to believe that she has a meeting then.

[2] e.g. Blackburn (1993), Gibbard (1990).

as facts which rationalize, *further* facts about what those facts rationalize—facts in some special domain of reality to which we have non-
empirical access. It seems to me that the governing insight from which one
must start is that cognition involves a fundamental *dualism* of factual and
normative judgements.[3]

Obviously this philosophical account of normative propositions—cognitivist but irrealist—calls for elucidation and extensive defence. It
encounters, for example, the deep-laid doctrine that all content is factual
content—together with related doctrines tying semantics to ontology.
These doctrines will not be touched on here, though some connected
issues about the epistemology of the normative will be spelt out a little further in Section 7. I mention them at this point to give an idea of the framework which I assume.

Our main topic, however, is the relation between reasons and reason
and the place of morality within the sphere of reasons. Many of us accept
some degree or other of rationalism about the epistemic and the practical.
We think that there are pure principles of theoretical reason—some of us,
probably a smaller number, think there are pure principles of practical reason. 'Pure principles of reason' in these two cases means something like:
normative propositions about what there is reason to believe or to do, our
knowledge of which does not depend upon empirical knowledge but is
attainable by rational insight and accessible to any rational being.
Rationalism is the view that there are such propositions, knowable, to put
it in an old-fashioned way, by the faculty of reason.

But are there pure principles of evaluative reason? Does anything stand
to evaluative reasons as (many think) pure theoretical reason stands to
epistemic reasons and pure practical reason stands to practical reasons?
That seems far less clear. My mother comes across an old photograph of
her childhood home—she has every reason to be moved. Is it reason that
tells me that? Some sort of rational insight accessible to any rational
being? Is it derivable from facts about the actual world and some fundamental evaluation known to reason? On the contrary. 'Le coeur a ses
raisons que la raison ne connaît point.' *That* seems unchallengeable.
Pascal's famous remark was made in another context but it is entirely
applicable to this one.

---

[3] Thus I agree with Alan Gibbard (1990) that factual and normative claims are to be
sharply distinguished but do not follow him in his expressivist conception of the normative.
Another basic point on which we agree is that moral claims are evaluations. Our difference
here is about what sort of evaluations moral claims are, i.e. what feelings one is judging reasonable in making a moral judgement. See Essays VII and VIII.

It lends plausibility to emotivism about evaluations, and hence about morality if morality consists of evaluations. But, as already noted, it does not entail emotivism. The plausibility it lends to emotivism comes from certain background assumptions which we alluded to earlier in this section. But just as one can be a cognitivist about evaluations without being a realist so, I think, one can be a cognitivist about evaluations without being a rationalist. The latter claim will become clearer, I hope, in what follows.

If it is right, and if morality does consist of evaluations, the connection between morality and reason cannot be quite as simple as a pure rationalism about morality would suggest. This is not to say that there is no truth in rationalism about morality at all. How much truth there is remains to be seen. We shall also be concerned with another question: if moral judgements are evaluations, what is their relation to *practical* reason? It is a question about the relation between reasons to act and reasons to feel.

One might put the two questions as follows. If moral propositions consist of propositions about what there is reason to feel, specifically, about what there is reason to blame or feel guilty about, then

(1) How does reason bear on moral propositions?
(2) How do moral propositions bear on practical reasons? What status does the following inference have: if X is morally wrong then there is reason not to do X?

4. We have many ways of disapproving actions—holding an action *morally* wrong is only one. An action may be bizarre or tasteless, but not morally wrong. To call it morally wrong is a more serious matter: it amounts to blaming the agent. Blaming is an act or attitude whose notional core is a feeling in the way that feeling sorry is the notional core of apology. That is, these feelings are invoked as appropriate by the person who blames or apologizes even when he does not actually feel them.[4]

Let us call this emotional core of blame 'the blame-feeling'. We shall be more concerned with the idea that blame has an emotional core than with any particular characterization of the emotion or emotions involved. Important as it is to get the character of this emotion right,[5] the pertinent thesis for present purposes is that blame has an emotional core. To say that

---

[4] There is a wider sense of the word 'blame', in which we may for example blame the car's faulty brakes for the accident, in other words, identify them as its relevant cause. But blame in this wider sense involves no reference, even notional, to a core of feeling. If I blame the faulty brakes, I am not saying that it is reasonable or appropriate to have that feeling towards the brakes.

[5] Their content is discussed in Essays VII and VIII.

something is blameworthy is to make an evaluation—it is to say that it is
reasonable to feel the sentiment of blame towards it. If we now characterize the morally wrong as that which is blameworthy, i.e. that towards
which it is reasonable to have the blame-feeling, we can go on to characterize the other moral concepts. The morally right is that which it would
be morally wrong not to do. Similarly, we can say that 'X is morally obligatory', or 'X morally ought to be done' will hold just if non-performance
of X is blameworthy. Of course we admire people for going beyond the
morally obligatory—'beyond the call of duty'—even though we do not
blame them for not doing so. We can say that admiration of such actions
is moral admiration, because we admire them for the reasons that impelled
them, and those reasons are moral reasons. For example lack of consideration for others' feelings, when it reaches a certain point, becomes blameworthy thoughtlessness. On the other hand, there are degrees of care for
others' feelings which go well beyond what we would expect, on pain of
blame, from people in general—but which we still admire when we meet
with them. (There are also excesses of solicitude of course.) The outstand-
ingly and the ordinarily thoughtful person are both impelled by the same
reasons—consideration for others' feelings. And we can say that those reasons are moral reasons—as against, say, prudential or aesthetic reasons,
since their absence from a person's mind beyond a certain point becomes
blameworthy. Finally the virtues fit into this framework. They respectively
involve sensitivity to various types of reason for acting which we recognize
as *moral* reasons. And they are traits of character which we could be
blamed for not attempting to attain or lose, when it is possible for us to do
something to attain or lose them.

5. So morality can be 'characterized', as I have put it, in terms of the
blameworthy. Does this mean that 'morally wrong' can be *defined* in terms
of the blameworthy? That would be a stronger claim. The stronger claim
may give an immediate impression of definitional circularity.
'Blameworthy' means 'ought to be blamed'—is this 'ought' itself not a
moral 'ought'? If it is, then we won't be able to define 'X is morally wrong'
as 'The doer of X ought to be blamed'—even if their equivalence (or some
refinement of it) is a priori.

However, we should not accept that the 'ought' in this case is indeed a
moral ought. It is rather the 'ought' of evaluative reasons—that is to say,
it is definable in terms of reasons to adopt a feeling, or feeling-based attitude. To say that an action is blameworthy is to say that there is adequate
reason, taking everything into account, to blame the agent for doing it—
it is to say that blame is a fully reasonable response. That is an evaluative

claim. It may *also* be true that one has a moral obligation to blame people for their moral wrongdoing—that when it is *reasonable* to feel the sentiment of blame towards someone it is also *morally obligatory* to blame them. But that would be a separate claim.[6] On the characterization of 'morally obligatory' which we are considering, it would be the claim that it is fully reasonable to blame a person who does not blame people for their moral wrongdoing.

So far then, we have found no circularity in the suggestion that morality can be defined by means of the notion of blameworthiness. Nonetheless, I don't think that 'morally wrong' can strictly speaking be *defined* in terms of blameworthiness. The reasons for this have to do not with the circularity already discussed but with a circularity which arises from the fact that the concept of moral wrongness enters into the intentional content of the blame-feeling.

The blame-feeling requires a belief—that its object is something that has been done or omitted but *morally* ought not to have been done or omitted.[7] It requires it, one might suggest, in the way that fear requires that the object be dangerous. Certainly one can feel guilt about doing something one does not really believe to be morally wrong, just as one can fear something which one does not really believe dangerous. But in that case one's response is open to criticism, indeed self-criticism, as irrational.[8] The blameworthy and the morally wrong are indeed equivalent but the semantically prior term is 'morally wrong'. 'Blameworthy' means something like 'meriting that evaluative response which is appropriate to the morally wrong', and so it is circular to define 'morally wrong' in terms of 'blameworthy'.

6. There is a defence against this point which I am going to consider in some detail (though I will finally reject it). It defends the definition of 'morally wrong' as 'blameworthy', as follows. There is a *disanalogy*, it says, between the dangerous and the morally wrong. The dangerous can be

---

[6] A false one I should think. What is morally obligatory is an action (public or private) not a feeling. It might be morally wrong to convey blame to someone who is in an emotionally distressed state even if they are blameworthy. Or it might be expedient to refrain from self-blame when time is short and things need to be done, even though the feeling is reasonable. Or perhaps bygones must be bygones—as sometimes in negotiation with violent activists—so that the act of blame is inopportune even though the blame-feeling is justified.

[7] Of course the belief may be false—and the morality invoked may be the morality of thieves.

[8] Fear of fictions is not irrational. But there is supposed to be a philosophical problem about that case. One response to it, for example, is to argue that one does not really fear a fiction but imagines or makes-believe that one is fearing it (see Walton 1990).

characterized independently, as that which is liable to harm or damage. But, this defence says, in the case of moral wrongness no independent characterization can be given. To say that the object must be morally wrong for blame to be justified is correct. But it does not give an independent characterization of the object, any more than to say that the object must be amusing for amusement to be justified, or boring for boredom to be justified, gives an independent characterization. To say that something is boring is to say no more than that the proper and informed response to it is boredom—that it is boredom-worthy, one might say. Likewise, saying that something is morally wrong is saying that the proper or just response to it is blame: it is blame-feeling-worthy. In neither case do we appeal to an external standard but only to an internal standard—the standard of what people of competent sensibility would feel. Thus the semantically prior term is 'blameworthy', not 'morally wrong'.

On this view holding that something is morally wrong remains a perfectly objective judgement and forms the intentional content of feeling the blame-sentiment towards it. But then holding that something is boring is a perfectly objective judgement, and forms the intentional content of feeling the sentiment of boredom in relation to it. Evaluations in general are genuine judgements because they are accountable to standards of correctness—but the standards can be entirely internal. We distinguish between having an emotional response and judging it justified, even when there is no external criterion of justification such as danger in the case of fear. For example in the case of boredom and amusement there is no external criterion, but there is a difference between saying 'I am bored/amused' and saying 'This is boring/amusing.' Similarly with other terms of evaluation—'irritating', 'despicable', 'frightening', 'moving', 'boring', 'tasteless', 'contemptible', 'admirable', 'despicable', 'desirable', 'hateful', 'frightful', 'horrific', and so on. In each of these cases having the feeling goes, when certain other resources of concept-possession are in place, with a normative disposition—a disposition to make the corresponding evaluation. For example, when these resources are in place, to feel bored is to experience the feeling as reasonable—to experience the object as boring. Where defeating considerations are absent, it is to judge that it *is* boring.

The element of defeasibility underpins a distinction between the object seeming boring to me and its being boring—generally, between the object seeming to be φ-worthy and it's being φ-worthy. Without that general distinction the force of normativity that comes with raw feeling would encounter no resistance and generate no objective evaluative thought. What puts in place the distinction? An evaluator is justified in judging that an object is φ-worthy if

(i) the object makes him feel φ (or, if he is imagining a case, he can see that it would)

(ii) his total state of relevant evidence gives him no warrant to think that other competent evaluators will not or would not feel φ in these circumstances, and thus would not be inclined to judge the object φ-worthy.[9]

The evaluator does not just feel the emotion; feeling it as he feels it, without defeating information about himself or others, he judges it to be *appropriate*, and is committed to holding that other evaluators of competent sensibility would also feel it. If he feels the object of evaluation is not one of which he is a good judge, or that his own state is wrong, he will disqualify himself. 'I must say I was rather bored—but I was feeling tired/distracted/probably didn't understand what the point of it was/don't know much about Dutch flower painting' etc. Similarly, he may disqualify others—as incompetent judges of the subject, or as being in the wrong state. And the content of their judgements, in cases in which he himself feels confident, will for him be an important test of their competence.

I will call (i) and (ii) taken together the internal or 'hermeneutic' criterion of an evaluation. It provides, via (ii), what is needed to make the distinction between an object seeming to be φ-worthy and it's being φ-worthy. I call it internal or hermeneutic because the only materials it calls on are experience of φ, imagining of circumstances in which one would experience it, reflection on it and intersubjective comparison. That discipline is in play when we judge that what bored or amused us, or what aroused in us the blame-feeling, is not after all boring, amusing or blame-feeling-worthy. It is a hermeneutic discipline since its ground is what can intelligibly, understandably, produce a given emotional response. Evaluative judgements, then, are accountable to spontaneous feeling—but the spontaneity in question is that which survives experience, reflection, and intersubjective comparison and agreement. The standard it puts in place is an ideal of competent emotional response. No external criterion is required—and in particular, according to the line of thought we are considering, none is required in the case of the blameworthy.

Let us say that hermeneutically disciplined normative judgements about appropriate feeling are 'purely affectively grounded', and that the concepts which they predicate are 'purely affectively grounded' normative concepts. The defence which we are considering says that 'That is morally wrong' is nothing but an affectively grounded judgement, like 'That is boring/

---

[9] 'Total state of relevant evidence' is explained in Section 7.

amusing/irritating'. It says that the concept of wrongdoing is a purely affectively grounded concept.

7. Before examining this defence further it will be useful to consider the epistemology of the normative, and in particular the connection between judgement and convergence, a little more broadly.

The commitment one incurs in making an evaluation, to the claim that other judges who suffer from no disqualifying defect or limitation would confirm one's judgement, arises because evaluation is judgement. It is not a feature of *evaluative* judgement alone; it is a feature of judgement as such. When I judge, I enter a commitment that inquirers who scrutinized the relevant evidence and argument available to them would converge on my judgement—unless I could fault their judgement or their evidence. Faulting an inquirer's *judgement* would involve identifying some relevant internal weakness or inadequacy in his judging propensity on the subject in question, sufficient to justify me in discounting the judgement. That can include weaknesses of taste or sensibility, and distortions produced by special pleading or wishful thinking, etc.—not just faults of logic. Faulting the inquirer's *evidence* would involve showing that the information input into his judging process is faulty or restricted in such a way as to vitiate his assertion on the subject in question—that is, in such a way as to justify me in discounting it, even if I can find no fault in his judgement. The critical standards for fault-finding are those which normally apply. Thus the commitment is that if relevant data (where data are relevant at all) went on being collected, and reasoning rescrutinized, inquirers who did not fall out of consideration through demonstrable faults of evidence or judgement would stably converge on agreement with the judgement.

When I speak of 'entering a commitment' I mean that we are not called upon to give grounds for expecting this convergence, over and above our grounds for the judgement itself. Rather, the existence of the commitment shows itself negatively. If I come, in one way or another, to have reason to doubt that my judgement would attract convergence, I thereby come to have reason to withdraw it. When those grounds for doubt become strong enough, they force withdrawal.

What case can be made for this claim? The first relevant point is:

> (1) It is irrational to judge that: p but there is insufficient reason to judge that p.

There is of course no self-contradiction in a proposition of the form 'p but there is insufficient reason to judge that p'. Indeed it can be true. But to judge such a proposition true would be irrational. I cannot rationally judge that p while also judging that there is insufficient reason to judge that p.

Now this only shows that if I judge that p *I* am rationally committed to holding that there is sufficient reason to judge that p. It does not on its own show that if I judge that p I must hold that *anyone* who holds that there is insufficient reason to judge that p is faulty either in judgement or in evidence. But consider next the following principles.

(2) Given a total state of relevant evidence [E] x is justified in holding that there is sufficient reason for x to think that p if and only if (for all y)(if y is in [E] then y is justified in holding that there is sufficient reason for y to think that p).

(3) If p then any evidence that justifies x in judging that there is insufficient reason for x to think that p is either

(i) also insufficient to decide whether or not it is the case that p,

or

(ii) is misleading inasmuch as it justifies x in denying that p.

Since x's judgement that he has such-and-such evidence may be rational but wrong 'evidence' in (2) and (3) refers to the total set of factual propositions, relevant to the question whether p, which x can rationally *take* to specify x's evidence on that question. And where the question can be settled without evidence [E] will be null.

Now suppose I judge that p and that another thinker, y, does not hold that there is sufficient reason to judge that p. By (1) I am committed to judging that I have sufficient reason, and thus (in cases where evidence is required) sufficient evidence, to judge that p. Adding (2) and (3) I am committed to one of three conclusions. The first possibility is that y's evidence is faulty for reason (3i) or (3ii). That is, it is either insufficient or misleading—partial or distorted in some way. The second possibility is that y has not considered the question whether p—or else is faulty in judgement. That is, he doesn't just fail to consider the question whether p; he refuses to accept that p although the total relevant evidence available to him justifies him in holding that there is sufficient reason to believe that p. (If his total relevant evidence is the same as mine the conclusion that he has not considered the question or is faulty in judgement follows by (2)). The third possibility is that it is my own evidence or judgement which is faulty. In that case, by (1), I must withdraw my judgement that p. So given (1), (2), and (3) if I judge that p I am committed to judging that any thinker who refuses to judge that p is faulty in evidence or judgement.

It is the *judgement* that incurs the commitment—not the judgement's *content* that entails it. I am not defining truth in terms of convergence.

There are—of course—factual judgements which would be true if made, but on which convergence could not occur because sufficient relevant evidence could not be collected. But just because evidence for them is not available, they could not be *justified*, even though they would be true. Equally, whenever we accept a judgement—however good our evidence and reasoning for it—the possibility always remains open that we are wrong in doing so and hence wrong also in thinking that impeccable inquirers would converge to stable agreement on it. The convergence commitment is compatible with as radical a form of defeasibility as one likes.

Nonetheless there is here a fundamental asymmetry between normative and factual judgements.[10] In the case of a factual proposition there is the simple possibility that there may not be enough evidence to pass a verdict, however long and expensive the inquiry. The point arises from the very idea of a world within which we are situated and in which we interact epistemically with other objects. Such a world cannot be fully transparent to us. There are limitations on our possible epistemic interactions in it.

In the case of normative propositions no such point applies. The metaphysics of the normative domain provides no basis for the idea of fundamental normative propositions which we could never be justified in recognizing as true.[11] Corresponding to this distinction between normative and factual propositions there corresponds a distinction in their epistemology. It is the distinction between a dialogical epistemology, which can operate with a purely hermeneutic criterion as discussed in Section 6 and the epistemology of correspondence. The hermeneutic criterion and

[10] At this point I should explain my use of the terms 'fact', 'factual judgement', and 'factual proposition'. There is a broad or nominal and a narrow or ontologically substantial use of the word 'fact'. In the broad nominal sense 'the fact that' is simply a device of nominalization, equivalent to 'its being the case that'. In the narrow sense to talk about facts is to engage in an ontology which carries with it a corresponding epistemology. It is the narrow sense of 'fact' that I use in contrasting factual and normative propositions.

The correspondence theory of truth holds that truth is correspondence with the facts in this narrow, ontologically committed sense. It may be that a narrow notion of truth is current in ordinary discourse, of which the correspondence theory is true. That would be a narrow, ontologically substantial notion, and one would not be able to predicate it of normative propositions—a different term would be needed, such as 'correct' or 'valid'. On the other hand, on a minimalist view, truth is a broad, nominal notion (see Horwich 1990). The minimalist can endorse 'the proposition that p is true if and only if the fact that p obtains', if he uses 'fact' as well as 'true' in the broad nominal sense. But however one opts to use the word 'true', the important point is the difference in the epistemology and ontology of normative and factual propositions, which I refer to below as the difference between a dialogical epistemology and an epistemology of correspondence.

[11] By 'fundamental normative proposition' I mean 'normative proposition knowable independently of deduction from premisses which included a factual proposition'. A normative proposition deduced from decidable normative premisses together with some undecidable factual proposition would of course also be undecidable.

the dialogical epistemology which describes it applies to all fundamental normative propositions, not just fundamental evaluations. My grounds for asserting a normative proposition turn in the first instance on what I am spontaneously inclined to think, do, or feel. They are corrigible by further reflection and discussion. One route by which they are corrigible goes via the convergence commitment. Corrigibility underwrites the distinction between what seems to me to be true and what is true: it allows one to treat normative claims as genuine judgements. It also underwrites the same distinction in the case of factual propositions; but whether I am justified in asserting a factual proposition turns on whether I am justified in holding that I am appropriately linked to what it asserts to be the case. (I may be default-justified in holding that I am so linked; but if I have grounds for holding that I am *not* so linked these will be grounds for holding that I am not justified in asserting the proposition.) Such a notion of breakdown of evidential linkage simply does not apply in the case of fundamental normative propositions.

This view of normative propositions is what I described earlier as cognitivism without realism.[12] It does not hold that there is something which *makes* normative statements true or false, or correct or incorrect—in the realist's correspondence sense. In particular, a normative proposition is not *made true* by some fact to the effect that verdicts on it would ideally converge. That is not its truth-condition: it has no non-trivial one. A comprehensive truth-conditional semantics can include normative sentences within its remit, but it should be understood minimalistically. It employs minimalist or nominal notions of truth, reference, and predication, even

---

[12] It has affinities with views developed by Crispin Wright in (Wright 1992) but differs in an important respect. Whereas my claim is that the convergence commitment is incurred by the act of judgement itself, Wright argues (1992, 1996) that it is a certain concept of *truth* as representation or 'fit' that carries with it a convergence commitment. To judge true in that sense is to incur the commitment. But he holds that the concept of truth applicable to ethical judgements does not involve the notion of representation. The concept of truth which is applicable there, he suggests, allows that a person may, without irrationality, judge that an ethical proposition *p* is true while *also* judging that convergence of fault-free thinkers (thinkers who suffer from no 'cognitive shortcoming') cannot be expected to occur on that judgement. I agree with Wright that ethical truth involves no notion of 'fit' to a domain of reality. But if what has been said here is correct that is irrelevant. *No* notion of *truth* allows a person to judge a proposition true without incurring the convergence commitment, because the convergence commitment arises quite generally from the *rationality* of judgement rather than any particular notion of *truth*.

Note however that the convergence commitment provides no quick route to eliminating relativism—where that is understood as the view that truth is relative to some framework or whatever. If relativism is true about a class of propositions, then in judging some proposition in that class I am judging it to be true relative to a framework or whatever. In that case the commitment is that other competent judges would judge it true relative to *that* framework. They and I might still judge it false relative to some other framework.

though stronger notions are applicable to some of the terms and sentences with which it deals.

We can now return to the thread dropped in Section 6.

8. There can be normative judgements about what there is reason to feel which are purely affectively grounded, because such judgements are still subject to an internal or hermeneutic standard. They are grounded on an affective response but subject to the convergence commitment which arises from (1)–(3), that is, from principles which connect the concept of a judgement to that of a reason for judgement. But not only evaluations are disciplined hermeneutically—all normative judgements, be they epistemic, practical, or evaluative, are so. Epistemic normative judgements are grounded on a normative disposition to acknowledge reasons to *believe* which plays the role in their hermeneutic epistemology which a disposition to acknowledge reasons to feel plays in that of evaluations. Practical normative judgements are similarly grounded on a disposition to acknowledge reasons to act. In each of the three cases there are fundamental normative propositions—propositions not derivable from others in combination with factual premisses.

In what sense then are fundamental practical and epistemic propositions given by reason and evaluative ones not? Why do we want to say that evaluative reasons are not given to reason? One may respond that our notion of reason is the notion of something that thinkers and choosers can respond to whatever their capacities for feeling may be. Reason yields reasons which all thinkers and choosers have in common, whatever their capacities and reasons to feel.

On closer inspection things get more complicated. Consider this general principle (the 'Feeling/Disposition Principle'), which links evaluative and practical judgements:

> (FD) if there is reason to feel ϕ then there's reason to do that which ϕ disposes to.

Thus:

> If there's reason to be frightened of x, then there's reason to avoid x.
> If there's reason to be bored by x, then there's reason not to attend to x.
> If there's reason to admire x, then there's reason to praise, reward x.
> If there's reason to blame x, there's reason to withdraw recognition from x or impose a penalty on which continued recognition depends.
> etc.

Should we say that (FD) is a pure principle of practical reason? It is a fundamental principle about what there is reason to do. Is it then given to reason? Reason is that which yields reasons which all thinkers and choosers have in common, whatever their capacities to feel. But instances of (FD) are intelligible only to those capable of experiencing the relevant feeling. At the limit a pure practical reasoner with no capacity to feel would find no instance of (FD) intelligible—an impossible limit no doubt, but illustrative of the point. So let us give the following content to the denial that there is such a thing as *pure* practical reason. It is the denial that there are any fundamental practical propositions *other* than those derived from affectively grounded evaluations via (FD). One might call this a strict sentimentalism about evaluative and practical propositions, without any degree of rationalism.[13]

9. The desire for X disposes to actions which one believes will result in one's attaining X. So, by (FD), if there is reason to desire G, then there is reason to do that which one believes will result in one's attaining G. This has a superficial resemblance to two popular theses about practical reason: the desire-satisfaction model of practical rationality, according to which one has reason to act just if the action promotes the satisfaction of one's desires, and the instrumentalist or relativist conception, according to which a reason for action is always relativized to an objective. But it differs in at least two ways. In the first place it does not assert the biconditional: that there is reason to do that which one believes will result in one's attaining G if *and only if* there is reason to desire G. Secondly, it is cast not in terms of what one desires but in terms of what one has reason to desire. In contrast both the desire-satisfaction and the instrumentalist model of rationality share a defect—they short-circuit the normative connection between feelings on the one hand and action on the other, by dropping out the intervening role played by evaluations. It is not raw unprocessed emotions and desires that come to the court of practical judgement. It is evaluative judgements, about what there is reason to feel and to desire, that come to it.

Thus it simply does not follow deductively from the fact that I desire X and α-ing is a way of achieving X that there is reason for me to α. The question is, whether there is *reason* for me to desire X. It is true (as we acknowledged earlier) that what I desire is a defeasible criterion of what there is reason for me to desire, just as what I am bored by is a defeasible criterion of what there is reason to find boring. But it would be a fallacy

[13] It is not emotivism in the expressivist sense because it is consistent with taking evaluative and practical normative propositions to be genuine contents of judgement.

to treat that criterial relation as though it sustained a deduction. And only if there is reason for me to desire X and α-ing is a way of achieving X can we go on to argue via (FD) that there is reason for me to α.

The problem with instrumentalism is similar but sharper. Instrumentalism adds a further term to the reason to act relation, namely, a set of objectives, *O*: *the fact that p gives x reason of degree d at time t to α relative to O*. And it says that I ought do that (an) action which there is strongest reason to do relative to *my* objectives. But this is likely to be false. It is false if there is no reason to pursue my objectives, or just reason on the whole not to. Of course it will be true if my objectives coincide with those which there is most reason for me to pursue. But to think that this must be true is a pretty heroic assumption. The trouble again is that we are being served up objectives in raw, unevaluated form.

However the sentimentalist need endorse neither the desire-satisfaction nor the instrumentalist models of practical reason. He has a route from evaluative to practical judgements, via (FD), which brings in neither of these. But is it sufficiently broad? How does it make sense of the connection between judging that something is morally wrong and judging that there is reason not to do it? Or of the connection between ideals—of excellence in activity and character—and reasons for action? Just as morality stands to the blame-feeling so ideals of excellence stand to the feeling of admiration. Judgements about what is morally wrong and about what is excellent are evaluative judgements about what one has reason to blame and what one has reason to admire. But whence comes the principle that there is reason not to do what is wrong, and not just to blame it, or that there is reason to pursue excellence and not just to admire it?

These two principles, like (FD), are *bridge-principles* which take us from a species of evaluative judgement, grounded in its characteristic affect, to a practical judgement, about what there is reason for someone or everyone to do. Indeed all fundamental practical propositions are bridge-principles; they must all, to be intelligible, invoke an evaluation. So long as we restrict attention to (FD) the purely sentimentalist position has some plausibility. But what kind of grounding do these other bridge-principles have?

Suppose we identify a person's well-being with that which the person has reason to desire. Then formal egoism, the principle that every person has reason to promote his or her own well-being, comes to be a special case of (FD). On the other hand another bridge-principle, crossing the same gap, is the 'principle of universal concern', to the effect that any agent has reason to promote any subject's well-being. This principle is no more derivable from (FD) than the perfectionist principle of excellence is.

We can characterize the argument between sentimentalist and rationalist as being about whether there are true bridge-principles other than (FD). Rationalism about practical reason is the view that there are true bridge-principles other than (FD), principles which are known by pure rational insight. Perfectionism and the principle of universal concern are possible examples. To take the rationalist view of either of them is to hold that it is knowable by any rational being—whatever the *evaluations* proper to that being's community of sentiment might be. In other words, whatever that rational being's affective nature might be, and whatever it might thus have reason to desire or admire, and whatever would therefore constitute its well-being or excellence—it would be able to see, by its reason alone, the truth or otherwise of the perfectionist principle or the principle of universal concern. But the admirable, like well-being (the desirable) would still be evaluative notions. Pure practical reason would still deal in bridge-principles from evaluations to reasons for action, just as pure theoretical reason deals in bridge-principles from facts to reasons to believe.

10. The judgement that a particular piano performance is not merely technically accurate, but beautiful, insightful, profound, has its own internal discipline, grounded in what we spontaneously admire. By (FD) it sustains the practical conclusion that there is reason to praise, reward. But that judgement in itself does not tell me, for example, whether I should learn to play like that, or whether I ought to put any proportion of the resources I control to the promotion of piano-playing like that. To get a conclusion about reasons for action we need a bridge-principle—which a perfectionist ethic seeks to specify.

What of the *moral* source of reasons for acting? Here too, by (FD), we get the conclusion, where there is reason to respond with the blame-feeling, that there is reason to blame—to exclude and offer renewed recognition by punishment.[14] The sentimentalist could add that there is reason to avoid wrongdoing if being blamed by oneself or others is bad for one, that is, one has reason to desire to avoid it. In that case it will be an open question whether avoiding the morally wrong thing is something one has reason to do—it will turn on whether being blamed is bad for one. Similarly it will be an open question whether achieving the admirable is good for one—something one has reason to desire.

In the case of the admirable I find that quite plausible. That an achievement is admirable gives me reason to desire to achieve it, as against applauding it in others, only if it will be good for me, conducive to my

---

[14] See Essays VII and VIII for further discussion of the characteristic disposition of the blame-feeling.

well-being, to achieve it. In this sense, I am not a perfectionist.[15] In contrast, the principle of morality, as against the principle of perfectionism, strikes me as correct:

(M) if α-ing is morally wrong then there is reason not to α.

(M) states the principle partially[16] but not elliptically—there is no hidden condition. To agree to it is to agree that morality is, in one familiar sense at least, categorical.[17] But is that consistent with the purely affective concept of wrongdoing? Well, the defender of that concept is not necessarily a sentimentalist overall. He can hold that (M) is a bridge-principle evident to pure reason, even though the concept of the morally wrong is purely affective. To refute his view of the concept of moral wrongdoing we must argue that (M) is a conceptual truth, a principle 'constitutive of the concept' of moral wrongdoing. Only then can we conclude that that concept is not a pure affectively determined concept, like the concept of the admirable, or the desirable.

Is (M) correct at all? Of course it is a controversial claim. Some philosophers would deny that (M) is unconditionally true. They would argue that to transform (M) into something true we need at least to add some further condition to the antecedent, for example about what the agent desires, or has reason to desire, or what is in his interests—or what promotes the general good, perfection, etc. So the correct principle would have the form

if α-ing is morally wrong and C(α), then there is reason not to α.

More specifically, if the condition is agent-relative,[18] concerning say the agent's desires or interests, it would have the form

if α-ing is morally wrong and C(α, x), then there is reason for x not to α.

However, given that the morally wrong is the blameworthy, that which there is reason to blame, (M) becomes

if there is reason to blame a person who αs, then there is reason not to α.

---

[15] i.e. in Tom Hurka's sense (see Hurka 1993).

[16] Partially because it says nothing about the comparative strength of reasons generated from the moral source. Note that given (M) and the definition of 'morally right' above it will follow that if X is morally right then there is reason to do X.

[17] In David Brink's sense it is authoritative, whether or not supreme. See Brink (1997: 255).

[18] See Essay III for an account of this concept.

And this is just the contraposition of

> (M′) if there is no reason not to α, then there is no reason to blame a person who αs.

I submit that (M′) is an obvious truth as it stands. One simply doesn't count as giving reasons for blaming a person *unless* one is giving reasons why that person should not have done what he did. If I can establish that there was no reason for a person not to α I *have*, unconditionally, established that that person was blameless in doing α. I do not have to establish that any further condition obtains, as I would have to if (M) needed to be expanded by a further condition in the antecedent as suggested above.

Moreover, the unconditional truth of (M′) is a constitutive feature of the concept of blame. Compare the following principle:

> If X is not dangerous—has no power to cause injury or harm—then there is no reason to be frightened of X (X is not fear-worthy).

Just as one can argue that there is no reason to fear a thing (a spider, say) because it has no power to cause injury or harm, so one can argue that a person deserves no blame, because there was no reason not to do what he did. The principle about the dangerous can be seen to be true just by reflection on fear and what there is reason to fear. Someone who hasn't grasped that if a thing is not dangerous then there's no reason to fear it hasn't grasped the constitutive relation between the concept of danger and the concept of fear. But this shows that the concept of what there is reason to fear, the 'fear-worthy', is not a purely affectively determined concept. It has a conceptually constitutive external criterion which is external in the sense that, when it comes to determining whether a thing is fear-worthy, our common evaluative responses can be defeated by evidence that it has no capacity to harm. The hermeneutically grounded judgement that spiders are frightening/fear-worthy can be defeated by showing that they are not dangerous—there is nothing to fear. Similarly, the blameworthy is not a purely affectively determined concept. It too has a conceptually constitutive external criterion, which is not a matter of reflecting on our common evaluative responses, and which can defeat them. But in this case the criterion is applied not solely by appeal to evidence but also by appeal to practical reason.

11. The standard of moral right and wrong is thus not fixed solely by the hermeneutics of the blame-feeling. The proposed definition of moral wrongness in terms of blame-feeling-worthiness which we have been considering does express an important insight: our spontaneous sentiments of

blame, shaped by reflection and discussion, shape our judgements of moral right and wrong from the inside. But our concept of moral wrongness allows—via (M)—for an external shaping influence as well, from practical reason as such.

It leaves a place for practical reason to plug in an external criterion, but it makes no determination as to whether there *is* anything with substantive content to plug in, or if there is, what it is. However, we need to have a view before us as to what if anything plugs in if we are to study the relation between morality and practical reason. So suppose our view is that there is just one principle of pure practical reason—the principle of universal concern.

What does it mean to say that this is the only principle? We recognized (FD) as a bridge-principle, but gave a reason in Section 8 for denying that it was a *pure* principle of practical reason. A very strong formulation of the reason would be this: a principle which requires an affective capacity for direct or first-personal knowledge of its truth (as against knowledge by testimony, say) is not a pure principle of practical reason. (FD) can only be known through its instances; and each of those instances can be known directly only by someone with the appropriate capacity. By the same argument, (M) is not a pure principle of practical reason. It can be known directly only by someone with the capacity to experience the blame-feeling—just as the principle about fear, that if there is reason to fear something, then it is dangerous, can be known directly only by someone with the capacity to experience fear.

But can this same reasoning not be applied to the principle of universal concern itself? That says that every agent has reason to promote every subject's well-being. Is not the concept of well-being affectively determined, being the concept of what the subject has reason to desire?[19] And does this not mean that an agent without the capacity to desire cannot know its truth directly?

One can imagine a number of responses to this, some of them unflinchingly Kantian. My own inclination is to accept that the concept of well-being, or the desirable, is affectively determined—so on the very strong criterion of pure practical reason the principle of universal concern is not a principle of pure practical reason. But on that very strong criterion nothing is—if I am right in arguing that all practical principles are bridge-principles with one of their piers grounded on some evaluation or other. If

---

[19] To identify the notion of a subject's well-being with what the subject has reason to desire is a substantial claim, of course. For example there are sentient subjects whose well-being has an authoritative claim on our concern—can they be said to have reasons to desire? I believe they can—see Essay VI, Sect. 3, and appendix.

we want a viable concept of pure practical reason, this criterion is too strong. What is relevant, rather, is that pure rational insight (as distinct from insight into hermeneutic principles of the emotions), as well as the affective capacity presupposed in grasping the concept of the desirable, is required for direct knowledge of the principle of universal concern, and that the principle is not derived from any other more fundamental practical proposition. In that sense it is a pure principle of practical reason.

To say that it's the only such principle is then to say that it *arbitrates* on what we have reason to do as no other principle does. What I mean by this is that it alone can defeat all affectively grounded reasons for acting. That of course makes the claim that it is the only principle of practical reason a very large one. Here I will only illustrate what it would imply for one particular set of affectively grounded responses—moral ones. In this case the arbitration works via (M): an activity which there is no reason not to do cannot be morally wrong—and the principle of universal concern, as the sole principle of practical reason, arbitrates on whether there is reason to do something.

But this does not mean that all practical reasons must be *derived* from it. If there is a principle of pure practical reason, a substantive external criterion of moral wrongness, its bearing on our moral judgements can and should be thought of in a conservative-holist, rather than a linear-foundationalist, way. The guidance given for action and evaluation by our internally determined judgements of blameworthiness has default status—neither more, nor less. It is legitimate guidance, in the absence of a well-made case against it; but it is corrigible by practical reason. Our ethical tradition emerges largely from human feelings of admiration and blame. It may nevertheless be shaped in its evolution by reason. Even where those feelings strongly cluster, for example feelings of blame around homosexuality, we can detach from them, stand back, and ask what is wrong with homosexuality. At this point we ask, for example, what harm a consenting homosexual relationship does, either to those involved or to others.

Structurally, the external standard of practical reason functions in much the way that standards of scientific method do. In each case they operate on an *existing* ethical or cosmological tradition, whose sources lie in the one case in substantive emotional responses, and in the other, in dispositions to substantive beliefs about the world.

With this in mind, let us return to the concept of moral wrongness. It is not *definable* in terms of the blame-feeling because it is not a purely affectively determined concept—it keeps a space open for criteria of practical reason. It is true that a thing is morally wrong just if it is blameworthy but that is because a thing is worthy of blame only if it is morally wrong, just as a thing merits fear only if it is dangerous. To acknowledge a reason for blaming or fearing a thing one must judge it to be morally wrong or dangerous; and this is a non-vacuous condition, unlike 'to acknowledge a reason for admiring something one must judge it to be admirable'.

'Wrong', in the moral sense of the word, is a semantically simple predicate. It is semantically simple in the way that 'yellow' is.[20] Moreover the explanation strikes me as similar in each case. Just as 'wrong' signifies a concept which is not determined purely affectively, so 'yellow' signifies a concept which is not determined purely sensationally. In the one case the concept *wrong* leaves a space for correction by criteria of practical reason, in the other, the concept *yellow* leaves a space for correction by criteria of theoretical reason.

Compare the following two principles:

> (i) If X arouses in me the blame-feeling, then, *ceteris paribus*, I am justified in judging that X is wrong
> (ii) If X produces in me a visual experience as of X's being yellow, then, *ceteris paribus*, I am justified in judging that X is yellow.

They seem to me to be roughly right, and partially constitutive, respectively, of the concepts *wrong* and *yellow*. They are epistemic norms[21] which partially constitute those particular concepts.

Each of them is a defeasible entry norm for the concept, containing provision for defeat in the *ceteris paribus* clause. In each case, the warrant provided by the norm may be defeated in two ways. It is defeated in the first way if something in my total state of relevant evidence warrants the view that I am not currently a competent judge of the matter in question. That possibility is already provided, as we emphasized earlier, by the internal or hermeneutic discipline which regulates pure affectively determined judgements involving such concepts as 'amusing', 'boring', and 'irritating'. Because these are pure affectively determined concepts the corresponding predicates are not semantically simple. '*x* is amusing/boring/irritating' is analysable as meaning something like 'There is reason to be amused/bored/irritated by *x*.' There *could* be judgements

---

[20] 'Yellow' was Moore's example in *Principia Ethica* (Moore 1903) but the comparison he drew (in Sects. 6 and 7) was between 'yellow' and 'good'. It was the ethical term, 'good', rather than the moral term, 'wrong', that he took to be semantically simple. I think he was mistaken in taking that view, and also mistaken in attempting to *define* 'right' or 'duty' in terms of 'good' (e.g. Sect. 89). This is not to deny that the good is prior to the right; however the view proposed here is closer on these points to Mill than Moore, even though it does not follow Mill so far as to hold that the moral can be defined, as against characterized, in terms of the penal sentiment of blame. (For more on Mill's view see Essay VII.)

[21] 'Norm' here is short for 'true normative proposition'.

which were similarly determined, wholly internally, by visual experiences of colour. Then '*x* is yellow' would mean something along the lines of '*x* would produce an experience of yellow in a normal person in normal conditions', where the normality of oneself and the conditions is the default assumption. But colour judgements are not like that, any more than moral judgements are. The concept *wrong* has an exit norm, as well an entry norm, provided by principle (M). Analogously, the concept *yellow* is the concept of a colour, and the concept of a colour is the concept of a categorical property of perceived and unperceived, even unperceivable, objects.

These exit norms put moral and colour judgements within the remit of general considerations of practical and theoretical reason. Thus if general considerations of practical reason, together with empirical data, show that there is no reason not to do X then it will follow that X is not morally wrong. Similarly, general considerations of theoretical reason, together with empirical data, may issue in a theory of the properties of objects which comes into tension at one point or another with the pattern of our colour judgements, insofar as these are regulated solely by their internal, perception-driven, standard. At the limit they might issue in a theory of the categorical properties of nature onto which our colour predicates cannot be satisfactorily mapped, but which *can* explain our experiences of colour. That would amount to a case for an error theory of colour judgements. Could there be a similar extreme in the ethical case—one in which general considerations of practical reason lead us to conclude that we should withdraw from making moral judgements entirely? A utilitarian might conclude, in some possible worlds at least, that blaming people never promotes the general good to any degree, and hence that there is never reason to blame. He or she might then argue, contrapositively via (FD), that the blame-feeling is never reasonable and hence that nothing is morally wrong. (Some people seem to think this argument holds in the actual world.) However, the second step in this argument would be unsound. You cannot use a principle of practical reason in that way. What was said earlier in this section was that practical reason *arbitrates* on what we have reason to do, in the sense that its reasons can defeat reasons generated by (FD). But to defeat them is not to strike them down as wholly null: they are defeated but they remain reasons. So there is no contrapositive move to the irrationality of the blame-*feeling*, even if the conclusion that *acts* of blame are never justified is right. Where that latter conclusion, that acts of blame are never justified, would leave the institution of morality, is something that requires extended consideration. On the face of it however, something much stronger is needed to get the genuinely error-theoretical conclusion that nothing is ever morally right or wrong—perhaps a nihilist account of practical reason which then worked through M or a strengthened version of M.

I have tried to indicate, in this last section, why it is that 'yellow' and 'wrong' are semantically simple predicates. The explanation, I have suggested, rests on certain points about the epistemic norms which constitute the concepts *yellow* and *wrong*. How do the points about the concepts connect with the point about the words? This question could be answered fully only within the framework of an account of concepts and a semantic theory. I have in fact been assuming such a framework.[22] The framework takes it that the semantics of a language is given truth-conditionally; within that theory the semantic clauses for 'yellow' and 'morally wrong' will state

> x satisfies the predicate of English 'yellow' just if x is yellow
> x satisfies the predicate of English 'morally wrong' just if x is morally wrong.

A person can grasp those clauses, and thus the meaning of 'yellow' and 'morally wrong' in English, only if he possesses the concepts *yellow* and *morally wrong*. The framework further takes it that grasping a concept is acknowledging a pattern of defeasible entry and exit norms which constitute that concept. These constitutive norms come at the level of an account of concepts, or cognitive roles, not at the level of semantic theory. They are not analytic on the *predicates* 'yellow' or 'morally wrong', in the way that 'A father is a male parent' or 'Tomorrow is the day after today' are analytic on 'father' and 'tomorrow'. One can consistently hold that the predicates are semantically simple while holding that the concepts they express are constituted by a complex pattern of entry and exit norms. Thus the relevant interconnections between reasons to blame and reasons to act constitute the concept of the morally wrong, even though 'morally wrong' is a semantically primitive, indefinable predicate.

[22] I touch on some but by no means all of the issues it raises in Skorupski (1997*a*).

III

Neutral versus Relative: Philosophical Utilitarianism and Practical Reason

1. The first part of this essay (Sections 2–5) examines the distinction between 'neutral' and 'relative' reasons, a distinction which plays a role in a number of the essays in this book. A special case of it, which has been much discussed, is the distinction between agent-neutral and agent-relative reasons. It is quite common at the moment to make 'agent-neutrality' a necessary condition of an ethical position called 'consequentialism' and to contrast that with 'deontology', which is held to be 'agent-relative'.[1] Both these tendencies, I shall argue, regrettably obscure useful distinctions. This will prompt us to consider the contrast between deontological and teleological ethics more widely, and also to consider that much abused term, 'utilitarianism'.

The final section of this essay (Section 6) moves beyond these questions, which mainly turn on finding a perspicuous terminology (always important in philosophy of course). It considers the relationship between what I shall call 'philosophical' or 'generic' utilitarianism and pure practical reason. Contrasting those reasons for action which stem from pure practical reason with reasons for action which stem from evaluative reasons—reasons to feel—it proposes that the former are agent-neutral.

Sidgwick famously argued that there is a dualism in practical reason. He held that two 'axioms' could *independently* be exhibited as rationally evident and fundamental: that of the Rational Egoist, the axiom of

Sections 1–5 of this essay are derived from two papers: 'Agent-Neutrality, Consequentialism, Utilitarianism: A Terminological Note' and 'Neutral versus Relative: A Reply to Broome, and McNaughton and Rawling', respectively in *Utilitas*, 7 (1995: 49–54, and 8 (1996: 235–48). The second paper was a reply to criticisms of the first by Broome (1995) and McNaughton and Rawling (1996). I have taken account of their comments in preparing Sects. 2–5 but have omitted specific responses to and criticisms of their views. I am grateful to them, and to Roger Crisp, Berys Gaut, and Brad Hooker for comment and criticism.

[1] David McNaughton and Piers Rawling have defended this view in detail–they cite a number of authors who have adopted it. See McNaughton and Rawling (1991, 1995, 1998). Its critics include Jonathan Bennett (1989) and John Broome (1991: 5–6).

Prudence, and that of the Utilitarian, the axiom of Rational Benevolence.[2] It could not be ruled out, according to Sidgwick, that in some circumstances these axioms might recommend incompatible courses of action—in which case there would be 'an ultimate and fundamental contradiction in our apparent intuitions of what is Reasonable in conduct'.[3] Drawing on Essay II ('Reasons and Reason') I will propose that Sidgwick was quite right to hold that these two 'axioms' are independent. They have different sources; Rational Prudence is not just a corollary of Rational Benevolence. Yet, just because they have different sources, it remains true that philosophical utilitarianism is the sole principle of *pure* practical reason. Thus although the two principles, of rational egoism and philosophical utilitarianism, are indeed independent there is, contrary to Sidgwick, no dualism of *pure practical reason*.

2. Let us begin with a definition of agent-neutrality. It is in the spirit of Thomas Nagel's seminal account in *The Possibility of Altruism*.[4]
    Consider the schema
        if it were the case that Py that would give x reason to y for some predicate 'P', where 'x' ranges over agents and 'y'
        ranges over actions (including inactions) open to x.[5] We will call 'P' a *reason-predicate* and say that if the schema is true in the case of a particular predicate 'P' for all agents and actions, 'P' *expresses* a reason for action.

Definition:
    (i) If 'P' contains a free occurrence of 'x' then it is an agent-relative reason-predicate. If it does not, it is an agent-neutral reason-predicate.
    (ii) A reason for action which is expressible by an agent-neutral reason-predicate is agent-neutral. A reason for action which is not so expressible is agent-relative.

This strikes me as a useful distinction. It makes clear, for example, the difference between Sidgwick's rational egoist and the utilitarian. Indeed the credit for seeing how (in essence) this distinction clarifies the issue between

---

[2] Sidgwick (1893: 387).   [3] Ibid. 507.
[4] Nagel (1970: chs. VII and X). In this book Nagel uses the terms 'objective' for 'agent-neutral' and 'subjective' for 'agent-relative'. In Nagel (1986: 152–3) he adopts instead the terms 'agent-neutral' and 'agent-relative' but gives the same account of the distinction, referring back to his previous discussion. However in ch. IX of the latter book he introduces a class of 'deontological reasons' which he takes to be agent-relative (165–6). On my argument here, treating the particular reasons Nagel has in mind as agent-relative is a mistake.
[5] Thus the domain of 'P' is the set of action-types open to the agent; it is fixed when the value of x is fixed.

them should go to him.[6] The rational egoist and the utilitarian respectively believe that the following (enriched by an account of what determines the strength of their respective kinds of reason) are the sole foundations of ethics:

> Rational egoist: $(x)(y)$(if it were the case that y probabilized a benefit to x that would give x reason to y)
> Utilitarian: $(x')(x'')(y)$(if it were the case that y probabilized a benefit to x'' that would give x' reason to y).[7]

Then there is the irrational egoist, whose sole principle is:
> $(x)(y)$(if it were the case that y probabilized a benefit to ME that would give x reason to y).

His view is that benefits to HIM are, as such, agent-neutral reasons for action. He does not derive his principle by substituting the indexical expression 'ME' into the utilitarian's or rational egoist's principle. He takes it as primitive. Sidgwick rejects this view as irrational because he sees that what makes my benefit an agent-neutral reason for action cannot be the fact that it is MY benefit. If it is an *agent-neutral* reason for action that must be because it is that: a benefit—not because it is *my* benefit.

This train of thought involves an interplay between the concepts of agent-neutrality and universalizability. The irrational egoist's reasons are agent-neutral but not universalizable, in the sense that his principle has a non-incidental rigid designator, 'ME', in the reason-predicate: one which cannot be eliminated without losing his fundamental thought.[8]

With these Sidgwickian points in mind let us now characterize a reason as impartial when it is both agent-neutral and universalizable. Impartiality, then, is a stronger notion than either agent-neutrality or universalizability on its own.[9]

---

[6] e.g. Sidgwick (1893: 420–1). See also Mackie (1976) and Schneewind (1977) (which I review in Skorupski 1979).

[7] Read these two theses as follows.

Rational egoist: for every person x, and every action y open to x, if it were the case that y probabilized a benefit to x that would give x reason to y.

Utilitarian: for every person x', and every person x'' (x' may be identical with x''), and every action y open to x', if it were the case that y probabilized a benefit to x'' that would give x' reason to y.

Similarly for other principles below.

[8] 't' is a rigid designator if it does not make sense to suppose that t (literally) might not have been t: as in 'I might not have been me.'

[9] This way of using 'impartiality' can be questioned. McNaughton and Rawling (1996) suggest that it 'has the disquieting consequence that deontology, because it contains duties of special relationship, is not an impartial moral theory' (324). (Note, incidentally, that unlike Nagel (1986) they thus include duties of special relationship within

3. On the definition of Section 2 there are no grounds for classing principles as agent-relative just because they are 'deontological'. We will come back to that term shortly. For the moment let us simply take it to mean 'principle concerning what is morally right (i. e. morally obligatory) or morally wrong'. Thus consider 'It is (morally) wrong to kill innocent people.' In reason-giving terms that entails at least this:

> (i) $(x)(y)$(if it were the case that y was the killing of an innocent person that would give x reason not to y).

But here the reason-predicate is agent-neutral, so the reason for action it expresses is agent-neutral because it is expressible by an agent-neutral reason-predicate.

Many 'deontological' principles are agent-relative—'It is wrong to neglect one's children', for example. Nor is this accidental. It arises from the role played by morality in ethical life. Agent-relative moral duties can arise from people's status or office, their relations and their previous interactions or agreements. Nonetheless, as well as these there are agent-neutral moral duties, such as the duty not to kill the innocent, whoever they may be. Morality is not *inherently* agent-relative. Some moral principles are agent-relative but some are not.

There is, it is true, a difference between the principle that it is wrong to kill innocent people, and the principle that you should minimize the killing of innocent people. Situations are possible in which one would minimize the killing of innocent people by killing an innocent person: the principle that killing the innocent is wrong entails that it is wrong in those situations too. But it is a mistake to handle this distinction as a difference between agent-relative and agent-neutral reasons. It is, in particular, a mistake to treat it as though it could be exhibited as the distinction between

'deontology'.) They find this disquieting because they agree with 'many philosophers' who 'regard impartiality as a minimum *desideratum* for any moral theory'. Hence they prefer a characterization of impartiality according to which impartiality consists in giving *due* weight to rival interests—that weight which moral considerations require.

I agree that mere theoretical neatness or brevity should not distort our use of crucial prephilosophical moral terms. But I don't think that is happening here. Consider someone who feels an obligation to give her child the best possible education. Assume that that education will give the child a cultural advantage over other children. One might well say, nevertheless, that she is doing what she has a duty to do, or is at least 'permitted' to do, but one would not say that she is showing, at least in this decision, an impartial concern for the education of all children. This, some of us feel, is a case in which one is not obliged to be impartial; or indeed a case in which one is obliged not to be. McNaughton and Rawling would prefer to describe the situation as one in which the mother is indeed being impartial; she is giving due moral weight to the interests of her child as against others'. I don't see that ordinary moral thought favours their usage as against mine. Indeed I suspect that an insistence that morally right action is always impartial is more misleading than not—it raises suspicions about distorting ideals of what it is to be moral that may lie behind it.

(ii) $(x)(y)$(if it were the case that y was the killing of an innocent person by x that would give x reason not to y)

and

(iii) $(x)(y)$(if it were the case that y increased the number of innocent people killed that would give x reason not to y).

The reason-predicate in (ii) is indeed agent-relative, while the reason-predicate in (iii) is agent-neutral. But that does not show that the *reason* expressed by the reason-predicate in (ii) is agent-relative. For (ii) has exactly the same force as (i) in which the reason-predicate is agent-neutral. That is, 'x ys and y is the killing of an innocent person' and 'x ys and y is the killing of an innocent person by x' are analytically equivalent. There is no possible world in which one of them is true and not the other. And it's a priori that there is not.[10]

In general, any agent-neutral reason-predicate, 'Ry', can be converted into an agent-relative predicate, 'y is an R-ing by x'. That does not show that it expresses an agent-relative reason. The question is whether you *can* express the reason with an agent-neutral predicate. For example the predicate 'y promotes the interests of x's grandfather' expresses a genuinely agent-relative reason because you cannot express it with an agent-neutral predicate. 'y promotes the interests of MY grandfather', if taken as expressing a reason not expressible by the previous predicate, would express a reason like the irrational egoist's—irrational familyism perhaps. In contrast 'y is the killing of an innocent person by x', 'y is the promoting of general good by x', etc. do not express agent-relative reasons.

Just as I may be an irrational egoist or an irrational familyist, I may be an irrational 'deontologist'. That is, I may hold it wrong for ME to kill innocent people—but refuse to see this conviction as an instance of a universal principle that it is wrong for anyone to kill innocent people (or an instance of or deduction from any other universal principle). In that case, my conviction is not impartial, on the definition in Section 3. However that is not because it generates reasons which are agent-relative; it is because it is not universalizable. It strikes me, as it struck Sidgwick, that universalizability is a condition of rationality—that is not to say, of course, that the position of these irrational thinkers is literally unintelligible, or

---

[10] It is also wrong to interpret 'You should not kill innocent people' as 'You should ensure, to the best of your ability, that you do not kill innocent people' (as McNaughton and Rawling have suggested). There may be ways of ensuring that, *other* than by not killing innocent people; the latter principle entails that there is some reason for one to act in those ways, whereas the former does not. In other words, 'x does not kill innocent people' and 'x ensures that x does not kill innocent people' are *not* analytically equivalent.

refutable by mere reflection on the meaning of words. (Note also that thoughts like 'What other people do is up to them—*I'm* not the sort of person who tells lies' are consistent with universalizability just because they appeal to the *sort* of person I take myself to be.)

4. What then about agent-neutrality and 'consequentialism'? I suggest that 'consequentialism' is best used to refer to a view about the relation between the theory of the morally right (that which is morally obligatory, a moral duty) and the theory of the ethical good. Consequentialists take a theory of good to be basic. They hold that actions (tokens or types) can be said to have a degree of goodness or badness, and that the goodness or badness of actions is determined by the intrinsic goodness or badness of their consequences, including therein the intrinsic goodness or badness, if any, of the actions themselves. They then hold (and this is what makes them consequentialists) that an action (token or type) is right just in virtue of being best, optimal (i.e. that is what *makes* it right). Or that it is right just in virtue of the fact that the agent, given his information state, should rationally have believed it to be optimal, etc. Or again that a type of action is right just in virtue of the fact that it would be optimal for an agent to do it most of the time, or for everyone to have internalized the injunction to do it regularly, etc.[11] They may hold this as a definition of (morally) 'right', or as a substantive moral position.

Now we can extend the distinction between neutral and relative to the good. It is then the distinction between what is good for x and what is good *tout court* (we will come back to this in Section 6). The rational egoist holds that while there are things that are good for each person, there is nothing that is good *tout court*. If the rational egoist then defines 'right action for x' as 'optimal action for x' (or in one of the more complicated consequentialist ways mentioned in the previous paragraph), he is a consequentialist, but an agent-relative one. Since a theory of the good may generate agent-neutral or, as with Sidgwick's rational egoist, agent-relative principles of right action, agent-neutrality in its principles of right action is not a necessary condition of consequentialism.

But if there can be agent-relative forms of consequentialism, can we trivially reduce all principles of right action to the maximization of some agent-relative value?

Someone might say '*My* doing the *right* thing has a special value for *me now*, which is maximized by acting rightly now, even if that ensures that I will often act wrongly in future.' Presumably that is sustainable only if the

[11] I mean to include here forms of 'rule-consequentialism' such as that defended by Brad Hooker (Hooker 1999).

value is relative not just to him but to the time at which he speaks[12]—but what intelligible value could that represent? Waiving that point there is a more obvious thing to be said. It is not the value to oneself *derived* from doing the right thing that *makes* it the right thing. Something else must make it the right thing, whether or not it comes down to consequences of some kind, and *then* one can derive an agent-relative value, such as self-respect, from doing the right thing. So the rightness of an action cannot be reduced to its optimizing some agent-relative value derived from doing the right thing.

It would make sense to use 'deontology' in its original sense, to refer to the theory of duty—morally right and wrong action, the morally obligatory, the morally forbidden and permitted. Instead of talking about 'deontological principles', which would properly be principles in this theory of morality, we could simply have talked about *moral* principles and said that *moral* principles may be either agent-neutral or agent-relative. Likewise, it would make sense to use 'teleology' to refer to the theory of ends, of what is desirable—the good, whether it be neutral or relative. What shall we then call the view that deontology is not at all derivable from, or in any way correctable by, teleology? Sticking to some established usages at least, we can call this *pure deontological ethics*. Kant's ethics is purely deontological in this way:

the concept of good and evil is not defined prior to the moral law, to which, it would seem, the former would have to serve as foundation, rather the concept of good and evil must be defined after and by means of the law.[13]

Consequentialism, or *pure* teleological ethics, in contrast, affirms that deontology is wholly *derivable* from a theory of intrinsic ethical value.[14]

But there is also a mixed position according to which moral principles are not derived or derivable from a theory of the good but are correctable by it. In my view this captures what is right in the intuitions of those who propose a pure deontological ethics, while giving due recognition to the fundamental role of teleology. So I suggest that it should be classified as teleological but not consequentialist, that is, not purely teleological.[15]

---

[12] See Sect. 5 for the notion of temporal relativity.　　　[13] Kant (1956: 65).

[14] One can endorse teleological ethics while holding that the primitive concept, in terms of which intrinsic ethical value is defined, is that of a reason for action. Good and bad would still on this conception be defined prior to the *moral* law, though not prior to the notion of a reason for action.

[15] I defend this position in Essays II, V, VII, and especially VIII, Sect. 8. (In his discussion of these terms Rawls says that deontological ethics 'either does not specify the good independently from the right, or [it] does not interpret the right as maximizing the good' (Rawls 1971: 30). That would seem to make the mixed position a species of deontological ethics, though it depends on what one means by 'interpret'.)

At any rate no thesis about agent-neutrality versus agent-relativity should be a defining feature of pure deontological ethics. The defining feature should simply be its claim that there are valid moral principles which are not in any way accountable to a theory of intrinsic ethical value, of what is good and bad. Why should one think that the distinction between the right and wrong and the good and bad is unclear, or that it has anything to do with the distinction between agent neutrality and relativity?

Consequentialism is a species of teleological ethics. But if we classify the mixed position as teleological, a teleological ethics need not be consequentialist. Certainly it need not be consequentialist in the particularly simple, or simple-minded, form of proposing a deontology whose sole proposition is that a right action is a best action. This was G. E. Moore's view—and he held it to be true by definition of 'right':

'right' does and can mean nothing but 'cause of a good result,' and is thus identical with 'useful'; whence it follows that the end always will justify the means, and that no action which is not justified by its results can be right.[16]

Mill, on the other hand, was not a definitional consequentialist of this kind, since he defines 'moral duty' as that which it is morally wrong not to do, and 'morally wrong' as that which a person ought to be punished for not doing—'if not by law, by the opinion of his fellow creatures; if not by opinion, by the reproaches of his own conscience'. Further, he thinks that people ought to be punished in one of these ways for their action or inaction when it is optimal to do so.[17] It is certainly not true by definition that it is optimal to punish people for not doing the optimal action. It may or not be—for a utilitarian that is a matter for inquiry, drawing on our everyday experience, or where possible our scientific knowledge, of human beings.

[16] Moore (1903: 147). As he notes, this has the consequence that 'we never have any reason to suppose that an action is our duty: we can never be sure that any action will produce the greatest value possible' (149). Thus his analysis of duty conflicts with Kant's and Hegel's insistence on what Hegel calls the 'right [or law] of the subjective will' (see Essay VIII, Sect. 3): *viz.*, that it must always be possible for a moral subject to achieve reflective awareness of, insight into, what his or her duty in a concrete situation is. And this is also a problem for some more sophisticated forms of consequentialism.

[17] Mill (1963–91), x. 246 (*Utilitarianism*, ch. 5, para. 14). See also Essay VII.

It seems to me that Mill did not hold that the morally right action is the optimal action even as a substantial, *non*-definitional thesis. Here I disagree with Roger Crisp (Crisp 1997), who lays particular emphasis on Mill's well-known, and apparently 'act-utilitarian', statement of the utilitarian creed in *Utilitarianism* (ch. 2, para. 2). However, whatever one thinks of this and other non-equivalent statements of utilitarianism by Mill, one should remember how important the idea of supererogation is to his social and political liberalism. In a supererogatory action one goes beyond one's duty, doing more good than just doing one's duty would do. Since Mill thinks there are such actions he cannot think that it is always one's duty to do the best thing.

But how then to use the term 'utilitarianism'? I agree with those who wish to use it, in one respect, narrowly—to refer exclusively to a theory of ethical value. Utilitarianism puts forward an 'ultimate principle of Teleology', in Mill's words.[18] If this is taken strictly, it makes it an open question whether the utilitarian should promote a consequentialist deontology at all, in any of the forms mentioned above. He has to reject *pure* deontological ethics, but he could adopt the mixed position, which says that though our moral principles are not derived or derivable from his principle of Teleology they are nevertheless correctable by it.

In another respect, however, I suggest that we could usefully use the word 'utilitarianism' widely. *Classical* utilitarianism held that all happiness and only happiness is good, and that the goodness of a state of a world is the simple aggregate of happiness in it.[19] But it is useful to have a name for the whole class of teleologies which hold that the good is some positive impartial function of the well-being of all individuals and of nothing else. (An impartial function is one generated by an impartial principle in the sense defined above.) Classical utilitarianism is a particular—and particularly simple—member of this class. But perhaps the whole class could be referred to as 'philosophical' or 'generic' utilitarianism.

'Philosophical' or 'generic' utilitarianism abstracts from classical utilitarianism by allowing (1) functions other than the aggregative function of classical utilitarianism from individual well-being to good—so long as they are positive and impartial functions and (2) different interpretations of well-being to the classical utilitarians' view of it as consisting exclusively of happiness. This generic view captures what many find plausible, even inescapable, in classical utilitarianism.[20] Whether or not one does in fact agree with this plausible element in utilitarian thought, one can at least recognize it as expressing a unitary and substantial ethical idea. Thus generic utilitarianism abstracts on classical utilitarianism in a natural way—in the way that shifting from the Euclidean paradigm of geometry to a class of geometries of which Euclid's is only one does—by allowing certain axioms of the original theory which always seemed a bit dubious

[18] Mill (1963–91), viii. 951 (*System of Logic*, VI.xii.7).

[19] It is natural to take Bentham, Mill, and Sidgwick as classical utilitarians. Admittedly Sidgwick also considered the option of maximizing average utility (and of course admitted a separate principle of rational egoism), while Mill, in distinguishing higher and lower pleasures, placed in doubt the meaningfulness of talking about 'aggregate utility'. Moreover Fred Rosen (1998) has argued that neither Bentham nor Mill took the Greatest Happiness Principle to require maximization of the sum total of happiness, while David Brink (1992) has argued that Mill was not a hedonist. Nonetheless I think the natural view of these three philosophers as classical utilitarians is the right one.

[20] Compare Thomas Scanlon's discussion of what he calls 'philosophical utilitarianism' in Scanlon (1982).

to be varied. The term 'generic utilitarianism' captures this abstracting and generalizing development and maintains a satisfying link with a historically real movement of thought.[21]

5. It is not only with respect to reasons to act, and in relation to the agent, that a distinction between 'neutral' and 'relative' reasons can be made. Analogous distinctions can be made with respect to reasons to act in relation to time, and (to generalize in another way) with respect to reasons to believe and reasons to feel. The distinction between agent-neutral and agent-relative reasons is just one member of a class of such neutral–relative distinctions. Reasons are relations between a fact, a person, a time and a type of action, belief or feeling. (In all cases they will come in degrees of strength and the degree of strength will in some way turn among other things on facts about probability; but we shall continue to ignore that.) When I believe that I have reason to do, think or feel something, that will be because I have certain beliefs about what the facts are. Thus reason-relations, more fully spelt out, will look thus:

> if it were the case that p that would give x reason at time t to do α/believe that q/feel ϕ.

How far can we generalize the neutral–relative distinction? Well, for example, reasons to act can be *temporally* neutral or relative. Consider the schema

> if it were the case that Py that would give x reason to y at time t.

If this schema is true in the case of a particular predicate 'P' for all agents, actions and times 'P' expresses a reason for action. Then

> (i) If 'P' contains a free occurrence of 't' it is a temporally relative reason-predicate. If it does not, it is a temporally neutral reason-predicate.
> (ii) A reason for action which is expressible by a temporally neutral reason-predicate is temporally neutral. A reason for action which is not so expressible is temporally relative.

It's at least as important to notice that the relative–neutral distinction can also be applied to reasons to feel and reasons to believe. Take first the case of reasons to feel. The fact that Sylvia has done *me* a good turn gives *me* a reason to feel grateful but it doesn't give *you* a reason to feel grateful.

---

[21] One may try another word to label it—but words like 'welfarism' and 'humanism' carry their own misleading freight of meaning. For a discussion of welfarism see Crisp and Moore (1996).

Call it a 'patient-relative' reason—'patient' stands to passion as 'agent' stands to action. To extend the definition from agent-relativity to patient-relativity consider the schema

if it were the case that Py that would give x reason to feel ϕ with respect to y,

where 'x' ranges over patients, 'y' ranges over objects with respect to which x may have feelings, and 'ϕ' names some particular type of feeling. If this schema is true for all patients, objects, and times, 'P' expresses a reason for feeling ϕ. Then

(i) If 'P' contains a free occurrence of 'x', it is a patient-relative reason-predicate. If it does not, it is a patient-neutral reason-predicate.

Example: the fact that y is a garage which has charged x for a repair which y has not carried out rationalizes x's irritation with respect to y. Since this is true for all x and y, 'y is a garage which has charged x for a repair which y has not carried out' is a patient-relative reason-predicate, expressing the reason for irritation.

(ii) A reason for feeling which is expressible by a patient-neutral reason-predicate is patient-neutral. A reason for feeling which is not so expressible is patient-relative.

Patient-relative reasons to feel are an important topic for ethics. Among other things, they can give rise to agent-relative reasons to act, as in my example of gratitude. But there are also patient-neutral reasons to feel: aesthetic and moral evaluations, which concern what there is reason to admire or to blame, are patient-neutral. To say that is, I believe, to make something like the Kantian claim that these evaluations are universally legislative. The claim is stronger than saying that they are 'universalizable' in the sense used earlier. For a patient-relative reason, like my reason for being irritated with the garage, is also universalizable in that sense. Similarly, anyone who is suddenly reminded of a very significant part of their past life has good reason to be moved. People who find themselves, or a group to which they belong and with which they identify, the butt of denigrating or belittling humour have reason to be annoyed. These are universal but patient-relative reasons. In contrast, to say that aesthetic and moral evaluations legislate universally is to say that they are not patient-relative: they assert that there is reason for anyone, not just those persons who stand in a certain relation to the object, to admire or blame it. (A patient-neutral moral evaluation may concern an agent-relative practical

maxim: for example that it's blameworthy to give preference to one's rela-
tives in making appointments.)

Finally the distinction can also be made for reasons to believe, though
this case is not so important for ethics. A possible schema would be

> if it were the case that *Py* that would give *x* reason to believe that *Fy*.

The definition of thinker-neutral and thinker-relative reasons to believe
would proceed as before—turning, that is, on whether '*P*' contains a free
occurrence of *x*. Thus for example the fact that a person hears his name
being called by someone else gives him reason to believe that that other
person wants to attract his attention.

In all these cases, when the fact that does the rationalizing for me now
is a *relative* reason for action, feeling, or belief that's because it's an indexical fact (or a '*de se*' fact[22]) about me, or about the present time. And its
indexicality is essential to its rationalizing force. I have to know that it's *my*
name that's being called, that it's *now* time to go to the meeting, that *I*'m
the person who was helped by Sylvia, etc. (Similarly the rational egoist has
to know that it's *his* benefit that will be advanced.) I don't have to know
any such indexical fact, about who I am, what relations I stand in, or what
time it is now, to know that if it's obligatory to contribute to famine relief,
there's reason—reason for me now—to contribute to famine relief; or that
if it's wrong to kill the innocent, there's reason for me now not to kill the
innocent. Here is another way of seeing why it's misguided to try to make
a characterization of deontological ethics turn on the difference between
agent-neutral and agent-relative reasons. Roughly: I don't have to know
who I am or any other fact about me to know that it's wrong to kill innocent people, and hence that *I* have reason not to kill innocent people.
That's because this is *not* an agent-relative reason.[23]

6. We can now pull together some threads. I want to propose that philosophical or generic utilitarianism is the sole principle delivered by pure
practical reason.[24]

---

[22] If one accepts the analysis offered of 'de se attitudes' in David Lewis (1993). (I should
confess that I'm skating over some well-entrenched difficulties about scope and reflexive
reference here.)

[23] If there's reason not to tell a lie just because it's a lie, and 'lying' means 'saying something one believes to be false', then that reason is agent-relative. One doesn't have to know
'who one is' to grasp that one has it in a particular case, but one still needs to know *something* about oneself, *viz.*, that one believes some particular thing to be false. This indexical
fact is open to reflexive awareness but the point remains that there is a particular indexical
fact about oneself that one needs to know.

[24] Mill would have agreed. He says that 'Teleology, or the Doctrine of Ends . . . bor-
rowing the language of the German metaphysicians, may also be termed, not improperly,

'Reasons and Reason' (Essay II) outlined conceptions of *morality*, the *good* and *pure practical reason* which will make further appearances in the essays that follow. It argued that moral judgements are evaluations— judgements about what there is reason to feel; specifically, judgements about what is blameworthy.[25] It also outlined an account of the good according to which an agent's good is what there is reason for that agent to desire.[26] So judgements about the good are also evaluations; patient-relative evaluations which give rise to agent-relative practical reasons. Finally, it postulated, at that stage for the sake of discussion, that the sole principle of pure practical reason was what was there called 'the principle of universal concern'. That principle is what we have now called 'philo-sophical' or 'generic' utilitarianism.

To say that this principle is a principle of pure practical reason is not to deny that the notion of an individual's good which it deploys, the notion of what is desirable for that individual, is affectively determined. The con-cept of the good can be grasped only by a thinker with the capacity for desiring things. But that capacity is not sufficient for insight into the prin-ciple. On its own, it only delivers the *hermeneutic* principle, that if there is reason for x to desire that p there is reason for x to do whatever probabi-lizes that p. Since the characteristic disposition of the desire that p *is* the disposition to do whatever probabilizes that p this is a special case of the FD principle (Essay II, Section 8). But philosophical utilitarianism says more than this. It says, agent-neutrally, that if there is reason for x to desire that p there is reason for *anyone*, y, to do whatever probabilizes that p. Moreover, from the standpoint of that principle *alone*, no particular indi-vidual's good stands out as having a greater rational claim on one's delib-eration than any other's. This principle cannot be got from the hermeneutics of any affective attitude; it can only be based on a disposi-tion of pure practical reason.

In Essay VIII I follow Kant in identifying practical reason and will. So a disposition of practical reason becomes a disposition of the will and a disposition of *pure* practical reason becomes, unlike instances of FD, an

the principles of Practical Reason' (Mill 1963–91), viii. 949–50 (*System of Logic*, VI.xii.7). Of course he holds that its basic principle is not just philosophical utilitarianism but the particular implementation of it which is represented by classical utilitarianism. In Essay V I consider the case for an alternative stronger view, one which determines the distributive structure of generic utilitarianism by means of a principle which I call 'Threshold Justice'. Thus in saying that philosophical utilitarianism is the sole principle of pure practical rea-son what I mean is that *at least* it, and perhaps more strongly some species of it, is the sole principle.

[25] This account of morality is further discussed in Essays VII and VIII.
[26] This is further discussed in Essay VI, Sect. 3 and appendix.

unconditional disposition of the will. That is, it is a disposition to act *irrespective of what one has reason to feel.*

A principle of pure practical reason is one which is reflectively grounded (dialogically grounded, in the sense discussed in Essay II, Sections 6 and 7) on such an unconditional disposition of the will. Hence the question whether philosophical utilitarianism is the sole principle of pure practical reason is the question whether it is so grounded, and is the only principle so grounded.

I submit that it is so grounded. We discover reflectively that there *is* something we can spontaneously will unconditionally: its content is impartial regard for the good of all individuals. It invites us to constrain and correct our maxims in some way by the requirements of philosophical utilitarianism.[27] But can one exhibit it as the only principle that is so grounded?

As Thomas Nagel has often said, there is something ethically effective in the thought that others are just as real as me: the 'full recognition that one is only a person among others'.[28] Why should this be? Surely the ethical force can't arise from a merely ontological observation? Surely the rational egoist, and indeed the irrational egoist, could agree with *that*. That is, no logic forces them, in virtue of their position, to a literal denial of the existence of others. True. Yet there is more to this particular ontological insight—the ontology of persons and the ethics of persons seem to interfuse. A further ethical reflection on the bare ontological point serves to divide the rational from the irrational egoist: when one asks the irrational egoist the Sidgwickian question, 'What's so special about *you*?', one is drawing his attention to the fact that he 'is only a person among others'. That is, the point one is making can be expressed in that formula. His only answer to the question is 'I'm me'—but other people could equally say that. The point has real force because there *is* a frame of mind which in practice denies it.

However it is not the frame of mind of the *rational* egoist. The rational egoist recognizes the equal reality of others in *this* sense. Still, in so far as he denies the existence of the agent-neutral reasons acknowledged by the utilitarian, a further ethical reflection on the ontological point has force against him. In this mode the thought that others are equally real can be experienced as a moving and liberating insight—one could say a spiritual

---

[27] This of course is to give familiar Kantian lines of thought a philosophically utilitarian twist. I am not suggesting that Kant himself should be interpreted in this way (but cf. Hare (1993)). And I am certainly not suggesting that the constraining and correcting of our maxims works in a 'linear' way, i.e. by *derivation* from the principle.

[28] Nagel (1986: 159).

experience; its core is still in some sense ontological but it comes to have an ego-transcending ethical force.

So I think the insight expressed in the formula that 'other persons are just as real as oneself' can, in this way, bring into view the existence of agent-neutral reasons (or simply *is* the vivid, non-notional acknowledgement of such reasons). But that does not show that there are no fundamentally relative reasons.

Whether there are fundamentally relative reasons may seem to be connected with the question: are there *ultimate* indexical facts? However, whatever scope there may be for discussing this second question it had better not undermine the existence of fundamental relative reasons. I may know that John Skorupski is due to address the meeting at noon without being prompted to action either (a) because I fail to realize that it's now noon, or (b) because, suffering from amnesia, I fail to realize that I am John Skorupski. Whether or not these thoughts that I fail to have express *sui generis* facts, the important point is that they're essential to the logic of deliberation. Whatever one may conclude about the ontology of indexical facts isn't going to change that. Nor will it undermine the existence of ultimate and fundamental patient-relative reasons, or their connection via FD with agent-relative reasons.

So there are fundamental agent-relative reasons—practical reasons which are in no sense *derived* from the agent-neutral standpoint of philosophical utilitarianism. In particular, the principle of the rational egoist can be seen as fundamental in this way. It is in fact an instance of FD; the rational egoist says that there's reason to promote one's good, and if one's good is whatever one has reason to desire, that becomes: if one has reason to desire that p, there's reason to do whatever will probabilize that p. Moreover we can split FD up into two parts:

(FDF) If there's reason to feel ϕ there's reason to desire to do that which ϕ characteristically disposes one to desire to do.

(FDD) If there's reason to desire to α (or to bring it about that p), there's reason to α (to do that which will bring it about that p).

FDD channels all the connections between reasons to feel and reasons to act which are expressed in FD.[29] It is not surprising, then, that a principle connecting reason to desire with reason to act (which very roughly plays the same role as Kant's hypothetical imperative)[30] should seem to have an importance in ethical theory commensurate to that of philosophical

---

[29] Incidentally the truth of FDD shows that one needs to qualify the equation of 'my good' with 'what I have reason to desire'. See Essay VI, appendix.

[30] Only very roughly—see Essay VII, n. 24.

utilitarianism (which corresponds in this structure to his categorical imperative).

But I have also argued that FD is not itself a principle of *pure* practical reason. This explains why the dispute between the rational egoist and the philosophical utilitarian tends to be associated with the dispute between sentimentalist and rationalist. The truth, however, as Sidgwick said, is that both principles, that of the rational egoist and that of the philosophical utilitarian, are correct and fundamental, neither being derived from the other.

Yet this does not produce a Sidgwickian dualism of *pure* practical reason. As far as pure practical reason is concerned philosophical utilitarianism (or perhaps some species of it) is the only fundamental principle. Pure practical reason is simply the perspective in which the evaluatively generated reasons of particular individuals receive impartial recognition.[31] To say that philosophical utilitarianism is its only principle is to say that it alone arbitrates on what we have reason to do, in the sense that it alone can defeat reasons generated by the various bridge-principles arising from the hermeneutics of feeling.

But defeating them is not striking them down as null. When they are defeated the principle which expresses them remains true. So there is no argument from philosophical utilitarianism to the irrationality of agent-relative feelings and desires, or the nullity of agent-relative reasons for action based on them. In that sense the principle of Sidgwick's rational egoist, as interpreted here, is both independent and true. That certainly leaves a question, for believers in impartial reason, about when and how far impartial reason defeats such reasons, but it's hard to see what one could say about it that would be both abstract and general and yet non-trivial.

---

[31] Hume acknowledged the perspective, somewhat reluctantly: 'Tis seldom men heartily love what lies at a distance from them, and what no way redounds to their particular benefit . . . Here we are contented with saying, that reason requires such an impartial conduct, but that . . . our passions do not readily follow the determination of our judgement' (Hume 1968: 583). Of course Hume thought he had a sentimentalist way of getting behind this kind of 'reason', taking it to be nothing more than a 'general calm determination of the passions'. (But what is achieved by that description, other than a verbal victory?)

IV

Value-Pluralism

1. INTRODUCTORY

A view with some considerable influence in current moral and political philosophy holds that there is a plurality of values, all of them fundamental and authoritative and yet, in some genuinely disconcerting way, *in conflict*. I shall call it 'value-pluralism'.

It is a philosophical thesis. It does more than record the fact that choice often involves conflicts, moral and other, and that choosing can be a difficult and sometimes even an appalling thing to do. That experience any serious ethics must acknowledge. It is basic, but it is not a surprise, philosophically or otherwise; whereas the claim of the value-pluralist is meant to be philosophically surprising and significant. Further, value-pluralism is to be distinguished from what Mill, Moore, and Rawls call 'intuitionism' in ethics: the view that there is no single moral principle to which all principles of conduct must conform, but a number of moral principles all equally fundamental.[1] 'Deontological pluralism' would be a good term for this view; it is a philosophical thesis, and certainly not uncontroversial—but value-pluralism is meant to go beyond it. The question is how. There are two main suggestions. One is that, at least in some cases in which fundamental values conflict, there is no rationally determinable answer to the question which should take precedence. The conflict is *inarbitrable*. Another is that in some such cases one does wrong whatever one does.

First published in David Archard (ed.), *Philosophy and Pluralism*, Cambridge: Cambridge University Press, 1996: 101–15. I have omitted or revised passages which overlap with Essays II and III. I am grateful to David Archard and John Broome for critical comments.

[1] Mill (1963–91), x. 206—'the intuitive school'; Moore (1903: p. x—'the common doctrine, which has generally been called by that name'); Rawls (1971: 34). The term 'intuitionism' is often used to refer not just to the thesis that moral principles are irreducibly plural, but to that conjoined with two further theses: that these plural principles concerning right and wrong are known by rational or a priori 'moral intuition' and that there is no overarchingly authoritative principle of pure practical reason, or of good (as envisaged by the philosophical utilitarian, the rational egoist, the Kantian, etc.) In Sect. 3 I refer to the conjunction of these three theses as 'rational intuitionism'.

Wrongdoing is *inescapable*. Both suggestions take value-pluralism beyond simple deontological pluralism—this essay considers both of them.[2]

The value-pluralism we are to consider is not a form of subjectivism. (This point is emphasized, for example, in Gray (1993)). It grants the 'objectivity' of normative propositions. What does this involve? There is a familiar sense in which a person's *judgement* can be more or less objective: it is objective to the extent that it is free of personal bias, prejudice, and the like. My judgement of how well my daughter plays the piano may in that sense be less objective than the examiner's. But what do we mean when we ask about the objectivity or otherwise of normative *propositions*?

Firstly, it is a question of whether they are genuinely that—propositions. A proposition is a judgeable and therefore truth-evaluable content. Here my use of the word 'true' is intended to be non-committal on issues of ontology. A philosopher who wishes to stress the difference between propositions about facts and propositions about reasons, and to reject a realist ontology with respect to propositions about reasons, might want to reserve 'true' and 'false' for factual propositions, and use some other terms, such as 'correct' or 'valid' for normative propositions. I sympathize with this approach—however the relevant point about it for present purposes is that it still maintains the view that normative propositions are judgeable contents, evaluable for correctness or validity. Since this discussion will not need to go far into questions about the ontology of norms I will, simply for convenience, use the term 'true' broadly (i.e. to cover both 'factual truth' and 'normative validity', should that be the preferred fundamental terminology).

A good name for the view that normative claims are genuine judgements is 'cognitivism'. *Objectivism* is worth distinguishing from it only because it can usefully label a position which is stronger. It holds not only that normative claims are genuine judgements, but that some normative propositions are true. If we take 'norm' to mean 'true normative proposition', it says that there are norms. In contrast scepticism about norms holds that we cannot know whether there are norms (whether any normative proposition is true); nihilism holds that we do indeed make normative judgements but that there are no norms. (Any wide-scope negation of a normative proposition is true, or neither true nor false.)

Relativism, finally, as I understand it here, is a variety of objectivism, one which holds that the truth-predicate is a relational term with a place reserved for a term denoting a community, form of life, theoretical frame-

---

[2] One or both of them can be found in some measure in the writings e.g. of Isaiah Berlin, Alasdair MacIntyre, Bernard Williams, and Charles Taylor. John Gray has recently emphasized this side of Isaiah Berlin's thought (Gray 1993, 1995).

work, tradition, etc. If relativism is the correct view for a given class of propositions, then propositions in that class will not be simply *true*. They will be true-relative-to-k, where k denotes a community, form of life, theoretical framework, or tradition. So relativism about normative propositions is the view that there are indeed norms—true normative propositions—but that truth in their case is a relation to some such parameter. Value-pluralism may or may not be a form of relativism; the question will be considered in Section 5.

2. RELATIVITIES OF SITUATION

Reasons for action and feeling can have a relativity which is in no way connected with relativism as I have just defined it.

It concerns the relational character of reasons themselves. Consider: I have reason to look after my children, you have reason to look after yours. This reason is relative to the agent in the sense that it supervenes on a relation between the children and the agent. What gives x reason to look after y is that y is x's child. Such reasons for action are often called 'agent-relative'. Not all practical reasons are agent-relative—some are 'agent-neutral'. For example, everyone has reason, where possible, to come to the aid of a person in distress, irrespective of that person's relation to them.

A parallel distinction can be made for reasons to feel. Seeing an old photograph of the house from which her family was expelled will very probably be a moving experience for my grandmother. There is every reason for her to be moved. But there is not necessarily reason for someone unconnected with the family to be moved. For him, quite understandably, it might be just an old photograph. Again, dumb-Polack jokes are quite reasonably irritating to Poles. There's reason for Poles to be irritated—but there is not the same reason for non-Poles to be. The latter may reasonably disapprove of crass jokes in general, but feeling disapproval is not the same as feeling offended or irritated.

In each case what makes it reasonable or intelligible for the person to have the reaction, of nostalgic sentiment, or irritation, towards the object is a relation it has to the person. These are, as it were, *patient-relative* evaluations ('agent' and 'patient' corresponds to 'action' and 'passion').[3] But as in the case of practical norms there are also patient-neutral evaluations. Most importantly, aesthetic and moral evaluations, which concern what there is reason to admire or to blame, are patient-neutral.

---

[3] See Essay III, Sect. 5.

One obvious source of these relativities, practical and evaluative, is the diversity of people's histories and social relations. Agent-relative reasons for action, including agent-relative duties and obligations, arise from one's social status or office, previous commitments, accumulated emotional ties—from our concrete historical and social position in the world. I have these reasons for action because I am a parent or guardian, or the treasurer of the club; or I have agent-relative practical reasons which arise from patient-relative evaluations—because I have reason to feel grateful to you for past kindness I have reason to go out of my way to help you in a present predicament.

Another important source of relativity has to do with the diversity not of our positions but of our natures. I will refer to both of these as aspects of our *situation*. We are 'situated' in determinate, though mutable, positions and characters. What is desirable for you, what there is reason for you to desire, is patient-relative. If wealth will make you happy, that's a reason for you to desire it. It's not a reason for *me* to desire wealth—the relevant question in my case is whether wealth would make *me* happy. Unlike judgements about the admirable and blameworthy, judgements about the desirable are not patient-neutral. If a person's good is characterized in terms of what there is reason for that person to desire, judgements about a person's good—what is good for that person, will be patient-relative in this obvious way. And what there is reason to desire varies with one's nature. Wealth will make you happy but not me. The general form of the underlying judgement is: if y will make x G then there is reason for x to desire y. So a further question arises: is there just one such property G or a number of them? 'Is happy' may be used formally, to mean 'has a property which there is reason for him or her to desire that he or she should have'. But if it is used more concretely, the question will arise whether it is the only property that can stand in for G. What about knowing, or being free? And if we allow the possibility of a concrete plurality of categorial ends, as one might call them, is the list the same for all kinds of persons? Or even for all kinds of human beings? Perhaps the underlying form should be: 'if y will make x G and x is the kind of being for whom it matters to have G, then there is reason for x to desire y.' That would build, so to speak, a double layer of patient-relativity into judgements about a person's good.

A similar diversity arises with what ideals I should pursue; despite the patient-neutrality of the admirable. There is reason—reason for us all—to admire profound musical sensibility or great physical courage and endurance but it does not follow that all should seek to cultivate these ideals. Ends and ideals are both plural and differentially accessible, and of course people are often torn between them: anyone with a bit of ethical and aesthetic imagination has experienced that. Indeed plurality and torn allegiance in the realm of the desirable and the admirable is probably more important in most lives than moral conflict proper. You cannot pursue all the ends and ideals you could pursue. Even if you could be a violin virtuoso or a soldier and explorer you probably couldn't be both. But, as with true moral conflict, to recognize the existence and importance of such choices is not yet to endorse the interpretation of them proposed by the value-pluralist.

3. INESCAPABLE BLAME?

Relativities arising from diversity of situation are a main source of the diversity of obligations and commitments—within a culture and across cultures. They give substance to 'ethical life'. But value-pluralism involved the thesis that some conflicts of values are *inarbitrable*, or that in some conflicts of value wrongdoing is *inescapable*. Let us first consider the second of these ideas, the idea that there are conflicts in which whatever one does one does wrong.

The moral dilemmas most likely to produce a sense of the inescapability of wrongdoing seem to be conflicts between agent-relative obligations, or between agent-relative and agent-neutral obligations. A conflict between duty to family and duty to country or state would be an example of the former; a choice between saving the life of a relative or friend and saving the lives of strangers would be an example of the latter. Less dramatically, but perhaps closer to experience, there is the case of choosing a school for one's child, where many parents have felt a tension between what they see as the relative obligations of family and the neutral considerations of justice. Of course there can be equally difficult choices which involve agent-neutral considerations on both sides, such as whether to give in to hostage-takers in a case in which one has no agent-relative obligations to anyone involved. But I suspect that these dilemmas, equally difficult, nevertheless do not conjure up the thought of inescapable blame as the others do.

The most natural representation of this thought about fated, inescapable blame is a world-picture in which one is subject to separate laws, coming from distinct but severally authoritative sovereigns, all of them legitimately armed with punishments for transgression: these gods and those, the edicts of the gods and the necessary law of the State. I am only saying 'the most natural'—I can see nothing positively incoherent in the idea of a single source of legitimation which sanctions laws capable of throwing the agent into inescapable wrongdoing. However, while not positively incoherent, it seems to me to lack any plausible, self-sustaining *rationale*. The very legitimacy of the source is vitiated if it dooms agents to unavoidable blame. If therefore we think of morality as an integral, unitary system—as I believe we do—it becomes hard to understand the possibility that moral blame might be inescapable. Is it not anachronistic to conceive a plurality of ethical sovereigns? I think (to be blunt) that it is. Yet the world-picture that goes with that way of thinking depicts something psychologically real. Though our idea of the moral is the idea of an integral and unitary sovereign source of law, morality's content comes from disjoint sources—the blame-feeling, which has its own spontaneous natural objects, and ethical notions coming from pure practical reason.

A purely *rational* intuitionism cannot explain the feeling that one transgresses whatever one does, let alone endorse it, because it fails to take account of this plurality of sources. The irreducible and potentially conflicting obligations it envisages still fall into a system of morality with a single source—reason. But if we recognize that morality has sources both in the emotions (those which lie at the spontaneous core of blame) and in reason, then we do at least have materials for *explaining* the feeling. That does not mean that we can *endorse* it. It is an internal norm of the blame-feeling itself that to blame the unavoidable is unreasonable. So a sovereign which sanctions punishment of the unavoidable must lose legitimacy. And hence we cannot seriously endorse the idea of the inescapability of blame—punishability—unless we seriously believe in the existence of a plurality of separate sovereigns, issuing potentially conflicting laws. If there is such a plurality, then there can be situations in which I will be legitimately punished by one or another sovereign, whatever I do. But to acknowledge that morality has sources both in various clusters of spontaneous moral feeling and in practical reason falls short of claiming that those sources are separately *sovereign*. What could it mean to say they are? One does not have to be a rationalist to acknowledge that in conflicts between them reason is supreme. For saying that spontaneous moral feeling, or tradition, can come into conflict with practical reason is just a vivid way of saying that there can be good reason to override spontaneous moral feeling, or tradition. Or that there can be good reason to give preference to a less strongly felt cluster of obligations over one that is more strongly felt.

That leads us back to the other value-pluralist claim, that there can be conflicts which are rationally inarbitrable—conflicts in which there simply is no good reason to give preference to one side over the other.

We need to distinguish here the claim that there are conflicts of choice which no rational *decision-procedure* or *criterion* can decide from the much stronger claim that there are conflicts which are rationally inarbitrable. Value-pluralism has to say something more than that in some conflicts between values 'there is no overarching standard whereby their claims are rationally arbitrable'.[4] A rational intuitionist holds that there is no over-arching decision procedure or criterion at all. But he would not agree that that implies that conflicts are rationally inarbitrable. He would rightly point out that reason can be a matter of exercising judgement rather than applying decision-procedures or overarching standards.

A second obvious point is that both rational intuitionist and utilitarian could agree that there may be rationally inarbitrable choices. Where there is more than one best action, choosing between them is rationally inarbitrable. I ought to do A or B, but it's not the case that I ought to do A and it's not the case that I ought to do B. There is no right answer to the questions, ought I to do A or B—but there is no conflict either. It really is a matter of choice—perhaps indeed very distressing choice; but certainly no blame attaches to whatever choice one makes. What then is the value-pluralist saying? Apparently he envisages *strong dilemmas*, as I will call them, in which there is a plurality of justified but incompatible answers as to which course of action I ought to pursue. The answers are rationally inarbitrable: this must mean that there is adequate reason to accept each one of them, and no adequate reason to accept just one of them over the others. The situation differs from that in which there is simply a short list of optimal things to do. But what difference to moral life does this abstractly framed distinction, between strong dilemmas and choices between optimal actions, actually make? The only possible answer is that in the strong dilemma one incurs legitimate blame whatever one does. And the only way to give genuine substance as against bare logical coherence to the idea of inescapable blame (I have suggested) is to appeal to the anachronistic world-picture of separate and ultimate ethical sovereigns.

4. OBJECTIVITY AND IDEAL CONVERGENCE

In the previous section we were considering the idea that a single ethical tradition might generate strong dilemmas: there might be situations in which it gave incompatible, justified, and rationally inarbitrable answers as to what one ought to do, so that blame was unavoidable. But in political

---

[4] Gray (1993: 291).

theory value-pluralism is often advanced in a somewhat different context: as a response to the historical existence of *different* ethical traditions. There are familiar cases of ethical choice in which these different ethical traditions each produce unitary answers as to what one ought to do—but the several answers they produce conflict. One tradition says that you ought to do X while another denies that you ought to do X. The value-pluralist response is that the conflicting answers may *all* be justified. In this context the idea of inescapable blame is not usually mentioned; presumably the different ethical traditions give incompatible justified answers as to what is blameworthy as well as giving incompatible justified answers as to what one ought to do.

This is certainly the important form of value-pluralism in current political and cultural debate, rather than that discussed in the previous section. But can this form of value-pluralism differ from relativism? Before addressing the question we need to delve further into the philosophy of judgement and assertion.

To judge is judge the content of one's judgement true. This observation uses the notion of truth broadly (Section 1). Truth in this broad sense may be partially characterized as a property F such that for any judgement or assertion, J, if it is shown that there is no adequate ground to hold that J has F, reason (as against etiquette, discretion or whatever) requires withdrawal of J. The characterization appeals to the notion of rational justification for belief. It is partial because being rationally justified is itself a property of beliefs and assertions which satisfies it. But truth is not rational justification. A judgement may be true but not rationally justified, or rationally justified but not true. The two notions are distinct. In the domain of belief, however, both are required. An action or a feeling may be assessable as rationally justified or not, but neither is assessable as true or not. Whereas it is inherent to the notion of judgement that a judgement is assessable in both these ways.

Now value-pluralism holds that there can be true, incompatible but rationally inarbitrable normative judgements. Do the points just made about judgement rule that possibility out? Not straightforwardly. Suppose the value-pluralist holds that there are cases in which it is true that one (morally) ought to do X and that one ought not to do X; or true that one ought to do X and that one ought to do Y, where doing X is incompatible with doing Y. These normative judgements are not contradictory (without further assumptions) but they are in conflict. The value-pluralist holds that they may all be rationally justified, and that there may be no question of using rational judgement to determine what one 'really' ought to do. This is all consistent with the points about judgement.

Of course if the moral 'ought' connects with blame in the normal way then in these cases whatever the agent does incurs blame. He either fails to do what he ought to do or he does what he ought not to do. If one is influenced by the considerations about blame and avoidability aired in the previous section, one will not accept the possibility of such cases. But we must consider another kind of thought, which remains even if such cases are ruled out. It is that one person or tradition may *justifiably* come to the conclusion that (it is true that) one ought to do X and another person or tradition may *justifiably* come to the conclusion that (it is true that) one ought not to do X (or indeed that it's not the case that one ought to do X)—and that these views may be in *genuine conflict* yet not rationally arbitrable. I now want to propose that this thought should be dismissed too, because this kind of value-pluralism has to turn into a relativism which removes the conflict.

When I judge that *p*, I enter a commitment that inquirers who scrutinized the relevant evidence and argument available to them carefully enough would agree that *p*—unless I could fault their rationality or their evidence. Call this the *convergence thesis*.

Judging that *p* means coming or continuing to *believe* ('genuinely', 'fully') that *p*; the contrast is with guessing that *p*, acting on that assumption, delivering a verdict in a situation in which one has to (while nevertheless not being quite sure) and so on. As to *rationality*, I use that term here very broadly. I mean it to cover everything that is involved in the capacity, given a state of information, to judge of reasons of any kind (whether they be reasons to believe, to act, or to feel) to estimate their weight on the basis of that information state, and to respond appropriately. Rationality in this very broad sense can be contrasted with *receptivity*, the capacity to receive information. Further, one's rationality in this broad sense can be diminished in two broad ways. First it may be diminished by absences or defects in what I will call *spontaneity*, that is, in one's capacity for spontaneously appropriate normative responses.[5] Of course a person can have some capacities of spontaneity without having others, just as one can have some capacities of receptivity without having others. But secondly, even where there is no intrinsic weakness of spontaneity, one's broad rationality may nevertheless be diminished because of *interference* produced by such things as special pleading, wishful thinking, partiality to particular persuaders, exhaustion, inattention, and so on. Spontaneity is thus not the only contributor to a well-functioning rationality. Faulting an inquirer's rationality involves identifying an inadequacy which might be

[5] I have chosen the terms 'receptivity' and 'spontaneity' partly with Kant in mind, of course, but some important differences are highlighted in Essay VIII.

either a weakness in the relevant qualities of spontaneity or an interference, and which in either case relevantly affects his judging propensity on the subject in question—in such a way as to justify one in discounting his judgement. Faulting the inquirer's evidence, on the other hand, would involve showing that it is the *information input* into his judging process which is misleading or insufficient—whether that is because of the nature of the incoming message, or in virtue of some impairment of receptivity—in such a way as to justify one in discounting his judgement, even if one finds no fault in his rationality.

Finally, let me stipulate that one *enters* or *incurs* a commitment that *q* by judging that *p* just if judging that *p* rationally constrains one to accept that reasons for judging that it's *not* the case that *q* are reasons for withdrawing the judgement that *p*. I have put this negatively: when we incur a convergence commitment by making a judgement we do not have to give grounds for expecting the convergence, over and above our grounds for the judgement itself. The point is only that if we come, in one way or another, to have reason to doubt that our judgement would attract convergence among fault-free inquirers, we thereby come to have reason to doubt it. When those grounds for doubt become strong enough, they compel us to withdraw our judgement.

So now what case can be made for the convergence thesis? It follows from three plausible principles, which I recapitulate from Essay II, Section 7.[6]

The first is the principle of Rationality:

(1) It is irrational to judge that: *p* but there is insufficient reason to judge that *p*.

Though there is no self-contradiction in a proposition of that form, to judge such a proposition true would be irrational. That is, in judging that *p* I incur the commitment that there is sufficient reason for me to judge that *p*.

This on its own does not show that if I judge that *p* I must hold that *anyone* who holds that there is insufficient reason to judge that *p* is faulty either in rationality or in evidence. But consider next the following principles.

(2) The principle of the Universality of Reasons:
Given a total state of relevant evidence [E] *x* is warranted in holding that there is sufficient reason for *x* to judge that *p* if and only if (for

---

[6] But I have slightly altered them to allow for a distinction between justification and warrant (explained below).

all y)(if y is in [E], then y is warranted in holding that y has sufficient reason to judge that p).

(3) The principle of Evidence:

If p, then any evidence that warrants x in judging that there is insufficient reason for x to think that p is either

    (i) also insufficient to decide whether or not it is the case that p, or

    (ii) is misleading inasmuch as it warrants x in denying that p.

Since x's judgement that he has such-and-such evidence may be warranted but false 'evidence' in (2) and (3) refers to the total set of factual propositions, relevant to the question whether p, which x can warrantedly *take* to specify x's evidence on that question. And where the question can be settled without evidence [E] will be null. (That will be the case for all fundamental normative propositions, so the principle of Evidence is irrelevant to the argument in their case.)

As argued in Essay II (Section 7), it follows from these three principles that so long as I continue to judge that p I am committed to judging that any thinker who refuses to judge that p has either failed to consider the issue carefully enough or is faulty in evidence or rationality.

The argument relies on no particular conception of truth. The three principles which provide its premises—Rationality, Universality of Reasons, and Evidence—will hold irrespective of what philosophical conception of truth one propounds. In particular the argument in no way rests on defining truth in terms of convergence. There are many true factual judgements on which convergence of judgement could not occur because sufficient relevant evidence could not be collected; belief in them could not be warranted, even though they are true.

Also, even when we are *justified* in holding some belief it always remains possible that the judgement that we are *warranted* in our belief is mistaken and hence that our commitment to thinking that fault-free inquirers would converge on it is mistaken too. I distinguish between 'justification' and 'warrant': the former pertains to epistemic appraisal of the judger while the latter refers to a relation between his [E] and the propositions he could judge. One's belief is justified if holding it, in the circumstances in which one does hold it, opens one's epistemic virtue to no criticism—shows no irrationality. So the possibility that our own judgement, as well as our evidence, is faulty applies even in cases where the belief we have is justified. Our evidence may be misleading even though we had no reason to think it was. But also there may be some aspect of the evidence or its implications (or in general some relevant epistemic norm) which we have *missed*—without, in that overall context of reflection, being to blame for missing it. For example, there was no time to think carefully in that practical situation. Or that kind of intellectual option was not salient in our culture and would have taken a genius to detect, etc. In this way one's belief may not be warranted by one's [E] even though one is justified in thinking that it is, and hence justified in the belief.

It must be possible for one to be justified in making a judgement even if one has *not* fully eliminated the epistemic possibility that some relevant aspect of one's judgement is at fault. Otherwise the standard for justification would be set too high; it would require that one has some way of definitely ruling out that epistemic possibility, and has applied it, before one is justified in making the judgement. But even though an error of judgement is always in principle detectable through sufficiently careful self-examination and discussion, it does not follow that there has to be an effective procedure for detecting it, still less that the procedure must have been applied before we are justified in proceeding to judgement. Thus the convergence thesis is compatible with as radical a form of defeasibility as one likes.[7]

Both justification and warrant must in turn be distinguished from a third term of epistemic appraisal: *authority*. Justification pertains to the epistemic virtue of the judge, warrant to the objective normative relation between his [E] and the judgement—authority, in contrast, refers to his *trustworthiness* as a judge, the degree to which the fact of his judgement can be seen as a sign of its truth. Warrant, justification, and authority focus different epistemic interests: appraising the evidence, appraising the epistemic virtue of the judge, appraising the reliability of his judgement. Thus a judgement can be warranted, as well as justified, at any level of authority: for example my judgement that something is admirable may be warranted even if I am a very inexperienced judge and my information about the object is poor. Relative to the information I have I am warranted in the judgement I make. Yet the warrant I have is very easily defeasible. My judgement may be corrected by more information about the object or in ways that work on the spontaneity that produced it. Greater familiarity with that kind of object (e.g. a new fashion style, a wine, a song, a film . . .) may make me feel that it is not as admirable as I initially thought it. Comparison with the judgements of others, together with discussion of our disagreements, may have the same result. I lose my original warrant—but gain authority as a judge.

[7] However that when I judge that *p* I do incur the commitment that no enlarged [E] will remove my warrant for *p*. So if to an [E'] which warrants the belief that *p* we add e. g. sufficiently strong meta-inductive reasons to think that such an enlargement will occur, then in this new [E] I am *not* warranted in judging that *p*. Sufficient *experience* of fallibility can indeed undermine warranted belief.

Remember, finally, that we are concerned with full belief, judgement. There are many less committing attitudes to a proposition. Suppose you and I are in [E] but you seem to think that [E] warrants the conclusion that *p* and I don't. We may not really be disagreeing about what should be *judged*. It's just that you think it's worth going with the hypothesis for various purposes and I don't. That is more like a practical decision and there may be all sorts of considerations outside [E] that make our different practical decision equally reasonable. For example, you think it's worth buying the stock and selling tomorrow before the bill comes in. That may be because you're backing a hunch, because you're richer, or just less risk-averse, etc. We very often have to adopt some conjecture or other, or come to a verdict, to get on with practical life.

In contrast, if the disagreement is genuinely about whether [E] warrants the *judgement* that *p*, then at least one of us must be open to criticism in respect of rationality. Moreover each of us is committed to thinking that the other is open to criticism. For example, you think I'm being epistemically cautious beyond what reason requires; I think you're being less cautious than reason requires. Might we conclude after discussion that there's no answer in this case as to what reason requires, because rational requirement is a vague notion, and this is one of those cases affected by its vagueness? Indeed we might. The thesis that reasons are universal is not intended to deny that 'reason' is a vague concept. However, if we do come to that conclusion in this particular case, then in one respect you are the one who has to give way. You don't have to hold that it's *false* that [E] warrants the judgement that *p*—but you have conceded that you're not warranted in holding it to be true. Equally, I don't have to hold that it's *true* that [E] warrants the judgement that *p*, though I have to concede that I'm not warranted in holding it to be false. The difference is that you *shouldn't* believe that *p*, because you're not warranted in believing that [E] warrants the judgement that *p*, whereas I can maintain my refusal to believe that *p*.

So much by way of elucidating the basis of the convergence thesis. Notice that it is no way based on the model of truth as representation or fit, together with the point that accurate representing devices, aimed at one and the same state of affairs, are going to have to produce the same representation or fit. This is something of a watershed issue. Let me underline then that the crucial consideration is not the argument that accurate representing devices yield the same representation; it is, rather, the *Universality of Reasons*. (The other two principles are truistic, I think.) I take this to be a fundamental presupposition in all cognition and discourse. Cognition and discourse deal in reasons; the very idea of a reason is the idea of something which makes a universal claim. (Not necessarily an agent-, patient-, or thinker-neutral claim.) So judgement commits us to convergence because judgement requires reasons and reasons are universal. The contrast between the two arguments for convergence indicated here, from representation and from universality, goes to the heart of one's conception of the normative and through that to much else.[8]

Having set out this case for the convergence thesis we can return to the suggestion we were considering: that one tradition may warrantedly hold that one ought to do X while another tradition may warrantedly deny that one ought to do X, the conflict between their views being rationally inarbitrable even though both conclusions *cannot simultaneously be true*. We are talking here about warrant, as against justification in the sense defined above. Uncontroversially, each tradition may be justified in that sense, given its circumstances—that is, it may be that neither is open to charges of irrationality. And we are not talking about warrant relative to an [E], since the suggestion is meant to hold for *fundamental* normative judgements. The suggestion was that two such *fundamental* judgements, coming from different traditions, may conflict with each other yet both be warranted.

That is ruled out by the convergence thesis. If the judgements are genuinely in conflict, then at least one of the traditions has either failed to consider the issue in the way that's needed to get the right answer, or is faulty in its rationality.

5. VALUE-PLURALISM AS RELATIVISM

If the arguments of the preceding section are right, then the value-pluralism we were there considering has to turn into relativism—that is, into the doctrine that truth is relative and that apparently conflicting moral judgements may be true relative to different parameters, for example ethical traditions. Against that view of moral judgements arguments from the avoidability of blame do not apply. For attribution of blame will also be valid only relative to the parameter in question, and so as long as that parameter is held constant, it will not be the case that blame is unavoidable. There may be choices where whatever one does is blameworthy according to some ethical tradition or other, but this is irrelevant. Nor does the convergence thesis count against this doctrine. The point that a convergence commitment is incurred by any judgement is not in itself

---

[8] See Essay I. The argument from representation is Kant's *consentia uni tertio, consentiunt inter se*.

inconsistent with relativism. If a judgement is only true relative to some parameter k, then the commitment is that reasoners not faulty in evidence or judgement would agree that it is true relative to k.

But does anything make relativism plausible for *fundamental normative*, as against factual, propositions? This may seem a surprising question to raise. Is it not particularly with respect to the normative that relativism has proved tempting? Nevertheless, in the case of factual propositions there is a forceful and familiar kind of relativism which says that they can be true only relative to some theoretical framework. The standard argument for it is the supposed underdetermination of theory by data. On that thesis, there is more than one optimal overall theory, judged by *all* accessible data and *all* epistemic norms. Assuming that to be so, the relativist about factual propositions argues that the notions of truth—and of correspondence—make sense only intra-theoretically. Relative to a theoretical framework, you can ask which propositions in it are true, correspond to the facts; but you cannot ask which theoretical framework is true or corresponds to the facts.

Whether or not this relativism is finally tenable, there is at any rate an opening for it, provided by the underdetermination thesis, an opening which has no parallel in the case of the normative. For while factual judgements may be underdetermined with respect to all data and epistemic norms, there is nothing with respect to which *fundamental* normative judgements themselves are underdetermined. The parallel, rather, is this. Fundamental practical and evaluative norms, together with the 'data' of the circumstances in which we find ourselves, may underdetermine our non-fundamental, applied practical and evaluative judgements. More than one morality may be optimal by those fundamental norms, just as more than one overall theory (according to the underdetermination thesis) may be optimal by our fundamental epistemic norms. And if more than one moral framework is indeed optimal relative to fundamental practical and evaluative norms, then (the relativist may argue) a moral judgement may be true relative to one optimal moral framework and not true relative to another. But that is not relativism about fundamental as against applied norms—in fact we have made sense of it only on the assumption that there are non-relative fundamental norms.

As well as the possibility that those fundamental norms may leave space for more than one optimal application in the same circumstances, there is the more obvious possibility that in *varying* circumstances they may optimize different moralities. The repertoire of virtues optimal among hunter-gatherers or marauders may not be the same as that which is optimal in technically advanced industrial societies. Let us call these possibilities, that different moralities may be optimal in different circumstances, and that more than one morality may be optimal in the same circumstances, the *relativities of circumstance* (as against the relativities of situation discussed in Section 2).

The relativities of circumstance may seem to give more support to a kind of value-pluralism than do the relativities of situation. They highlight two things. The first is the historicity of moral schemes. That is hardly new. If value-pluralism boils down to this, it is a doctrine which would have been widely accepted in the nineteenth century. The other, slightly less familiar point, concerns the scope for indeterminacy in moral argument. There may be much in concrete moral discussion which is underdetermined by any plausible set of fundamental norms. Justice, for example, may dictate impartiality. And justice is plausibly a fundamental norm. But it may well be underdetermined by those fundamental norms what exactly impartiality requires. Yet one should not on this basis leap too quickly to a view of justice which relativizes it to ethical traditions. Suppose that the question, which of many incompatible impartial principles is the true principle of justice, is genuinely indeterminate in the sense that no answer can secure ideal convergence. If we come to see that, then shouldn't we, by the argument of the previous section, cease to assert any of these incompatible principles? It is not that in these circumstances there is more than one right theory of justice—there isn't one at all. There is only a shortlist of principles compatible with impartiality, among which no objective ranking can be sustained. By what magic, then, would it become determinate, 'relative to an ethical tradition', that a particular principle of justice on this shortlist is the one that is *true*?

People situated in a concrete tradition may perhaps be justified, relative to their historic state of evidence and argument, in holding the principle of justice they do. But that is a different point, about justification not truth. Were we to reach the view, for example by reflecting on conflicting concrete or philosophical traditions, that there is only an optimal shortlist of principles, then it would seem to become a question of choosing (if necessary) among the principles on the list, rather than of arguing about which is true.

If there is nonetheless a case for arguing that principles of justice are socially *relative* and not just *indeterminate*, the argument will have to be stronger. It will have to take a constructivist view of the particular case of justice. In other words, it will have to argue that principles of justice stronger than mere impartiality are not normatively fundamental but 'artificial'. No such principle can secure ideal convergence of *judgements*—yet general *consent* to some such principle may nevertheless be forthcoming within a given ethical community. A constructivist view will then say that if that consent satisfies some or other specified conditions it becomes normatively binding for that community. On this view it is then *true*, relative to that community, that that is what is just.

This constructive view of justice must still treat the normative authority of consent reached under appropriate conditions non-constructively. That is, the fundamental and non-relative normative principle comes to be this: where appropriate consent is reached within a community on a distributive principle that lies within a shortlist of acceptable principles, it is obligatory, in that community, to obey that principle. Defenders of a politically germane kind of value-pluralism (or equivalently, as it turns out, value-relativism) have to argue along some such lines as these.

PART II

The Good

V

Value and Distribution

1. Many important trends in recent moral and political philosophy oppose classical utilitarianism and seek to develop alternatives to it. The opposition advances on a variety of fronts. There are those who develop alternatives to utilitarian ethics and politics, as (in their very different ways) Rawls or Nozick do.[1] These philosophers propose substantive ethical or political principles which are at odds with the classical utilitarian's in a clear-cut way.

There are also more indirect lines of opposition. Some oppose the attempt to propose foundational ethical principles or criteria as such, preferring to explore moral practices from within. They distinguish between immanent clarification and critique (good) and theorizing and the propounding of 'abstract' theses (bad). There is an important truth in this, but it is also true that moral practice is no unified thing: it is riven with disagreement, reflectiveness is a part of it, and reflection unavoidably issues in a quest for comprehensive legitimating perspectives, of which the utilitarian's is one. Such perspectives are not artificial growths which wither if ignored; they are among the strongest shoots thrown up by moral and political discourse.

In diametrical contrast comes a line of attack which itself stems from a completely general thesis: the epistemological thesis that all practical reasoning must be instrumental—concerned with what means most efficiently realize non-rationally specified objectives. Morality must then be somehow fitted into that: as the rules of a game played between instrumentally rational players; but the question always arises why a player should obey a rule when it does not advantage him to do so.

The present essay proposes an alternative to classical utilitarian principles of distribution, but it does so from a point of view more sympathetic to classical utilitarianism than are any of those just mentioned. A classical

First published in M. Hollis and W. Vossenkuhl (eds.), *Moralische Entscheidung und rationale Wahl*, Munich: Oldenbourg, 1992: 191–207. I am grateful to the editors, and to Nick Baigent, Jim Griffin, Alan Hamlin, and Bob Sugden for helpful discussion.

[1] Rawls (1971); Nozick (1974).

utilitarian believes that an individual's life, or a social state consisting of many individual lives, can be more or less good. Further, each can be seen as a *distributed* good, in the sense that it is made up of parts which can be good or bad, and the value of the whole depends solely on the value of the parts, that value being measurable in principle on an additive scale. Whether it is right to see the matter in that way, or whether an individual life or a state of society should be seen, in a certain strong sense, *holistically*, is a question to which we shall return. However if we do see them as distributed goods, there will arise the substantive question of how the value of the parts is consolidated into a single value, the value of the whole. I shall call a principle which provides an answer to that question a *consolidation principle*. Maximizing aggregate utility is one such principle.

In each case, that of the individual life and that of the social state, the assumption that one can speak of a single, consolidated value at all is no truism. But if we grant it, it certainly becomes a truism that the best life or social state is the one which has the highest value. Assume further, with the utilitarian, that the value of a life is fully determined by the levels of well-being at every period within that life, and that the value of a social state is fully determined by the levels of well-being of all the individuals who comprise that state. Assume also that well-being can be fully cardinalized, and objectively compared across individuals and times. (We shall return in due course to these initial assumptions.) Should one further accept, with the utilitarian, that the values of an individual life or of a social state are simply the aggregate of the distinct levels of well-being comprising it? I shall argue that we are not compelled to do so, even under these assumptions, and that an alternative consolidation principle, the 'Principle of Threshold Justice', is more attractive.

But before broaching the question I must indicate two broad points on which the utilitarian tradition seems to me to be right; for if it is not right on these there is little point in pursuing the specific disagreement with classical utilitarianism on which I wish to focus.

Utilitarianism must, when thought through, differ from any attempt to found ethics on instrumental rationality; in the division between those who recognize 'categorical'—non-instrumental—principles of practical reason, and those who believe that there are no objective ends and that reasons for acting obtain only as relativized to specified objectives, utilitarianism belongs firmly on the former side. The principle of utility is a categorical criterion of conduct; though on any sensible form of utilitarianism it will normally enter into deliberation only 'indirectly'—mediated through many tiers of practices and attitudes which are not themselves categorical, but are shaped by tradition, circumstance, and human nature.

I do not find the appeal to a categorical principle unacceptable; the Humean, and modernist, assault on categorical reason seems to me to derive from unsound epistemology and philosophy of mind. Nor does it seem to me wrong to think that categorical principles of practical reason are heavily mediated in their application to conduct, as the indirect utilitarian does. Compare the case of science. To say that there are some final criteria of theoretical reason by which scientific theorizing is judged, is not to say that every step of scientific theorizing is immediately judged by them, or that it intelligibly could or should be. A theoretical step takes place in the setting of a cognitive tradition. The same goes for a practical policy—that is the element of truth in the idea that creative ethical criticism is immanent critique—though there is no automatic step from conservative holism to political conservatism.[2]

There is however an important point on which the framework within which I shall argue differs from the utilitarian tradition. Well-being in that tradition is interpreted hedonistically. But a person's good has components other than happiness, even when happiness is maturely understood. Knowledge of one's situation, autonomy—the ability and freedom to pursue one's own life within one's own domain—are ingredients of a person's good, on all fours with and irreducible to happiness.[3] 'Well-being' and 'utility' are purely formal terms, intended as stylistic variants on the notion of an individual's good, of what is worth pursuing for his sake. The distributive question with which this essay is concerned appears separate. We shall see however that the two issues—the content of well-being and the aggregative conception of distributed value—are intertwined.

2. How much is implied by the notion of general good, the good of all? At least this much: that the good of all be impartially considered—'everybody to count for one, and nobody for more than one'. Thus far, we travel with the utilitarian—Thomas Scanlon terms the view that the ultimate standard of moral reasoning is perfectly impartial concern for the good of all individuals, 'philosophical utilitarianism'.[4] It holds, in Scanlon's words,

---

[2] See also Essay VIII, Sect. 8.   [3] These points are argued in my (1989: ch 9).

[4] Scanlon (1982). Scanlon also sets out very tellingly the broad considerations which appear to make philosophical utilitarianism compelling. Philosophical utilitarianism is one very natural stance to take up in the context of a thoroughly naturalistic view of human beings. But he thinks there is another, equally natural stance: 'contractualism', which takes as central 'the desire to be able to justify one's actions to others on grounds that they could not reasonably reject . . . Reasonably, that is, given the desire to find principles which others similarly motivated could not reasonably reject' (ibid. 116).

Such a desire differs from the desires postulated in simple Hobbesian or sceptical contractualism. 'Reasonable' is not here understood as that which is efficient in relation to the

that all

that counts morally is the well-being of individuals, no one of whom is singled out as counting for more than the others, and . . . all that matters in the case of each individual is the degree to which his or her well-being is affected.

So it seems that a variety of ways of further articulating the general good is consistent with philosophical utilitarianism, each meeting the requirement of impartiality, but carrying potentially divergent implications for the distribution of the good. Scanlon's suggestion, however, is that philosophical utilitarianism leads to classical aggregate utilitarianism:

If all that counts morally is the well-being of individuals, no one of whom is singled out as counting for more than others, and if all that matters in the case of each individual is the degree to which his or her well-being is affected, then it would seem to follow that the basis of moral approval is the goal of maximizing the *sum* of individual well-being. Whether this standard is to be applied to the criticism of individual actions, or to the selection of rules or policies, or to the inculcation of habits and dispositions to act is a further question, as is the question of how 'well-being' itself is to be understood.[5]

This puts the issue on exactly the footing which interests us: the question concerns the nature of the ultimate standard—what policies and habits best promote well-being, and what the elements of well-being are, are further questions. Yet does 'philosophical utilitarianism' indeed force *aggregate* utilitarianism as the ultimate standard?[6] Keeping closely to Scanlon's formulation, the three principles of philosophical utilitarianism are

> (1) all that counts morally is the well-being of individuals,
> (2) no one individual is to be singled out as counting for more than others, and
> (3) all that matters in the case of each individual is the degree to which his or her well-being is affected.

Principle (1) states that the general good is determined exclusively by individuals' goods. Principle (2)—the requirement of impartiality—will be analysed more carefully in a moment; its intuitive import is that one cannot give a differential weighting to the well-being of an individual *because of who that particular individual is, or of his relation to oneself*. Principle (3) is the most difficult to interpret. It should I think be taken to mean that an

agent's overall objectives. What is reasonable is relative to a structure of norms; but then further discussion must obviously require some analysis of the content of those norms, and of how far people can be expected to live up to norms—and it is open to the philosophical utilitarian to argue that the final test of what is reasonable is the criterion of general good.

[5] Ibid. 110.

[6] Scanlon only says that 'some form of utilitarianism appears to be forced on us' (109–10).

increase in any individual's good counts as an increase in general good; insofar as it further says that nothing else about the individual matters it simply repeats (1). Putting the same point in another way: if the well-being of an individual is improved, and the well-being of no individual is diminished, there is an increase of general good.

This yields the Pareto Principle: whenever an individual's well-being can be improved without reducing the well-being of anyone else, general good would be increased by that improvement. The Pareto Principle certainly rules out some consolidation principles—strict egalitarianism, for example. But it does not yield aggregative utilitarianism. Aggregate utility as a consolidating principle constitutes a particular implementation of the notion of general good, going beyond what is required by (1)–(3).[7] Another consolidation principle would be the 'lexical' version of Rawls's Difference Principle (also known as 'leximin'):

first maximize the welfare of the worst-off representative man; second, for equal welfare of the worst-off representative, maximize the welfare of the second worst-off representative man, and so on until the last case which is, for equal welfare of all the preceding n-1 representatives, maximize the welfare of the best-off representative man.[8]

Leximin provides another particular implementation of the notion of general good: seen in this way, it is a version of philosophical utilitarianism.[9] But is either leximin or aggregate utilitarianism the *right* implementation?

3. Impartiality as understood here can be analysed into two requirements—universalizability and agent-neutrality. Universalizability disqualifies any principle for whose expression a term rigidly designating a particular moral individual or group is indispensable. Where an impartial principle is so stated as to contain such a term, the occurrence of the term

---

[7] It might be urged that the classical utilitarian's basic thought is that well-being is 'the only thing that's good', and that if well-being is 'the only thing that's good', one must maximize its total. But 'well-being is the only thing that's good' could mean—implausibly strongly—that good is a simple additive function of well-being, or it could more weakly mean that good is a function of well-being and nothing else. Even within the tradition of classical utilitarianism (Bentham, Mill, Sidgwick) maximizing average utility was suggested as an alternative to maximizing aggregate utility—and that is already incompatible with the implausibly strong version of the utilitarian's basic thought. So I think it's fair to propose (1)–(3) as capturing the really plausible core of utilitarianism.

[8] Rawls (1972: 83).

[9] Amartya Sen uses the term 'welfarism' or 'Pareto-inclusive welfarism' (1982: 328, n. 2) for a position which roughly corresponds to philosophical utilitarianism. But he builds into it claims which are not part of philosophical utilitarianism as here envisaged e.g. a hedonistic conception of well-being and the assumption that welfarist criteria should be directly applied in the formation of policy.

must be dispensable—the principle must be 'universalizable': restateable as, or derivable from, a general principle in which no term rigidly designating that moral individual or group occurs. Agent-neutrality, on the other hand, rules out picking out individuals by the relation they stand in to the agent. Where an action is recommended by an agent-neutral principle, the fact that people affected by the action stand to the agent as fellow members of a family, lineage, nation, or whatever will form no part of the reason, identified by the principle, for doing the action.[10] A principle can be universalizable but not agent-neutral ('Everyone ought to obey their own father'), or agent-neutral but not universalizable ('Everyone ought to obey God'—assuming 'God' to occur essentially in this).

Whatever consolidation principle is accepted by the philosophical utilitarian it must be impartial in this sense and it must also be Pareto-efficient. That fits aggregate utilitarianism and Rawlsian leximin, but it also fits the principle which I call *Threshold Justice*. This holds that one should maximize aggregate utility subject to a threshold below which no individual is allowed to fall. A principle of this general form, I shall argue, is rationally preferable as a consolidation principle to both aggregate utility and leximin. I shall consider its analogues in the case of prudential reasoning and reasoning under risk; but it will certainly not be possible to consider all aspects of the issue in a single essay. In particular, the various questions which arise when one attempts to implement the idea of a threshold constraint within a concrete social setting, or individual life, will not be pursued here.

Threshold Justice is not to be understood as a general theory of justice. The object of such a 'theory' would be to describe comprehensively how the ideal of justice should be invoked in practice. It would belong not to the level at which we discuss ultimate standards of practical reason, but to the practical level at which actions, characters, and institutions are discussed and assessed; many concepts—need, desert, equity, fair procedure, rights, etc.—come in at that level. Since Threshold Justice refers to a consolidation principle, not a theory of justice proper, the name is potentially misleading; on the other hand a consolidation principle will underlie and inform the complex and concrete notion of justice which develops from it. Thus one might speak, in the same way, about utilitarian or Rawlsian justice without implying that the utilitarian's or the Rawlsian's detailed recommendations for just procedure will be limited to prescribing maximization of aggregate utility, or adherence to the Difference Principle.

[10] The notion of rigid designation is borrowed from Saul Kripke. 't' is a rigid designator if it does not make sense to suppose that t (literally) might not have been t. For a definition of agent-neutrality see Essay III.

Nevertheless in practice, it seems to me, our ideas of social justice—that is, of the broadest distributive constraints which should be observed wherever possible in the formation of social policy—are much closer to the Threshold conception than to utilitarianism or the Difference Principle and thus more easily rationalized by it than by them.[11] Threshold Justice is also a major strand in liberal thought, in the shape of the ideal of a 'social minimum' which should be guaranteed where possible to all citizens;[12] the idea that social justice requires that every citizen be guaranteed some minimum standard of material well-being is one of the least controversial of popular political ideas, in contemporary liberal democracies at least—though the question of how high that standard should be set is of course very controversial. Unlike leximin, Threshold Justice does not proscribe any improvement, however massive, to someone's position when it is offset by a deterioration, however small, in the well-being of someone less well-off. And unlike the principle of aggregate utility, it does not allow indefinite worsening of a person's position so long as that is offset by compensating gains of well-being to others. Of course it is open to the utilitarian or the Rawlsian to argue that the Threshold conception should be seen not as an ultimate consolidation principle but as a derived principle of justice, which is itself grounded, for reasons of empirical circumstance, on the maximization of aggregate utility or on the Difference Principle. However I believe that that becomes implausible once one sees it as a possibility that Threshold Justice *itself* could constitute the ultimate standard. The crucial question therefore is whether Threshold Justice can indeed be regarded as constituting the ultimate articulation of our idea of general good. Is there not something disconcertingly arbitrary about it—who is to say at what level the threshold is set? And how should we act when no option which maintains every individual at or above the threshold is available to us— when every option entails that one or more individuals fall below?

In reply to the first of these questions it should be stressed that there is no reason why an ultimate ethical notion should be fully determinate, or lend itself to smooth and simple mathematical treatment. On the contrary, there ought to be something *surprising* if it turns out that way—if our notion of general good turns out to be fully articulated by something as crisp and neat as 'Maximize aggregate well-being', or 'Maximize the

[11] There is some empirical evidence for this. See Frohlich, Oppenheimer, and Eavey (1987), Lissowski, Tyszka, and Okrasa (1991), Lissowski (1994), and Lissowski and Swistak (1995) (the article by Lissowski is in Polish but has an English abstract).

[12] Lockian or natural-rights liberalism recognizes it as much as Millian or 'philosophical-utilitarian' liberalism. See Nozick's discussion of the 'Lockian proviso' (Nozick 1974: 178–82). The difference—insofar as these are 'left' and 'right' versions of liberalism—would come on the question of what level the threshold should be set at.

well-being of the least well-off'. (Similarly, the criterion of simplicity is an ultimate standard of good theorizing: but there is nothing simple about what simplicity in concrete cases is—no easy way of replacing the theoretician's judgements of relative simplicity by a mechanical rule.)

Still, the question remains of how ideas about the threshold level are fixed. There are many possibilities to be explored. The threshold may be variable; it may be fixed by natural milestones such as, for example, the level at which 'essential physical needs' are met, or the level at which meaningful exercise of personal freedom becomes possible; or by these in combination with culturally relative understanding of what is an essential physical need, or a meaningful exercise of personal freedom. It may crawl behind or jerkily follow average or aggregate well-being. All these possibilities should be explored in detail, but the task will not be undertaken here. Our concern is with the abstract possibility of a threshold requirement in the distributive specification of general good; not with the question of how that abstract feature might be deployed in a multiplicity of concrete cultural contexts.

The second question—what happens when all options are sub-threshold—is a cogent one. One obvious possibility is that when a particular threshold is unattainable a lower one comes into operation. In that case, is the succession of lower thresholds finite? If so, what policy is to be followed in cases of extreme urgency or overwhelming deprivation, when every one of them becomes unattainable? Perhaps in that desperate case one just maximizes aggregate utility? Again we cannot follow through the various possibilities; for the purely provisional sake of simplicity we shall assume that general well-being is maximized subject to a threshold, and simply maximized where the threshold cannot be met.

4. One of the most striking aspects of Rawls's construction of a theory of justice is his linking of rational choice theory with principles of just distribution.[13] The just principles are those which an instrumentally rational man would choose in the Original Position; thus principles of justice turn out to depend on one's view of what principle of rational choice should be adopted there. However the link Rawls forges (or has often been thought to forge) seems too strong. It would not, for example, be actually inconsistent to hold that maximizing expected utility is always the rational procedure to adopt in one's prudential decisions, while accepting the Difference Principle as an account of justice—though one could not then

---

[13] He is of course not the only person to have done this. John Harsanyi is another pioneer—see the essays in Harsanyi (1976).

justify the Difference Principle by reference to Rawls's hypothetical Original Position.

On the other hand, the formal analogies remain suggestive. It would be philosophically satisfying if formally analogous cases produced analogous responses—even if it is not logically required that they should do so. There are in fact three formally analogous cases to consider. There is the case of social morality (under certainty). Here we seek the greatest general good, and the question is, what consolidation principle determines the general good? Aggregate utility gives one answer, leximin another, Threshold Justice a third. Then there is the case of prudence under certainty. We seek the best life, and the question is what consolidation principle takes the well-being of particular periods of a life into the value of the whole life? Once again there is aggregate maximization, leximin, and threshold-constrained maximization, applied this time over the periods of a single life. Thirdly there is deliberation (prudential or moral) under risk: here we have maximization of expected benefit, maximin, and maximizing expected benefit subject to the requirement that the worst possible outcome of the chosen action does not fall below a particular threshold.

Prudence (under certainty) is surely the case where simple maximization is at its most plausible. Individuals, as critics of classical utilitarianism often point out, are 'separate'; but the periods of a life are all part of one life. So if it is the *separateness* of individuals that undermines simple maximization of aggregate utility, there would not, it seems, be a similar objection to simple maximization within a single life. But it is worth exploring the matter with some care.

Let us translate the three tenets of philosophical utilitarianism to the prudential case. We then have

(4) all that counts prudentially for me is my well-being across all the periods of my life;

(5) no one period is to be singled out as counting for more than others;

(6) all that matters (prudentially) as regards each period is the degree of my well-being in that period.

(5), the requirement of impartiality, will now consist of universalizability with respect to time and temporal neutrality. Thus universalizability in this case requires that no term rigidly designating a particular time should appear indispensably in expressing the force of a prudential consolidation principle. That leaves open the possibility of what economists call pure time-preference; it is ruled out, however, by temporal neutrality, which stipulates that the fact that periods of well-being affected by my present action stand to the present moment in a particular relation (of relative proximity, or whatever) should form no part of my reason for doing the action.

Let us call the analogue of Philosophical Utilitarianism encapsulated in (4)–(6), Philosophic Prudence. It requires me to maximize the value of my life taken as a whole. Of course, given a preference ordering across *whole* possible lives, I choose the best. But how do I arrive at such an ordering? This is the question for which a principle consolidating the well-being of the various periods of a possible life into a single value appears to be required.

The consolidation principle analogous to Threshold Justice would be to maximize my aggregate intertemporal well-being subject to a threshold below which no period of my life is allowed to fall. Can one give some plausibility to this?

Imagine a man who has a seriously incapacitating accident. He can be kept alive and conscious on a life-support machine but his potential for experience, thought, and action is drastically reduced. He can still derive a small amount of pleasure from life, for example by watching television soap opera, but he can derive no more. Imagine that at any moment this gives him just enough pleasure for him to prefer to continue watching than to cease to live. The pleasure remains constant (there is a device which wipes his memory so that all the episodes can be run in a circle without boredom ever setting in). Imagine that medical science has so progressed that it is possible to keep him alive on the life-support machine, at that level, indefinitely. Since we are not applying time preference this means that his aggregate well-being can be increased indefinitely.

Contrast a different life: of three score years and ten, in which he knows the happiness of friendship, love, and family, is able to lay great plans and fulfil them brilliantly, and ends his life honoured and loved. Whatever the value of this life, it seems that it must have some finite value (a few more years of honoured retirement would have made it even greater); hence, on a purely aggregative approach, it seems that a sufficiently extended period of television-viewing on the life-support machine would have exceeded it. Should he then, given the choice, prefer the sufficiently extended television-viewing life? It does not seem to me at all obvious that he should. It seems perfectly reasonable to choose the life of three score years and ten.

But there is no direct path from this response to rejection of the simple maximization model. Remember that we are not assuming a hedonistic conception of well-being. We have accepted that autonomy and knowledge of one's situation are also ingredients of well-being, and perhaps other things too; it may be that life on the machine is drastically lacking in these. On the other hand happiness *is* an ingredient of well-being as well as these other things—must it not therefore, when it accumulates in sufficient quantity, outweigh the others?

It cannot be taken for granted that it does, and that means that the preference for the life of three score years and ten is not an unambiguous counter-instance to the view that Philosophic Prudence requires simple maximization. When we introduce a plurality of personal goods it becomes evident that the cardinalist assumption to which we have so far adhered is too simple (and for reasons which have nothing to do with the methodology of measurement). In fact it would already be too simple if we simply modified hedonism in the manner of John Stuart Mill, by allowing for pleasures of different quality. Mill's modification is wise and justified; it brings to our attention the possibility that there are discontinuities among kinds of happiness or pleasure which make it impossible to place all possible states of a person's happiness onto a single additive scale. The likelihood of such discontinuities is even greater when we take such things as knowledge and autonomy into account.

Such discontinuities would still allow for an ordering of a person's states but not a cardinalization of them. It is possible, as James Griffin notes, that

so long as we have enough of B any amount of A outranks any further amount of B; or that enough of A outranks any amount of B. Both of these forms bring with them the suspension of addition; in both we have a positive value that, no matter how often a certain amount is added to itself, cannot become greater than another positive value.[14]

And he shortly after notes as plausible that

fifty years of life at a very high level of well-being—say, the level which makes possible satisfying personal relations, some understanding of what makes life worth while, appreciation of great beauty, the chance to accomplish something with one's life—outranks any number of years at the level just barely worth living— say, the level at which none of the former values are possible and one is left with just enough surplus of simple pleasure over pain to go on with it.[15]

The explanation, in his view, lies in discontinuity. So long as there is enough 'simple pleasure' any amount of higher 'prudential values' outranks any further amount of simple pleasure; or perhaps, enough higher prudential value outranks any amount of simple pleasure. But prudential value taken as a whole can still be ordered on a single scale and we should prefer the greatest amount.

---

[14] Griffin (1986: 85).   [15] Ibid. 86.

I agree that it's plausible that some forms of life, in which we receive certain higher qualities of well-being, may be discontinuously higher in well-
being than other forms of life in which those higher qualities of well-being
are not received—however much lower quality of well-being is received.[16]
Consider Milrates. Unlike Socrates, he does not go so far as to consider
the unexamined life to be not worth living. But he is persuaded that the
examined life—with sufficient levels of physical well-being—outweighs in
value the pleasant but unexamined life, however far the simple pleasures
of the latter are extended. A no doubt simple-minded model of this would
be the following. There are, say, two prudential values, reflective insight,
and physical well-being. Below a certain level of physical well-being,
insight is of no or subordinate importance to Milrates. He prefers any
increase of physical well-being to any increase of insight. But as some
(vaguely defined) level of physical well-being is achieved, insight becomes
dominant. He now prefers increases of insight to increases of physical
well-being, however great. Below the switch-over level, there is a lexical
ordering with physical well-being dominating insight, above it the lexical
ordering is reversed, with insight dominating well-being. Perhaps similar
things could be said for personal goods such as active accomplishment, or
autonomous participation in communal life.

Milrates' schedule of personal good takes us beyond the simple 'pleasure–pain cardinalism' of the Benthamite tradition and correspondingly
undermines the aggregate-maximization account of Philosophic
Prudence. There is no sense, in his case, to the idea of maximizing an overall *aggregate*. It becomes harder to get at the specific issue we are concerned with. However it does not become impossible, since there can still
be cases in which simple pleasure–pain cardinalism has application. After
all I can and do decide such things as that this second ice cream was just
as pleasant as that first one, so that two were twice as pleasant as one. In
this kind of case my considered report on my quantum of enjoyment is
authoritative. In similar vein, I might judge that a certain amount of mild
physical discomfort is just worth one ice cream. So far, it seems that such
simple pleasures and pains can be put on a single additive scale.

Let us then abstract from putative higher values such as friendship, love,
insight, autonomy, accomplishment. Consider only 'simple' pleasures and
pains. Certainly a life consisting only of such simple pleasures is worth living. When a person is reduced to such pleasures alone, by incapacitating
illness or injury, we deplore his misfortune but we do not think life's value
to him is as nothing. Consider then the following question. Suppose a

---

[16] This is discussed further in Essay VI.

period of pain to be the necessary and sufficient condition for an addition of life lived at such mildly pleasurable levels of well-being. For any period of physical pain, however intense and lengthy, *must* there always be some addition of mildly pleasurable life sufficiently long to make acceptance of the period of pain prudentially reasonable? For me the answer is no.

Undoubtedly it is hard at this point to keep various strands in our thinking separate. Remember that we are not allowing for the perspectival effects of time preference. (Imagine that the decision is being made on behalf of someone else—perhaps the incapacitated person who has suffered an accident.) But does sufficient pain perhaps induce a transformation of quantity into quality? A 'deeper pain' (corresponding to a 'higher' pleasure) which no amount of simple pleasure can outweigh? 'Deeper pain' would be incommensurably worse than any amount of physical well-being. Certainly, if there are higher pleasures there may be 'deeper' miseries—the loss, presumably, of something discontinuously preferable to simple pleasure would not be outweighed by any amount of simple pleasure. But sheer physical pain is not a loss of this kind.

Consider the question again from a third-person point of view. Is an intensely painful operation justified for indefinitely extended just-pleasurable life? Suppose one is asked that question by a doctor, about an incapacitated relative who cannot decide for himself. The question, it seems to me, does not get easier as the length of just-pleasurable life, secured by the operation, is extended further. However long the extension, a feeling remains that the end secured, though not *pointless*, cannot override the horror of the means. Simple pleasure *is* worth while—and is not incommensurable with physical pain—nevertheless, it is still not obvious that a period of intense pain should always be accepted in return for a sufficiently extended period of mild pleasure.

But then would an intensely painful operation be justified, say, to restore a senile patient's powers, reopening deeper possibilities of life for him? That would indeed be an agonizing choice for a relative to have to make. In this case one might well ask oneself whether the patient, his powers restored, would be happy to have undergone the operation. That is to say, he himself, having undergone the operation, would again be able to think of his life as a single, unified life, and to place the recovery of powers achieved through great pain on a scale of preferences which reflects the unity of that life in no simply additive way.

What emerges from this? Certain elements of a good life are incommensurable with simple pleasure and pain; they create discontinuities which prevent complete cardinalization. I suggest that every element of this kind which might be at all plausibly proposed—for example, autonomy, knowledge of one's situation, accomplishment, even friendship or love (in the full sense)—in fact require self-consciousness; they require that I should see myself *as* a self, with a life to lead. The two features—the presence of plural goods inducing discontinuities and the presence of self-consciousness—go together and together compel one to see the value of a human life holistically.

If we try to envisage an impaired human existence in which only the simplest pleasures of physical well-being are psychically possible, we have to think away the higher powers of self-government, disinterested accomplishment, friendship, and love. But in doing so we simultaneously, I suggest, whittle away the basis for thinking of that existence as a unified human life, a single whole; it becomes, rather a genuinely distributed good—a sequence of pleasurable experiences. So an acid test for simple aggregate-maximization only becomes possible where the idea of a unified life, and with it the distinct concept of Philosophic Prudence, i.e. concern for the flourishing of *one's own* life, as against impartial concern for distinct periods of experience, fades. But then at this point it also seems to me that the grip of aggregate-maximization loosens. The upshot that finally emerges, then, is that where there is not a genuinely distributed magnitude the policy of aggregate maximization is inapplicable, and where it is applicable it is questionable.

5. The analogue of Threshold Justice in the case of risky decision is: maximize expected utility subject to the worst possible outcome not falling below a certain level. This is the principle of *threshold-constrained maximization* for decision under risk (the Threshold Principle for short): 'maximize expected utility subject to a threshold; where the threshold cannot be met just maximize.' As in the case of Threshold Justice, a fuller discussion of the principle would investigate more closely the way in which thresholds are related to the overall structure of benefits and risks—their spread and level. There is also the question of how one should act if every available option carries the risk of unacceptable (sub-threshold) outcomes; the same possible answers are available as were considered earlier.[17] There may be a succession of lower thresholds, determined in complicated ways by overall level and spread; when none can be met one maximizes expected utility. But the simple statement of the Principle does I believe pick up an important feature of our actual decisions. Some worst-case scenarios are just too bad. Thus, as between an action with a slightly

---

[17] Life, of course, always presents a tiny chance of disaster whatever one does. So in stating the Threshold Principle one must assume that the deliberator who follows it brackets out this continuous small 'background noise' of risk.

higher expected utility, but a slight risk of a catastrophic outcome, and one with slightly lower expected utility, but no such risk, the latter would I think be commonly preferred, and in my view, rationally preferred. A financial adviser should not simply assume that clients automatically prefer high-risk investments with higher expected utility. It is obviously relevant, for instance, what proportion of one's investment is at risk. The common advice is that one should take on a speculative investment only if one could walk away with equanimity from the worst-case result.

This phenomenon should be distinguished from simple 'risk-aversion'—understanding that as temperamental preference. Such preferences obviously do exist, but the disposition which we are now considering is not, in my view, one of aversion to gambles as such. It is a question of rational dispositions under risk: does the rational risk-taker impose a constraint on his choices, in the form of a threshold below which possible losses must not fall, as well as an objective, that of maximal expected benefit? I believe that in making risky choices he should attend to the constraint as well as the objective. Where the expected value of a gamble is equal to that of a certain gain, but the gamble's worst outcome is at or above the threshold, such a policy recommends indifference between the two. A preference for the certainty would then be temperamental.

Let me add that I do not mean to lay excessive weight on the distinction between temperament or feeling on the one hand and reason on the other. It is not sharp. Reactions can be understandable and the understandable reaction sets the norm of what is not unreasonable. For example a reaction of anger in particular circumstances would be regarded as quite understandable; but beyond a certain point it becomes unreasonable and even irrational. Risk-aversion can be unreasonable and even irrational in the same way. What should be resisted, however, is the assumption that unconstrained maximizing of expected utility sets the norm from which temperamental preferences for or against risk produce deviations.[18]

6. We finally return to Threshold Justice itself. In our discussion of Philosophic Prudence we were led to distinguish between a holistic and a distributed conception of the value of an individual life. If the goodness of

[18] Threshold-constrained maximization violates the 'sure-thing principle'; it would produce the pattern of decision-making exemplified in the so-called 'Allais paradox': see the appendix. It should be remembered that a person's 'utility' or 'well-being' is being defined here in terms of his good—what there is reason to pursue for his sake. So utility is not to be understood formalistically as that whose expected value a person can be described as maximizing, if his behaviour can be represented by the 'rationality' axioms underlying Bayesian decision theory. The sure-thing principle and the independence axiom in Bayesian theory are penetratingly criticized in McClennen (1988).

a life is a holistic value, one cannot add up the goodness of all periods of that life because they cannot be measured on an additive scale. One must estimate its value directly, considering it as a unitary whole. Under these circumstances it does not make sense to talk of maximizing the aggregate value of the life, and hence no contrast can be made between that consolidation principle and one of maximizing subject to a threshold. However, there may nevertheless be dimensions of its goodness which can be additively scaled; the value of a life whose goodness was confined entirely to that dimension would be a distributed good, and in that case the threshold conception became plausible.

On the face of it, since the value of a social state is determined by the goodness of the lives comprising it, it must be a distributed good. But perhaps this is not so clear. What is certainly true, by philosophical utilitarianism, is that only factors relevant to determining the goodness of the individual lives which comprise a social state can enter into determining the value of the social state. However it is consistent with that to hold that the overall value cannot intelligibly be arrived at by adding up the value of individual lives, because the numbers representing the value of individual lives cannot meaningfully be added.

This is not that old chestnut, the supposed general impossibility of interpersonal comparison, according to which any statement that one person is better-off than another is purportedly meaningless. Such comparisons certainly can be made, even if only vaguely and only within limits. The point at issue is the incommensurability of different kinds of good, which already crops up within one life. If the good of insight and the good of physical well-being cannot be added up within one life, they cannot be added up across two.

Suppose A and B both have the cross-over preference schedule between insight and physical well-being which Milrates had in Section 4. In that case aggregate maximization as a consolidation principle has no application, since we cannot meaningfully add the numbers which represent A's and B's levels of well-being. Suppose further that resources are only adequate (1) to afford to both of them a just-pleasurable state of well-being, at which further increase of physical comfort is still valued above insight—or alternatively (2) to afford to just one of them a sufficiently high level of physical comfort for a life of insight. Each of them would prefer the insightful life to an extended life containing no insight, but equal in well-being to the aggregate well-being of the two lives of just-pleasurable physical comfort. (It will be remembered that we have allowed addition in the special case where only physical comforts are at stake.) Can we conclude that the social state which consists of just one of A and B, resourced at a level of physical well-being sufficient for a life of insight, is better than the social state consisting of both, at just-pleasurable levels of well-being?

From what standpoint would that judgement be made? In the case of a single person, we can appeal to his own ideal preference-ordering (the one he ought to have, given his psychology). But there is no collective self, with all human lives as periods or moments in it, which sees itself as a self and generates its own preference-ordering. The two elements which went into treating the value of a single life holistically come apart here. There is incommensurability, but though there are two similar psychologies there is not a single psychology, a life unified by a single point of view, to generate a single preference ordering. Aggregate maximization gets no grip, but neither is there a holistic social value to maximize.

Threshold justice can be extended to the case where incommensurabilities as well as interpersonal comparisons are involved. In the case we are considering, I suggest that we should prefer the social state in which A and B lead lives of rudimentary physical comfort to the one in which just one of them leads a life of insight. A natural higher threshold is that which provides the life of insight for both of them; but where that cannot be achieved, the lower threshold of adequate physical comfort should be applied.[19] The analogous recommendation in the case of risky decision would be that each individual, given a choice between the certainty of a merely comfortable life and a lottery offering equal probabilities of a life of insight and instant death, should choose the certainty of a merely comfortable life.

The liberal sees social good, 'the good of society', as a distributed good; there *is* no single social being whose point of view makes it into a holistic value, and it is a dangerous metaphysic which talks as though there is. Threshold justice is the complement of this conception: the threshold being set at the highest natural point possible—ideally, at the level which makes possible citizenship and meaningful private attachments. There is, then, after all a sense in which individual rights are part of the basic structure of the general good: they correspond to the threshold provision which a society at a given level of material affluence and cultural advancement is able to provide.

---

[19] I am assuming that A and B already exist and that the decision to be made is how to distribute resources between them. It is not a question of whether to bring into existence two people who will live just-pleasurable lives of physical comfort or one person whose life will include insight as well as adequate physical comfort. In the latter case my intuition goes the other way.

APPENDIX

The Allais 'Paradox'

Consider the following case given by Maurice Allais (all the monetary sums in the table should by now have a nought or two added to take account of inflation!).[1]

	s_1 probability of s_1: 0.01	s_2 probability of s_2: 0.10	s_3 probability of s_3: 0.89
a_1	$500,000	$500,000	$500,000
a_2	$0	$2,500,000	$500,000
a_3	$500,000	$500,000	$0
a_4	$0	$2,500,000	$0

The table presents two possible situations of choice: between the pair of actions a_1 and a_2, and between the pair of actions a_3 and a_4. The monetary value, to the chooser, of the various possible outcomes is represented in dollars; and the outcome depends on the action he chooses, and on whether the state of the world in which he is choosing turns out to belong to s_1, s_2, or s_3. The probabilities of these respective states, as assessed by him, are shown.

Allais found that most people, given the choice between a_1 and a_2, prefer a_1. On the other hand, given the choice between a_3 and a_4, most people prefer a_4. Now this pair of choices (call it 'the Allais response') appears on the face of it to be inconsistent with Bayesianism (i.e. the policy of maximizing expected utility), and more specifically, with one of the axioms in L. J. Savage's formalization of its underlying theory, namely, the 'sure-thing principle'.

Suppose the monetary sums shown in the table measure the utility accruing to the chooser in the various possible outcomes. That is, the utility of the outcomes is determined only by the money received in them, and hence the difference between the expected utility of a_1 and a_2 is the same as the difference between the expected utility of a_3 and a_4. The Allais response is then inconsistent with maximizing expected utility, because if the expected utility of a_1 is greater for the agent

I am indebted to John Broome for discussion of this issue—it has improved what I have to say in this appendix but also raised more questions than I can answer. I hope to come back to some of these in future.

[1] Originally in Allais (1953). See also Allais (1979) (the collection in which this appears also contains an English translation of the full-length memoir which Allais 1953 presents in summary). There is a useful collection of papers, together with a survey of the issues, in Gärdenfors and Sahlin (1988).

than the expected utility of a_2, the expected utility of a_4 cannot be greater than the expected utility of a_3. Likewise it is inconsistent with the sure-thing principle—which holds that the choice between two actions cannot be influenced by consideration of outcomes in which both would have the same pay-off—because the pair a_1, a_2 is differentiated from the pair a_3, a_4 only in the third column, where, as can be seen, pay-offs are equal within each pair.

On the other hand the Allais response *is* consistent with the Threshold Principle discussed in Section 5. This recommends that one should maximize one's expected gain subject to a threshold constraint when that constraint can be met; when it cannot be met, that is, when no available action eliminates the possibility of sub-threshold outcomes, one should simply maximize. So if the $0 outcome is below the chooser's threshold whereas the $500,000 outcome is not, the Principle recommends a_1 over a_2. But since the possibility of a sub-threshold outcome cannot be avoided in the choice between a_3 and a_4 the Principle recommends simple maximization of expected utility in that case. If we assume that the chooser follows the Threshold Principle, and fixes a threshold above $0 when confronted with the first situation of choice, that will explain why he chooses a_1 over a_2 while nevertheless choosing a_4 over a_3. (He might fix a threshold above $0 because he is interested in improving both the aggregate of his utility and its threshold across possible outcomes, and the offer of a choice between a_1 and a_2 gives him the option of choosing *both* an increased aggregate of utility *and* a raised threshold.)

The Bayesian must either (1) try to explain the Allais response in a way which shows that it contains some element of irrationality—an error of reasoning, or something not fully thought through—or (2) he must try to show that it is not in fact inconsistent with the sure-thing principle.

(1) Savage takes the first line in his discussion of the case.[2] He says that his own first reaction conformed to the Allais response, and then he goes on to describe a way of presenting the example which caused him, on reflection, to reject that first reaction as wrong.

The two situations described in the table could also be realized, he points out, 'by a lottery with a hundred numbered tickets and with prizes' as in the following schedule:

| | | Ticket number | | |
		1	2–11	12–100
situation 1	a_1	5	5	5
	a_2	0	25	5
situation 2	a_3	5	5	0
	a_4	0	25	0

---

[2] Savage (1954: 101–3).

Here each action is the purchase of a ticket in the particular lottery specified on the corresponding row, the prizes being stated in units of $100,000. Savage now argues thus:

if one of the tickets numbered from 12 through 100 is drawn, it will not matter, in either situation, which gamble I choose. I therefore focus on the possibility that one of the tickets numbered from 1 through 11 will be drawn, in which case situations 1 and 2 are exactly parallel. The subsidiary decision depends in both situations on whether I would sell an outright gift of $500,000 for a 10 to 1 chance to win $2,500,000—a conclusion that I think has a claim to universality, or objectivity. Finally, consulting my purely personal taste, I find that I would prefer the gift of $500,000 and, accordingly, that I prefer [action] 1 to [action] 2 and (contrary to my initial reaction) [action] 3 to [action] 4.[3]

So Savage—rightly—looks for a perspective which 'has a claim to universality, or objectivity', and from which the reversal of his original preference for a_4 over a_3 seems, as he says, the correction of an error. But need there be any error? In this revised presentation the Threshold Principle may once again recommend the Allais response. If the outcome of $0 is below threshold, while outcomes of $500,000 and $250,000 are at or above threshold, it may recommend that one chooses a_1 in situation 1 and a_4 in situation 2.

(2) The second possible response for a defender of Bayesianism is to deny that the Allais response manifests a failure to maximize expected utility. Thus for example one may cite the *ex post* disappointment involved in choosing a_2 and ending up with nothing when one could have guaranteed $500,000 for oneself by choosing a_1, or the *ex ante* anxiety involved in choosing a_2 over a_1. Either way, on this view, option a_2 is not fully described by the tables, since the costs of actual anxiety or possible disappointment are not shown. When these costs are taken into account it may turn out that the Allais response is both reasonable and consistent with Bayesianism.

Both these lines of defence seem weak when one sees that the Allais response may be explained in terms of a *systematic pattern of choice*—one which features constraints, in this case threshold constraints, as well as goals. What is then required is some case for thinking that *this* systematic policy has less claim to rationality ('universality, or objectivity') than *Bayesian* policy. But what could that be?

Constraints as well as goals are a constant feature of our deliberations. Most obviously, moral considerations usually enter into deliberation in just this way: presenting some line of action as compulsory or prohibited irrespective of one's objectives.[4] Nor is it plausible to represent judgements about what is morally obligatory as though they were judgements about what will maximize something, or judgements about what is morally wrong as though they were judgements about what will guarantee a suboptimal outcome (see Essay II). Moral considerations characteristically enter into deliberation as constraints; there is no defect of

---

[3] Savage (1954: 101–3), 103.

[4] Nozick (1974: 28–33) brings out the point very clearly (though he is concerned primarily with rights).

rationality in this form of deliberation just because it takes into account both goals *and* constraints.

It seems to me that the same applies both to the purely prudential case and to deliberation about the general good. In the prudential case there is no defect of rationality in a policy which seeks to maximize well-being subject to a constraint—in this case a threshold below which one's well-being is not allowed to fall at any time or in any possible outcome.[5] Following this policy need have nothing to do with temperamental aversion to risk or fear of disappointment. It may simply express the rational thought that the distributive *shape* as well the overall *amount* of well-being in one's life matters. Specifically, the thought is that elimination of 'spikes' of suffering, however short or improbable, comes into rational deliberation as a consideration *distinct* from the maximizing of total well-being. One has in mind a threshold as well as a total, though the level at which the threshold is fixed may well be related in complex ways to the attainable totals.

When we turn to deliberation about the general good the analogous thought is expressed by the principle of Threshold Justice. In reckoning the general good, elimination of spikes of suffering, in however small a number of cases, is a consideration *distinct* from the maximizing of total well-being. These thoughts certainly seem to have as much claim to rationality as their pure maximizing alternatives, and I would urge that they have more.

John Broome elegantly defends the sure-thing principle, arguing that the Allais response is either inconsistent with Bayesianism and irrational or rational and consistent with it after all.[6] He also defends a principle which he calls the 'Principle of Personal Good'[7]—in effect this means that he accepts the standpoint of philosophical utilitarianism, as analysed in Section 2 above. And further, he wants to allow considerations of fairness to enter into deliberation *about the good*. This combination of views leads him to conclude that being treated unfairly is a harm to a person, in the specific sense that it *diminishes (other things equal) their well-being*.

Now this seems a very counter-intuitive conclusion. Suppose that in possible world A I am treated more unfairly overall than in possible world B. Suppose, however, that if we take into consideration all components of well-being (categorial ends whose realization in one's life constitute well-being) *other* than the putative component of 'being treated fairly', life for me in A comes out neither more nor less good overall than life for me in B. Should I nevertheless choose, from a prudential point of view, possible world B? I think not. Suppose that life for me is slightly better in A than B, by all these other components of my good. Then it seems to me that I should choose A over B (assuming that only *I* am treated more unfairly therein, and, of course, that no other morally relevant constraint rules out A).

---

[5] The qualifications mentioned in the essay apply: the threshold applied may depend on the outcomes available and the background noise of risk mentioned in n. 17 is ignored.

[6] Broome (1991: ch. 5).   [7] Ibid. ch. 8.

In other words, being treated unfairly does not as such, or intrinsically, diminish one's good. Of course it does usually *produce* a diminution of one's good, because it typically (not invariably) means that one ends up with a lesser benefit than if one had been treated fairly. But that does not make fair treatment a *constituent* of one's good.

I agree with Broome about the principle of personal good. I also agree with him about the importance of fairness. However I think that considerations of fairness enter into deliberation as moral constraints rather than as constituents of the good. (For example, one might think that a particular way of distributing the budget for school skiing trips would produce most well-being overall, but would be unfair, and so must be ruled out.) So the analysis of what fairness requires belongs to deontology, the theory of morality, rather than teleology, the theory of the good.

Nevertheless I have also argued above that the consolidation principle from individual to general good which we should adopt is some version of Threshold Justice. That *is* a claim at the level of the theory of the good, and is incompatible with the argument Broome develops for the 'utilitarian' (i.e. aggregative) principle of distribution. Broome's argument raises many interesting questions for discussion; for present purposes however the relevant point is that the sure-thing principle figures essentially in it as a premiss. As I have suggested above, this principle ceases to look plausible when one realizes how systematically and pervasively (in the three dimensions of persons, time, and risk) we take account of constraints as well as goals in our deliberation.

Broome acknowledges the attraction of non-aggregative consolidation principles; he seeks to take them into account by making *fair treatment* a component of individual good. But this wrongly moves fairness from its proper domain of morality to the theory of the good, and has the counter-intuitive consequence that 'fair treatment' becomes a categorial end—an intrinsic component of well-being. I suggest that we do better to reject the sure-thing principle.

VI

Quality of Well-Being: Quality of Being

It is an old idea that there is quality as well as quantity of well-being—that a distinction (perhaps a number of distinctions) can and should be drawn between higher and lower human goods. The implications of the idea differ according to the wider ethical framework in which one places it. But since virtually everyone thinks that a notion of individual well-being plays one or another major role in our ethical thought the questions at stake—whether it makes sense to distinguish between higher and lower goods, and what it might mean to do so—are of wide interest. In this essay I want first to examine the idea as such (Sections 1–3) and then to consider its place within a moral philosophy which takes the ethical standard to be the well-being of all, impartially assessed (Section 4).

1. THE MEASURE OF WELL-BEING

A good starting point is a thought-experiment of a kind to which James Griffin alludes in his discussion of incommensurability in *Well-Being*.[1] Suppose I am diagnosed as having an illness whose slow development will be imperceptible over many years. At some time in the future however it will reach a crisis-point which involves no physical discomfort but is almost immediately fatal. There is a cure for this illness—say an operation or a drug—but it has a serious consequence. It will reduce my mental powers and general energy permanently. I will come to have, as the consultant puts it, 'something like the mental age of a very small child' and I will also be limited in the amount of physical exercise I can take without exhaustion. After the cure, he explains, I may retain a more or less glazed memory—a remembering as through frosted glass—of the greater powers I currently enjoy, and of their exercise, but I will thenceforth only have a

Published in Roger Crisp and Brad Hooker (eds.), *Well-Being and Morality: Essays in Honour of James Griffin*, Oxford: Oxford University Press. I am grateful to the editors and to John Broome and Jonathan Riley for very helpful comments and criticisms.

[1] Griffin (1986: ch. 5), 'Are There Incommensurable Values?'

limited range of enjoyments, interests, affections. Physical warmth and comfort, food, melody, colour, stories, straightforward human affections and communication will now be everything to me. I will no longer have the developed forms of recollection and anticipation, reflectiveness and insight, physical powers and active accomplishments which I now have and will continue to have if I do not take the cure.

On the other hand medical science has progressed to a point at which my life after the cure can be maintained indefinitely. Moreover I have the resources to maintain it at a level which gives me a constant positive flow of well-being for as long as I like. I will not be a burden on others. By setting up contracts with an insurance company and a firm of solicitors which will act as my legal guardians, I can so invest my assets as to produce a cash flow which will cover the costs of care for as many years as I want. The only catch is that if I decide to have the cure I must have it straightaway. I cannot delay.

So I have a choice. I can choose not to have the cure. Or I can choose to have it, in which case I will be able to live an enjoyable life for as long as I like. Is it unreasonable to refuse the cure?

One might argue that it is, in this way. If I do not have the cure, I will lead a life which achieves a certain overall amount of well-being. It is however a finite amount—it could have been greater if I had lived a little longer, had another packet of popcorn, etc. By hypothesis, if I have the cure I will be able to live as long as I like, receiving a constant flow of well-being. So it seems that I will be able to live long enough to exceed the amount of well-being I achieve in the life without the cure. And it is surely unreasonable to prefer the lesser amount of well-being in one's life over the greater.

However, many feel that it is not unreasonable to refuse the cure; I am one of them. (If it is unreasonable not to have the cure, is it reasonable to have the operation or take the drug anyway, even if one is not ill?) This view could be defended in a number of ways, of which the following are three (a fourth, the 'perfectionist' response, will be discussed in Section 2).

(1) It may be said that it is reasonable at any given time to discount future benefits in proportion to their futurity, that is, their distance into the future from that time. That being so, the present value of a flow of well-being at a given level may always sum, however long the flow goes on for, to less than the present value of the finite amount of well-being achieved in my life without the cure. So the principle that it is unreasonable to prefer the lesser amount of well-being in one's life over the greater will not show that I should have the cure, since the assessment of amount must be applied to the present value of the alternatives before me.

(2) It may be said that the person who survives the cure is not really me. So at any rate the *prudential* principle that it is unreasonable to prefer the lesser amount of well-being in one's life over the greater cannot be applied to show that I should have the cure.

(3) It may be said that the notion of amount of well-being is being used equivocally.

I will not consider the first response, which appeals to the rationality of pure time-preference. To my mind pure time-preference can seem rational only on certain desire-satisfaction models of well-being which are themselves indefensible.[2] The second response raises issues which we shall have to come back to. However the response which will mainly concern us is the third.

Let us distinguish between *measure* and *quantity*. The measure of well-being for a being over a period of time in a possible situation will be a code which represents where the well-being in that possible period stands in an ordering; whether it is greater than, less than, or equal to well-being in another possible period. Whenever it is meaningful to consider whether the well-being of some being in a possible stretch of life is to be preferred, dispreferred, or regarded as indifferent to its well-being in another possible stretch (assuming no considerations other than its well-being to be at stake), it is also meaningful to attach codes to the two stretches of its life representing the comparative measure of well-being in them.[3] With 'measure' thus understood, the principle that it is unreasonable to choose for oneself a lesser measure of well-being is unchallengeable.

But the argument above does not show that I can achieve a greater measure of well-being by having the cure. The measure of well-being need not be additive; it may be incorrect for that reason to assume that the measure of well-being in a period can be represented as the sum of measures of

---

[2] Pure time-preference affirms the rationality of discounting future benefits by their very futurity, rather than by the greater riskiness which may be associated with their futurity. Perhaps it is programmed into us by evolution, since it's a simpler survival programme than explicit discounting for risk. But *that* explanation of pure time-preference undermines its rationality, since we can and do explicitly discount for risk. See Nozick (1997: Sect. IV).

Our thought-experiment assumes that no greater risk attaches to life after the cure than to life without it. (It may indeed be less.) One may of course question whether such a thought-experiment is not affected by worries about the risk involved in placing oneself in other people's hands, however reputable the insurance company and the firm of solicitors. But I think we can reasonably put this issue to one side.

[3] The codes may be real numbers but that does not mean that the ordering is representable by a real-valued utility function, for we are allowing the possibility that it contains lexically discontinuous preferences.

well-being in its sub-periods.[4] And there is one particular possibility here which we must consider further: that the well-being achieved in my uncured life may be *discontinuously* greater than that achievable in any life in which I have had the cure. Discontinuity of this kind, lexical superiority in an ordering, is one of the forms of so-called 'incommensurability' which James Griffin distinguishes in his consummate clarification of that subject.[5] In discussing it Griffin notes as plausible that

fifty years of life at a very high level of well-being—say, the level which makes possible satisfying personal relations, some understanding of what makes life worth while, appreciation of great beauty, the chance to accomplish something with one's life—outranks any number of years at the level just barely worth living—say, the level at which none of the former values are possible and one is left with just enough surplus of simple pleasure over pain to go on with it.[6]

He describes this as a situation in which 'enough of A [those higher constituents of well-being] outranks any amount of B [a surplus of "simple pleasure"]'.[7] There are two problems with this description.

In the first place this thought-experiment, like the thought-experiment with which we started, does not show that *any* life containing this amount of the various higher constituents to well-being outranks any life containing only a surplus of 'simple pleasure'. We are told that the fifty-year life includes satisfying personal relations, some understanding of what makes life worth while, appreciation of great beauty and the chance to accomplish something with one's life—but not how much surplus of simple pleasure it contains. Suppose the surplus is reduced and starts to go negative. Is it obvious that the resulting lives, however richly endowed with those constituents of well-being (A), continue to outrank any number of years of simple pleasure (B) alone—even as they come to have very small and then negative amounts of B: perhaps many years of pain following on the fifty years of very high well-being?[8] It is surely far from obvious.

On the other hand, so long as there is *enough* simple pleasure in one's life and not too much pain, it is still possible that a sufficient amount of

---

[4] It may be incorrect anyway: it is not obvious that summing the well-being of sub-periods of a life, even if that were possible and even within a single life, would be the right way to assess the measure of well-being in that life—for example, if the well-being in its sub-periods varied immensely (see Essay IV). However the distributive issues this raises do not I think affect the example we are considering, since we are assuming that life after the cure will produce a *constant* flow of well-being.

[5] Griffin (1986: 85–9).   [6] Ibid. 86.   [7] Ibid. 86.

[8] I may be reading Griffin unfairly here. He characterizes discontinuity on the previous page in this way: 'so long as we have enough of B any amount of A outranks any further amount of B; or ... enough of A outranks any amount of B' (p. 85). Perhaps the phrase 'so long as we have enough of B' should be read as having the second disjunct in its scope as well as the first.

the higher constituents of well-being (*A*) produces a combination good enough to outrank *any* further surpluses of simple pleasure (*B*) if those surpluses are combined with big enough reductions of *A*. But now the second point is that it does not immediately follow that there is a discontinuity. Another possibility to be considered is that as simple pleasure increases, its marginal value, measured by the rate at which it is rational to substitute it against the higher constituents of well-being, decreases. If that is a real possibility, then Griffin's thought-experiment does not establish a discontinuous preference for higher well-being.

However he also describes the case as one in which

we have a positive value that, no matter how often a certain amount is added to itself, cannot become greater than another positive value.[9]

In talking here about adding a certain amount to itself he must be referring to an amount of *well-being*. And it is for this additive metric of well-being that I want to reserve the term 'quantity'. Consider the amount of 'simple pleasure' I get from eating a particular bar of chocolate, and suppose you find by asking me that I get an equal amount of pleasure from eating a similar bar of chocolate the following day. If that is so, we should also conclude that the quantity added to my *well-being* by the pleasure of eating the two bars is exactly twice that contributed by the pleasure of eating one bar. For even if such pleasure is only one constituent of well-being why should equal amounts of *it*, as against equal amounts of that which gives it, have diminishing marginal utility? We can see why successive units of chocolate consumption may produce diminishing quantities of pleasure. In contrast, the suggestion that I get twice as much pleasure, but not twice as much well-being, from eating the two bars would take some explaining. Thus in this particular case we can legitimately shift to talking about the quantity of well-being contributed by consumption of a bar of chocolate and compare it with that contributed by the consumption of two or three. In this local case you *can* 'tot up' well-being, in Griffin's phrase.[10]

Nor does the point apply only to uncomplicated pleasures like eating bars of chocolate. Suppose you are a person to whom great painting matters deeply. If the satisfaction you get from spending an hour looking at Michelangelo's work in the Sistine Chapel is equal to that which you get from an hour looking at Tintoretto's in the Scuola di San Rocco, then

---

[9] Ibid. 85.

[10] Thus I agree with Griffin that additive talk about a person's well-being can make sense independently of assessments of that person's subjective probabilities (Griffin 1986: 98–102).

going to both Rome and Venice and seeing both makes (other things being equal, looking at too many pictures may diminish satisfaction of course) twice as great a contribution to your well-being as seeing just one of them. And saying that it makes twice as great a contribution to your well-being has an implication. It means that you should be willing to make twice as great a sacrifice of well-being to seeing both. The rate at which you substitute quantities of well-being from other sources to achieve constant increases of well-being from this source should not fall. In general, to say that the quantity of well-being generated by some particular activity or state A increases at a constant rate is to say that its contribution to well-being does not diminish at the margin, as measured by the rate at which it is rational to substitute it against quantities of well-being derived from some other activity or state B.

In describing the thought-experiment with which we started I said that life after the cure would afford a constant positive flow of well-being for as long as one likes. What this means, then, is that the *quantity of well-being* accrues at a constant rate day by day. It is perfectly imaginable that it should do so—in my post-cure state I will experience each day as neither more nor less satisfying than the last; nor will anything other than my experienced satisfaction any longer make a difference to my well-being. And now we are indeed forced to say that our preference for life without the cure implies that we hold a life without the cure to be discontinuously or lexically superior to any life after it. We cannot equal the measure of well-being in life without the cure by adding constant quantities of well-being to life after the cure.

So the measure of well-being is a function of the quantity of well-being derived from various sources and of some other feature of those sources— perhaps the 'quality' of well-being derived from them? That fits, at least roughly, the picture which John Stuart Mill had in mind in his famous discussion of the issue—which is why I have used the word 'quantity' in the way I have. Jonathan Riley has noted the point.[11] 'The most straightforward way to capture the quality/quantity distinction' (he says) 'is in terms of a lexical hierarchy of . . . aggregation procedures, one procedure for each kind or quality of pleasure.'[12] On this most straightforward interpretation the measure of ethical value for the Millian utilitarian will be pleasure—but with any quantities of higher-quality pleasures outranking any quantities of lower-quality pleasures.[13]

---

[11] Riley (1988, 1993).   [12] Riley (1993: 295).

[13] One should not say that in this interpretation a unit of higher pleasure is equal to an infinite amount of lower pleasure. For the notion of a 'lexical' preference implies that it is reasonable to prefer a unit of higher pleasure which is combined with *more* rather than *less*

This is *too* straightforward in that it implies that the smallest decrease in higher 'pleasure' always outweighs any increase in lower 'pleasure' (i.e. whatever one's existing 'consumption' of the two may be). If, in our thought-experiment, we prefer life without the cure that does indicate the presence of some lexicality or discontinuity in our preferences but not, so far, of a lexical hierarchy as simple as that. Still, the straightforward model suffices to show the coherence of distinguishing between quantity of well-being and some other aspect of it, also relevant to its measure. I shall not be concerned with how the model might be made more realistic. My main concern will be with what it is to think of this other aspect of well-being as a matter of its *quality*.

In distinguishing quantity and measure of well-being we have not yet shown that any notion which deserves the name 'quality' of well-being is required. Does our thought-experiment show that my actual life is higher in 'quality' than life after the cure? Why not content ourselves with saying that the measure of well-being cannot be represented additively? Why should a discontinuity indicate that something turning on 'quality' is at stake, where difference of quality does not just mean difference of kind or sort, but implies assessment in terms of a normative notion of 'higher' and 'lower'? Suppose that below a certain level of consumption of X, Alpha discontinuously prefers X to Y, while above some other level he switches over to a discontinuous preference for Y over X. Which enjoyment is superior in quality—X or Y? One might say that if there are such lexical switch-overs qualitative superiority is simply undefined. But even if switch-overs never take place, even if Riley's model of a lexical hierarchy fits people's preferences tolerably well, why should that sustain talk of quality of pleasure? Suppose that Alpha discontinuously prefers heroin to poetry at certain levels of heroin and poetry consumption, and that he never discontinuously prefers poetry to heroin. Suppose indeed that this is true of all those who have sufficient experience of both heroin and poetry. Does this show that taking heroin is qualitatively superior to reading poetry, or does it just show that heroin is addictive?

It may not show that taking heroin is qualitatively superior, because the lexical preference for taking heroin may not be rational. It may simply signify addiction. So in examining how a normative notion of quality of well-being works we must look in particular at how it is connected with the rationality of preference. Having done that we shall be able to reconsider in Section 4 how qualitative distinctions enter into the measure of well-being and what discontinuities in it they may generate.

lower pleasure. But adding units to a countable infinity still only gives you a countable infinity.

2. QUALITY OF WELL-BEING

We do think and talk about well-being, contentment, happiness and plea-sure in qualitative terms. For example, notions such as purity, elevation, depth, refinement, sublimity, and their opposites enter into our assess-ments of a person's enjoyments (including their pleasures).[14] We can easily understand what it means to say that A has more contentment in life than B, but that the contentment involved is a pretty shallow, simple-minded, low, crass, or even base kind.

A person who is satisfied with such kinds of contentment is thought to be undiscerning or lacking in finer feeling. It seems that the higher forms of well-being are those which require higher capacities or powers of dis-cernment and sensibility. Their full measure is not accessible to someone who does not have those powers.

The powers involved are rational and moral powers, capacities of rea-son, imagination, and sensibility and thus of character. It does not follow that higher enjoyments must be of an intellectual or a moral kind in the normal sense. Take the pleasure of an omelette and a glass of white wine on a radiant Mediterranean morning. It offers no deep human insight. Nevertheless to enjoy it to the full one must have active capacities—of attention, concept-formation, discrimination, imaginative synthesis, and recollection. Full enjoyment involves—for example—the idea of perfec-tion in omelettes, discriminating attention paid to the look, taste, and smell of this particular omelette, a synthesizing grasp of how perfect omelette, glass of wine, and radiant morning come together into a greater whole. The same can be said for higher enjoyments which involve physical activity such as sport or dance. Whether one enjoys these as participant or observer they involve the same powers. They may also involve moral insight into qualities of character or indeed the possession of these quali-ties. Exercise of these mental and moral powers is infused into the sheer animal enjoyment of physical movement and competitions and trans-

---

[14] Enjoyment *v.* pleasure: in this paper I use the term 'enjoyment' technically, to mean receipt of well-being. I do not use it to refer to an experienced state of pleasure, content-ment, or satisfaction. The truth or falsehood of hedonism is not at issue in the present dis-cussion. I do not mean to exclude accounts of well-being which make it possible that one is well-off in some respect without being aware that one is. Indeed anything like a correct sub-stantive account of well-being seems to me to have that consequence. Hence, in the techni-cal sense of 'enjoyment' adopted in this essay one can *enjoy* an element of well-being, such as the respect of people one respects, without realizing that one has it. Equally one can take pleasure in the false belief that one enjoys it. This technical sense can certainly diverge from ordinary use—for example, it is odd to talk of *enjoying* the sorrowful recollection of a death, even if (as I would agree) it can be an intrinsic part of one's well-being to mourn.

forms it, in the way that full enjoyment of the omelette involves an infusion of higher awareness into the animal enjoyment of sensuous life. Again when a mother plays with her baby son the kernel of her enjoyment is a simple animal pleasure: she responds to a small other which, in the most primitive sense, stands to her as 'mine'. Seeing another as 'mine' in this sense is a thing some non-human animals can do just as competing is. Mental and moral powers transform that kernel—infusing it with the awareness that this is in some fuller sense my son, my responsibility, and to some extent my creation, that he has a life ahead of him, much to discover, perhaps to suffer as well as to enjoy, etc. In particular they infuse it with an ethical sense of the innocence and humanity of the relationship involved, of its situatedness in time, of projects from which it came and to which it will lead. So too in the case of the omelette, come to that—it can include an ethical-aesthetic sensibility of transience, of the location in time of an experience and a self.

The general pattern, then, is one in which a variety of simple animal enjoyments, enjoyments open to human animals, is transformed or sublimated by developed intellectual and moral powers. This is not to intellectualize higher enjoyment, or moralize about it. But neither should one deny that there are hierarchies of quality in enjoyment, in which enjoyments involving forms of intellectual, spiritual, or moral insight come high. We spend a lot of time discussing how worthwhile particular kinds of enjoyment are and in the same spirit we spend a lot of time discussing the relative worth of various human achievements—here too the same considerations, about the range and impressiveness of the powers involved in the achievement and the enjoyment it affords, enter in.

Does this count, one might now ask, in favour of a 'perfectionist' view? Is talk about the quality of well-being really talk about the quality of the being whose well-being it is? Is it that we want to raise ourselves in the qualitative scale of beings, even at the cost of a reduction to the quantity of our well-being?

We should distinguish two points. On the one hand there is the epistemological truism that the criterion of higher well-being is what people who have, in developed form, the relevant powers of mind prefer. On the other there is the ethical claim that human development is something that matters in itself, an intrinsic goal in its own right, that there is an ethical imperative to become a person of developed higher powers: to 'raise oneself in the qualitative scale of beings'.

The truism is the inevitable starting point of any discussion of qualitative distinctions in well-being. It is what brings the notion of quality in. A criterion of quality in well-being is the criterion of what persons of greater discernment can enjoy and those of lower discernment cannot. I will come back to the questions this raises in Section 3.

The second thought is a version of perfectionism. I agree with Thomas Hurka's proposal to make it a defining characteristic of perfectionism that it takes excellence to have ethical value as such, irrespective of the contribution excellence makes to well-being.[15]

Thought-experiments like the one from which we started may well suggest it. In fact we can now see, in this version of perfectionism, a fourth response distinct from the three considered in Section 1: one should not have the cure because it lowers one in the qualitative scale of beings. It is better to be Socrates—or Elizabeth David—dissatisfied than a fool satisfied. Would one want to be the kind of person for whom a bag of crisps and a diet coke would be just as good as a perfect omelette on a crisp morning, because the discriminating capacity and power of attention was lacking? Would one want to be that kind of person even if perfect omelettes and radiant mornings were very hard to come by? If not, is that not because one wishes not to sink to a lower level of being?

To be able to experience higher enjoyments at their full value is to feel the banality of a life without them. In their absence, lower enjoyments leave a sense of dissatisfaction or frustration. That being so, does the welfarist, for whom well-being is all, not have to argue that if higher enjoyments are not available, then it is positively unreasonable to develop the capacities for their enjoyment? Must he not deny that it is better to be Socrates dissatisfied?

But to say that Socrates is dissatisfied is not to say that he is bereft of enjoyments. Many particulars of life may strike him as frustratingly mediocre, it is true; but the mental and moral powers which produce higher enjoyment work holistically. Their development—so long as they are being exercised—sublimates the whole experience of life.[16] It does not follow that such development is worth buying at any price. If for example a side-effect of developing these powers was chronic incapacitating pain which made their exercise impossible, it would not be worth it. If we

---

[15] See Hurka's very clear discussion and defence of perfectionism in Hurka (1993). A perfectionist may focus (as Hurka does) on excellence of achievement rather than the standing or status of the achiever. But it is hard to keep these separate. If excellence of achievement is not to be valued for the quality of well-being that it brings, is it not valued for the quality of being it brings—the standing of the achiever in the qualitative scale of beings, as measured by ideals of being?

[16] This is a version of what John Rawls called the 'Aristotelian principle' (Rawls 1971: §65), but my emphasis here is on the qualitative difference in enjoyment which development brings (and, to repeat, I do not assume that 'enjoyment' must be understood hedonistically).

amend our thought-experiment in this way it becomes much more diffi-cult. It is not obvious that possession of such powers in a condition of personal suffering which makes their exercise impossible is to be preferred to life after the cure. The latter life is still worth living and in these cir-cumstances it may well be that it makes sense to live it.

We are now better placed to see how discontinuity comes in. There is no *conceptual* connection between the idea of a higher enjoyment and the idea of a discontinuous preference. Our criterion of a higher enjoyment is that beings of greater discrimination show a greater preference for it than beings of lesser discrimination—it is not required that they prefer it *lexically*. Does a more discriminating person *lexically* prefer a perfect omelette to any amount of salt and vinegar crisps? Not necessarily. The point is only that the discriminating give it a degree of preference that the undiscriminating do not.

But neither is discontinuity an irrelevant notion. If the exercise of higher powers sublimates experience holistically, then a whole life in which they are exercised may be discontinuously preferred to one in which they are not. The reason is that if I have developed powers and am able to exercise them, my experience and sense of myself is transformed as a whole. What is lexically preferred is a life in which I have those higher powers and can attain the enjoyments they open up to me to a life in which I do not or can-not.

So we can explain why it may be reasonable to eschew the cure without appealing to perfectionism. But another point lends perfectionism some plausibility. Higher powers, and achievements requiring them, call forth admiration and respect. They have a value in their own right: they are admirable in themselves. That is true; on the other hand it is also true that the value they have has no *direct* implication for action, other than in giv-ing one reason to applaud. To deem something admirable is to see reason to admire it: to find a certain affective response, that of admiration, rea-sonable and justified. It does not directly entail that there is reason to achieve this thing ourselves, or to put resources towards other people's achieving it. Consider a brilliant violin performance (say). It has aesthetic value whether or not it contributes to well-being and its aesthetic value is independent of the well-being it generates. There is reason to admire it; but only if it contributes to well-being is there reason to seek to emulate it, to allocate resources towards maintaining the skills required for such perfor-mance, and so on. It may connect with well-being in more than one way. Excellent achievement may be itself, as Griffin suggests, a part of well-being. And whether or not it is, there is pleasure in being that which one admires and displeasure in failing to be. And obviously achievement can benefit others. But these connections between the admirable and reasons for action work via well-being; while perfectionism short-circuits the connection.

So it seems to me that what is admirable in character and achievement generates reason for action only through the effect it has on well-being. Mill seems to take an even more strongly anti-perfectionist line—holding that the very constitution of the admirable is a matter of its effect on well-being:[17]

> I hold that the very question, what constitutes . . . elevation of character, is itself to be decided by a reference to happiness as the standard.

That is too strong: what there is reason to admire in a particular field turns on the criteria internal to the judging of excellence in that field and does not necessarily refer to the happiness produced. (Unless of course the happiness produced is itself one of the criteria of excellence in it.) The passage continues, however, with a weaker statement:

> The character itself should be, to the individual, a paramount end, simply because the existence of . . . ideal nobleness of character, or of a near approach to it, in any abundance, would go further than all things else towards making human life happy; both in the comparatively humble sense, of pleasure and freedom from pain, and in the higher meaning, of rendering life, not what it now is almost universally, puerile and insignificant—but such as human beings with highly developed faculties can care to have.[18]

This statement may also seem to indicate a departure on Mill's part from hedonism; however though it would indeed (to my mind) be right to reject hedonism I do not believe that that is what Mill is doing here, any more than his preference in *Utilitarianism* for the life of Socrates dissatisfied over that of the satisfied fool is a rejection of hedonism. But be that as it may, there is certainly in this passage a rejection of perfectionism. And whether or not one agrees with hedonism one can hold, with Mill, that quality of being matters ethically (i.e. to reasons for action) only inasmuch as it makes a difference to the measure of well-being.[19]

---

[17] He did not have to. A utilitarian needs only to hold that all reasons for action derive from, or are correctable by, facts about well-being—he does not also have to hold that reasons to feel derive from the same source, or are even correctable by it. They can have their own, *sui generis*, rationale.

[18] Mill (1963–91), viii, 952 (*System of Logic*, VI. xii. 7).

[19] Mill discusses the value of nobility of character in similar vein in *Utilitarianism*, ch. 2, para. 9 (Mill 1963–91: x. 213–14). Cf. his explanation of what he means by 'higher natures' in a paper he wrote for Harriet Taylor 'On Marriage' (Mill 1963–91: xxi. 37–9): 'I mean those characters who from the combination of natural and acquired advantages, have the greater capacity of feeling happiness, and of bestowing it.'

3. TWO VIEWS OF WELL-BEING

The passage from Mill also embodies our earlier criterion of qualitatively superior enjoyment. It is what 'human beings with highly developed faculties can care to have'—but human beings with less highly developed faculties do not care to have as much or at all.[20] What is being suggested is a *criterion*—in other words, the suggestion is at the epistemological, not the definitional, level. This difference of levels should be kept in mind when we examine the notion of well-being as I want to do now. Let us consider two broad approaches to well-being; call them the *ideal-preference* view and the *reason-to-desire* view.

The ideal-preference view is actually a genus of views. The idea is that to characterize well-being one must start with preference—or with desire, or with contentment—and then idealize it by attaching some condition, C. Characterizing well-being then consists in producing some a priori true equivalence of the form 'ϕ promotes x's well-being if and only if x would choose to ϕ—or desire to ϕ, or be content with the result of ϕ-ing—in condition C.' Or again: 'g is an ingredient of (human) well-being if and only if human beings would choose g, desire g, be content with g, in condition C.'

In contrast the reason-to-desire view holds that an individual's well-being consists in whatever that individual has non-instrumental reason to desire, reason to desire for itself.[21] In talking of reasons to *desire* we are dealing with affective reasons, reasons to feel, not with practical reasons, reasons to act. Indeed this characterization of individual well-being relies on distinguishing between reason to desire and reason to pursue,[22] for it would otherwise obliterate the distinction between good in general and individual good. If there is such a thing as the good in general at all, it is not a priori that the good in general is equivalent to one's own good—but it *is* a priori that if there is a good in general, then there is reason to pursue whatever forms part of it. It does not follow that the good in general

---

[20] In *Utilitarianism* the 'test of quality, and the rule for measuring it against quantity' is 'the preference felt by those who, in their opportunities of experience, to which must be added their habits of self-consciousness and self-observation, are best furnished with the means of comparison' (Mill 1963–91: x. 214; ch 2, para 10).

[21] More accurately, his well-being consists in whatever there's reason for him to desire for itself *under some categorial end*. One can think of categorial ends as ingredients or elements of well-being (James Griffin's 'prudential values'); so, for example, your pleasure and your knowledge of your situation are distinct ingredients or elements of your well-being. See the appendix to this essay.

[22] By the FD principle (see Essay II, Sect. 8) if I have reason to desire g, then I have reason to pursue g. But the principle leaves the truth of the converse open.

must also form part of one's own good, since one's own good is defined in terms of what one has reason to desire, not what one has reason to pursue. Note also that to characterize the individual's good in terms of what that individual has reason to desire is not to endorse a desire-satisfaction model of practical reasons. This characterization of individual good, unlike the desire-satisfaction model of practical reasons, leaves open the possibility that there can be reason to do something that does not satisfy one's desires (however idealized) and that recognition of such a reason can lead one to act simply *from* recognition of it. (I may have no particular reason to *desire* your good but I still have some reason to lend it a helping hand.)

Henry Sidgwick held the reason-to-desire view of well-being:[23]

Putting aside the conceivable case of its being my duty to sacrifice my own good, to realise some greater good outside my own existence, we may say that my good on the whole is what I 'ought' to desire: but—since irrational desire cannot be dismissed at once by voluntary effort—we cannot say this in the strictly ethical sense of 'ought'. We can only say it in the wider sense, in which it merely connotes an ideal or standard, divergence from which it is our duty to avoid as far as possible, though, even when it is distinctly recognised, we may not always be able to avoid it at will.[24]

But as the first clause shows, Sidgwick does not distinguish firmly enough between reason to desire and reason to pursue. As we have just noted, the fact that I may have reason to pursue something other than my good does not entail that I have reason to desire something other than my good. Thus we don't need to put the 'conceivable case' aside. This is not the only infelicity: Sidgwick is quite right to say that the notion of 'ought' involved is not the 'strictly ethical [that is, moral] sense'; but having made the point he reconfuses it by suggesting that our good on the whole is a standard divergence from which it is our *duty* to avoid.

After a passage comparing the reason-to-desire view with a 'full-information' version of the ideal-preference view—hedging his bets about the latter's a priori correctness but dismissing it as a strict analysis—Sidgwick offers a reformulation:

I conclude, then, that '*my* ultimate good' must be taken to mean in the sense that it is 'what is ultimately desirable *for me*,' or what I should desire if my desires were in harmony with reason, assuming my own existence alone to be considered,—

[23] I quote the *Methods of Ethics* from its 5th edn. However the whole section from which these passages come (ch. IX, Sect. 3) was thoroughly revised for the 6th edn. Reading the revised version of the section and then rereading the 5th edn. version I am now not sure that the 'reason to desire' view of well-being can be attributed to Sidgwick, even in the 5th edn.

[24] Sidgwick (1893: 111).

and is thus identical with the ultimate end or ends prescribed by reason as to what ought to be sought or aimed at, so far as reason is not thought to inculcate sacrifice of my own ultimate good.[25]

Again a conflation of reason to desire with reason to pursue is strongly suggested, if not positively endorsed. Setting that aside, there is also an ambiguity in Sidgwick's 'what I should desire if my desires were in harmony with reason'.

To say that my desires are in harmony with reason may simply mean that I desire what there is in fact reason for me to desire. In that case saying that what is desirable for me is what I should desire if my desires were in harmony with reason is simply a circuitous way of saying that it is what there is reason for me to desire. It makes no improvement on the simple statement that y is desirable for x, good for x, part of x's well-being, just if x has reason to desire y. On the other hand 'x's desires are in harmony with reason' may mean something rather different: that x's desires are not such as to lay x's reasonableness open to criticism, show some rational failing on x's part. Understood in this way we would have a version of the ideal-preference view, a normative, not a reductive, version but still a version. It would offer the following as an a priori equivalence: what there is reason for me to desire is what I should desire if my rationality could not be faulted and I was equipped with all relevant information.

We need to know the aim of this counterfactual account. What I have reason to desire depends on the facts. That is, the relation I consider when I reflect on what there is reason for me to desire is of the form *the fact that p gives x reason (of degree d at time t) to desire* φ. (Call it the 'reason-to-desire' relation.) Now, in the counterfactual account, is rationality so defined as to include the ability to recognize the truth of statements of that form? Alternatively, does the notion of relevant information invoked by the counterfactual account include information about which statements of that form are true? If the answer to either of these questions is affirmative, then the account can throw no light on what it is for a fact to give a person reason to desire something. So if that is its aim it is redundant. But the answer is unlikely to be affirmative, because the idea which underlies the counterfactual is likely to be this: what one has reason to want is determined by one's actual underived wants (perhaps subject to some rational systematization) and the facts. Now counterfactual facts about how it would be rational to systematize one's wants presumably supervene on facts about one's actual underived wants (and about other things). So if this *is* the aim, then again why should one bother with a counterfactual

[25] Ibid. 112.

account? If one accepts this underlying idea, then what is actually needed is more direct: a theory showing how facts about x's underived wants, together with other relevant facts, determine conclusions about what x has reason to desire.

This is a better route in any case, since there are well-known general problems for such counterfactual explications—problems which arise even when they are proposed not as strict analyses but as a priori equivalences. In the present case, the difficulty may be put thus. What there is reason for x to desire in a particular case may be opaque or hidden from x in a whole variety of ways—even if x is perfectly rational in the sense of incurring no criticism on that score. The counterfactual account attempts to deal with this by idealizing x's information. But now we encounter the following systematic problem: it is logically possible that there is reason for x to desire g only because x is ignorant of some of the facts in virtue of which there is reason for x to desire g. In this logically possible case the set of facts on which 'there is reason for x to desire g' supervenes, $F_1 \ldots F_n$, is such that x does not know every single one of $F_1 \ldots F_n$ to hold. Yet when we add to the set the further fact that x knows every single one of $F_1 \ldots F_n$ to hold, we find that 'there is reason for x to desire g' does not supervene on the new set of facts; that is, relative to this new set of facts it's not the case that there was reason for x to desire g. Now what does the counterfactual account imply in this case? It implies that if x knew every single one of $F_1 \ldots F_n$ to hold and reasoned properly x would desire g. But, *ex hypothesi,* there would in this case be no *reason* for x to desire g. This is already odd. But further, on the counterfactual account, to say that there would in this case be no reason for x to desire g is to say that if x *knew* that he knew every single one of $F_1 \ldots F_n$ to hold and reasoned properly he would *not* desire g. To avoid contradiction, the proponent of the counterfactual account must respond that knowing does not entail knowing that one knows (presumably he would also need to argue that believing does not entail believing that one believes). He can then try to develop a notion of relevant information in which one can fail to have the *relevant* information by having *more* information than that, as well as *less*. But why bother? Why not just go directly to an account of what facts give x reason to desire what objects?

An ideal-preference account of the reason-to-desire relation looks no more promising than an ideal-belief account of the reason-to-believe relation. What is needed is a *direct* theory of the reason-to-desire relation—of when it is that a given being has reason to desire something, of the facts on which reasons for that being to desire supervene. This is a substantive task for ethics, as a theory of the reason-to-believe relation is a task for epistemology. One may well suspect that ideal-preference accounts of well-being will either turn out to presuppose the reason-to-desire relation or fail.

In contrast the reason-to-desire view seems to me to offer not only an a priori equivalence but a strict analysis, or definition, of personal good or well-being.[26] There is, indeed, an obvious difficulty: what about the well-being of animals not able to reason? Can they be said to have reason to desire anything?

We have a notion of flourishing or well-functioning: in terms of that notion we can characterize a notion of good for some kinds of entity—as whatever makes an entity of that kind a flourishing or well-functioning specimen of its kind. Fertilizing is good for the lawn and oiling for the saw. It makes no sense to say that lawns have reason to desire fertilization, or saws oiling. But while this is clearly right it does not seem to me (perhaps contrary to some Aristotelians) that *that* notion of good is the notion of well-being with which we are here concerned: the ethically significant notion with respect to which one can talk of quality. It does not seem unreasonable to say that well-being in this ethically significant sense is a notion that applies only to beings that can be said to have desires.

But can all such beings be said to have *reasons* to desire? One response is to answer in the negative and then suggest that we can nevertheless form the notion of what there is reason to do for their sake, on their behalf, in their interests, as their trustee. But these notions implicitly invoke the good or well-being of the being in question. For example, what there is reason to pursue on x's behalf is just what there is reason to pursue with the good of x in mind.

Moreover this negative answer is too intellectualistic about reasons. Animals can be said to have reasons. The cat may have reason to wait by the hole—it's a mousehole. The fox wants to find the chicken coop and it has good reason to want that. One can say without strain or metaphor that the cat's or fox's well-being consists of what it has non-instrumental reason to desire.

More needs to be said. But suppose we allow that some version of the reason-to-desire account can be defended as a *definition* of individual good.[27] That does not mean that it gives us a substantial *criterion*, or defeasible warrant, for judgements about what human good and its ingredients are. And here is where the notion of an ideal preference has its proper place.

---

[26] Subject to the qualification made in the appendix to this essay.

[27] In general the point of view adopted here is that the good should be defined in terms of reasons: individual good in terms of reasons to desire, general good in terms of reasons to promote or pursue. So an individual's good is part of general good just if whatever there is reason for an individual to desire there is reason for all to promote or pursue.

The primitive criterion of what there is reason to desire is what one does desire—the primitive criterion of what there is reason to feel in general is what one feels. One does not simply have a feeling, one experiences it in the normal case, in the absence of defeating considerations, as a *reasonable* feeling, a *correct* response. But of course the primitive criterion is also a crude criterion, since although what one desires is a warrant for judgements about what one has reason to desire, it is an easily defeasible one. What one would desire after experience and self-examination and discussion with others would provide a less easily defeasible—but still in principle defeasible—warrant. Yet defeasibility does not stop reflection on what one desires, or what competent judges desire, from being an indispensable tool of inquiry in deliberation about one's good.

It is in this sense that Mill's 'what human beings with highly developed faculties can care to have' is a criterion of higher well-being. The relevant faculties are attention, concept-formation, discrimination, imaginative synthesis, recollection, insight . . . And to say that they are more highly developed in a person is to say that that person is better at making qualitative judgements, in particular, qualitative judgements about what constitutes and what contributes to well-being, and how. This is no vicious circle, however; it is a perfectly innocent epistemic interaction between judgements about well-being—about what there is reason to desire—and judgements about who is a good judge of well-being. The interaction is made possible by two general conditions of objectivity for discourse about the rationality of feeling and desire, namely, that feelings themselves should be primitive criteria of what there is reason to feel and that an assertion or judgement incurs a commitment to convergence of judgements. Conditions of these two kinds, involving the spontaneity of a particular kind of normative response, and a convergence commitment, characterize the dialogical epistemology (the epistemology of self-examination and discussion) which is proper to all normative judgements.[28]

To sum up. A being's good is defined in terms of what there is *reason* for that being to desire. More or less refined criteria of its good can be given in terms of what it *does* desire, what it would desire in certain conditions, what beings of that kind do or would desire. Such criteria, however, being defeasible cannot provide a characterization or explication in terms of a priori equivalence of the concept of personal good. Likewise, the criteria governing the concept 'qualitatively higher good of a being of kind K' are given in terms of what beings of kind K, in whom capacities relevant to

---

[28] See Essay II, Sect. 7, and Essay IV, Sect. 4.

judging what there is reason to desire are developed, desire or would desire—more than K-beings in whom these capacities are less developed. The more well-informed and cognitively or affectively equipped for the judgements in hand these K-beings are, the less is their judgement open to defeat.

In chapter II of *Value-Judgement*[29] James Griffin contrasts two models of judgements about what he calls 'prudential value'; a 'taste' and a 'perception' model. 'The perception model gives priority to a judgement of value: desired *because* valuable . . . The taste model reverses the priority: valuable *because* desired.'[30] Griffin thinks that both are false pictures and I agree. I also agree with Griffin that particular objects are desirable because they fall under 'prudential values', or categorial ends (as I would call them) under which we reflectively acknowledge objects as *worth* wanting—ends such as pleasure, say, or knowledge of one's situation, or perhaps accomplishment. One can say a bit more about these two models. The notion of a spontaneous normative response—what one acknowledges as worth wanting, as reasonably desired, when the clutter of delusive self-images and distorting ideals is cleared away—belongs to the epistemology of judgements about well-being, not their semantics. If one believes that concepts are patterns of epistemic norms, then it belongs also to an account of the epistemic norms which constitute the concept of well-being. At this level, the taste model is wrong because it ignores the primitively normative element in desire or in any feeling, its criterial role in judgements about what there is reason to feel, and the defeasibility of these judgements by non-convergence. However the perception model, I am inclined to say, is more wrong, because it imports a quite irrelevant epistemology. That it is reasonable to desire one's happiness, for example, any reasonable person will acknowledge; but this acknowledgement in no way derives from 'perception' or 'non-perceptual intuition' of some special non-natural domain of fact.

4. QUALITY AND IMPARTIALITY

We can return now to our questions about the quality of well-being and its measure.

The criterion of higher goods is that they are what beings of highly developed faculties would, under certain conditions, care to have. Does it follow that they are goods for beings of less developed faculties? That there is reason for beings of less developed faculties to desire them?

[29] Griffin (1996).   [30] Griffin (1996: 20).

Let us say that a good is *accessible* to a person x if x has the personal capacities required to enjoy that good to the full. It is *available* to x if x could obtain it. If a good g is both available and accessible to x, then certainly there is reason for x to desire it: it is a good-for-x. Is there reason for x to desire g if it is accessible but not available? Suppose x is a fine pianist to whom a very high ratio of the potential enjoyment offered by piano-playing is accessible. But suppose that enjoyment is unavailable because he is up a creek without a piano. Is it then reasonable for him to want to play the piano? Apparently it is. His desire to play the piano is not unreasonable. It may, indeed, also be reasonable for him to desire to diminish or eliminate this desire, since it makes him unhappy and it is quite reasonable to desire to avoid unhappiness. Nonetheless, a case like this provides no counter-example to the principle that if a higher good g is accessible to x, then there is reason for x to desire g.

Suppose on the other hand that I am thoroughly unmusical. The enjoyment of piano-playing is not accessible to me at all. Is there intrinsic reason for me to want to play the piano? No. Piano-playing is in this case no part of my good. But what if it is possible for me to overcome my lack of musicality by undergoing some training? It remains the case that there is no intrinsic reason for me to want to play the piano—but there may now be intrinsic reason for me to want to undertake the training whose result will be that I acquire such a reason. For a Butlerian desire for one's own well-being in the abstract, so to speak, is a reasonable desire to have. If this training will make a superior form of enjoyment, that of piano-playing, accessible to me—and if the opportunity to play the piano will be available to me in circumstances that produce a net gain to my well-being—there is instrumental reason for me to want to undertake the training.

This further condition may not be satisfied, though. A good may be accessible to me without being available to me, or without being available to me on beneficial terms. If it is accessible but unavailable, its unavailability may well make me miserable and dissatisfied. Thus it does not follow from the fact that I *can* do something to make it accessible to me that I should want to do so. The absence of any such desire on my part may be quite reasonable. A higher good g may not be a part of my good and it may not even be rational to want it to be. Equally, a good g may be a part of my good as things actually stand, even if a more developed version of me would not be content with g. It may even be unreasonable to want to develop myself in such as way as to make myself dissatisfied with g—if there is no net benefit to me in doing so.

These points having been made, we can finally consider how the distinction between quality and quantity of well-being fits into a certain conception of ethical value—one which equates it with the well-being of all, impartially assessed. One may think of the broad class of views which fit this description—of which classical, aggregative, and hedonistic, utilitarianism is just one—as *generically* utilitarian. They all make the ethical value of a state of affairs a positive and impartial function of the well-being of all individuals in it and of nothing else. By an 'impartial function' I mean one which expresses an impartial distributive principle, and by that in turn I mean a principle which is both agent-neutral and universalizable.[31] Impartiality in this sense is compatible with giving the well-being of some beings greater weight than that of others, so long as that weight supervenes on some agent-neutrally characterizable property of them. In other words it is a more inclusive concept than that expressed in the classical utilitarians' 'Everybody to count for one, nobody for more than one.' And this leads me to the final question I want to consider.

It can be introduced by asking how, in an account of general good, we should measure the ethical value of animals' well-being. Do we or should we give the well-being of animals less weight than the well-being of humans? Or should we think of the criterion of general good as a measure in which everybody, including animals, counts for one: but into which judgements about the *quality* of animal well-being are fed?

How should qualitative judgements about well-being feed into the function from individual to general good? To fix ideas, consider an example. Suppose that beings of highly developed faculties place the pleasures of scientific discovery or artistic creation so far higher than those of material well-being that (above a certain threshold of physical comfort and security) they would not give up a certain amount of the former for any amount of the latter, however large. Suppose, however, that beings of considerably less developed faculties do not share this assessment. We now ask, how much of the enjoyment of the less developed beings may be sacrificed to maintain more highly developed beings' higher enjoyments?

On the account we have given, the verdict of the more highly developed beings is the one on which to rely in assessing the relative value of higher and lower enjoyments. It provides the criterion, though a criterion is always of course defeasible. By hypothesis, these beings would be prepared to sacrifice any amount of the lower enjoyment, down to a threshold of physical comfort and security, for a certain amount of the higher. Does it then follow that general good is increased by sacrificing all the lower enjoyment of less developed beings, down to that threshold, so long as that releases that amount of the higher enjoyments to beings able to access them at their full measure?

[31] See Essay II.

Obviously the answer depends on what distributive principle one builds into the criterion of general good. On a number of such principles, including plausible descendants of classical aggregative or average utilitarianism, ethical value will be measured by a function whose effect is that value is maximized against increasing resources (in our hypothetical case) *first* as sub-threshold levels of well-being are eliminated, *then* as lexically preferable higher-quality enjoyments are made fully available to those who have access to them, and finally, as lexically inferior lower-quality enjoyments are made fully available to those who have access to them. But this will not hold for all positive and impartial functions. It will not hold, for example, for a distributive principle which requires that maximization be constrained by a leximin principle.

Of course this thought-experiment makes a substantial assumption about what lexical preferences highly developed beings may be expected to have. Still, in the related example with which we started many of us prefer not to take the cure—and this is best explained and justified as a discontinuous preference for a superior quality of life, irrespective of the quantity of qualitatively lower enjoyment available in another. Or so I have argued.

What then of our ethical view of animals? Does it illustrate a related lexical discontinuity? It is not easy to say. However, a case for that interpretation can be made. Some fairly common moral assumptions go vaguely like this: insofar as we raise animals and have responsibility for them, we should ensure that they have a pleasant life. But it is not wrong to kill them humanely for a wide range of human purposes, including eating. And we seem to envisage no clear limit to the number of animals that can be slaughtered to avoid the certainty or even the risk of a small number of human deaths. These common assumptions seem to assume that the well-being of animals has ethical value. On the other hand they give animals a very different moral standing to human beings.

The moral rights and wrongs of killing cannot be straightforwardly derived from considerations of ethical value, even in a (sensible) teleological ethics. And further it is at least a grave possibility that common views about the morality of killing animals are wrong. However, those views, as they are, are consistent with something like the following underlying conception. Many animals are capable of enjoying well-being. But the enjoyment which they can experience is not sufficiently transformed by higher capacities to be fused into a single life, that is, a life-for-oneself as against a more or less contented succession of experience, with nothing to bring the experience together into experience for-a-self. This view of animal experience may of course be wrong for some animals—but arguments to that effect seem to be arguments for revising our view about the rights and wrongs of killing them.

There are other possible accounts of these common moral conceptions. Let me consider just one. Jeff McMahan distinguishes between *the value of a life* and the *worth of the individual* whose life it is.[32] The former refers to the measure of well-being in a life; it is 'the extent to which the life is worth living'. The latter 'is determined by the nature of the subject of the life—by the particular properties and capacities that make that individual the kind of thing that he or she is'.[33] McMahan is concerned with the morality, that is the rightness or wrongness, of killing. And, invoking the superior worth of human individuals, he envisages a two-tiered account which distinguishes between a morality of interests which applies to animals and a morality of respect which applies to humans.

I want to ask a rather different question about this distinction between the value of a life and the worth of an individual. How does it affect the measure of ethical value? May it be the case that in assessing general ethical value the well-being of individuals of greater worth should be given greater weight than that of individuals of lesser worth?

That would infringe the principle that every being capable of enjoying well-being is to count for one. But it could still be impartial, so long as differences of worth supervene on properties of the individuals which give rise to agent-neutral reasons for discrimination. What then might these properties—the bases of the worth of an individual—be? McMahan mentions 'capacities for rationality, autonomy, free choice, imagination and creativity, the use of language, deep personal and social relations, empathy, and so on'.[34] So this looks very much like the list of capacities required for enjoyment of qualitatively higher forms of well-being. And the question to ask is why this should give greater weight to the well-being of the individuals who have them, as against giving them access to forms of well-being which already and intrinsically have greater weight in the sense of being qualitatively higher. Would this not be a sort of double counting?

Certainly we admire such capacities. But even if someone deserves greater admiration, does that mean that his or her well-being should be given greater weight in the assessment of general good? It might, on certain forms of mixed perfectionism[35] (depending on the distributive criterion the perfectionist used). But we have rejected perfectionism.

---

[32] McMahan (1995). He says that a similar distinction is drawn in Regan (1983).
[33] McMahan (1995: 10, 11). [34] Ibid. 12.
[35] 'Mixed perfectionism' attaches ethical value to things other than excellence, such as well-being, as well as excellence.

So it seems to me that we can stick to narrow impartiality. The appearance that our moral views give animals lesser weight as beings can be explained away. What we in fact believe is that they have lesser capacity for enjoyment. We believe (perhaps wrongly for some species) that their capacity is so much lower as to make it a mere reaction of contentment or otherwise to the stream of experience. Suppose we go back to our original thought-experiment and ask what attitude to take to a 'cure' which would reduce us to such low level of capacity for enjoyment—even with the enjoyment indefinitely guaranteed. This would be a much more dramatic decline than the possibility originally presented, the possibility of being reduced to the 'mental age of a very small child'. For in that original case one survives the cure in a full sense. One retains a sense of self and of a life extended in time which is one's life. But in this new thought-experiment one cannot be said to retain any such sense. If I have this new cure what survives is still me; I have not ceased to exist. But there is no longer a life which is mine in the sense of being for-me. In this case, and in this latter sense, the response which said 'this is no longer me' does seem appropriate: it is not literally true that I no longer exist but it is true that there is no longer a life-for-me. It does not seem to matter how brief or long this succession of experience is. All that seems to matter is that if it takes place at all, it should be an experience of contentment rather than suffering. But since it does not matter how brief or long it is, it does not matter whether it takes place at all.

APPENDIX

Is My Good what I have Reason to Desire?

1. Suppose you and I go to a piano recital. You admire the performance immensely; at the end of it you leap to your feet and applaud. I, on the other hand, have had a bad day at the office, or (as a music critic) I have been to far too many piano recitals recently . . . for one reason or another, at any rate, I just don't *feel* that admiration. I don't think the performance was bad—I can see that it was just as admirable as you think it was. Still, *seeing* that great admiration is justified is not the same as actually feeling it: a feeling may be lacking, for all sorts of reasons, even when one can see, cognitively grasp, that it would be entirely justified. In this case I am just too jaded to feel the admiration which in other circumstances I might feel, and whose reasonableness I can still appreciate.

2. In Essay III, Section 6 I suggested that the FD principle stated in Essay II (Sect. 8) could also be put in a two-part form:

(FDF) If there's reason to feel φ, there's reason to desire to do that which φ characteristically disposes one to desire to do.
(FDD) If there's reason to desire to α (or to bring it about that p), there's reason to α (to do that which will bring it about that p).

Let us look more closely at these two principles, starting with FDF.

I find your admiration and thus also, by FDF (applause being one of the characteristic dispositions of admiration), your desire to applaud, entirely reasonable. But I neither admire nor desire to applaud. I am just feeling too jaded. Would it then contribute to my well-being to applaud? Quite possibly not, though it probably would not detract from it either. I applaud dutifully, but it would not be true to say that I'm better off for applauding, whereas you, responding spontaneously, get very real expressive pleasure from applauding.

Yet there *is* reason to admire and thus, in particular, reason for *me* to admire; hence also by FDF there is reason to desire—reason for *me* to desire—to applaud. Since it's nevertheless quite possible that applauding would not contribute to my well-being or good it follows that it is not true that *whatever* I have reason to desire would contribute to my good. If FDF is sound, we need to qualify the simple equation of my good with what I have reason to desire.

3. Consider Bishop Butler's distinction between 'particular passions'—desires for particular objects—and 'cool self-love'—desire for my own well-being. When we desire a particular object, o, we desire it under a desired characteristic, D—it might for example be pleasure or avoidance of pain, knowledge of my situation or at one-ness with a person who was close to me. I want that glass of beer because of the pleasure I expect to get from drinking it. I want to know what you think of me, or what my illness is, because in general I want to know how I stand—irrespective of whether it will be pleasant to know. A mother visits her son's grave to commune with his memory, even if that brings painful feelings in its train.

Particular objects are always desired under such desired characteristics—in these cases, pleasure, knowledge, at-one-ness. And the desired characteristics themselves may, but need not be, objects of *general* as against particular desire. Not that a particular object o must always be desired as a *means* to the attainment of the desired characteristic D under which it is desired; it may be desired for its own sake. There is the possible case in which I desire o only as a means to attaining D and because I believe that o will give me D, but there is also the possible and common case in which I desire o for *itself*—*under* the idea of it as yielding D. The point is important, for example in refuting some common arguments for the idea that all motivation is 'really' selfish. It is also important that a person may lack the reflectiveness to desire some such D in itself, even while desiring particular objects under the idea of them as yielding this D. For example I might not have become reflectively aware that I desire o under the idea of 'achieving knowledge of my situation'. Indeed I might not have the *general* desire for such knowledge, as against particular desires for objects under it; I might even resist the suggestion that this is the idea under which some of my particular desires fall. Self-insight is required to identify desired characteristics and there is no reason to think it must be easy.

Still, this seems true: there is no reason to desire *o under the idea of it as yielding D* if there is no reason to desire D.

So when is there reason to desire D? A defeasible criterion for the claim that one has reason to desire D is that one would be happy or satisfied with it if one got it and knew oneself to have it. (Being happy or satisfied *with* D in this sense is not necessarily experiencing happiness *in* having it, finding it to be pleasant—it is, rather, not wanting one's state to be otherwise in respect of D but on the contrary, wanting it to stay that way in that respect.) The criterion is defeasible, since one can be misled through ignorance or deformation of one's desires into being happy with a situation.[1]

Let us say that a D which there is reason for a person to desire is a *categorial end* for that person. It may be that there is more than one categorial end. It may be that the list is not the same for everyone. It may be that different items on the list do not have the same rational weight for different people. These are questions calling for treatment in their own right. Here we can make the most permissive assumption, that there is a plurality of categorial ends which may differ for different people. It will still be objectively true or false that a given D is a categorial end for a particular person—in other words that that person has reason to desire D.

Suppose it's true for a particular person and a particular D*. Then it's also true that there is reason for that person to desire a particular object, *o*, when there is reason for him to believe that *o* will bring D*. We can say that my good comprises my categorial ends, appropriately weighted in relation to each other for me. Alternatively we can say that it comprises that set of Ds which there is (appropriately weighted) reason for me to desire. My actions promote my good to the extent that they contribute to realizing these categorial ends.

4. Since, in the example of Section 1, I won't get expressive enjoyment by applauding and (for the sake of argument) I won't promote any other of my categorial ends by doing so, applauding does not promote my good. Nonetheless, by FDF, it's true that there is reason for me to desire to applaud. What follows from this, then, is that there can be reason for me to desire *o* and yet no reason for me to desire it under a categorial end—some D which I have reason to desire. For while there is indeed reason for me to desire expressive enjoyment, applauding in this case won't give me expressive enjoyment.

5. Now turn to the following case. The performance is actually very boring and I can see that—in the sense that I can see that boredom is an entirely reasonable

---

[1] As discussed in Sect. 3 of the essay, giving a criterion is not the same as giving a characterization. One cannot characterize *having reason to desire D* in terms of a counterfactual about what a person would *in fact* be happy with. It is not even obvious that there is some way of characterizing it normatively, i.e. supplying an a priori true biconditional which has normative concepts on the right-hand side.

reaction for anyone to have. Quite unreasonably, however (as I admit), I find myself enjoyably fascinated by it. Do I have reason to leave or to desire to leave? Yes: in the sense that I can see by FDF that it is reasonable for anyone to want to leave and, by FDD, that it is reasonable to leave. And 'anyone' includes me. Yet surely I should stay, since I am enjoying it. It seems as though I can accept, with good warrant, that it is reasonable to leave and yet rightly allow that acceptance no rational force in deciding me to leave.

I accept that my affective response is somewhat unreasonable in the sense that it's criticizable. My spontaneity would be better tuned, apter, if instead of getting some unaccountable enjoyment from this particular performance I actually found it as boring as it really is. And yet, *given* that I respond to it with criticizable enjoyment rather than justifiable boredom, I have no reason to leave.

So FDD is wrong or at least ambiguous. One could bring out the ambiguity by distinguishing 'there is reason for *x* to *y*' and '*x* has reason to *y*'. If you suggest that we leave, I might say, perhaps a bit shamefacedly: 'I can see that this is very boring. I guess there's good reason to leave. Yet somehow I'm getting a perverse kind of enjoyment from it, so I think I'll stay.' Here I concede that there is reason to leave, yet one might say that *I* don't *have* that reason—it doesn't 'apply' to me, because I'm getting an admittedly unreasonable thrill from the performance.

What seems to matter is what you are actually going to enjoy—what will be worth while for you, in that it will promote one of your categorial ends, such as pleasure. So perhaps one should amend FDD to

(FDD') If there is reason to desire to *x* (or to bring it about that *p*) *under one or another of one's categorial ends*, there is reason to *x* (to do that which will bring it about that *p*).

Given our definition of personal good, that would turn FDD into the rational egoist's formula for practical reasons. To endorse it is not to endorse rational egoism, since the formula supplies only a sufficient, not a necessary and sufficient, condition on having a practical reason—one could also accept other principles of practical reason, which might override it. However FDD' itself requires further discussion before it is accepted, and I will not pursue the discussion further here.

PART III

Morality

VII

The Definition of Morality

1. We use such terms as *good, bad, right, wrong, should, ought,* in many ways other than moral: good evidence and bad argument, right answers and wrong notes, novels which should be read, and policies which ought not to be adopted. The moral is a sphere of the practical and the practical itself only a sphere of the normative. Norms guide us in all we believe, feel, and do. Do these normative words then have a specifically *moral* sense? If so can it be defined?

I think they do have a moral sense. That calls for some supporting argument, but I shall not go into it here.[1] I want rather to consider an attempt to define that sense. It is not a definition which illicitly reduces the normative to the non-normative. It purports rather to define *moral* senses of goodness, rightness, wrongness, and obligation in non-moral but still normative terms. 'Definition', however, will turn out not to be quite the right word. We shall see, I think, that 'moral' is strictly speaking indefinable, and why it is undefinable. Nevertheless, I shall defend the spirit of the definition; even though 'moral' cannot be defined I shall argue that we can still *construct* its sense (as one might say) using only non-moral normative concepts.

These issues of definition and construction are not my sole topic. I shall also broach (but no more than broach) deeper philosophical questions which lie behind them and give them their interest: questions about how morality is to be situated within the larger sphere of the practical, how it is related to such categories, putatively distinct from it, as the ethical, or the rational; what basis moral judgement has in reason and feeling. I shall also discuss some particular questions about the nature of moral

First published in A. Phillips Griffiths (ed.), *Ethics: Philosophy Supplement 35,* Cambridge: Cambridge University Press: 121–44. I am grateful to Berys Gaut, James Griffin, A. Phillips Griffiths, Matthew Kieran, Dudley Knowles, and Christopher Martin for comments on this paper.

[1] An alternative view is that they are univocal but always implicitly relativized (at the semantic level) to some contextually understood practice, project or objective. What follows assumes that that is not so.

punishment and blame. But it is with the issues of definition and construction that I begin.

2. The definition I have in mind is to be found in Mill.[2] The relevant remarks are to be found in his discussion of the concept of justice in chapter 5 of *Utilitarianism*. Having observed that the idea of something which one may be constrained or compelled to do, on pain of penalty, is central to the idea of an obligation of *justice*, he remarks that this idea nevertheless 'contains, as yet, nothing to distinguish that obligation from moral obligation in general':

> For the truth is, that the idea of penal sanction, which is the essence of law, enters not only into the conception of injustice, but into that of any kind of wrong. We do not call anything wrong, unless we mean to imply that a person ought to be punished in some way or other for doing it; if not by law, by the opinion of his fellow creatures; if not by opinion, by the reproaches of his own conscience. This seems the real turning point of the distinction between morality and simple expediency. It is a part of the notion of Duty in every one of its forms, that a person may rightfully be compelled to fulfil it. Duty is a thing which may be *exacted* from a person, as one exacts a debt. Unless we think that it might be exacted from him, we do not call it his duty . . . There are other things, on the contrary, which we wish that people should do, which we like or admire them for doing, but yet admit that they are not bound to do; it is not a case of moral obligation; we do not blame them, that is, we do not think that they are proper objects of punishment . . . I think there is no doubt that this distinction lies at the bottom of the notions of right and wrong; that we call any conduct wrong, or employ, instead, some other term of dislike or disparagement, according as we think that the person ought, or ought not, to be punished for it; and we say that it would be right to do so and so, or merely that it would be desirable or laudable, according as we would wish the person whom it concerns, compelled, or only persuaded and exhorted, to act in that manner.[3]

These brief remarks of Mill will lead us into a good deal of analysis and discussion. But before taking up more subtle issues, including subtle issues about circularity, let me remove the impression of blatant circularity which may seem to lurk—to be almost explicit—in Mill's words.

If I define 'X *ought* to do Y' as 'X ought to be punished in some way for non-performance of Y', I use the word I am defining in my *definiens*. Mill does not quite put it this way, since what he defines is 'duty', 'right', and

---

[2] It has recently been refurbished by Alan Gibbard (Gibbard 1990: ch. 1, 40–5, ch. 7). For a comprehensive discussion of Mill's view see Lyons (1976).

[3] Mill (1963–91), x. 246 (*Utilitarianism*, ch. 5, para. 14).

'wrong'.[4] But he clearly takes it that 'X is (morally) right' = 'X (morally) ought to be done', and 'X is (morally) wrong' = 'X (morally) ought not to be done.'

The apparent circularity is avoided if the 'ought' in the *definiendum* is a moral one, while the 'ought' in the *definiens* is not. It's pretty plausible that this is Mill's position. Thus in the *System of Logic*[5] he says that general utility is the first principle of Teleology, or Practical Reason—the normative doctrine which, in combination with 'laws of nature', produces the Art of Life. Morality is one 'department' of this Art, the others are Prudence and Aesthetics (the 'Right, the Expedient, and the Beautiful or Noble'). So general utility stands outside Morality, as the final source of practical-rational oughts. (The position is still consistent with there sometimes being a *moral* obligation to act directly on grounds of general utility. General utility can play a bit-part within, as well as being the ultimate animator without.)

3. The distinction between the moral ought and a more fundamental practical ought is plainly indispensable to anyone who seeks to define morality in the manner of Mill. Further issues about this practical ought, however, can remain open. Obviously it is not essential to agree with Mill that its determining principle is general utility. A contractualist, for example, who based his practical ought on self-interest, limited sympathy and self-interest, instrumental rationality, or whatever, could still adopt the Millian definition as an account of what makes an ideally agreed rule a *moral* rule. Since there can be ideally agreed rules which are not moral rules (e.g. to purely cooperative coordination problems), a contractualist criterion of the moral is required, stronger than that of simple ideal agreement.

Again, the definition can be adopted whatever view one takes on the epistemological status of the practical ought. One may hold that it is grounded in a structure of objective norms, or like Gibbard,[6] one may believe that it expresses the attitude of the person who issues the ought, and is not constrained to reflect any such structure. One may identify it with the ought of practical rationality as such, or one may take some other view, involving, for example, a broad notion of the ethical and a narrow notion of the moral.

---

[4] Note that in defining these as he does he differs from those contemporary consequentialists who follow Moore rather than Mill, defining 'morally right action' and 'moral duty' directly in terms of optimal consequence—with predictably disconcerting results (Moore 1903: Sect. 89).

[5] Mill (1963–91), viii (*System of Logic* VI. xii. 6&7).   [6] Gibbard (1990).

The last distinction is made by Bernard Williams.[7] He treats the moral as a particular form—a somewhat pathological one—of the broader category of the ethical. We shall consider later whether the institution of morality is as peculiar as he makes it (Section 9). But for the moment note only that, while Williams offers no *definition* of morality, his view is like Mill's at least in this, that he thinks morality's central concept is moral obligation—and its fundamental assumption is that penalty, specifically, the penalty of guilt and blame, is appropriate for non-compliance with moral obligation.

Where Williams usefully reserves the word 'moral' for the narrower notion, and the word 'ethical' for a broader one, Mill uses 'moral' itself, and its cognates, in broader and narrower ways. The definition he provides is of *narrow* morality, as one may call it, corresponding to Williams's 'moral', as against his 'ethical'. But when Mill speaks, as he often does, of the processes of moralization his concern is ethical—for example, in this remark: 'the moralization of the personal enjoyments we deem to consist, not in reducing them to the smallest possible amount, but in cultivating the habitual wish to share them with others'.[8]

Our conceptions of moral education and moral life go well beyond narrow morality. Much beyond the simple carrying out of duties attracts an admiration which is still *broadly* moral. In this broader sense, moral education, as Mill pre-eminently understood, is an education of the affections as well as of conscience and will, transcending 'the notion of Duty'. Narrow morality itself—the system of practices to which adherence should be exacted on penalty of blame—is conditioned by the state of ethical development of a society:

the domain of moral duty, in an improving society, is always widening. When what once was uncommon virtue becomes common virtue, it comes to be numbered among obligations, while a degree exceeding what has grown common, remains simply meritorious.[9]

So while the test of utility is not in Mill's view in any way itself relative, the historicity of social forms and human dispositions, on which he placed great stress, means that narrow morality inevitably is so.

He thinks that in an improving society its domain widens. One might think in contrast that it narrows, for example because the general good no longer requires the sanctioning of various classes of action with moral penalties. On a sufficiently utopian view of present or future human

---

[7] Williams (1985: ch. 10).
[8] Mill (1963–91), x. 339 (*Auguste Comte and Positivism*).
[9] Ibid. 338.

nature, its domain could shrink to zero. Another attitude to morality, distinct from this, though it can be combined with it, is that of the subversive thinker (by now a somewhat jaded character) who views morality as a device of repression and self-delusion to be thrown off by the strong spirit. The utopian and the subversive can agree on the *definition* of morality while asserting its present or eventual nullity.

One might even, consistently with the Millian definition, hold morality to be null on conceptual grounds. Thus, while holding that the moral is defined in terms of guilt and blame, one may also hold that guilt and blame presuppose pure voluntariness, or 'autonomy', and that these are incoherent concepts.

These various views of morality have this much in common: they all take what I shall call below an 'external' view of it. (That is not quite true of the last—one could hold morality to be incoherent without viewing it from any other normative standpoint, or holding any other such standpoint to be coherent.) I shall defend externalism in this particular sense, and the spirit at least of Mill's definition, even though I shall reject it as a strict definition. As to the philosophical context which I shall sketch out for the definition, that will be Millian in three further respects—in envisaging a domain of ethical, or ethical-aesthetic, ideals which are relatively independent of (narrow) morality; in agreeing that the fundamental ought is that of practical reason as such; and in holding further that the standard of practical reason is impartially conceived general good. (But this is not to accept the utilitarian's notion of *aggregate* or *average* utility as the right account of that good—those classical utilitarian notions of distribution are determinate and disputable versions of the more general, determinable, concept of distributive impartiality.) I shall not defend these Millian features; they will be provided simply as a backcloth which I find persuasive and against which the concept of the moral, together with its distinctive concepts (blame, penalty, moral freedom) can be viewed in their true proportions and proper role.

4. In the passages I quoted, Mill's most usable words are that

We do not call anything wrong, unless we mean to imply that a person ought to be punished in some way or other for doing it; if not by law, by the opinion of his fellow-creatures; if not by opinion, by the reproaches of his own conscience.

Let us drop the reference to law, and concentrate on the reproaches of conscience and the opinion of our fellow-creatures. We lose nothing by doing so, and we leave space for the possibility that something not morally wrong should nevertheless be punished by law. The key notion then is that of punishment by guilt and blame. Allowing further that guilt—the reproaches of one's own conscience—is identical with self-blame, the single notion involved is that of blame. This identification will do for the moment; but it would be more accurate to identify guilt with what I call below the 'blame-feeling', directed at oneself. (We *feel* guilt.) Blame in general will shortly be considered in more detail. But for the moment we have two central thoughts. The first is the definition of the morally wrong as the blameworthy. The second is that blame, whether by self or others, is itself penal. They need not go together, but they do in Mill, and I shall be discussing both; but we begin with the first.

Consider then the following definition:

> (M) *x* is morally wrong if and only if the agent ought to be blamed (by himself and others) for doing *x*.

This will also furnish a definition of '*x* is morally obligatory', given that the latter means 'not doing *x* is morally wrong'.

But it may be a bit too simple. As Alan Gibbard notes,[10] we seem to allow that an action may not be blameworthy even though it is morally wrong—his example is speaking rudely to a friend out of a paroxysm of grief. So he proposes the following definitions:

An act is *wrong* if and only if it violates standards for ruling out actions, such that if an agent in a normal frame of mind violated those standards because he was not substantially motivated to conform to them, he would be to blame. To say that he would *be to blame* is to say that it would be rational for him to feel guilty and for others to resent him.[11]

Would we, in Gibbard's example, say that the speaker acted morally wrongly? Another response, which maintains the straight equivalence of wrong and blameworthy actions, is that though speaking rudely is indeed usually wrong, the speaker in the particular case envisaged by Gibbard cannot be said to have acted wrongly. On the other hand, if we do want to say that the speaker in Gibbard's case acted wrongly yet should not be blamed, that is surely because we think he was not in a 'normal frame of

---

[10] Gibbard (1990: 44).

[11] Ibid. 45. Note that Gibbard defines being 'to blame' in terms of what it would be rational for people to feel about the agent, not in terms of what it would be rational to feel or do, whereas Mill's definition seems to turn on whether it is rational to do a type of action: to blame in the sense of reaching, and presumably (given the punitive function) expressing, a verdict about what it is rational to feel about the agent. In this respect I think Gibbard's definition is better. So in M, to say that the agent ought to be blamed should be understood as saying that it would be rational for people to have those feelings towards the agent which are deployed in blame. See Sects. 7 and 9.

mind'—specifically, he couldn't help himself. The point could be taken into account by amending M to:

> x is morally wrong if and only if, to the extent the agent could have avoided doing x, he ought to be blamed (by himself and others) for doing x.

It is not clear that any reference to 'standards' is required—after all, is it really the case that, in every case of morally wrong action, there must be some standard (non-trivially understood) which is being violated?

However I shall not pursue these issues. The simple M is enough to raise the question—whether we have here something that at least in principle could be refined into a definition of the moral.

M, it may be said, is (subject to such correction) an a priori truth; but that leaves open the question of why it is. That it is so by definition of 'morally wrong' is only one possibility. Another is that it is so by definition of 'blame'. Blame, it may further be said—the characteristic moral penalty we are considering—has a definitive object. It is directed to that which is (believed to be) morally wrong. There is indeed also a wider sense. One can *blame* the dud calculator-batteries for a mistake in the bill, blame the weather for the train delay, etc. But in that wider sense M is simply false. Perhaps one ought to blame the weather, rather than British Rail, for the train delay. But the weather didn't act morally wrongly, though it did delay the train. And if British Rail was in *that* sense to blame, it still wouldn't follow that British Rail acted morally wrongly—though it might be appropriate to seek compensation. One can say such things as that Mary was to blame for the misunderstanding, but that one can't really *blame* her—she was understandably distracted by something else that was happening. Narrow blameworthiness turns on whether the agent could have helped doing what he did—a point we shall come back to.

Narrow blame is the concept invoked in M. But once that is clear, is it not also clear that the primitive term is 'morally wrong'? The agent of course ought to blame himself if his action is morally wrong. So M is true by definition—but by definition of (narrow) 'blame'. The moral itself is indefinable. At least it is not definable in *this* way.

5. There is a particular perspective from which this response has special force. It is reached only when morality is clearly disentangled from nature and divine command. But it goes beyond that crucial separation in asserting the *irreducible* reality of moral law, and the *indefinability* of moral concepts in non-moral terms. There can be, it adds, no external critical standpoint on morality. *Morality* is the governing normative standpoint. I

will call this internalism. It is internalist also in the sense that it does not allow as meaningful the question why I ought to do what I morally ought to do. In contrast, on the definition of morality under consideration that question can in principle arise. Internalism stands in contrast to a secular-naturalistic perspective which is shared by philosophers as opposed in other respects as Mill and Nietzsche. This naturalism also makes the crucial separation, so it does not commit Moore's naturalistic fallacy. But it views morality externally. It sees it as an institution criticizable from some ethical or rational standpoint outside it. (So it is not 'value-free'—it is a position *within* the philosophy of value.) And it looks for a genealogy of the moral and of moral phenomena such as conscience and blame. This is the perspective to which the Millian definition belongs.[12]

The internalist holds that the concept of the moral is indefinable in non-moral terms. I will now argue that he is right, but that internalism does not follow from the indefinability of moral concepts. The external normative perspective on morality can be maintained, even if 'moral' cannot be defined.

6. The charge against the Millian definition, M, is that it involves a subtle circularity. Blame is a response whose justifying base requires that the object be something that has been done or omitted but morally ought not to have been done or omitted. It requires it in the way that fear requires that the object be dangerous. One can feel guilt about something one does not really believe to be morally wrong, just as one can fear something which one does not really believe dangerous—but in these cases the response is pathological.

The externalist may reply that there is a disanalogy between blame and fear. The dangerous (as against the *fearsome*) can be characterized independently as that which is liable to harm or damage. But in the case of blame no *independent* characterization of its justifying base—'moral wrongness'—can be given. To say that the object must be morally wrong for blame to be justified is not to give an independent characterization of the object, any more than to say that the object must be fearsome for fear to be justified, or boring for boredom to be justified, is to give an independent characterization. Saying that something is boring—boredom-worthy—is saying that the proper or just response to it is boredom.

---

[12] A view not considered here is that the moral ought is a perspective irreducible to other oughts, but that neither it nor any other ought is the *governing* normative standpoint. That would make the moral ought incommensurable with non-moral oughts in a way that neither the internalist nor the externalist allows.

Likewise, saying that something is morally wrong—blameworthy—is saying that the proper or just response to it is blame.

But can the logic of 'morally wrong' be aligned in this way with the logic of 'boring'? To examine this more closely we will compare the concepts 'boring' and 'red', and then see how 'morally wrong' fits in.

At the semantic level 'visual perceptual experience (as) of red' is roughly definable as 'visual perceptual experience of the kind which a suitably sized red thing, optimally displayed to a relevantly normal observer, would cause that observer to have as part of his visual perception of that thing'. (Various refinements could be added.) This is analytic on the meaning of 'experience of red'. Thus 'red' is semantically primitive, and 'experience of red' is defined in its terms.

At the constitutive level, in contrast—the level of cognitive role, as against semantic content[13]—we have a norm partially constitutive of the concept red. That norm is something like this:

> When it visually appears to me that there is there an item which is red (a feature of the total visual experience is that an item looks red), then, in the absence of counter-evidence, I am justified in asserting that there's something red there.

So here the experience as of something red (a feature of the total visual experience) primitively provides a defeasible warrant for a verdict about the world—that it contains something red.

Compare 'boring'. At the semantic level, 'x is boring' is definable as 'x has properties to which the proper or just reaction is a feeling of boredom whose object is x.'[14] Thus unlike 'x is red', which is semantically primitive, 'x is boring' is definable. It is defined in terms of '(feeling of) boredom'. So it's certainly analytic that a feeling of boredom is a feeling of the kind which boring things, optimally displayed to a good judge, would cause that judge to have. But that is in virtue of the definability of 'boring', not in virtue of the definability of 'boredom'. The latter is the primitive expression.

Whereas at the semantic level there is this asymmetry, at the constitutive level there is at least some symmetry. There must also be asymmetry, if the semantics of expressions is fully fixed by the concepts, that is, cognitive roles, they express; it will lie in the *location* of the two concepts in the more general fabric of concepts—in particular in the fact discussed below, that

---

[13] The distinction between cognitive role and semantic content underpins the distinction I make between a 'construction' and a 'definition' of the concept of the moral. I discuss it in Skorupski (1997*a*).

[14] So 'boring' is ambiguous—as in 'That is a boring instrument.'

judgements about what is red are accountable not only to phenomenology but to a wider theoretical context. But the symmetry is that the norm which partially constitutes the concept of the boring is something like

> A feeling of boredom with x, in the absence of countervailing considerations, justifies the verdict that x is boring.

A further point will be of importance to us: in both cases the verdict incurs the *convergence commitment*. In issuing the verdict I commit myself to holding that qualified judges would either converge on the same verdict or would be suffering from some discernible error or failure of relevant information which would explain their disagreement. Now this commitment is a general feature of the act of assertion.[15] It is incurred by the act, not its content. With any assertion, if we acquire reason to think that this kind of convergence cannot be expected to occur, i.e. that fault-free divergence can perennially persist, we acquire reason for withdrawing the assertion. But, despite the existence of this general convergence commitment, the response itself—the experience of red or the feeling of boredom—defeasibly justifies the appropriate judgement.

Now we come back to the difficulty for the Millian definition. It is this: semantically, 'morally wrong' does not behave like 'boring'—instead, it behaves more like 'red'. If there is a connection between blame and moral wrongness at the semantic level, it is that 'blaming' (in the narrow sense) in part means 'considering to be morally in the wrong'. So '(morally) wrong', like 'red' and unlike 'boring', is the semantically primitive term.

We must conclude that Mill's account fails as a literal definition, at the semantic level. But it can still survive as what I call a construction of the concept of the moral. To see this and to see why blame is a penalty, we must consider the emotional core of blame.

7. Like welcoming someone or apologizing to them, the act of blaming has an emotional core. The welcome-emotion is feeling happy or good that you have come, the apology-emotion is feeling sorry for something I've done to you. I can often sincerely welcome or apologize without *feeling* the emotion, but the act always *invokes* the emotion—accepts its appropriateness. And sometimes it isn't enough to do the performance without having the feeling. You may not feel genuinely welcome, and you may feel that I am not as sorry as I should be. Blame similarly has an emotional core. I shall simply call it the *blame-feeling*, without broaching the many interesting questions about its relationship to other emotions. (A

---

[15] See Essays I, II, and IV.

little more about it will be said in Sections 8 and 9.) As with apology or welcome, the act of blaming can be effectively performed without the emotion being felt—but not always. A child, for example, may not *feel* blamed if the blaming is too evidently formal.

Though blame can be a public act it doesn't have to be—unlike apologizing or welcoming. Whereas having the sorry or the good-to-see-you feeling is not itself apologizing or welcoming, having the blame-feeling—when one has the appropriate moral concepts, and is not seeking to check the blame-feeling as inappropriate—*is* blaming. (These qualifications are required because, on the account I will give, the blame-feeling is a more primitive phenomenon than fully developed moral blame.)

With blame, as with apology and welcome, the core feeling has a justifying base—a set of beliefs without which it doesn't make sense for you to have the feeling. The question is whether the concept 'morally wrong' features intrinsically in that justifying set of beliefs. Compare feeling sorry. Here the thought that I have injured or offended you in some way features intrinsically in the justifying base. But it needn't have been a morally reprehensible way, and it needn't have been a voluntary or even an avoidable way.

With the blame-feeling, similarly, the thought that what was done was *morally* wrong need not enter the justifying base, though some more basic notion of wrongdoing must. Nor need the wrongdoing involve wronging someone, as apology requires injuring or offending someone. However a more important contrast with feeling sorry, for our purposes, is that the act which arouses the blame-feeling must be thought of as one which the agent could have *avoided* doing. It is not quite the voluntary that is here in question. For one can blame a person for things he did not do voluntarily—spilling the coffee, running someone over. These are still things that he could have avoided doing, with proper care. So I shall use the term 'avoidable' to cover all such doings, including those which are not in the full, intentional, sense, acts (and including omissions). A doing was avoidable when the agent could have done otherwise. Thus one constraint on the intelligibility of the blame-feeling is that its object must be a doing which is taken to be avoidable. We shall consider later what sort of constraint it is.

Another constraint on the intelligibility of the blame-feeling, of course, is that the doing must be thought to be wrong. But 'wrong' here is still pre-moral. At this pre-moral level wrongdoing is simply a doing which properly arouses the blame-feeling—a 'blame-feeling-worthy' doing—in the way that the boring is simply the boredom-worthy. 'Blame-feeling-worthy' is here a more basic concept than our actual, moralized, notion of the blameworthy.

A third constraint is that one must believe that the agent knew or could have known what he was doing. This condition will be relevant only in one of its aspects—that he knew or could have known the action to be wrong (see Sections 8 and 9).

What makes a space for the distinction between having an emotional response and judging it justified? It comes from the discipline set up by criteria grounded in experience of that response, reflection on it and inter-subjective comparison. Those criteria are in play when we judge that what bored or amused us, or what aroused in us the blame-feeling, is not after all boring, amusing, or blame-feeling-worthy. Let us call them 'hermeneutic' criteria, and the discipline they impose hermeneutic discipline, since their ground is what can intelligibly, understandably, produce a given emotional response. Not only emotional responses are disciplined hermeneutically—aesthetic responses and impressions of validity would be other examples. But it is with emotional responses that we are concerned here. The understanding in question is an understanding from within—a matter of *verstehen*. ('I can't understand why you find that funny.' 'I used to find that funny, but I really can't see what's funny about it any more.') So judgements which are disciplined hermeneutically, and in no other way, are finally accountable only to spontaneous feeling—but the spontaneity in question is that which emerges from experience, reflection, and inter-subjective comparison and agreement. The criteria formed in that process are enough to allow a distinction between what seems to me a just response and what is a just response, and thus to underwrite the judgements as *judgements*. But they are internal criteria—they do not shape the judgements by any controls other than those which flow from appeal to the ideal of an undistorted, 'adequate', or 'well-tuned' convergence on a spontaneous emotional response. Let us call such hermeneutically disciplined normative judgements 'purely response-determined', and the concepts which they predicate 'purely response-determined' normative concepts. On the analysis, so far, 'That was a wrongdoing' would be a purely response-determined judgement.

However the judgement 'this is (morally) wrong' is not a purely response-determined normative judgement. And as we have seen, in a certain semantic respect 'morally wrong' behaves like 'red' rather than like 'boring' or 'amusing'. Similarly, insofar as 'blameworthy' in its actual use is definable in terms of the morally wrong, it cannot be detached from the normal syntax that goes with that and aligned, as I aligned 'blame-feeling-worthy' in the last but one paragraph, with 'boring' and 'amusing'. The concept that stands to the blame-feeling as the concept of the boring stands to boredom is a simpler concept than the concept of blameworthiness we actually have. The externalist needs to explain this point. Whether the externalist view is reductive will depend on the explanation it gives. It will be reductive if it explains the asymmetry between 'boring' and 'morally wrong' in a way that does not at the same time justify it.

An analogy would be this. Someone who reflects on the intentional content of amusement may conclude that it is always some kind of incongruity that causes amusement. He may think of this as a substantive theory— incongruity being some independent relation in the objects. But we find, when we examine, that incongruity is not characterizable in a way that is at all independent of what we spontaneously find amusing. Incongruity is simply a purely response-determined concept in disguise. An explanation of 'morally wrong' which treated it in the same way, as a purely response-determined concept in disguise, would be reductive.

So we need to show why 'morally wrong' is not a purely response-determined concept, and that may in turn give us the material for a non-reductive construction of the morally wrong. The material is indeed available—it lies in the fact that verdicts about what is morally wrong, unlike verdicts about what is boring, are accountable to criteria which are independent of, and *externally* regulate, the blame-feeling. Boredom, amusement, irritation, etc. generate criteria internal to the response, which regulate verdicts about its propriety, set up the ideal of what well-tuned judges would feel, and in turn make space for judgements about whether a person is, say, irritable, or lacking in discrimination or sensibility (and thus in a particular context disqualified as a judge). But moral judgements are not disciplined *solely* in this hermeneutic way. They are, in this respect, comparable to verdicts about redness.[16] These latter judgements are indeed accountable initially to perceptual experience. But they are accountable also to criteria of theoretical reason. Those latter, external, criteria are mediated through a context of physical theory, a body of beliefs which can retrospectively override a judgement that something is red, even when that judgement is default-justified by perceptual experience. If, for example, we find that atmospheric conditions, or the relative speed of a body to the perceiver, can affect its apparent colour, then we may withdraw colour judgements which perceptual experience would otherwise have justified by default. At the limit, indeed, we could discover that nothing is red, even though we have sensations of red. That doesn't seem possible with 'boring' (i.e. that we have the very same feelings of boredom but 'discover' that nothing is really boring). But it does seem possible with 'morally wrong', precisely because 'morally wrong' is not a purely

---

[16] Kant classes moral judgements (in contrast to judgements concerning the beautiful) as 'logical' rather than 'aesthetic' for related reasons. See Kant (1987: Sects. 6 and 7).

response-determined concept. The institution of morality might be
shown, by criteria external to the hermeneutics of the blame-feeling as
such, to be redundant. Blame-feelings might never justify judgements of
blameworthiness, that is, moral wrongness. And the construction of the
concept of the moral must illuminate the ways in which that is *possible*—
though I shall argue in Section 10 that no such undercutting takes place.

8. But let us first go back to the blame-feeling, which is primitive to the
construction of the notion of the morally wrong. It has a justifying base,
which places hermeneutic constraints on its possible objects. These constraints, as with other feelings, are hermeneutic in that they limit what we
find intelligible. One cannot intelligibly, for example, be bored or amused
by a car tyre. There must be something about it which makes it boring or
amusing—and it is that total context (appearing at the fancy-dress ball
wearing a car tyre as a hat) which is boring or amusing. A car tyre in itself
cannot be the total object of boredom or amusement.

It is at this level, I believe, that we find the connection between blame
and avoidability. It rests on a hermeneutic constraint, which limits the
objects of the blame-feeling to (what are taken to be) avoidable doings.
That constraint underlies the central principle of narrow morality: the
blameworthy agent could and *ought to* have done better. The ought here is
the moral ought; so the principle's aprioricity is in part owed to the definition (or rather, construction) of the moral ought. But only in part,
because the principle also requires that the agent *could* have done better.
It may be suggested that the aprioricity of this stems from 'ought implies
can'. But this only pushes the question back to why *that* principle is a
priori. On the view I am suggesting its foundation is the hermeneutic constraint on the blame-feeling—the object of the blame-feeling must be an
agent who could have done better. Not every such agent is blamed, but
nothing can be blamed which is not such an agent. To blame anything else
is unintelligible, in the way that being bored by a car tyre is.

This unintelligibility is not to be further explained at the level of *reasons*.[17] One might try to explain, in biological or psychological terms, why
human beings have the blame-feeling, and one may also try to resolve the
feeling into other feelings. But insofar as such explanations go beyond the
hermeneutic domain, the domain of the directly or intrinsically intelligible, they address non-philosophical questions (perfectly good ones of
course). In contrast, one can simply seek greater understanding of the
blame-feeling at the hermeneutic level, by placing it in a wider group of

---

[17] The connection between blame and avoidability here proposed thus differs from views
which derive it from the *pointlessness* of blaming the unavoidable.

hostile or disparaging emotions, such as anger, disdain, contempt, suspicion, scorn, horror, frigidity. In all of these cases the object is something whose doing is thought to fall short, or expected to fall short, of what good doing of that kind would be. It *should* have been better, though this 'should' does not imply 'could'. (I can feel angry with a bent nail—it shouldn't have bent, it was faulty.) Anger, disdain, and the rest can certainly be aroused, quite intelligibly, by doings which the agent could not have bettered. Blame cannot. We may or may not feel there are moral grounds for inhibiting such feelings, when the agent couldn't have helped it, and may be hurt by them. But still these are not *hermeneutic* constraints, on the intelligibility of the feelings. In contrast, if someone expresses the blame-feeling towards a doing which he also claims not to think the agent could have bettered, our understanding is strained.

9. It is by reference to the blame-feeling that we should understand the penal nature of blame. Emotions are aroused by characteristic objects— but they also give rise to characteristic dispositions. To what then does the blame-feeling dispose? To exclusion of those towards whom it is felt from the moral community, to a withdrawal of recognition, however partial and temporary. That community is the community of agents who live by, observe, intelligible norms. Hence the ethical significance of the effort to understand other persons and cultures from within. And here lies the connection with avoidability: what prompts exclusion is the failure to avoid something which should have been recognized as proper to avoid, if one was freely responding to relevant norms. The wrongdoer is discredited, dishonoured as a 'self-legislating' member of the kingdom of ends.

The blame-feeling does not dispose, like anger, towards attack, like fear, towards flight, like frigidity, towards withdrawal of love, or like feeling sorry, towards reparation. It disposes towards ostracism, the cutting off of solidarity, the reduction of respect. There is an overlap here with disdain. But the blame-feeling *presupposes*, and then imperils, the wrongdoer's standing as a free self-legislator. while disdain does not suppose it in the first place. At the limit, the withdrawal of recognition becomes the attitude taken to a being which must be, not reasoned with as autonomous, but trained, or deterred, by external penalty and reward. At this limit the blame-feeling ceases, since its object must be thought of as a member, however errant, of the moral community. Without moral membership ostracism, withdrawal of membership, makes no sense. Blame is a penalty in itself, an internal penalty, inasmuch as it gives rise to this sense of threatened recognition, of casting out into the liminal region between the village and the bush, between the social order and the outer, hermeneutically unintelligible, world. Guilt is self-exclusion, one's own withdrawal of recognition from oneself.

As an act, blame puts this disposition to exclude overtly, even formally, on the record (though perhaps only between blamer and blamed), in the same way that overt greeting, welcome, or apology puts on record the corresponding disposition to make at home, or to make amends. Interestingly, the same sort of putting on record is not possible with anger or scorn. One can of course make one's anger or scorn explicit, but there is no socially recognized vehicle, instituted in forms of language, for being (performatively, so to speak) angry with someone or scorning them. And if one bypasses blame by saying 'I'm rather angry with you', one is in fact soft-pedalling, ducking past the judicial-penal element in blame, staying on equal terms with the other, being 'non-judgmental'. On the other hand, the old-fashioned habit of snubbing people one didn't approve of (cf. James on 'cutting dead')[18] was a close cousin of the practice of blame: it implied withdrawal of respect. Its withering is an aspect of our increasing focus on the morality of action and blame as against the ethics of character and approval—a natural development of the decline of status distinction. (The interaction of character and ethical approval with breeding and social status, as in the very meaning of words like 'gentle', 'noble', is insufficiently explored by 'virtue theorists', though they were clear enough to Aristotle. This abstraction from social realities can give their discussions a somewhat innocent air.)

The judicial-penal element, internal to blame as such, consists, then, in loss of recognition. External punishment, in family, school, or law, at least sometimes functions to restore recognition (not least by oneself). This aspect of the matter is picked up by those who say that external punishment is the wrongdoer's right; though recognizing it does not force us to deny the obvious deterrent function of external punishment.[19] And the inherently penal character of blame provides the key to understanding how blameworthiness comes to be detached from the blame-feeling; how it transcends the primitive, purely response-determined concept of blame-

---

[18] James writes:

No more fiendish punishment could be devised, were such a thing physically possible, than that one should be turned loose in society and remain absolutely unnoticed by all the members thereof. If no one turned round when we entered, answered when we spoke, or minded what we did, but if every person we met 'cut us dead', and acted as if we were non-existing things, a kind of rage and impotent despair would ere long well up in us, from which the cruellest bodily torture would be a relief; for these would make us feel that, however bad might be our plight, we had not sunk to such a depth as to be unworthy of attention at all. (James 1890: i. 293–4).

[19] Hegel is a source of this view, as of the notion of recognition which I have made use of in this section. See Essay VIII.

feeling-worthiness. It is *because* blame is penal that one can rationally raise the question of what *should* be penalized by means of it. Spontaneous blame-feelings thus come under the regulation not only of their own hermeneutic discipline, but also of external regulative forces—ethical ideals and practical reason as such. The content of these is not our main concern here, though I shall sketch out a view of them in the final section. The main constructive claim of this essay is that the concept of the moral emerges from this interaction—between hermeneutic criteria regulating the blame-feeling from within, and external criteria which come from sources independent of it and which seek, more or less successfully, to shape its penal effect to a larger context. This interaction is an important phenomenon on any view of what those external criteria are. Its presence explains why the concept of the moral cannot be reduced to the internal, hermeneutic criteria which partly constitute it, any more than the concept of redness can be reduced to the phenomenal criteria which partly constitute it. But to see the interaction one must recognize, as the externalist does, that there are indeed standards regulating blame other than those affectively determined by the blame-feeling itself.

10. If we accept that there is this interaction we must then also accept the logical possibility that morality might be superseded. External criteria might convince us that it is never rational to allot blame. We might become convinced, like the utopian and the subversive thinkers of Section 3, that the penal element which is incipient in the blame-feeling— the element of exclusion, which morality accredits and institutionalizes into a mode of social control distinct from formally prescribed external penalties—should, on the contrary be discredited and, so far as possible, decommissioned. More effective methods of pursuing our ethical ideals or practical-rational goals might be found. Blame-feelings might persist, being grounded in human nature—but instead of being harnessed in a social institution they would become surplus to requirements. They would be seen as non-rational survivals, unhelpfully 'negative' and 'judgmental' in their accompanying disposition to withdraw recognition and to exclude.

All of this is indeed *abstractly* possible, but perhaps it only has to be spelt out explicitly to seem unreal. It could also happen, however, that the overcoming of morality arose out of a deeper analysis of the hermeneutic of blame itself—it might be that that itself rested on some confused picture of things. The blame-feeling might be irrational in the same way as fear of unlucky omens, or disgust at taboo substances, or belief in the magical power of symbols. It would be prone to undercutting from rational reflection on its justifying base as such, irrespective of the efficiency or otherwise of harnessing it in a social institution.

The blame-feeling would be undermined in this way if there were philosophical reason to conclude that nothing is avoidable. The notorious argument here, of course, is from 'determinism'—but this will not sway those of us who regard *that* alleged incompatibility (of 'free will and determinism') as either an irrelevancy or a confusion. Is there, though, some more subtle incoherence in morality's dependence on the notion of avoidability?

Bernard Williams notes that blame, 'the characteristic reaction of the morality system' is 'directed to the voluntary'.[20] He highlights what I have also highlighted, that when we blame we blame for what the agent should have *recognized* as something to be avoided. We take it that the agent is responsive to the norms to which we also respond. But Williams thinks the agent would only have had reason to act otherwise if doing so would have promoted projects or concerns he in fact had—there are no reasons grounded in concerns which he is rationally *required* to have. So 'The institution of blame is best seen as involving a fiction',[21] the fiction that there are reasons for acting which apply to all agents, irrespective of their already existing motives. Now this fiction does not concern the voluntary, that is, avoidability, as such. It lies rather in the assumption that wrongdoer and moral judge respond in common to categorical norms, which transcend their possibly divergent motives. Williams rejects such 'absolutely "external"' reasons—ones that do not 'speak to any motivation the agent already has'.[22]

Here he represents Humean or Nietzschean presumptions, rather than Kantian or Millian ones. Autonomy, or (in Mill's less transcendentally charged phrase) 'moral freedom', involves something more than the instrumental notion of practical rationality. Moral freedom *is*, precisely, the disposition to respond to reasons whether or not they 'speak to any motivations the agent already has'.[23] Thus when Williams predicts that if

---

[20] Williams (1985: 177 and 178).   [21] Ibid. 193.   [22] Ibid. 223–4, n. 19.
[23] Williams is wrong in holding that Kant also thinks every reason must 'speak' to a *'motivation* the agent *already* has' (my emphases). It is truistic, of course, that a reason must engage with *something* 'already' in the agent, if it is to affect his belief or his action. It must engage with a capacity to recognize reasons and a capacity to respond to them. But it is not true, and Kant does not hold, that it must engage with an already existing *motivation*. A disposition to act (or believe) when one recognizes reasons to do so cannot as such be termed a motivation. To treat it so would simply beg the questions against the believer in what Williams calls 'external' reasons. Let me add here that in equating Kant's autonomy and Mill's moral freedom for present purposes I do not mean to suggest that they are identical. They have in common the idea of rational mastery of one's desires; but (among other things) Mill does not identify the moral with the rational—as the passages quoted in Sect. 2 suffice to make clear.

we achieve a 'reflective and non-mythical understanding of our ethical practices', 'the practices of blame, and more generally the style of people's negative ethical reactions to others, will change',[24] his prediction is grounded on the idea that what cannot survive non-mythical understanding is the (Kantian/Millian) ideal of autonomy or moral freedom—the capacity to recognize impartial claims of reason as authoritative, and to act from that recognition.

I do not agree. Moral freedom does not require the idealist underpinnings Kant gave it; nor is it the case that to be a naturalist one must be a Humean. On the contrary, a *properly* naturalistic, non-mythical, understanding of our hermeneutic notions would, among other things, scrap the mythopoeic 'science' of 'desire-belief psychology'.

This is not the place to defend such convictions; but if I am right, then neither determinism, nor the supposed impossibility of giving an account of categorical reasons without idealism, nor the Humean doctrine of motivation, is the problem. However Williams presents a further, independent, and important, line of thought. 'To the extent that the institution of blame works coherently,' he suggests, 'it does so because it attempts less than morality would like it to do.' Morality, he thinks, tends to seek more than the practices of blame require:

There is a pressure within it to require a voluntariness that will be total and will cut through character and psychological and social determination, and allocate blame and responsibility on the ultimately fair basis of the agent's own contribution, no more and no less. It is an illusion to suppose that this demand can be met.[25]

It is indeed an illusion to suppose that *this* demand can be met. I further agree with Williams that 'the institution of blame' does not require it. But then what is morality other than that institution? A firm distinction should be maintained here, between the principle of avoidability—that I cannot be blamed for what I could not have avoided—which is both central to morality and defensible; and, in contrast, the pressure which Williams identifies towards 'total' voluntariness. The former is deeply rooted in the hermeneutic of the blame-feeling. The latter arises not from anything essential to morality itself, but from that least compelling aspect of the Kantian legacy—its rigoristic moral egalitarianism.

To impose such rigoristic egalitarianism is not what morality 'would like to do' but what Kantians and many other modern moralists would like to do, under the influence of two governing ideas: that worth cannot reside in acts or qualities outside the agent's control and that all agents

---

[24] Ibid. 194.   [25] Ibid.

must be equal in their possession of that control, the control on which worth depends. It is this ideal, the ideal of pure egalitarian desert, which forces them towards the idea that all worth traces back to the transcendental exercise of moral freedom—and to the fetishism of morality that goes with it.

11. Blame presupposes moral freedom. You cannot be blamed for what you could not have *recognized* as something you should not do, or were unable to do *on the basis* of that recognition. But it is not true that all worth presupposes moral freedom. A quality of character or an action can have worth even though it is not the product of an exercise of moral freedom. A person's generosity and moral courage, for example, have value even if they are natural to him and do not result from any intervention of moral consciousness on his part. And his generous and brave acts are admirable even if they are products of spontaneous inclination rather than conscientious principle.

The reluctance to accept that stems, as Williams suggests, from a yearning for 'ultimate fairness'. This remains even when other misconceptions, as that all inclination is selfish, are removed. Natural qualities are unequally distributed, and the inequality does not stem from the efforts of the agents. Hence the attractiveness of transcendentalizing autonomy, and giving it the monopoly of worth. If every agent is transcendentally equal in autonomy, and nothing except autonomous action has worth, worth maps onto 'the agent's own contribution' in the way that pure egalitarian desert requires. But in fact autonomy—in the shape at least of its demythologized correlate, moral freedom—is also, just like generosity or moral courage, a natural quality of human agents. As with natural generosity and courage, its worth does not depend on its resulting from an exercise of moral freedom. We can to some, but only to a limited, extent, make ourselves more morally free, by our own effort. But that requires some moral freedom in the first place, not itself resulting from the agent's own effort. It is not required, for being free, that you should freely have made yourself free, nor is it a condition of your freedom's having ethical worth.

If moral freedom is a natural quality, then, as with generosity or moral courage, it is entirely expectable that some should have it more than others. This does not itself cause problems for the institution of blame. Diminished moral freedom means diminished blame. Neither the practice of blame, nor the institution of morality based on it, require 'ultimate' equality in the degree of moral freedom moral agents have. It is only required that they have some. But while that does not undermine morality, it does undermine those modern ideals of it according to which we are all, in respect of moral agency, equal—and which base our equal worth or dignity entirely on that. It is those ideals, rather than anything within morality itself, which produce the pressure to 'cut through character and psychological and social determination', to identify ethical worth with autonomous action, and to hold that all agents are—transcendentally speaking—equally autonomous. Seeing morality non-mythically certainly forces one to give up that, and thus for example, to rethink those varieties of the liberal ethic which rest on it.[26]

In eliminating the fetishism of morality, the external, genealogical, point of view on moral phenomena comes into its own. It dismantles the monopolistic concept of 'moral worth', replacing it by the diversity of valuations connected with admiration and blame. But it too has its characteristic dangers—the antipode of moral fetishism. It is pretty obvious (other than to the last discoverers of Nietzsche) that shallow suspicion of the supposed 'illusions' of morality is presently a much greater danger than fetishism. We need to find a way between fetishism and modernistic subversion, a way of redirecting suspicion from the innocent, and pre-eminently human, institution of morality to the rigoristic-egalitarian modern distortions of it. Like any other institution, of course, morality can be exploited for the exercise of domination. But it is not inherently an exercise of domination. If we direct suspicion to its proper targets, we shall not think that dismantling 'moral worth' is dismantling morality. And we shall better appreciate the relations between morality and other systems of human valuation, also rooted in spontaneous feeling, and disciplined hermeneutically.

As well as morality, whose emotional core is the blame-feeling, there is the system of *ends*, whose affective core is liking or desire. Then there is the system of *character-ideals*, whose core is admiration. Like morality, these systems are controlled by the ideal of undistorted, well-tuned convergence referred to in Section 6. Objective ends, such as happiness, or insight, or recognition and respect, are resilient categories under which we continue to desire objects—after experience, reflection, and discussion—despite the tensions which this plurality of categorial ends creates, and the perennial disagreements as to their relative importance. Objective character-ideals are constituted by what is in the same way, through the same tensions and disagreements, *admired*.

---

[26] It is however easy to overstate the importance of autonomy, and faith in the equal autonomy of all human beings, in the ethics (let alone the political economy and political sociology) of classical liberalism. See Skorupski (1993), and Essay XI.

There is interaction between these three systems, one kind of value spilling over into another. In particular, there is interaction between morality and the system of character-ideals. Not all ideals of character are virtues—not, for example coolness, wit, or sheer vitality; the admiration we feel for them is in some cases ethical, in some cases aesthetic, in some cases a mixture of the two. Note the asymmetry here which is obscured by the notion of 'moral worth': blame is a penalty, but admiration should not be moralized into a reward. We admire many character-traits and performances whose absence is not *blameworthy*—though it may become disestimable. We naturally admire physical courage and style. But we do not blame those who could have done something to reduce their timidity or frumpishness, but haven't bothered—though we may well, if we are honest with ourselves, admit that we think less of them.

In contrast, someone who could have done something to overcome his natural cruelty, but has not bothered, is blameworthy. A virtue is something narrower than the general notion of a character-ideal. It is a quality of character which we admire or can come to admire, and failure to develop which in oneself, where it is possible to do so, is—other things being equal again—blameworthy. Our notion of virtue draws on the resources of the system of character-ideals, and its core-sentiment of admiration. The moral shades into the ethical and the ethical into the aesthetic, along a spectrum with the blame-feeling at one end and simple admiration of human excellence at the other.

Behind these systems of valuation lies the background framework of practical reason. This is the larger structure of which Mill thought that morality is only a department. My division into morality, character-ideals, and ends corresponds fairly obviously, if only roughly, to his division into Morality, Aesthetics, and Prudence. But to call these only departments is misleading. They are more like fiefdoms, coming under the loose sovereignty of reason, but animated by their own independent spirit, without which reason would have nothing over which to rule. If the fundamental idea of practical reason is impartially conceived good, it is an idea that would remain empty without them; just as truth, the idea of theoretical reason, would remain empty without substantive valuations, similarly grounded in convergence, about what reasonings are justified and what explanations good.

This highlights a final point. One can be a rationalist about practical reason, without being a rationalist about moral judgements—judgements as to the blameable—or indeed about judgements as to the admirable or the desirable. *Their* material is drawn from various modes of feeling. That, I should add, is to reject a rationalist, but not a cognitivist, view of them.

They are genuine judgements. The point is that even where reason regulates and modifies them, as in the case of the blameworthy, it does not give them their primitive grounds. But to pursue this meta-ethical issue, or to map out general relationships between the various aspects of human valuation and practical reason is no task for today. I have been concerned here only with sketching how the moral fits in.

VIII

Freedom, Morality, and Recognition: Some Theses of Kant and Hegel

Kant affirms that no one transgresses the moral law in full freedom. Hegel says that punishment is the right of the transgressor. Both theses seem implausible, even bizarre. They are also in apparent tension; in that rightful punishment might be thought to presuppose that the transgression *was* fully free—while a punishment to which the transgressor has a right presumably *is* a rightful punishment. Nonetheless, despite this apparent implausibility and tension, both theses are true. Or so I shall argue; I shall also consider how they are connected. Although I draw on some important arguments of Kant and Hegel my aim is to isolate those parts of the arguments which are really necessary for the defence of the two theses and to show that these parts are sound, whatever may be said of the rest. My main interest, then, is in the two theses and their relationship, rather than in the interpretation of Kant and Hegel (though obviously I hope that such interpretative claims as occur below are indeed correct).

The conclusions will be broadly as follows. There is a freedom to which we rightly aspire: freedom as integrity—determination of the activity of the self by the self. Kant is right to identify this freedom with rationality, but, as Hegel says, too narrow in his conception of what that sort of rationality includes. Integrity encompasses the determinate rationality of the feelings as well as 'pure practical reason'. In particular, and because of this, morality and moral agency cannot be reduced to 'pure practical reason'. On the other hand, when integrity, freedom as self-determination, is understood in its full scope it is indeed the condition of recognition within the moral community, as both philosophers hold. Transgression is a failure of that self-legislating integrity and suspends that recognition. It divides the self, both internally and from its community. The right of punishment is the right to at-one-ment, to the restoration of integrity and

First published in this volume. I am grateful to Carla Bagnoli, David Bell, Gordon Finlayson, Axel Honneth, Adam Morton, Frederick Neuhouser, Peter Niesen, Robert Pippin, and Mark Sacks for helpful comment and criticism.

recognition: hence punishment is the transgressor's route back to this kind of freedom.[1]

These conclusions are argued for in Sections 1–7. Section 8 reflects further, in their light, on the place of morality, 'the peculiar institution',[2] within the domain of the ethical, and on how that institution, the system of distinctively *moral* evaluations, functions as an essential element in liberal individualism.

1. THE PARADOX OF TRANSGRESSION

It seems to flow from Kant's treatment of freedom and morality that one cannot freely transgress, and thus (transgression being by its very conception free) cannot transgress at all. I will call this the paradox of transgression.

In the *Groundwork* Kant says 'a free will and a will under moral laws are one and the same'.[3] The identity is deeply rooted in his thought. For will, for Kant, is nothing but the moving force of reason. And freedom is will.[4] A free action, therefore, is an action which is prescribed by practical reason and springs from that prescription. But further, Kant also thinks that *morality* is practical reason. The moral law is legislated by pure practical reason alone. The identity of a free will and a will under moral law follows from these two doctrines, which respectively connect freedom and reason, and reason and morality.

However, to *identify* free will with a will under moral law is too strong. What should we mean by 'action under moral law'? I shall understand it to mean action responsive to moral law. For example, if I have a cup of coffee to relieve my thirst I am not typically acting out of the belief that it is my moral duty to relieve my thirst. I am nevertheless acting under the moral law in this sense: my action *is* morally permissible, I can see that it is (though I don't necessarily reflect on that), I would have seen that it was

---

[1] I am concerned with punishment as a concept of morality rather than of law. The moral and juridical concepts must of course shade into each other; one cannot explain the distinction between criminal and civil law without appeal to the moral concept. In that sense the present discussion is relevant to legal punishment. But criminal law is justifiably concerned with matters of order, discipline, and sheer deterrence which are not directly relevant to the issues discussed here.

[2] See Williams (1985: ch. 10).   [3] Kant (1964: 114).

[4] Similarly Hegel: 'Freedom is just as much a basic determination of the will as weight [or rather, mass] is a basic determination of bodies . . . will without freedom is an empty word, just as freedom is actual only as will or as subject,' Hegel (1991a), 35 (§4, Addition). Cf. 41, §7: 'the *freedom* of the will . . . constitutes the concept or substantiality of the will, its gravity, just as gravity constitutes the substantiality of a body'.

wrong if it was, and refrained if I had seen that it was. Thus my action is under the control of the moral law even though it is not done *from* the moral law, that is, not done because I see that it is morally obligatory.

In having the cup of coffee I may also be acting fully rationally: that is, in a way that is rationally optimal—from the well-founded belief that this is what there is most reason to do.[5] In that case, if my desire to have a cup of coffee were equally strong but overruled by a better reason—for example, that having a cup of coffee would soon be followed by unpleasant palpitations—I would not have the cup of coffee despite having the same desire at the same level of strength.

But suppose, on the other hand, that my thought is: 'To hell with those palpitations, I'm going to have this coffee anyway.' From weakness, I drink the coffee, even though I can see that it would be better not to. In that case my action is less than fully rational and thus (to anticipate) less than fully free. Yet I have not done something I was morally obliged not to do—and it may still be true that if there had been some *moral* obligation not to have the cup of coffee, then I would *not* have had it. In that case, on our account of acting under the moral law, I *do* act under the moral law, but I do *not* act in full freedom.

Hence acting in full freedom is not identical with acting under the moral law. This account, then, departs somewhat from Kant. To maintain his identity Kant would have to say, about our example, that when I have the cup of coffee even though I know it's a silly thing to do I am also failing morally—acting against a moral obligation to preserve myself in my animal nature perhaps. In general he would have to treat any irrational action as immoral.

Nonetheless, the account we have given will still have the consequence that no morally wrong action is fully free—so long as fully free action is rationally optimal action, and so long as it's never rationally optimal to do something morally wrong. Both points will be defended in what follows. But let us first set up the paradox of transgression.

---

[5] Throughout this essay I use the terms 'rationally optimal' and 'optimal' in the following way. A *rationally optimal* action is an action which the agent would be justified in thinking to be optimal—given what he would be justified in believing to be the evidence at his disposal. An *optimal* action is an action which there is most reason for the agent to do (to which there is no alternative action which the agent has *more* reason to do).

I assume only that actions in a choice set can be weakly ordered by how much reason there is to do them. I make no assumption about how degrees of strength are assessed, whether they can be put on an additive scale, whether they are determined by consequences, and so forth. There can be more than one optimal action; in that case there is no reason for me to choose one rather than another of these, though there is more reason for me to do any one of them than any action which is not one of them. (The same applies to 'incommensurable' optimal actions, if that is a genuinely distinct category.)

It is a basic principle of blame that I cannot be blamed for doing a thing if I did it unfreely.[6] Now suppose that my action is morally wrong only if it is blameworthy. Then if we add the further proposition that whenever I act morally wrongly I have not acted freely it will become self-contradictory to say that any action is morally wrong. Nothing that is done is morally wrong: it was either free and thus not morally wrong, or unfree and thus not morally wrong.

However this is too strong if it is allowed that we may evaluate a particular action as morally wrong yet excuse the agent from blame, because of some limitation on his freedom.[7] (How deficits of freedom function as excuses will be considered in the next section.) In that case the premiss that my action is morally wrong only if it is blameworthy is false. But there will still be the paradox that nothing is blameworthy. That follows from the less contested principle that an action is blameworthy only if it is morally wrong. Given this principle, an action was either free and thus not morally wrong, hence not blameworthy; or unfree and thus not blameworthy.

Reinhold seems to have been among the first to make this kind of objection.[8] Allison suggests that in the following passage Kant reaffirms his analysis of freedom against criticisms of this type:

freedom of choice cannot be defined—as some have tried to define it—as the capacity to make a choice for or against the law . . . Only freedom in relation to the internal lawgiving of reason is really a capacity; the possibility of deviating from it is an incapacity. How can that capacity be defined by this incapacity?[9]

The point is powerful, but it does not dissolve the paradox. For if deviating from the moral law results from *incapacity*, how can it be blamed?

The obvious solution is to distinguish between freedom in Kant's particular sense of autonomy and practical freedom in general. This indeed seems to have been Kant's position. When Kant says that a free will is a will under moral law he must be understood to mean a will that is free in the sense of being autonomous. Only autonomous action is identifiable with action under the moral law. So if I am not acting under the moral law

---

[6] I use 'blame' in the narrow sense in which its intentional object is transgression, not in the wide sense in which a dead battery can be blamed for the car's failure to start (in that sense the blameworthy agent is simply the contextually relevant causal antecedent of the deplorable outcome).

[7] I assume throughout that the object of moral assessment is either a token action which has been done, or a possible action which is being considered in some fully determinate set of circumstances.

[8] See Allison (1990: 133 ff). The criticism is also made by Sidgwick (1888). I am much indebted to Allison's discussion of the issue.

[9] Kant (1991: 52).

my action is not, according to Kant, autonomous, but it does not follow
that it is unfree.

In that case, however, what is the connection between autonomy in particular and freedom in general? Kant's answer is that practical freedom is
the *possibility* of autonomy. A practically free agent is an agent who is
capable of autonomy. A morally wrong action *is* done freely—even though
it is heteronomous—in the sense that it is a product of the will (or in the
case of a controllable involuntary action, one could have refrained from it
at will). But, on Kant's conception, if we are talking about an agent who
has will (i.e. practical reason) at all we must be talking about an agent who
had the capacity to see what he should do and do it—he must have been
capable of acting autonomously, under the moral law, and doing so in this
determinate case, even though he did not.

Now I want to defend an account of autonomy, full or actualized freedom, along these Kantian lines (as I take them to be)—against the appearance it may present of being a merely verbal *tour de force*.[10] Then we will
consider what the paradox of transgression, and this roughly sketched
response, tells us about some concepts central to morality: freedom,
blame, and moral punishment.

2. WILL, REASON, AND FREEDOM

First let us look more closely at the connections between will and reason.

Both Kant and Hegel[11] affirm that will is nothing but reason in its practical aspect. Their claim can be defended by the following three points,
which seem to me to be true.

---

[10] I will defend the distinction between practical freedom and autonomy—but not the
'all-or-nothing' aspect of Kant's view: that if one has any degree of practical freedom, then
one is capable of autonomy. One can have some freedom without the capacity for full freedom.

[11] e.g. Hegel (1991a), 35–6 (§4, Addition):
[I]t must not be imagined that a human being thinks on the one hand and wills on the
other, and that he has thought in one pocket and volition in the other . . . The distinction
between thought and will is simply that between theoretical and practical attitudes. But
they are not two separate faculties; on the contrary, the will is a particular way of thinking—translating itself into existence . . .
what I will I represent to myself as my object. The animal . . . has no will, because it does
not represent to itself what it desires. It is equally impossible to adopt a theoretical attitude or to think without a will, for in thinking we are necessarily active.
See also Hegel (1991b), 100–2 (§§ 53–4). Here Hegel attributes to Kant the conception of
practical reason as will determining itself in a universal way (§53)—adding that 'the will certainly possesses this faculty, and it is of great importance to know that man is only free insofar as he possesses that will and employs it when he acts' (§54, Addition).

1. (*Efficacy of reason*) The conviction that α is optimal[12] can be the full explanation of why one does α. Such an explanation need be in no way elliptical, there need be no other antecedent of action that has to be made explicit.

2. (*Will as practical reason*) Fully willing what one does is acting under the conviction that one's action is optimal. One's action is then explicable as the product of that conviction in the way postulated in (1).

3. (*Irrealism about reason*) To acknowledge that there is reason to α in C is to reflectively accept a spontaneous impulse of the will—the impulse to α in C—as a universal maxim: i.e. to accept that there is reason for anyone in C to α. 'What there is reason to do is what one can universally will.'

Let me comment on these three points in turn.

(1) The first thesis is incompatible with Humeanism about action, that is, the view that if an account of the agent's reasons for acting does not ascribe to him a desire which he had, and whose satisfaction he believed the action would promote, then it must be at best elliptical. Humeanism is of course a very influential view in contemporary philosophy. I set it aside for by now familiar, though continuingly controversial, reasons (but this is not the place to try to disentangle the strands of scientism, over-simple empiricism, and sheer verbal manœuvre that underpin it).

(2) To 'fully will' what one does is to act voluntarily with no admixture of weakness of will—where weakness of will is doing voluntarily that which one sees is not the best thing to do.

It seems right to describe weakness of will as a case of free action which is not *fully* free. That is precisely why we describe it as a case in which the will is *weak*: it did not produce what it would have produced if it was stronger. (One might think to oneself retrospectively: 'I could see that X was the best thing to do—why on earth couldn't I *bring myself* to do it?' Or again: 'I just couldn't *control* myself.') So incontinent action seems to be action which is shaped not just by my idea of what action is optimal but also by something opposing or weakening it, inclination. It is less than fully free because I couldn't bring myself to do what I could see was the best thing to do—I wasn't giving the law to myself, I shared mastery over myself with inclination.

In weakness of will there is a settled limitation on, or occurrent disordering of, the capacity to act from what one believes there is most reason to do. Hence a wrong done through weakness of will is to some varying extent extenuated. The extent varies because we treat weakness of will as something which may itself be more or less controllable by an effort of

---

[12] See the definition of 'optimal' in n. 5.

will. 'I couldn't bring myself to do it—but if I'd tried harder perhaps I could have done.' To the extent that you *could* have overcome your weakness by trying harder you are not excused. That does not commit us to thinking, implausibly, that weakness of will can always be overcome by greater effort of will, so that the will always stands free of empirical limitations. Rather we picture a given will at a given time as having a certain normal driving power, which can be increased, but not indefinitely, by special effort (by assigning more drive to the will at the expense of other functions). Perhaps its normal driving power can be increased over time, by some process such as training, but that too has definite limits.[13]

(3) A belief about what action is optimal may be false in light of the full facts. It may also be *epistemically unwarranted* relative to the agent's actual information state. By (3), this epistemic fallibility must arise from an impairment of the agent's rationality or a failing or inattention in his application of it to the particular case. For irrealism about reasons says that the epistemology of judgements about reasons makes no appeal to a *receptive* faculty—a capacity for receiving signals from some putative normative sector of reality. It appeals only to the agent's own spontaneity (in the case of practical reasons, spontaneity of will) and reflective discussion thereof. If the agent reaches a conclusion about what is best to do which is not justified relative to his information state that cannot be because of a misleading input or a faulty receptive capacity which distorts or fails to register the input—in the way that misleading input or faulty reception can explain our misjudgements about the colour of a surface, the distance of an object etc.[14]

By (1) and (2) a fully willed action is an action which springs from the conviction that the action is optimal. By (3) judgements about what is optimal are in turn reflectively grounded in the spontaneity of the will. Thus Kant and Hegel are right to identify will and practical reason. But how in turn is will, practical reason, connected with freedom?

---

[13] Note that the notion expressed by 'voluntary' does not coincide with this notion of what is willed. In weakness of will I do something voluntarily which I *will* not to do—or I do something *in*voluntarily (such as showing my surprise) which I *will* to stop myself doing. In each case my will is insufficiently strong to stop me: something I do involuntarily may still be something I might have stopped myself doing by a greater effort of will.

[14] These comments rely on the epistemology of the normative which is set out in Essays I, II.7 and IV.4. They assume that one can be a cognitivist about reasons without being a realist about them. Thus the irrealist formulation in (3)—reflective acceptance of a spontaneous impulse of the will—is not intended to imply a non-cognitivist, 'voluntarist' or 'prescriptivist' view. It seems to me that reading Kant as an irrealist cognitivist is at least as plausible as a voluntarist reading (see Sect. 4 below, also Skorupski 1998*b*). However, irrespective of that interpretative claim, the thesis that will is practical reason stands in its own right and can in my view be defended without rejecting cognitivism about normative claims.

To act fully freely *at least* requires that one fully wills what one does: full willing is a necessary condition of full freedom. Therefore by (1) and (2) fully free action springs solely from the conviction that one's action is optimal. However, what if that conviction itself results from impaired rationality? Is one's action then fully free?

It can be maintained that freedom pertains exclusively to one's ability to carry out what one thinks is best, not to one's ability to reach a rational conclusion as to what is best. But I think it is more plausible to regard deficits of rationality in one's beliefs about what one has reason to do as also constituting restrictions on one's freedom. On this inclusive conception of freedom, doing what one thinks is best because one thinks it's best is not a sufficient condition for full freedom. Full freedom also requires that one's capacity for forming rational conclusions about what to do should not be impaired. Full freedom is thus a twin track—the capacity to recognize what is rationally optimal and the capacity to act on that recognition. The two capacities are captured by Kant's *Wille* and *Willkür*: *Wille* is practical reason, *Willkür* is its driving power.

Why, after all, should a weakness in one's capacity to *act* in accord with what one judges to be rationally optimal be a restriction on one's freedom, whereas an impairment in one's capacity to *judge* what is rationally optimal is not? Neither *Wille*, one's power of judging about reasons to act relative to an information state, nor *Willkür*, one's power of executing that judgement, is in principle outside our control in the way input and well-functioning receptivity are. Both *Wille* and *Willkür* are imputable aspects of our capacity to determine ourselves: I can try harder to reason well just as I can try harder to act on good reasons. If my reasoning is at fault, *I'm* at fault, whereas if the sensory input is misleading, or my sensory organs are at fault, *I'm* not at fault. In cases where there is some moral onus to reason well, and I fail to reason as well as I might have done if I had tried harder, criticism may turn into moral blame. So acting fully freely is acting under reason as such, i.e. doing what *is* rationally optimal, *because* it is. Freedom as self-determination is rationality.

Let us now simply define an autonomous action as an action which is fully free. And let us say that autonomy as a property of character is the capacity to act autonomously—to acknowledge reasons for action and to act on them.[15] This is a very strong concept. Are all human beings fully

---

[15] Allen Wood suggests that Hegel departs from Kant in treating autonomy as the 'highest or truest kind' of freedom, seeing it not as a 'possibility or capacity but a determinate way of acting'—Wood (1990: 39). I do not myself see why these aspects of Hegel's conception of autonomy involve a departure from Kant. Both philosophers take it that acting fully freely—autonomously—is doing the rationally optimal thing *because* it is the rationally

autonomous—do they all, in all circumstances, have the capacity to act autonomously?

Kant is an egalitarian about autonomy. He says that transcendentally all humans have absolute autonomy. I do not follow him in that. Autonomy is a limit-concept, to the realization of which in ourselves we can at best aspire. We fall away from autonomous action to the extent that we suffer from either weakness or distortion in the power to judge reasons or from weakness of will. And, to the extent that such weakness or distortion is something we cannot overcome by the application of effort, our character falls short of autonomy. Presumably no one is fully autonomous; certainly many fall far short of autonomy. Not only is there no 'transcendental' level at which all can be guaranteed to be absolutely autonomous; the empirical variations in people's autonomy are clearly very great. Serious ethics must always have this in mind. On the other hand, it must also recognize in autonomy an important ideal of character. And apart from its role as an ideal, it is also true that if one thinks there is good reason to be in the business of choosing, i.e. making right judgements about what there is reason to do, one must also think there is reason to be autonomous, fully free—to judge rightly and act on that judgement. Indeed this is one main reason for preferring the inclusive over the exclusive conception of freedom: it is the inclusive conception (well-functioning *Wille* as well as well-functioning *Willkür*) that we have reason to try to satisfy if we have reason to deliberate and choose. Again, though, I am not saying that there necessarily always *is* good reason to be in the business of choosing. Since maintaining one's capacity to choose can incur varying costs, the best thing to do in some circumstances may be to restrict one's full freedom or get rid of it completely.

Overall then, autonomy should be kept in its place. It is not something that we can be guaranteed to have, it is only one ideal among others and, even though it is a condition of fully rational choice, it is not always rational to try to achieve fully rational choice. Nonetheless, Kant is right to equate full freedom, autonomy, with rationality, and furthermore to see it as an aspiration implicit in the very activity of deliberation (as he does in *Groundwork* III).

---

optimal thing, though Hegel adds important further conditions, concerning at-one-ment in one's social relations, to the notion of full freedom. (Hence both philosophers have an account of autonomous action which is in some sense 'causal': though this is questioned by a number of interpreters, e.g. Pippin 1995: 104–5). Kant takes freedom, understood as a property of the person, to be the capacity for autonomous action, and there seems no reason to think that Hegel would disagree.

3. MORALITY, REASON, AND BLAME

To deliberate, then, is to act under the idea of full freedom. And now from that idea as such, according to Kant, morality itself can be unfolded. Few simultaneously defend both the unfolding steps required to complete this deduction—the step to the categorical imperative from the very idea of full freedom, and the step to substantive moral obligations from the categorical imperative. Some take the categorical imperative to express the universality of practical reason and its connection with the spontaneity and universality of willing, as captured in (1)–(3)—but rightly point out that no substantive moral obligations follow. Others endow the categorical imperative with putatively moral content, for example by highlighting the formula of humanity—in which case, as they equally rightly concede, the categorical imperative does not follow from the very idea of fully free willing. There is however also a middle ground possible, which I shall further defend in the next section and return to in Section 8. According to this middle ground pure practical reason yields a constraint of impartiality which goes beyond the mere universality of reasons though it still does not yield morality.[16]

To take that middle ground is to accept that Kant's ambition, of *deriving* morality from the impartial standpoint of pure practical reason—let alone from the very idea of full freedom—reflects a deep misapprehension of morality and its sources. Our distinctively moral convictions do not come only—by and large, they do not come at all—from pure practical reason. It is not pure practical rationality, the capacity corresponding to *pure* practical reason, that is called upon to recognize them, but rationality in a very much wider sense. This is a central truth of the Hegelian critique of *moralität*—it will be at the centre of our attention, in various ways, throughout the rest of this essay. So let us first consider why morality is not derivable from pure practical reason and then examine the broader notion of rationality under which moral judgements do fall.

Moral judgements are in the first instance evaluative not practical— they are judgements about what there is reason to blame rather than judgements about what there is reason to do. To blame is to judge that a

---

[16] Korsgaard (1985, 1996) defends the deduction of moral duties from the categorical imperative, but not the deduction of the categorical imperative from the universality of reasons. Allen Wood (1990: ch. 9) defends Kant against the strong claim that the categorical imperative is an 'empty formalism', but not against the weaker claims that (i) the categorical imperative is not deducible merely from the universality of reasons and (ii) it cannot yield a substantive doctrine of moral duties without a given context of 'ethical life' (*Sittlichkeit*). This is also the view taken here.

certain emotion, the blame-feeling, is appropriate towards the person blamed. Morality, that particular but not peculiar institution, rests on such judgements, judgements of guilt and blameworthiness, and the moral agent must be 'inside' those judgements, responsive to the hermeneutics of blame. The practice of blame is both a spontaneous and a collective emotional discipline by which personal and social life is regulated. For this reason, possession of pure practical reason is not enough to characterize a *moral* agent, an agent who is immersed in the practice, and thus the emotional presuppositions, of morality. Morality is not derivable from pure practical reason because it gets its content from these sentiments and their objects. As we shall see, however, that does not mean that pure practical reason cannot criticize it.[17]

Yet even if we abandon Kant's narrow rationalism about morality we can nevertheless affirm with him *the principle of moral categoricity*:

If α is morally wrong, then α is not rationally optimal.[18]

Although this principle cannot for us be the trivial consequence of *deducing* the morally obligatory from the rationally optimal, it can still be maintained. For emotions have their own hermeneutic principles, constitutively linking their justification, their intentional objects and the behaviour to which they dispose. By a hermeneutic principle I mean a principle whose truth one can see for oneself (as against learning of its truth by testimony) only by apprehending or grasping in one's own experience and imagination the emotion which it concerns. Moral categoricity can be derived from two such principles of the hermeneutics of blame, principles about what must hold of the object of blame if the blame-feeling is to be justified, viz.:

If α (that token action) is morally wrong and X does α freely, then X is blameworthy for doing α.

If doing α is rationally optimal (there is no action which X has reason to think there is more reason for X to do), then there is no reason to blame X for freely doing α.

The second principle is controversial—an externalist about morality may deny it.[19] And a weak externalism, which simply denies that this principle

[17] These claims about the connection between morality and blame draw on the case made in Essays II and VII.

[18] Granting that when a given action (or disjunction of actions) is morally obligatory any alternative to it is morally wrong, it will follow that a morally obligatory action (or disjunction) is uniquely rationally optimal, since not all available actions in a choice set can be rationally suboptimal.

[19] e.g. someone who is both a Humean about practical reasons and a contractualist about morality is committed by his position to denying it.

is an analytic truth, seems to me correct. But a full-blooded externalism, which denies its truth altogether, seems to me incorrect. Against such full-blooded externalism I am suggesting that this principle, like the first, is a hermeneutic principle of the blame-feeling. It is perhaps easier to accept that about a weakened version of it: if there's no reason not to do α, then there's no reason to blame someone for doing α. And that already yields a weak form of categoricity: if α is morally wrong there's some reason to do a. However I think the strong version is as much a part of the hermeneutics of the blame-feeling as the weakened version. In that respect guilt (self-blame) contrasts with regret—one may well have very good reason to regret 'having to do' something even while having good reason to think that it was the action there was most reason to do.[20]

These hermeneutic principles of blame, in combination with our analysis of autonomy, or fully free action, entail Kant's conclusion that no morally wrong action is fully free—even if we do not follow Kant in deriving morality from pure practical reason.

However I have only argued that if an action is morally wrong it is not rationally optimal. I have *not* argued that if it is rationally optimal then it is morally obligatory. That is not true. For a start there are cases like my having the cup of coffee (Section 1)—it may be rationally optimal but it's not a moral obligation. Then there is the case of supererogation. You throw yourself on the grenade to save others. You did not have a moral duty to do that, and those of us who just hit the ground are not blameworthy. Nonetheless the outcome of *your* action is predictably better—less death and injury. That being so there is no irrationality in your judgement that you have *more reason* to pursue this outcome than to hit the ground, even though you're not *morally obliged* to pursue it. You thought that was the best thing for you to do and you were not wrong. In each of these examples, the coffee and the grenade, the agent acts autonomously and under the moral law—as we have defined 'autonomously' and 'under the moral law'—but not from moral *obligation*.[21] Identifying the rationally

---

[20] Moral categoricity implies that there are no moral dilemmas in the strong sense envisaged by some: that is to say, situations in which one is blameworthy whatever one does. (For further discussion of this idea see Essay IV.) But of course there can be situations in which whatever one does one has reason to regret 'having to do'. (To regret having to do something is not the same as regretting doing it—the latter does indeed seem incompatible with thinking that one did what one had most reason to do.)

[21] Kant acknowledges that there are actions which have 'merit' but which it is not obligatory to do (and thus blameworthy *not* to do). He sees the merit in question as moral merit, inasmuch as he regards it as a '+' corresponding to the '−' of blameworthiness on a single scale, and not as something praiseworthy in a different, non-moral, dimension of praiseworthiness—see Kant (1991: 194). So he might well say that falling on the grenade is meritorious but not obligatory. The question, however, is whether his account of the relation

optimal and the morally obligatory would be sustainable only at the cost of denying the possibility of supererogation and moralizing every optimal action. But both of these distinctions, between the obligatory and the supererogatory, and the obligatory and the permissible, are fundamental features of our concept of morality.

Morality is categorical, though it does not follow from pure practical reason. And this categoricity presupposes that Kant is right in a further fundamental respect. It is a fundamental feature of our concept of the moral that *what is morally right and morally wrong in a specific situation is open to reflection* (as ever, of course, *defeasible* reflection). Here too Hegel would agree—he calls this the 'right [or law] of the subjective will'.[22] However (I'm speaking for myself now, not Hegel) the reflection involved is not, as Kant's narrow or pure rationalism leads him to suppose, *pure* reflection on what one can will. In the first instance it is reflection on what should be blamed. It becomes reflection on what should be willed via moral categoricity, which is itself, as we have seen, something that comes from the hermeneutics of blame, not from 'pure practical reason'.

So these fundamental Kantian truths, that one's moral duty is knowable by reflection, and that one cannot fully freely, that is, autonomously, fail in one's moral duty can be defended—without accepting Kant's rationalistic reduction of morality to pure practical reason.

4. BROAD AND NARROW ('PURE') PRACTICAL REASON

Now let's consider a broader notion of practical reason than Kant's. Let us say then, first, that *rationality* as such covers the whole set of powers

---

between a prescription of practical reason and an obligation *allows* him to say that. Does it allow him to say that there was *more reason* to fall on the grenade than to fall to the floor— even though only not running away (thus, *either* falling on the floor or on the grenade) was obligatory? And if he cannot say that, how can he account for the moral merit of falling on the grenade? Note that falling on the grenade to save our fellows is not something we have an obligation to do on some occasions but not all (as in Kant's conception of 'imperfect obligation'). We never have a moral obligation to do it.

[22] Hegel (1991*a*), 136 (§107); 108 (§132). See also the discussion of formal versus true conscience on 163–70 (§§136–9). Categoricity presupposes the right of the subjective will in that one of the claims from which we derived it—*if α is morally wrong and X does α freely then X is blameworthy for doing α*—incorporates it. This claim assumes that a moral agent who does α freely can *tell* that his action is morally wrong whatever his information state. If we allowed that an action could be morally wrong even though the agent could not tell it was, the claim would fail. But the 'right of the subjective will' says that an action cannot be morally wrong if we cannot tell that it is.

involved in the capacity, given a state of information, to judge of reasons of any kind (whether they be reasons to believe, to act, or to feel), to estimate their weight on the basis of that information state, and to respond appropriately. In this very broad (unusually broad) sense rationality may be contrasted with *receptivity*, the capacity to receive information. *Practical* rationality is then a correspondingly broad subdivision: the capacity to recognize reasons for action, weight them appropriately and act on them. This broad characterization is intended to include every aspect of practical rationality, that is, every aspect of deliberation or reflection about reasons for action (instrumental rationality is only a proper part). *Broad practical reason* is the totality of principles that express it. So it includes those hermeneutic principles internal to the feelings (sentiments, emotions, inclinations, and desires) which connect reasons to feel and reasons to act.

There is in particular one very important principle that does that (the Feeling/Disposition principle):

(FD) If there's reason to feel ϕ, there's reason to do that which ϕ characteristically disposes to.

It delivers a principle of practical reason for each feeling which is associated with a characteristic disposition.[23] And so it does so for the blame feeling and its characteristic disposition. Identifying, and understanding from within, that characteristic disposition of blame will be our central theme when we turn to the connections between blame, punishment, and recognition.

I have only said that reasons for action *sometimes* stem from feelings. One might think that they always do—that FD, together with other principles deriving from the hermeneutics of feeling, such as that of moral categoricity, exhaust the content of practical reason. Such *sentimentalism* about practical reason would be compatible with acknowledging that there is such a thing as practical rationality broadly conceived—a cognitive capacity to judge of reasons for action. More strongly though, and incompatibly with sentimentalism, one may also think that there is a narrower notion of *pure* practical reason, and corresponding to it a capacity of narrow or *pure* practical rationality: the capacity to recognize, weight appropriately, and act upon principles of pure practical reason.

---

[23] By the 'characteristic disposition' of a feeling I mean something narrower than the totality of behaviour it may cause. For example the characteristic disposition of fear is flight, the characteristic disposition of desire is trying to get. But fear may root you to the spot and desire may just make you tremble.

What would these be? The criterion or warrant for assertions about what there is reason to feel consists in spontaneous and reflectively acknowledged dispositions to feel, and the criterion for assertions about what there is reason to believe consists in spontaneous and reflectively acknowledged dispositions to believe; likewise assertions about practical reasons are warranted by spontaneous and reflectively acknowledged dispositions to *will*. Among these dispositions to will the ones that are epistemically relevant to assertions about *pure* practical reasons will be dispositions which are not *conditioned* in any way. For example they will not be conditioned on a disposition to feel via the FD principle. To take a particular instance: if I desire something I am characteristically disposed to pursue it. So by the FD principle, if I reflectively accept a desire as normative—that is, I accept that there is reason to desire its object—then I have reason to pursue the object. That is a practical judgement based on a conditional disposition of the will, and thus it is not pure.[24]

In deriving the formula of universal law Kant in effect claims to detect pure or unconditional dispositions of the will which we reflectively acknowledge. His claim must be stronger than a simple appeal to the universality of reasons. For to appeal to universality is indeed just to appeal to a formal point about the concept of a reason. For example, if the fact that I have reason to desire something gives me reason to pursue that thing, then for all x and for all y the fact that x has reason to desire y is a reason for x to pursue y. No unconditional disposition of the will is involved in acknowledging this.

However there can be a case for pure practical reason which starts from a stronger premiss than mere formal universality even while it falls short of establishing substantive moral duties. Just because the constraint expressed by the 'can' in 'what you can will' is not enough to deliver substantive moral duties, it does not follow that it expresses only a merely formal feature of the very notion of a reason, namely the universality of reasons. It can still be argued that this constraint—what one can will when one wills unconditionally—is real, because there *is* something which on

[24] One could break FD into two parts (cp. Essay III, Sect. 6 and Essay VI, Appendix Sect. 2):

(FDF) If there's reason to feel φ, there's reason to desire to do that which φ characteristically disposes one to desire to do.
(FDD) If there's reason to desire to α (or to bring it about that *p*), there's reason to α (to do that which will bring it about that *p*).

(FDD) broadly corresponds to Kant's hypothetical imperative—but a crucial difference is that it conditionalizes what there's reason to do to what *there's reason* to desire. This is one of the points at which Kant's failure to take proper account of the rationality of feelings weakens his analysis.

reflection one finds oneself willing unconditionally. The content of this unconditional will is *impartiality*, that is, not just universality but agent-neutrality. On this view the dispositions of the will are not completely eliminated when we consider it solely as will, in abstraction from whatever emotions and inclinations are particular to the self whose will it is. A disposition of the will, any will, remains when it is so considered: the remaining disposition is the disposition of pure practical rationality, the disposition to constrain one's maxims in some way by a requirement of impartiality.[25]

We will come to the vital question of how the requirement constrains them, how pure practical reason, so conceived, interacts with the totality of reasons for acting, in Section 8. The relevant point for the moment is that this view gives a content—impartiality—to the notion of pure practical reason. But it does not imply that there is a capacity for recognizing reasons for action which is independent of all emotional spontaneity. Rather, it invokes the notion of a kind of reason, or better, a kind of constraint on reasons, which could be acknowledged irrespective of what particular emotions and desires one experiences. Specifically, the notion of individual good, understood as what an individual has reason to *desire*, and thus (via FD) to pursue, provides the material which it constrains. Understanding the notion of individual good only requires grasp of the concept of, and thus experience of, desire; in the presence of this concept—the good—a concept delivered by spontaneity of desire, the content of pure practical reason will express itself as a *constraint* on the good. It will stipulate that the good of any one being is of no greater significance than the good of any other. The good of any being is good—not just good-for-that-being but simply good.

In this sense I agree with Kant not just on the point that to act freely is to act rationally—to do what one has most reason to think there is most reason to do, and to do it for that reason—but also on the claim that there is such a thing as pure practical reason. On the other hand, against Kant I have claimed (1) that what there is most reason to do comes from the totality of reasons for action—broad practical reason, not just narrow or pure practical reason, and (2) that impartiality, not morality, is the content of pure practical reason. Morality is an aspect of broad, not narrow

[25] There is also an interpretation of Kant's formula of universal law which in effect conditionalizes the 'could' in 'what you could will to be a universal law' to your background conviction about what has ethical value together with your views about the capacities and limits of human beings. That is a way in which we sometimes defend some moral principles ('What if everyone did that?'), but it presupposes a background of agreed anthropological and ethical assumptions. In examining what can be *unconditionally* willed, however, Kant says he is making no such presupposition.

practical reason, since its obligations are grounded not in what one can reflectively will but in what one can reflectively blame. The requirements of impartially conceived good, once recognized, have the potential to enter such reflection, and to defeat reasons for action arising from hermeneutic principles of blame—as they have the potential to enter any reflection on what there is reason to do. But that does not mean that moral obligations *derive* from those requirements.

Put another way, Kant is right to say that fully free action is self-determined action, but wrong to identify the self with pure practical reason. The self must rather be identified with the totality of its reasons, including those which come from its emotional spontaneity, not just the unconditional spontaneity of its will. Emotional spontaneity is as fully a part of the self as pure practical reason. To act fully freely, autonomously, to determine oneself, is to act from that integrated totality. Defenders of Kant can of course rightly urge that he recognized the ethical significance of the emotions in various ways.[26] But he did not recognize their significance in the *right* way. That is, he did not recognize that feelings are not things that, so to speak, we just have, aspects of our 'empirical character', but that they too have their reasons and are in this respect as imputable to us as are beliefs and actions. My emotional responses may be unreasonable—but then so too may be my beliefs and actions. Because Kant did not clearly acknowledge that there are evaluative as well as epistemic and practical reasons he failed to pin down properly the way in which such reasons translate into reasons for action and interact in deliberation with pure practical reason. In this crucial sense Kant does operate with an inadequate opposition between reason and inclination, and an inadequate conception of the difference between autonomy and heteronomy, as he is accused of doing from Schiller onwards. It is also this failure of insight (along with other well-known preoccupations, notably that worth cannot accrue to contingent qualities of the person) which underlies his doctrine that only action done from recognition of moral obligation has something called 'moral worth' (which is the only real sort of worth). Overall, together with his absolutist egalitarianism about autonomy, it is a major source of the one-sided Kantian distortions of ethical life.

---

[26] Much of this defence has focused on the doctrine that an action not done from duty has no 'moral worth'. Schneewind (1992: 327–8) gives a judicious summary and cites some of the literature; see also Allison (1990: ch. 10). I do think that Kant's account of this matter, even with all allowances made, is indefensible. But the issue here—the absence from Kant's ethics of a proper account of evaluative reasons—is different.

5. NO TRANSGRESSION IS FULLY FREE

Now let's return to the thesis that no transgression is fully free. The disagreements with Kant which I have just been highlighting do not let us off that hook. We are committed to the thesis as he is. Does it force us to conclude that all transgression results from weakness of will? Does that in turn imply that no transgression is blameworthy?

As noted earlier, we seem to distinguish between weakness as a *limitation* and an *aberration* of the will. It is a limitation when it is something which the agent cannot overcome and which is thus a reduction of his freedom—either as a settled feature of his character or as a temporary reduction which results from the circumstance in which he finds himself. Such limitation, of character or circumstance, may be a cause for shame and disdain, but the actions which result from it are not a proper object of guilt and blame. (Although *that* one has allowed oneself to get into such a state might be.) In contrast, weakness of will is an aberration when it is a case of giving in or flinching which the agent could have overcome in those very circumstances.[27] In the first case we have a *reduction* of moral agency and an *elimination*, in those circumstances in which the limitation obtains, of blameworthiness; in the second case we may have an extenuation or excuse, depending on how important it was to have tried harder, and how understandable that one didn't. (In these cases blame mixes with shame.)

But there is also the possibility of transgressions which do not stem from weakness. In these cases the agent does something which was not the morally required, and thus by moral categoricity, the rationally optimal thing to do—he does not do it, not through weakness, and despite recognizing the rationally optimal thing, but through not recognizing the rationally optimal thing.

Once again, this may arise either (i) through a settled limitation or a circumstantial impairment of his rationality which removes his ability to recognize the rationally optimal thing, or (ii) it may simply be an aberration which results in his not recognizing the rationally optimal thing even though he had the ability to do so. In the first case we have removal of blameworthiness, in the second the possibility of extenuation. Our notion

---

[27] This distinction does not involve 'contra-causal freedom' and is open to the compatibilist. It is simply the distinction between an ability which is *absent*, either permanently or because it's removed by the occurrent circumstances, and an ability which is not absent but not realised either. 'I could have potted that ball, refrained from that remark—it was difficult but not beyond me—I wasn't trying hard enough' versus 'I could not have potted that ball, refrained from that remark—I was blinded by the light, overcome by irritation.'

of rationality is broad not narrow—so the impairment or limitation may be rooted in limited emotional spontaneity. In particular, it may be rooted in a limitation of moral spontaneity—taken far enough such limitation may remove the agent from the field of moral beings, at which point he ceases to have the potential to transgress. (The cat is not morally blameable for torturing the mice.)

But finally we have the possibility on which we must focus. It is the case not of *failure* to recognize but of *refusal* to acknowledge the rationally optimal thing. In non-moral cases this might mean for example refusing to acknowledge that one's health has come to require that one give up certain favourite foods, that one isn't fit or able enough to take on some daring competitive thing, etc. In such cases one still falls short of Kantian autonomy or *full* freedom, even though in another sense one is quite free to eat or not to eat, to jump or not to jump. That is, *there is no limitation or impairment either of one's ability to recognize the rationally optimal action or of one's ability to do it; yet one does the non-optimal action without weakness of will.* The will is free and active, but not autonomous.

In particular it is this kind of transgression, in which the will is free and active, which is the central object of blame; and I will argue that it is in application to this kind of transgression that Hegel's account of punishment offers insight.[28] The transgressor has the ability, has it in the circumstances which actually obtain, to recognize the moral obligation which he transgresses and its categoricity—but he refuses to acknowledge it or its categoricity.

At some level he does recognize it, because, as Sartre might ask, how can he *refuse*, as against fail, to acknowledge it if he does *not* recognize it? His will/practical rationality is not weak—it is free and active. But it is at war with itself. It wills an action, and thus a maxim, against its own law, the law whose content and status as law it has it in itself to affirm. Thus in transgression the will is free but divided against itself. Its arrow is split, its

---

[28] Hegel says:
Where . . . the will is in a state of pure inwardness, the self-consciousness is capable of making into its principle either *the universal in and for itself*, or the *arbitrariness* of its *own particularity*, giving the latter precedence over the universal and realizing it through its actions—i.e. it is capable of being *evil* . . . both morality and evil have their common root in that self-certainty which has being for itself and knows and resolves for itself . . . The *origin of evil* in general lies in the mystery—i.e. the speculative aspect—of freedom. Hegel (1991a), 167 (§139)
Of course this sets a very high standard for moral agency, transgression, and punishment. As we have noted it is an empirical question how far human beings in general approach such moral agency: maybe much less than we would like to think. As we have also noted our concern is with moral rather than legal punishment.

sovereignty divided. It makes a particular law against its own moral law. Transgression is disintegration or division of the self.

Yet the division which has just been described exists *whenever* the self freely and actively wills something other than the rationally optimal; for example when it refuses to acknowledge the imprudence of trying to excel in some dangerous thing. Why then is there something phenomenologically special and important about *transgression*? How is it that moral wrongness, transgression, give rise to blame and punishment? The answer is that the concept of moral wrongness is given not by pure reason but by the blame-feeling. So to investigate the phenomenology of blame and punishment we must explore more fully that emotion—which lies at their core.

6. TRANSGRESSION AND BLAME

Blame as such is not an emotion. To blame someone is to find them blameworthy, thus, to make a judgement; where that blame is publicly expressed it is to perform a public act. Nonetheless the judgement and the act refer to an emotion, which I have simply labelled the 'blame-feeling'. To judge that someone is blameworthy is to judge that the blame-feeling towards them would be *reasonable*, whether or not one actually feels it.

In attempting to pin down an emotion one looks to its intentional content and the action to which it disposes. By these criteria the blame-feeling is not a species of anger, as some have suggested. It is not resentment, because resentment is specifically occasioned by what is taken as injury to oneself—resentment is the opposite of gratitude, one might say. If gratitude is reasonable, then it is reasonable to give thanks or a gift to the person to whom one is grateful; if resentment is reasonable, then it is reasonable to demand apology, the expression of regret, or compensation from the person whose action one resents. (Note, incidentally, that these are instances of the FD principle.) Gratitude and resentment are thus patient-relative feelings, constituting the realm of benefits and torts, whereas the blame-feeling is patient-neutral and constitutes the realm of right and wrong. If it is reasonable for anyone to feel it towards a certain object, it is reasonable for everyone to feel it towards that object.[29] It is the community or in the legal case the state that acts against the wrongdoer, not the victim. (While in the state of nature, Locke says, we all have the right to punish the transgressor, whoever the victim is.)[30]

---

[29] See Essay III, for a definition of 'patient-neutral' and 'patient-relative'.

[30] Locke (1988), p. 271 (*2nd Treatise of Government*, §7).

Indignation, it is true—'righteous indignation'—is patient-neutral: it is occasioned by what is taken to be wrongdoing, whether or not it involves injury to oneself. If it is reasonable for anyone to feel it towards a certain object, it is reasonable for everyone to feel it towards that object. Nevertheless it seems mistaken to make it the emotional core of blame, even though wrongdoing is its object. Rather, indignation is what people of spirit feel on witnessing a moral (or religious) violation. It impels them to right the wrong done, aggressing if necessary against the violator. To be righteously indignant about an action one must first find it blameworthy. But one may blame with regret or sorrow, not indignation. The difference between indignation and the blame-feeling lies not in their intentional object, then, but in the action to which they characteristically dispose.

The blame-feeling as such does not dispose to aggressive restorative action. It disposes to *withdrawal of recognition, casting out of the community*. (Which is why it may be accompanied not by indignation but by regret.) Guilt, self-blame, is the withdrawal of recognition from oneself.[31] The affinity of blame and guilt, in extreme cases, is to a kind of horror akin to the reaction to pollution. Like fear it disposes to the creation of distance between oneself and the object; but the difference is that the disposition of fear is to fly, whereas the disposition of the blame-feeling is to expel, outlaw, ostracize.[32]

Crucially, however, withdrawal of recognition is *not* a matter of ceasing to treat the guilty person as a moral being, of consigning them unambiguously to the realm of wild things. Blame is an inappropriate attitude to a wild thing to which the moral law cannot be promulgated. Rather, the blamed person is stripped of moral membership but at the same time remains a moral being: the outlaw exists in a liminal field which is neither the village nor the bush, forest, wilderness—even though these are the outer regions to which he has literally or metaphorically been expelled.[33]

[31] Consider the very telling idiom 'I couldn't live with myself if I did that', mentioned by Christine Korsgaard (1996: 101); also her remarks on 'conscience', 'consciousness'.

[32] Compare Williams (1993: 119–23) who seems to me much more accurate in his account of shame than of guilt. I do not find it plausible that the 'primitive basis' of guilt is fear on the part of the blamed at the anger of the blamer. In certain cases, though by no means all (cases of free choice of evil *as* evil, one might say), it can seem closer to the truth to say the blame-feeling itself is primitively akin to fear—though for the reasons given above it still remains distinct from it. Williams's distortion of guilt seems to me to connect with his suspicion of 'modern conceptions of morality' and a general tendency to treat these conceptions as more distinctive of modernity than they really are.

[33] In Hegel's thought *recognition* is a ubiquitous determinable category; its constant feature is the idea of membership, mutual awareness, or acknowledgement, in a social unit of self and others (including, so to speak, a unit of self and self). As used in this essay, however, it refers determinately to recognition as a free moral agent, a member of the community or 'kingdom' of such agents. One may lose recognition in this determinate respect while

In these respects guilt and blame contrast with shame and disdain. Central to those latter feelings is the notion of personal standing, status, or rank. The behaviour to which disdain disposes is not exclusion from the community but demotion within it, not withdrawal of recognition as such but loss of status. Shame, disdain directed towards oneself, is the experience of loss of standing in one's own eyes. It is interesting that with loss of standing there is no analogue to the recognized antidote, so to speak, which is provided for exclusion by repentance. Presumably that is because standing requires properties of the self which can be beyond the control of the self whereas membership requires compliance. Blame relates to the quality of the will, something redeemable of whose redemption one can give a sign; whereas disdain need not. A shameful defect is not necessarily, or even typically, a defect of will and it may not be possible to remedy it by effort. I may be ashamed of my ugliness, inability to stand my ground, or lack of wit; but it makes no sense to repent of them. And if shame and guilt are related in this way, as demotion to expulsion, it is also understandable that they should interfuse. Their interfusion is a characteristic of aristocratic or caste society; their radical differentiation and the downgrading of shame and disdain as public disciplinary categories is the characteristic of liberal individualism.

Many societies connect transgression to impurity or pollution, and associate with them rituals of cleansing such as the scapegoat carrying its burden of evil into the wilderness.[34] Christianity's heaven and hell take integration into the community or expulsion from it to their furthest limit: this life becomes a liminal phase preceding final integration or expulsion.[35] But we should not infer that the very notions of wrongdoing and punishment depend on such religious or magical extensions. They remain the root notion of criminal as against civil law even when law is shorn of magic and religion. It is more plausible to hypothesize that shame and

still retaining it in other determinate respects: for example as a being which is not just wild, or as a being rather than a thing. (Actually the wild in traditional cultures is by no means undifferentiated in respect of recognition: animals, ancestor-spirits, etc. feature in overlapping circles of reciprocity.)

Note also that it is no part of my argument that a being has moral claims on us only if it has recognition as a free moral agent.

[34] However, the magical transfer of guilt does not really satisfy the dialectic of atonement; it is rather an attempt to escape it. (Another interesting point about the magical identification of guilt with impurity is that pollution can have unexpected connections with the sacred: the impure transgresses law, the sacred is above it. The gods do morally atrocious things as an indication of their divinity.)

[35] The contrast with Brahmanical Hinduism is interesting: transgression leads to demotion of caste in the next return; final release is nothingness, not membership of the ideal moral community. This is the ritualization of aristocratic ethics.

guilt are elementary structures of human sensibility.[36] They grow into spontaneous disciplinary systems which maintain solidarity and prohibition, whether or not they are also developed into more explicit or codified systems of law and expected behaviour enforced by instituted sanctions. Indeed such artificial or conventional disciplines psychologically presuppose them and could not sustainably replace them.

7. THE DIALECTIC OF ATONEMENT

Blame, then, is the withdrawal of recognition; guilt, self-blame, the withdrawal of recognition from oneself. They involve the idea of a community, actual or ideal, under an autonomously shared moral law, and of expulsion into a domain outside the law. How are we to connect these points with the necessity and the 'right' of punishment, understood as a category in the phenomenology of moral life?[37] Understood in this way the rationale of punishment is a dialectic comprising the moments of (i) transgression and expulsion, (ii) liminality and repentance, and finally (iii) annulment and atonement: at-one-ment of the self with itself and with the community.

(i) Withdrawal of recognition. The expelled transgressor enters a liminal position, neither in the community of moral agents nor in the wilderness to which the law is not promulgated. He is not a wild thing outside the law. He has a will which is divided, heteronomous, but not unfree. It maintains the rights of subjectivity and renewed recognition.

(ii) Liminality and repentance. The transgressor recognizes the moral law as his law, and thus his own dividedness. He suffers through this recognition, through the split in himself which it forces him to acknowledge, and through the process required to restore wholeness: recognizing the

---

[36] I have tried to get at their ideal types, of course. In practice these emotional structures, together with those of indignation, resentment, fear, etc. can be more or less acute, more or less encouraged, more or less differentiated or intermingled.

[37] As mentioned in n. 1, legal punishment is a multi-purpose phenomenon. None of what follows is meant to deny that the forms of coercion conventionally counted under legal punishment may involve major and variable considerations of deterrence, education—even preventive detention. These coercive instruments of law could be included in the 'right' (i.e. law) of the criminal only in the minimal or abstract sense that (i) if they are rational and the criminal wills rationally he wills that they should be used, and thus used against him and (ii) if he can be said to be a criminal at all he must be capable of willing rationally.

Though Hegel appeals to this basic starting point he goes well beyond it to an insightful phenomenology of punishment, specifically in the idea that punishment annuls and transcends the crime.

transgressing self as oneself but at the same time going on from it or beyond it—'superseding' it.

(iii) Recognition, return to the community: atonement. This at-one-ment with the community is also at-one-ment of the will: re-identification of the individual will with the moral will, return to autonomy.

But why does (iii) require (ii)—why does at-one-ment require the suffering of repentance?[38] Generally, if I fall short of full freedom through some passing aberration of rationality I simply *resolve* to try harder. Why should resolve not be enough in the particular case of moral transgression? Why must repentance involve not just a *resolve* to do better but a particular sort of suffering—*guilt*, perhaps expressed in freely undertaken penance—at what one has done?

Suffering is required to 'annul the sin'—or rather, to anneal the self: moral punishment (punishment as penitence) reforges the arrow of the will through pain. But then the question simply becomes, why should this reforging, in the particular case of transgression, require pain?

What kind of explanation are we asking for here? What is being called for may be more like a *justification*. Pain is bad, so must it not be outweighed by a compensating good? And if the compensating good is a firmly resolved will, would it not be better if that could be achieved without the pain, for example by a simple, painless but effective, resolution? Is it just that, as a matter of fact, effective resolution requires pain?

In similar spirit we might ask why, if, unintentionally, one has grievously injured someone it is not enough to compensate but also necessary to *feel* sorry—that is, to undergo that pain. Or we might ask why the pain of grief is necessary for recovery after the loss of a close relative or friend. Why do people not just experience it but feel the *need* to experience it, so that they are so to speak locked in and unable to move on and beyond if for example the body is lost and cannot be buried?

In none of these cases is our attitude to the suffering instrumental, a case of taking your medicine because no less painful remedy is available. Grief and penitence are particularly comparable in this respect. Each is embraced for itself, not as an instrument but as a friend, and each restores wholeness by annealment. Repentance identifies with the transgressing self as oneself but at the same time goes on from it or beyond it, grief at the loss of another identifies with that other as a part of oneself but at the

[38] At-one-ment, the condition of being at one, is the original sense of 'atonement'. Other patterns or metaphors associated with punishment include (i) redemption: an obligation 'owed' to society; non-payment puts one in bondage until redeemed; (ii) propitiation: an action which incurs the wrath of the gods is calmed by gifts. These appeal to an emotional logic distinct from that of the dialectic of atonement, though they are intertwined with it.

same time goes on from it or beyond it. (Though in each case the healing of the wound may still leave the knife point inside it.) But at this point explanation, at any rate at the hermeneutic level, has to stop. It is a fact about us that repentance, regret, grief are ways of restoring ourselves with ourselves and others, and that we find them necessary and good.

The first element in the Hegelian thesis that punishment is the right of the transgressor is the claim that what is punished is a breach of the transgressor's own law, the law affirmed by his own will in its universal shape. However this in itself does not explain why that will should prescribe *punishment* for the transgression. But as Hegel also says, punishment annuls the crime. I suggest, then, that this is best understood along the lines just developed. It is not an appeal to cleansing magic (bleaching the stain) but rather to the structure of feeling which underlies that cleansing symbolism. Punishment annuls the transgression in that it anneals the transgressor, restoring him to wholeness. It is the 'negation of the negation': the transgressor is in denial, the pain of repentance is the denial of that denial. Thus, secondly, punishment is the transgressor's right in the way that grief is the right of the mourner. It is a right to be reintegrated, reunified in one's freedom, through the human processes which must be gone through to achieve that result—and which are inseparable from it in just the way that Hegel so rightly underlines:

In the present discussion, we are solely concerned with the need to cancel transgression—not as a source of *evil*, but as an infringement of right as right—and also with the kind of *existence* which transgression possesses, which must also be cancelled. This existence is the true evil which must be removed, and the essential point is [to discover] where it lies.[39]

8. MORALITÄT AND SITTLICHKEIT

Hegel's treatment of freedom, morality, and reason is strongly continuous with Kant's. It is no more possible to transgress in full freedom on Hegel's view than on Kant's, and the reasons why it is impossible are the same: will is practical reason, full freedom is rationality, in full freedom the subject's will affirms the validity of the moral law.[40] On the other hand Hegel criti-

---

[39] Hegel (1991a), 125 (§99)—I have put the word 'transgression' in place of 'crime'.

[40] 'In doing my duty, I am with myself [*bei mir selbst*] and free' (Hegel 1991a), 161 (§133 Addition H). It may be thought that Hegel's views on the absolute right of world history (e.g. §345) imply the possibility of fully free transgression. Cf. Wood (1990: 234–6, on Hegel's amoralism. However, it seems to me that Wood makes Hegel's view needlessly paradoxical. If Hegel is to be consistent he should not say that it can be right not to do one's duty. He should instead say that there are critical periods of history in which duty lapses—

cizes the rationalism of Kant's conception of reason and the empty subjectivity of his conception of duty. The conclusions to which we have been
led, though they have not followed Hegel's path, support Hegel both in his
agreement and in his disagreement with Kant—with one potential but
crucial exception.

The way in which they support the points on which Kant and Hegel
agree—that will is practical reason and that transgression is never fully
free—was outlined in Sections 1–3. In Sections 4–5 I argued that Kant was
right in identifying personality[41] with practical rationality but wrong in
identifying practical reason, the broad notion required for this identity to
hold, with *pure* practical reason. This criticism of Kant at least parallels
Hegel's accusation that Kant's concept of reason is itself rationalistic. For
since broad practical reason encompasses the totality of reasons for
action, including those which link evaluative and practical reasons, broad
practical rationality must correspondingly encompass emotional spontaneity. Only within this comprehensive conception of rationality can one
identify selfhood and self-determination with rationality, and only in
terms of it can one understand the hermeneutic of moral wrongdoing and
punishment. I further urged (Sections 6–7) that Hegel provides a largely
sound account of that hermeneutic.

However I also accepted that pure practical reason has a content:
impartiality. If that is right it will not be possible to dismiss any appeal to
it as an 'empty formalism'.[42] Perhaps Hegel would deny that it can be said
to have such a content: this is the potentially crucial point of disagreement
mentioned above. On the other hand, one can read him as arguing only the
following two points: (i) that the attempt to derive moral obligation from
the a priori idea of a rational requirement as such is empty, and (ii) that
even a constraint of impartiality (or Kant's formula of humanity understood in some such sense) cannot be used to *derive* moral obligations. In
that case I think his claims can be defended. We have already discussed the
first claim. The second claim requires us to take stock of his contrast
between *Moralität* and *Sittlichkeit*.

The terms are usually translated respectively as 'morality' and 'ethics'
or 'ethical life'. But for present purposes these are unsatisfactory trans-
lations: it is better in this context to translate *Sittlichkeit* simply as

in which the (positive) *Sittlichkeit* of the time cannot in some aspect be endorsed. In those
periods one cannot affirmatively do what is considered one's duty and so cannot in that way
be 'with oneself'.

[41] Personality in this sense is still not the same as actual or empirical character, since the
latter comprises what the individual is actually disposed to think, feel, and do, as against
his or her determinate rational potential.

[42] Hegel (1991), 162 (§ 135).

'morality' and *Moralität* as 'morality conceived as pure practical reason', or 'morality conceived from the standpoint of pure ethical theory'—taking pure ethical theory and pure practical reason to come to the same thing. For *Sittlichkeit* is the moral institution—the received ideas and practices about the blameworthy, with their embodiments in custom and law and their tradition—either positively or ideally conceived. While when Hegel talks of *Moralität* he is talking of a certain modern, individualist, and rationalistic, conception of morality, and the outlook and practice arising therefrom, rather than of morality as such.[43]

This conception purports to derive moral obligations from pure practical reason. Hegel takes as its characteristic form the Kantian notion of a self-legislating subject evolving, entirely from its own a priori reflection, the content of the moral law. And he thinks that notion is doomed to emptiness by its own purism. Now it seems to me that even though pure ethical theory is not empty of content there is a sense in which Hegel is right.

Ethical theory is not empty of content—it has the notions of impartiality, the good, the desirable at its disposal; it can investigate them in abstract terms or apply them to the critique of a moral tradition. Yet Hegel is right to hold that moral obligations are neither derived nor derivable from any theses which pure ethical theory alone can deploy: 'From this point of view, no immanent theory of duties is possible.'[44] This is as good a criticism of utilitarians or contractualists, insofar as they try to do that, as it is of Kant. Pure ethical reflection can deflect and reshape a moral tradition, but it cannot give rise to a moral tradition, or rebuild it from the foundations by a process of radical doubt. It operates on an *actually existing* moral tradition, grounded in the hermeneutics of blame and collectively or dialogically developed. (Just as canons of scientific method operate on an existing cognitive tradition which is grounded in default presuppositions about the world and collectively developed.)

To drive this home, let's imagine a hypothetical *ethical* agent and contrast him with moral agents. Let's imagine this merely ethical agent as someone who has pure practical reason but experiences no guilt or blame feelings, or respect (in the Kantian sense) for moral agency, and (for the sake of starkness let's suppose) no shame or disdain, or regret. The ethical

---

[43] Ideal *Sittlichkeit,* towards which (Hegel thinks) modernity develops, incorporates the right of the subjective will (of insight into the moral law) on which *Moralität* insists, but reconciles the moral [*sittlich*] disposition with the moral [*sittlich*] order. This is the ideal morality of modern times (in Hegel's view; cf. Essay XI). It would be useful to reserve the term 'ethical life' not as a translation of *Sittlichkeit* but for a broader use, covering all aspects of the evaluation of character, activity, and outcome, not just the moral.

[44] Hegel (1991), 162 (§135).

agent is not to be confused with that much-invoked figure, the purely instrumental agent. He acknowledges the rationally constraining force of impartiality, but has no moral or quasi-moral sentiments. He has other sentiments, and we are not assuming that he is perfectly rational, i.e. fully free—he may suffer from weakness, distortion, or lack. When the ethical agent sees that he has not done the best thing, he *resolves* to do better—at least as effectively we do—but he experiences no guilt, shame, or regret. And perhaps he is inclined to lament that others do experience these evidently painful but apparently unproductive feelings.

How does the merely ethical agent differ from us, and would it be better or worse to be like that? (Although this is the only conception of ethical life which some ethical theorists seem to present I think that it is actually very hard concretely to imagine someone who is fully like that.)

First of all he suffers an epistemic deficit, because he knows the aim, the general good, but has no moral compass. So quite often where we experience moral constraints on our action, that is, we 'immanently' experience *duty*, he won't know what is the *best* thing to do. True, this assumes that the moral constraints we experience do on the whole point in the right direction—but then according to the Hegelian standpoint of conservative holism, or reason in history, that is a default assumption which we rightly make.

Also, he will lack understanding of others' moral sentiments and the capacity to judge their reasonableness or otherwise. So he will not make what we see as appropriate decisions—for example because he won't appreciate that someone has a reasonable moral expectation (say to be invited to stay for Christmas) which must be respected. Put another way: he will have to rely on a moral agent to outline to him the morality-dependent costs and benefits.

But, other than epistemically, is he worse off? On our account, to lack moral sentiments is not to lack freedom—except insofar as the inability to judge of reasons to blame is itself an impairment of the practical rationality with which we have identified freedom. Still, what the ethical agent mainly lacks is not freedom but humanity, that is, a capacity of mutual recognition described above, recognition as the attitude of respect for moral spontaneity, which we certainly value profoundly.

But, standing still further back, one might nevertheless ask whether the system of morality is *on the whole* a good thing for us or a bad one. Is it a good thing to entrench the emotions of respect, guilt, and blame into a social discipline, or should we try, so far as possible, to release people from them?

The question must come from some conception of ethical value, and it must assume that there is an alternative. To think morality is dysfunctional one must have an ethical end in mind which is not itself moral. For example a utilitarian might claim that the blame-sentiment should be downgraded as dysfunctional, perhaps after some level of social development has been reached. Blame and guilt are after all hostile feelings which cause pain, even if their other face, respect, is something which we deeply desire to have.

Yet, on any conception of ethical value, isn't the idea that we would be better off without the social authority those feelings presently carry utopian? We can split this into some further questions. First, can human beings reach a level of practical rationality at which the need for any discipline, spontaneous or artificial, drops away? This might be the case in a community of sufficiently well-motivated ethical agents. But if, as seems obvious, the answer as far as human beings are concerned is 'no', the choice must lie between spontaneous systems and costly and repressive artificial ones, and then within the spontaneous, between the system of guilt and blame and such other systems as that of shame and disdain.

Again, it is surely obvious that to eradicate all spontaneous emotional systems of self-discipline in favour of artificially imposed systems of social control will not make human life better, on any reasonable understanding of what makes human life good. But that still leaves open the question whether we have the best balance of disciplinary sentiments in our actual ethical life. Might it not be better for us to shift away from our system of guilt and blame towards a system of shame and disdain?[45]

A society which shifted emphasis towards the latter would also have to shift—how far is hard to tell—from modern individualism and modern respect, i.e. the moral respect which, we think, can be gained or lost irrespective of one's standing or popularity in society or one's achievements in life. One can think of two ways a 'shame culture' could go: towards hierarchy and some sort of modern recreation of aristocratic ethics, or towards an egalitarian collectivism regulated by shaming rituals and 're-education' (as with the Red Guards).

Aristocratic ethics assumes that people are irredeemably unequal in the dominating hierarchy of what makes one noble—and indeed, as Nietzsche emphasized, positively relies on the 'pathos of distance'. Collective shame-culture relies on the shaming discipline of the group and in effect removes the right of the subjective will—personal responsibility or conscience. The system of morality, realistically understood, allows one to differentiate the degrees of freedom people bring to moral agency, while nevertheless holding on to the idea that the moral law is internally promulgated to (almost)

---

[45] Nietzsche's question, also pursued by Bernard Williams, e.g. in Williams (1993).

all. It is not true that liberal individualism has to rely on the dubious claim to *equality* of respect.[46] But it *is* true that it relies on moral agency having a *sufficient* presence, scope, and gravitational attraction to make personal responsibility work as the spontaneous regulating core of liberal order— to establish the right of the subjective will. In that way the categories of morality: self-legislation, guilt, blame, respect, and recognition are indispensable categories of liberal ethics. Yet critics, such as Alasdair MacIntyre,[47] may be right to urge that liberal individualism itself has a tendency to make pure ethical theory so dominant that it begins to put those very categories in question. In that case liberalism needs to learn a lesson of self-restraint or historical sense in regard to the moral tradition, and Hegel is certainly one of the places to go to learn it.

[46] See Essay XI.   [47] MacIntyre (1981).

PART IV

Politics and the Ideal

IX

Liberal Elitism

1. THE LIBERAL AND THE POPULIST

'Liberal elitism' is mostly a derogatory term. In this country such British institutions as the *Guardian* newspaper, the Anglican hierarchy, do-gooders associated with universities and the media—the 'liberal establishment'—stand accused of it. Or more accurately, they *used* to be accused of it. There is an analogous stream of criticism in the United States. It often comes from the free-market populist Right. But it can also come from the Left insofar as that dons a populist mantle; though in the past left-wing movements in politics inherited, from the European and particularly German response to the enlightenment, a substantive non-populist legacy in their conceptions of the good society and the developed human life.

It would be a mistake to dismiss the coupling of liberal and elitist values as a politician's device. On the contrary, the connection is historical and it runs deep. The classical liberals of the nineteenth century held that stable and progressive liberal order absolutely requires the flourishing, and due social influence, of moral and intellectual (not just technical) elites. This was one of their central themes as they anticipated the emergence of mass democracy. It is a significant fact about the subsequent development of liberalism in this century that we should have lost sight of it: in the market place of politics 'liberal elitism' has become a term of abuse, in the academy, by contrast, the interpretations of liberalism which are currently most influential—to the point where many writers now take them effectively as definitive of what liberalism is—would make 'liberal elitism' a contradiction in terms.

The simple response is that liberalism differs from populism; the former opposes authoritarianism (restriction of freedom)—it is the latter which opposes 'elitism'. How then come the two to be confused?

There are two exceedingly influential tenets which belong, one might say, to the philosophic deep structure of populism; forming a major

First published in D. Milligan and W. Watts Miller (eds.), *Liberalism, Citizenship and Autonomy,* Avebury, 1992: 134–56. I am grateful to Gordon Graham for helpful discussion.

element in 'the spirit of our age' they penetrate political and social thought, and thought about morality and the arts, extraordinarily widely—but they are hardly discussed explicitly outside philosophical circles. The first tenet is that you cannot deliberate about ends and values; the second tenet is that the ends and values of all individuals deserve equal respect. It is further essential, for populism, that the second tenet be understood negatively, as deriving from the first—individuals deserve equal respect *because* there can be no ground for giving them unequal respect—the ultimate ends and values of individuals are simply unappraisable. This being so, all attempts to evaluate ends become unenlightened prejudice or mere snobbery.

Populism as a force in politics includes currents other and more obvious than these two tenets: in particular, insofar as it tends to majoritarian imposition of conventional ends and mass values it shifts away from liberalism. Such imposition is not an unintelligible outcome of the two tenets, though it is not an automatic one; for if ends are held to be unappraisable, the effective social result may well be a tyranny of conventions. Since the dissenting individual cannot defend his ends and values by claiming them to be superior, he seems to glory in difference and eccentricity as such.

There are various other complications. For example, any political doctrine must recognize a category of anti-social ends. The more attractive side of the populist spectrum identifies this with the liberal notion of harm to others.[1] The way in which populism opposes elites must also be kept clear. It does not hold that all are equal in point of energy, or of technical, organizational, or usefully innovative skills.

However it is the two underlying philosophical tenets that I want to discuss. Obviously there is considerable scope for confusion with liberalism here. The second tenet in particular causes confusion with liberalism because the ideal of equal respect is an important part of the liberal heritage. In the populist version the second tenet is derived from the first; in classical liberalism, I shall suggest, it was derived from religious or metaphysical or at least regulative principles which are now difficult to sustain. We shall have to return to that difficulty by the end. But though classical liberals founded equality of respect on the potentially equal rational autonomy, or responsibility, of all individuals, that did not prevent them from recognizing that individuals are far from equally rational and autonomous in empirical fact. Hence the importance, for classical liberal-

---

[1] Liberalism and populism were thoroughly interfused in 'Thatcherism': it had a modern-populist vein but it also had a more deeply English and Evangelical doctrine of self-management and improvement—an important constituent of English liberalism in the 19th cent. Though these elements blended they also warred with each other.

ism, of the idea of progress, and of the idea of elites which lead that progress in a peaceful and socially stable way.

Elitism, as I shall use the term here, will be opposed to populism: it denies the first tenet, and the second understood as following from the first. It holds, then, that there can be substantive and not merely instrumental deliberation on moral, cultural, and spiritual questions, that some individuals are more penetrating judges of these questions than others, and that some are intellectually or morally more creative than others. Second, it affirms that such individuals are socially vital and must exert a due influence through the recognition of their authority in their sphere. This one may call moderate or liberal elitism.

The critical question for liberalism is how that authority is to take effect. Should the gifted few be formed into a Church, Vanguard Party, Caste—an estate of society, with formal powers? To answer in the affirmative would be to endorse a strong elitism to which liberalism is opposed—but the transition from moderate to strong elitism is not clear-cut, though it is vital for liberalism, because institutions can in practice approximate more or less closely to the formal establishment of such an estate. There is a spectrum, and the liberal ideal unequivocally opposes elitism of the strong kind. Yet on the other hand classical liberals of the nineteenth century were just as unequivocally elitists in the moderate sense; they certainly held that due social influence of superior spirits was a precondition of stable and progressive liberal order. Thus in practice the important and difficult question was where to establish the healthy point on the spectrum, the question, for example, between Matthew Arnold and John Stuart Mill.

It still is an important and difficult question, and in practice the institutions and the controversies of contemporary liberal democracies recognize it as such. But it is difficult to get it stated in philosophically clear and robust terms, because in the twentieth century liberalism has staged a long intellectual retreat, which is perhaps only now ending and turning. Modernist (as against classical) liberalism—an embattled and distinctly ingratiating doctrine—has grounded equality of respect precisely in the populist way: basing equality of respect and 'ethical neutrality' on the uncriticizability of ends. I shall argue that this is a modernist heresy, which must be renounced as certain other philosophical aspects of the modernist inheritance must be renounced.

I begin by outlining the nineteenth-century view (Section 2), proceed to contrast it with current 'liberal' wisdom (Section 3), and finally turn to outlining the philosophical foundations which provide (as it seems to me) true grounding for essential liberal positions (Section 4).

2. VICTORIAN VALUES

The nineteenth century is the classical phase of liberal thought. This was something more concrete—more complex, tempered, and nuanced—than the liberalism of John Locke or of Adam Smith; classical liberalism had experienced the French Revolution and it had imbibed romantic conceptions of the autonomous self. These liberals wanted no return to the *ancien régime*; they stood by the doctrines of 1789. But they had been sensitized to the dangers of revolutionary populism. In opposition to Jacobinism and Rousseau they asserted the fundamental separateness of civil liberty—freedom from political and social constraint—and political liberty, the right of equal participation in democratic process. The problem, as it had emerged in the later stages of the revolution and its Bonapartist sequel, or as it could be observed in the democratic institutions of America, was the danger posed for civil liberty by political liberty—the potential for despotic legislation in a democratic State.[2]

One fundamental ideal of classical liberalism is the rational autonomy, or in other words the responsibility, of the individual. That ideal provides a rationale for democracy;[3] but further, and potentially in counterbalance to democracy, it entails equal protection under the rule of a system of law containing effective safeguards for the so-called 'negative' civil liberties. It is, again, rational autonomy, conceived as the core of citizenship, that drives liberalism into a concern with social justice. The liberal's conception of justice encompasses threshold as well as formal elements: procedural fairness, equality of opportunity, impartial enforcement of legal rights—but also a level of universal provision which ideally enables all to develop the capacities for free and responsible citizenship.

On the question of what that enabling threshold of provision must be, and what the role of the State is in providing it, nineteenth-century liberalism witnessed a shift towards ever more generous and interventionist ideas. The question continues to divide social from free market liberals,

---

[2] This was particularly a theme of French liberals such as Constant, de Staël, Guizot, Tocqueville. Thus Tocqueville refers as a matter of course to 'la race ordinaire des révolutionnaires français qui, par liberté du peuple, ont toujours entendu le despotisme exercé au nom du peuple', *Souvenirs*, in Tocqueville (1964: xii. 182).

[3] Which is not to deny the well-known ambivalence of classical liberals towards universal franchise. The *ideal* provides a rationale for democracy: it envisages autonomy of all persons as both a capacity and a freedom, a freedom not fully realized without equal political rights. But one cannot simply assume that the equal freedom should be fully realized when the equal capacity has not been. (Mill's view of democracy as an educative instrument, and its relation to his elitism, are usefully surveyed in Garforth 1980: ch. 4.)

but liberalism as such maintains the idea that threshold provision is *enabling*—motivated by what is necessary to release the individual's powers. Within those constraints it endorses markets and competition. In that respect it differs from socialism, which values collective action just because it is collective and economically egalitarian—though social liberalism became ever harder to distinguish from socialism at the turn of the century, and now socialism becomes ever harder to distinguish from social liberalism.

However, our concern is with a set of problems which the great dividing controversies about social justice have tended to obscure.

Classical liberals worried on the one hand about whether liberal values could, on their own, cement allegiance to a sustainable social order—they worried on the other hand that mediocre and conventional values would readily fill the gap with a too rigid and too brittle cement. On the one hand, the vision of a babble of voices descending from discussion through controversy to denunciation and violence; on the other, rigid elimination of effective discussion, and imposition of social conformity—by the State or by civil society itself. How should one steer between a crisis of allegiance, rightly feared by conservatives, and descent into mediocre stagnation? The solution was a social order which would give full scope to the moral influence of outstanding individuals. The ability of gifted individuals—conforming and non-conforming—to make their influence felt was an absolute precondition of liberal pluralism and of liberal progress. In its absence fragmentation would indeed be overcome, but at an insufficiently high level of excellence and liberty: the 'Chinese stationariness' to which Mill more than once referred.

Such fears were no monopoly of post-revolutionary liberals: they were a refrain of many nineteenth-century thinkers, echoed in Marx's Asiatic mode of production, taken to extremes in different ways by Carlyle or Nietzsche. The liberal version of this widely influential conception was that outstanding individuals were indeed essential, but could claim no authority beyond what they could establish by example and persuasion. Of course it is just here, as we have noted, that the crucial problems lie. Still, the issues of principle, at least, emerge with brilliant clarity in Mill's assimilation and criticism, over the middle fifty years of the century, of its most characteristic and stimulating social philosophies.

On Liberty announces the importance of gifted individuals in ringing terms:

No government by a democracy or a numerous aristocracy, either in its political acts or in the opinions, qualities, and tone of mind which it fosters, ever did or could rise above mediocrity, except in so far as the sovereign Many have let themselves be guided (which in their best times they always have done) by the counsels and influence of a more highly gifted and instructed One or Few. The initiation of all wise or noble things, comes and must come from individuals; generally at first from some one individual. The honour and glory of the average man is that he is capable of following that initiative; that he can respond internally to wise and noble things, and be led to them with his eyes open.

Such leadership cannot however be imposed or exacted.

I am not countenancing the sort of 'hero-worship' which applauds the strong man of genius for forcibly seizing on the government of the world and making it do his bidding in spite of itself. All he can claim, is freedom to point out the way. The power of compelling others into it, is not only inconsistent with the freedom and development of all the rest, but corrupting to the strong man himself.[4]

The average man can be relied upon to see the rightness of the way when it is pointed out—that is his 'honour and glory'; in the very next paragraph Mill adds that

If a person possesses any tolerable amount of common sense and experience, his own mode of laying out his existence is the best, not because it is the best in itself, but because it is his own mode.[5]

He thinks that people in general, outside 'backward states of society in which the race itself may be considered as in its nonage', already do possess the necessary amount of 'common sense and experience'.[6] They are not all as creative, as morally discerning or as brave as a minority among them, but they have the rational capacity and mental spontaneity to recognize and follow 'genius, mental vigour and moral courage'—when they perceive it.

This estimate of the common man is the backbone of Mill's various resistances: to state authority, to bureaucracy ('A bureaucracy always tends to become a pedantocracy'), to conventional majoritarian opinion, to the Saint-Simonian idea of a 'pouvoir spirituel'. It is the groundwork of that pluralistic analysis of European progressiveness which he shared with French liberals. Progress and liberty depend on a salutary antagonism of social forces:

No one of the ancient forms of society contained in itself that systematic antagonism, which we believe to be the only condition under which stability and progressiveness can be permanently reconciled to one another.[7]

---

[4] Mill (1963–91), xviii. 269 (*Liberty*, ch. III, para. 12).   [5] Ibid. 270.

[6] Ibid. 224. Laying out one's own existence is good, insofar as autonomous living is itself an ingredient of well-being. But it is only one ingredient: lacking common sense and experience one can make a big enough mess of one's life for the gain of autonomy to be cancelled by miseries and missed opportunities.

[7] Mill (1963–91): xx. 269 ('Guizot's Essays and Lectures on History').

The capacity of the average man to learn his own lessons from others and to apply them himself, the recognition that some minds are more critically or creatively equipped than others, the need to safeguard conflicting tendencies, were Mill's guiding themes in his encounters with conservative philosophy in his youth and with socialism at the end of his life. They required, Mill thought, an educated class with leisure to engage in free inquiry but they did not require a class formally constituted in institutions with defined social powers.

Coleridge in England, the Saint-Simonians in France, had proposed an institutionalized intellectual and moral elite—but it was the Coleridgean rather than the Saint-Simonian formulation which impressed him, as it impressed so many Victorians (the Arnolds, F. D. Maurice, Gladstone). Coleridge had taught the need for a '*clerisy* of the nation, or national church': a 'permanent class or order', distributed throughout the country, and funded by the State.[8] He was to be honoured, Mill thought,

for having vindicated against Bentham and Adam Smith and the whole eighteenth century, the principle of an endowed class, for the cultivation of learning, and for diffusing its results among the community . . . On this subject we are entirely at one with Coleridge . . . and we consider the definitive establishment of this fundamental principle, to be one of the permanent benefits which political science owes to the Conservative philosophers.[9]

The fundamental principle owed to Conservative philosophers, and asserted against Bentham and Adam Smith, was the public endowment of learning! But Mill's assessment of Comte and the Saint-Simonians showed

---

[8] The 'final intention of the whole order', according to Coleridge, was

to preserve the stores, and to guard the treasures, of past civilization, and thus to bind the present with the past; to perfect and add to the same, and thus to connect the present with the future; but especially to diffuse through the whole community, and to every native entitled to its law and rights, that quantity and quality of knowledge which was indispensable both for the understanding of those rights, and for the performance of the duties correspondent. Finally, to secure for the nation, if not a superiority over the neighbouring states, yet an equality at least, in that character of general civilization, which equally with, or rather more than, fleets, armies, and revenue, forms the ground of its defensive and offensive power. (Coleridge 1976: 43–4)

Or again:

The proper *object* and end of the National Church is civilisation with freedom; and the duty of its ministers, could they be contemplated merely and exclusively as officiaries of the *National* Church, [and not also as Christian ministers] would be fulfilled in the communication of that degree and kind of knowledge to all, the possession of which is necessary for all in order to their CIVILITY. By civility I mean all the qualities essential to a citizen. (ibid. 54)

[9] Mill (1963–91), x. 150–1.

the limits on how far he would go. 'Their criticisms on the common doctrines of Liberalism' seemed to him 'full of important truth'[10] but their
practical policies amounted to liberticide. 'M. Comte has got hold of half
the truth, and the so-called liberal or revolutionary school possesses the
other half.' It is, he conceded to Comte,

without doubt the necessary condition of mankind to receive most of their opinions on the authority of those who have specially studied the matters to which
they relate . . . [but] in order that this salutary ascendancy over opinion should be
exercised by the most eminent thinkers, it is not necessary that they should be
associated and organized.[11]

This states, with characteristic succinctness, the guiding outlines of
classical liberal elitism. But it undeniably leaves important and pressing
questions of practical balance open to debate. Let us turn to some contemporary encounters with that same debate.

3. POPULIST VALUES

In a recent 'CounterBlast' pamphlet, *Universities: Knowing Our Minds*,
Mary Warnock asserted that universities

must be seen as the *source* of new knowledge, the *origin* of that critical, undog-
matic, imaginative examination of received wisdom without which a country cannot be expected to have its voice heard, and from which ultimately all intellectual
standards flow. It is this critical and imaginative function that is in danger, if civil
servants and Ministers show themselves unable to accept the intrinsic *authority* of
the learned, the academic and the scholarly.
    There is nowhere else that such intellectual authority can come from but the
universities themselves. This is an area where the concept of the free market is simply not applicable.[12]

The *Times Higher Education Supplement* commented in a leader as follows:

[T]he central thrust of Mary Warnock's argument is that Government and people
should respect the *authority* of higher education. But liberals as well as, perhaps
more than, Thatcherites are incapable of such respect.
    Both are incapable because it is the nature of the modern world to question
and inevitably to compromise all authority whether religious, political, social,
cultural, or intellectual. It deconstructs to reconstruct. And higher education is

---

[10] Mill (1963–91), i (*Autobiography*), 173.
[11] Mill (1963–91), x (*Auguste Comte and Positivism*), 313–14.
[12] Warnock (1989: 42).

probably the most subversive of all modern institutions. There is no place now for deference. . . [liberals] refuse to respect the authority of higher education because they recognize its gathering diversity, its deepening social and economic commitments, its intimate relation to our culture, which prevent it standing apart from or above Government and people. The university is embraced by the affectionate familiarity of our democracy. If it had to be deferred to, in the eyes of liberals it would have failed.

[Conservatives] refuse to respect the authority of higher education because, deep down, they fear its capacity for enlightenment and emancipation . . . [the subversive qualities of universities must be] confined to the technical sphere.[13]

Now one may well consider it a dangerous exaggeration to say—the classical liberalism outlined in our previous section would so consider it—that intellectual authority can come from 'nowhere else' but universities. The universities are major reservoirs of intellectual authority and indeed of moral authority, of people competent, desirous, and funded to take part in the collective process wherein benchmarks of intellectual and moral discussion are fashioned and maintained. But they are not, and never should be, the sole source of such authority: they have a responsibility to that process but it could never be even largely, let alone wholly, confined within their walls.

Similarly, it is far too quick on Mary Warnock's part to pass from recognition of the indispensableness of authority in the setting of standards, to the assertion that this is an 'area where the concept of the free market is simply not applicable'. In one quite particular sense it is truistically not applicable: a standard, or a quality-ordering, is something logically distinct from a price which clears the market at a particular level of supply and demand. It is not the market which determines what the relative quality of different kinds of apple is. However it does not yet follow that the market has no role to play in determining what kinds and qualities of higher education, or apples, should be supplied and at what price.

Of course the supply of higher education is a very different thing, involving much more complex issues for liberal theory, than the supply of apples. The respective role of State, university, and student in determining what is taught and researched in universities is a major question of public affairs, drawing together economic, historic, and philosophical issues.

And undoubtedly the issue of moral and intellectual authority is one of them. On this issue classical liberalism is patently on the side of Mary Warnock. It most certainly does not deny that the process of setting and maintaining standards requires authority; it positively affirms that truly authoritative voices should make themselves heard and be given due weight.

[13] *Times Higher Education Supplement*, editorial 10 Nov. 1989, no. 888: 40.

The liberals envisaged by the *Times Higher Education Supplement* have a remarkably Jacobin and populist strain. Of all institutions in that modern world whose nature is to 'compromise all authority', the university, we are told, is (probably) the most subversive. Liberals, according to the *Times Higher Education Supplement*, welcome that probable fact—they welcome the university being prevented from 'standing apart from or above Government and people'—they sentimentally contemplate the spectacle of it being 'embraced by the affectionate familiarity of our democracy'.

Outside the 'technical sphere' of scientific and technological innovation (no small sphere!), the university's function seems to be to emancipate by deconstructing and subverting. We are told it deconstructs to reconstruct—but we are not told how religious, political, or cultural reconstruction can proceed, unless the authoritative claim of some specific proposals as to what construction should take place comes to be recognized. For in these fields, as classical liberalism clearly saw, majority opinion is not necessarily right just because it is majority opinion.

What then do we make of the *Times Higher Education Supplement*'s editorial view of liberalism? What it in fact presents us with is not classical liberalism but modernist populism—a spirit which, in so many different ways and dimensions, emerges precisely in reaction against classical liberalism; just as classical liberalism itself emerged partly in reaction to the Rousseauesque, or sentimental-'subversive', side of the Revolution.[14]

It would be absurd and unfair to over-analyse a brief editorial comment. Let us directly address the spirit which seems to inform it. Emancipation, in this familiar modernist vision, is an essentially negative process, a process of eliminating prejudice, undermining false consciousness, discarding artificial constraint, subverting the mythology of the rational self. What then is left at the end of that process? The sentimental innocent motivated not by corruptly civilized *amour-propre*, but by undomesticated *amour-de-soi* and *pitié*? The existential self arbitrarily choosing its projects? Or its close cousin, the economic individual who efficiently services his elementary, incorrigible, pre-given ends?[15]

---

[14] Modernist populism: the phrase is not meant to suggest that modernism as such is populist—many of the earlier artistic and philosophical modernists held strongly elitist attitudes. It is closer to the truth to say that the *interplay* between elitism and populism contributes one of the main dialectics at work within modernism—with the reaction against classical liberalism the factor common to both sides.

[15] Rousseau is a pivot between the ideals of sincerity and 'authenticity'(see Trilling 1972). His ideal should be distinguished from the later classical-liberal ideal of spontaneity, as exemplified in ch. 3 of Mill's *Liberty*. However the noble savage remains an eminently concrete character in comparison to the existential chooser or the economic man: both

Modernist authenticity, in opposition to liberal rationality, is the common theme of all these variations. Liberal rationality posits a human potential for self-mastery which can be realized and positively developed, or denied and degraded; and it assumes substantive—and plural—conceptions of human good, which are discovered as part of self-discovery. Culture, on this view, is a product of human beings which, in some of its forms, can imprison them, yet in some form is the indispensable agent of their emancipation. It has *both* these powers. To find the forms which emancipate, instead of imprisoning, is for the liberal the critical problem. There is no truly human development in a pre-cultural or anti-cultural State: that basic thesis of nineteenth-century historicism was as much accepted by Mill, let alone T. H. Green, as by Hegel or Comte. Modernist authenticity on the other hand sees culture as a mask or a cage to be discarded at will, freeing a naturally preformed, or alternatively an existentially blank, individual.

Its theme is subjectivist: about human ends and about reason. Ends are simply given by one's desires, or alternatively, they are existentially chosen. At any rate they are not duly and reasonably shaped by common reflection on what human ends can and should be. There is no *point d'appui*, in historically evolving human nature, which enables such shaping. Since there is not, how can there be such a thing as the rational culture of the feelings, or a positive autonomy which results from mastering one's feelings by the help of that culture? Reasoning reduces to the 'technical sphere': beyond lies, in ideological camouflage, the will to power. Or to approach the same points from a more prosaic but equally modernist angle: if all truths divide into the strictly definitional and the strictly empirical, and if an unbridgeable gulf lies between ought and is, what space can be found for a philosophical anthropology inquiring into norms for thought and action, and grounded in reflection on human nature? Equality of respect follows, in the sense that nothing merits *inequality* of respect; merely technical gifts, however useful, being clearly not morally relevant.

'There is no place now for deference.' The healthy and liberating achievement recorded in that must be fully and gladly granted. Could anyone decently wish a return to forelock-touching or humbugging arrogance? But that major moral advance of this century should not obscure

Rousseau and Mill envisage an organic human nature, mutable by civilization (even though their attitudes to civilization differ); both contrast strongly with modernist conceptions of the self as sheer nothingness, or as an abstract bundle of exogeneously given desires. Such conceptions have recently been criticized by 'communitarian' critics of modern liberal theory; it is important to see that this criticism would largely miss its mark if directed at the historical tradition of liberalism, however well taken it is when directed at deviations from it induced by the spirit of populist modernism.

an associated, less major, but still important fallacy. For 'deference' is one of the magical words of modernist populism, possessing the inverse alchemical power of changing gold into base metal. There can be an un-self-abasing deference: to the authority of an educated judgement, to the legitimacy of reason as reason, which can be recognized (and is more easily recognized) in full confidence of one's own standing. It is, to quote Mill once more, not 'the blind submission of dunces to men of knowledge, but the intelligent deference of those who know much, to those who know still more'.[16] It might be better to say, to the claims of knowledge and reason as such—but only if one remembers that abstractions make claims only in concrete relations between human beings.

Closely associated with this inverse alchemy are the other fallacies of modernistic liberal populism, which centre on failure to be clear about the relationship between rationality or objectivity and coercion: as that rational constraints or requirements would be coercive just because they are constraints or requirements, or that toleration (liberal 'neutrality') presupposes moral scepticism because if there were a right answer it would be all right to impose it on people.[17] There follows in turn the idea that politics and ethics can only be an agreement between, or more likely a restraint clamped upon, instrumentally rational individuals. All these are quite fundamental differences between liberal theory as it is represented today in English-language political economy and philosophy, and the European liberalism of the nineteenth century.

4. LIBERAL VALUES

It is one thing to identify the philosophical syndrome from which modernist liberalism flows, another to refute it. For there is a great, in fact a historic, philosophical question at stake, which deeply underlies the syndrome. Does not scepticism about the objectivity of rational requirements, and scepticism about the liberal conception of rational autonomy, flow

---

[16] Mill (1963–91), x. 314.

[17] For all the historical and philosophical penetration in his discussion of these issues, Isaiah Berlin is guilty of this—see his *Four Essays on Liberty*. He regularly conflates objectivism with monism, and further, with the imposition of certainty; and subjectivism in turn with pluralism and fallibilism. But objectivism, fallibilism, and pluralism can go together, and this is essential in a proper appreciation of Mill. Cf. Berlin's 'John Stuart Mill and the Ends of Life' in Berlin (1969) and the other essays and introduction. (Added note: I realize that Berlin's 'value-pluralism' is intended, as John Gray has recently emphasized (Gray 1995) to differ from subjectivism and relativism. Essay VIII discusses whether the doctrine can indeed be distinguished from relativism, while Essay XI considers its significance within modern liberalism's strategy of 'epistemological detachment'.)

inexorably from a naturalistic viewpoint? Does not that viewpoint gain ever greater power? Can it by now be even *intelligibly* denied?

It is from the German tradition—from Kant and Hegel to the Frankfurt School—that we receive the most heroic and ambitious defence of reason, or rather, *Reason*. But in that tradition the distinction between 'Reason' and mere Understanding, though it means very different things to different thinkers, is always bound up with the rejection of naturalistic empiricism. Philosophers in that tradition have held that naturalism produces its own downfall, by undercutting objectivity and reason, and they have striven to liberate themselves from naturalism. Such efforts, however, very easily appear quixotic, not to say desperate: naturalism is but Weber's iron cage seen in its philosophical aspect. A victory for 'Reason' accomplished at the cost of radically unintelligible metaphysics can never end the war.

The real question is whether one should accept those terms of debate at all—for all the tremendous influence they have had, outside as well as inside philosophy. They stem from the romantic critique of enlightenment—but must one accept that critique in the shape of a single package deal? At this point we are returned again to Mill, and to the classical liberal's selective absorption of romantic cross-currents.[18] For to free the cultural and spiritual insights of German idealism from their leaden suits of metaphysical High Talk was exactly what Mill attempted in his classical essays on Bentham and Coleridge. He sought to assimilate 'Germano-Coleridgean' conceptions of self, culture, and society into the liberal tradition, while rejecting idealist metaphysics and the conservatism which (as he thought) went with it.

It is important to remember here that Mill was no more a Humean in epistemology than he was an eighteenth-century *philosophe* in his political thought. His version of naturalistic empiricism was not a rehearsal of Hume, just as Hegel's version of idealism was not a rehearsal of Kant.[19] He did not have an instrumentalist conception of reason. He believed that autonomy as a capacity, or in his words 'moral freedom', was a matter of mastery of the passions by the rational self. He made the German ideal of self-development his own.

---

[18] But the question is further discussed in Essay XII.

[19] I do not mean to press the analogy too far—Hegel's philosophy includes an extended meditation on and critique of Kant, whereas the philosophic radicals generally, and Mill in particular, almost totally ignored Hume (generally dismissing him as a Tory sceptic). Revealingly, Hume was brought back into discussion by Green: it was precisely the anti-rational(ist) strain of his naturalism, and the sharpness of his dichotomies, which appealed, for quite different reasons, both to 19th-cent. idealists and to 20th-cent. conventionalists.

Not that Mill succeeded in showing how reason can be naturalized, any more than Hegel succeeded in showing how nature can be an objectification of Reason. We cannot go back to Mill or to Hegel, but the question remains: whether classical liberalism, with its belief in rational autonomy, and in the historical progress towards it of all human traditions, can flourish in a naturalistic (deGeisted) framework.

An important strand in modernism is the conviction that it cannot. It goes back to the first dissatisfactions with the classical liberal synthesis, which date back to the 1870s and 1880s. On the story which then began to emerge, the points had been switched by Kant and from then on the advance guard of philosophy had travelled on German idealist rails. The story was told, in Britain, by Green—but many agreed with it who felt, unlike Green, that the eventual destination was not a rehabilitation of idealism, stabilizing the liberal ideal—but the collapse of idealism, and Nietzschean free-fall. The important point, on either scenario, was that the classical liberal-bourgeois synthesis, which sought to reconcile naturalism, historicity, and Bildung—allegiance and continuity with criticism and individuality—(as in Mill's essays on Bentham and Coleridge) is incoherent and doomed. And the supposed impossibility of sustaining objective reason on a naturalistic base was the core of this rupture.

We have reached the deepest issue dividing classical liberalism from the pallid liberalisms which scuttle on the hostile landscape of modernist thought. What is no longer clear, however, in the 1990s as against the 1890s, is that modernist thought has the advantage. On the contrary, many signs suggest that we are again witnessing an intellectual sea-change. Some of them are social rather than intellectual or philosophical—the technical imperatives of science-based, post-industrial societies, the patent failure of 'actually existing' socialism. But such factors never march alone; they intermix with a profoundly changing intellectual climate.

In some respects this is generally recognized, but in other respects, it seems to me, its implications, or its opportunities, have not been properly seized. That is true of a great deal currently said about the 'postmodern' situation. The question, in a nutshell, is whether the situation is postmodern or postmodernist.

'Modernity', referring to the period recognized by such usages as 'modern European history' or 'modern European philosophy', is of course not the same as 'modernism', the cultural phase of the first half of this century. Correspondingly, the postmodern may refer to what follows modernity as such, or more modestly, to what follows twentieth-century modernism. Complicating the issue is the fact that an important element in modernism is its own self-image as postmodern, i.e. as the beginning of a new epoch succeeding that which lasted from the Renaissance and the seventeenth-century growth of science to the twentieth century. And a major part of this self-image was a reaction against the triumph of bourgeois liberalism, which appeared as the ever more strident and shallow keynote of the modern era.[20] If modernity witnesses the growth of liberalism, modernism, in many if not all ways, is the period of its eclipse.

Postmodernity, as many conceive it, seems in some ways to constitute a liberal come-back. Zygmunt Bauman, for example, suggests that 'liberty, diversity and tolerance' are the keynotes of postmodern culture, replacing 'liberty, equality and fraternity'.[21] He may be right. Romantic nationalisms and communalisms, socialist economic egalitarianism, were nineteenth-century products of industrialization and of the *ancien régime*'s decay as much as classical liberalism was. Gradually they over-powered it, worked out their own momentum—and it may well be that in the advanced industrial societies they now face decline. Perhaps equality and community, having outstripped liberty, are now giving way before it. Not that the crossing of cultural identities with unequal access to material well-being will lose any of its explosive power. But in the long run, nothing dismantles it more surely than multicultural, mass-affluent, market society. It domesticates compelling, life-constituting, cultural difference into optional life-styles; it transforms essence into accident. 'Liberty, diversity, and tolerance' is the culture of options, but there *is* loss as well as gain: once choice has been installed you cannot choose to remove it—though you can try shutting your eyes to it.

How, though, does this postmodern liberal dispensation—if that is what it is—stand in relation to the older clash between modernist populism and classical liberalism? Have the questions which exercised classical liberals, about the sustainability of diversity, of allegiance, of creativity and rationality, dissolved?

Maybe the newer liberal order has an easier battle to fight, because liberty and diversity have been shown to pay off in very much the way that nineteenth-century liberals' analysis of progress envisaged, and because the resulting affluence and technical mastery can provide mass culture, elite culture, every kind of culture, in greater quantities, and more ecumenically and dispassionately, than those old liberals ever dreamed. Taking that perspective one might well hold that liberalism is being

---

[20] Among many studies of this transition Carl Schorske's (Schorske 1981) is particularly gripping. The essay on Klimt's paintings for the University of Vienna ('Gustav Klimt: Painting and the Crisis of the Liberal Ego') describes an incident in which the clash of liberal rationalism and emerging modernism crystallized with exceptional clarity.

[21] Bauman (1990). He is rather suspicious of this new trinity.

regenerated not by the return of its ancient myth of rational autonomy, but by the exhaustion of competing illusions. Postmodernity would then be the continuation to full crisis-point of the subjectivist and convention-alist assumptions of modernism,[22] together with a rejection of all its 'transcendent' strains—be they spiritual/mystical on the one side, or constructive/utopian on the other. Many of those who regard 'postmod-ernism' as a novel (anti-) philosophical stance are in effect seeing it in just this way.

It seems to me a profoundly mistaken perspective. Liberal politics require a positive groundwork no less than they ever did, and 'postmod-ernism' understood in this way cannot provide it. No doctrine of the polis can survive in the form of pure criticism or negation. Sooner or later it must place weight on load-bearing pillars of its own: in liberalism's case, rational autonomy and rational legitimation. Thus the challenging ques-tion for liberals is what in classical liberalism is truly dead and what returns to vitality as modernism in the narrower twentieth-century sense dies. *This* question is purely philosophical.

I am not proposing to discuss complex issues about objectivity and rationality, which are central to current philosophy, in a few pages! But I would like to bring into outline some theses which seem to me to lie at the heart of a naturalistic vindication of reason and, simultaneously, of the classical-liberal conception of liberty of thought and discussion.

I am morally free to the extent that I can resist desires when there is rea-son to do so. The more I can recognize good reasons and act on them, the more I can bring motives under rational scrutiny and control, the greater my freedom. This is the ideal of rational autonomy. But if autonomy is a capacity to recognize and act on rational principles and categorial ends, there must be objective rational principles and categorial ends, and it must make sense to talk of recognizing them. Can that make sense in a natural-istic framework? The challenge is to show how the final ground of all deliberation about ends and norms can and must be habits of reasoning

---

[22] Assumptions carried to full crisis-point: a goodly proportion of academic philosophy for three or four decades after the 1920s was in effect an effort to embrace the subjectivist and conventionalist assumptions while neutralizing their subversive impact. This was one major source for the attractiveness of the doctrine that logical, mathematical, and a wide range of other a priori truths are analytic—automatic byproducts of the conventional structures of language; on this doctrine the deep structures of language themselves could somehow determine criteria of rationality. Hence the doctrine's collapse lays bare the true challenge the assumptions pose for any attempt to ground the concept of rationality. Another case in point would be the ever more sophisticated (and in my opinion, doomed) attempts to provide an emotivist account of ethical judgements which does not subvert them. (I discuss some of these aspects of modernism in analytic philosophy in Skorupski 1990–1.)

and desiring, to which we are naturally disposed. Norms which authentically express such dispositions of reasoning must have an objective—though defeasible—claim on our reasoning.

This proposal contains an epistemological thesis, that the objectivity of rules of reasoning is soundly grounded on natural dispositions, and an anthropological thesis, that there are such natural dispositions. Modernism attacked both, in both cases by highlighting sharply and exclusively ideas which already had a venerable history—coming into prominence whenever an anthropological view of man and society has taken hold (in the eighteenth century, or the Athens of the sophists). A primitive naturalism which conflates is and ought, and dogmatizes about a constant human nature, inspires a counter-emphasis on the unbridgeable gulf between is and ought, and an assault on the idea of human nature. There is only variable culture constituted by convention alone.

But this criticism must itself be criticized, as nineteenth-century historical sense criticized both the primitive-naturalistic and the sceptical counter-currents of enlightenment. It did not deny human nature, essential species-being, but only insisted on its dialectical and progressive historicity. To envisage an evolution of forms of life does not in itself prevent the naturalization of reason: reason can still be seen as constituted by those spontaneous and irreducible constraints on thinking which immanently shape the evolution.

When the idea of dialectical evolution, which replaced the idea of cross-cultural and unchanging natural norms, itself comes to be replaced by the idea of non-rational changes of convention, the normative becomes the stipulative—and comes within a step from self-destruction. For the idea of an a priori or rational requirement *is* the idea of a norm not subject to my (or 'our') choice. But that is the idea that liberal thought cannot confidently do without. To ground itself it needs a pragmatic conception of norms of reasoning—a conception of them as norms that compel reflective assent, appearing as a constraint on one's thinking not as something that one chooses; constraints which remain when dialogue and criticism has stripped irrelevant compulsions away.

Since a normative claim which survives criticism at a given time may not do so in the long run, whenever we appeal to a principle as natural in this sense we necessarily commit ourselves forward: to the view that it will survive future criticism—even as we recognize the blank possibility that it may not. The idea of 'man as a progressive being', progressing via a historically unfolding self-discovery, enters into the very essence of rational norms. The inescapable regulation, both of our thinking and of our affective responses, by standards of reason commits us to a notion of what normally constituted human thinkers and feelers—whose thinking is not irrelevantly distorted or screened, and who explore their most spontaneous dispositions philosophically—will continue to experience as requirements on thinking. Free convergence becomes a signal that we have reached normative bedrock but the fact of agreement never entails the truth of what is agreed. At any point we can only appeal to what at *that* point appears as a reflective equilibrium. There is no vantage point from which we can see what would be the result in an indefinitely extended long run, yet our regulative ideal is what would survive criticism in that indefinitely long run. So agreement can at no point be deemed indefeasible, however long it has persisted, and even where we can form no picture of what new information or further reflection would undermine it.

But not everyone is equally sensitized to, or gifted in divining, common human norms. There are better and worse judges. That introduces no *vicious* circularity: there are people whom we recognize, in a particular department of human responses, as registering more sensitively, or in the light of better information or greater reflection, natural dispositions which we also share. They are better attuned to the common voice, and their better attunement can guide them into complexities of discrimination or elaboration far from common.

These related points about objectivity, undistorted convergence, and fallibilism constitute, I suggest, the deepest level of argument for liberty of thought and discussion; they are the focal point of a defence of the coherence of naturalism and, simultaneously, of a demonstration of how it can underpin philosophical liberalism.[23] Contrast this historical and naturalist picture of objectivity with the legacy of modernism. On the one hand the idea of a progressive and dialogical convergence; on the other the denial of any such natural regulating norm or progressiveness, and the alternative picture of convention, contract, or complicity, between bare individuals from whom a common human nature, regulating dispositions towards convergence, has been stripped out.

It is easy to see how the naturalistic and historical vision blends with the classical liberals' moderate elitism. For on the one hand classical liberals affirm that there are better judges, who see further, and whose natural influence must be in no way impeded or checked, but progressively broadened and deepened. On the other hand, they deny that those judges are equipped with special vision of an esoteric Platonic domain—what they

---

[23] I discuss connections between naturalism and liberalism in Mill's thought in Skorupski (1989: ch. 1, specifically on liberty of thought and discussion, see ch. 10, Sect. 10), also in Skorupski (1998a).

respond to are standing human responses common to all. (Balanced in different ways—monism is no part of this: there may be plural equilibria.)

But how does this vision lie with the liberal ideal of equality of respect? For many old liberals, a recognition of the evident empirical inequality of human beings coexisted uneasily with belief in their equality as creatures endowed by God with guiding conscience, or—in the Kantian surrogate for Protestantism—as transcendentally rational agents. In modernist liberalism, as we have seen, the foundation for equality of respect is entirely negative—but such formalistic sleights of hand, we have suggested, render it defenceless against robustly populist assaults.

It is indeed axiomatic that there should be equality of respect, understood as a concrete attitude to one's fellows. The practical meaning of the axiom is that no one is privileged by caste to go to the front of the queue, that it is not your class or race or descent that matter—that no one need defer on such grounds as these—that every human being is properly addressed with unauthoritarian civility. It is this simple recognition of common humanity, not a metaphysical doctrine, which (so we must hope) can suffice to cement liberal order.[24] Nor is there any need to insist that in a good and civilized state of society moral and rational inequalities will be utterly overcome. It is enough that conditions can be reached in which the great majority realizes, in sufficient measure, all those moral and intellectual qualities which make up the common sense (in its deepest meaning) required of liberal citizens.

The binding tenets of liberal order have a 'preceptoral' character which is at odds with many currently popular images of what liberalism is.[25] The question of liberal policy is the question of how this should be realized in substantive institutions. Mill's contrast between 'freedom to point out the way' and 'the power of compelling others into it' is healthy but rudimentary. Anyone can point. But between coercion and *laissez-faire* there are many grades of influence and persuasion. What is required of civic culture—to what extent should the community foster, by allocation of

---

[24] This is discussed more fully in Essay XI.

[25] The term is David Marquand's (1987: 251). He suggests that 'reductionist individualism'

can encompass only two ways of living together in society, and therefore only two conceptions of politics and political man and only two modes of social change. One is the communal mode, and the other the exchange mode . . . Society is either a kind of hierarchy, held together because those at the bottom obey those at the top, or it is a kind of market, held together by the calculating self-interest of its members.

His preferred third mode is 'preceptoral', 'persuasive', 'educational', 'moral': in effect, as it seems to me, the classical liberal ideal which I have been contrasting with modernist liberal populism.

resources, certain public cultural goals? Should museums be publicly funded, or the arts or sciences ('curiosity-driven research'), or higher education? And how far? These are questions of practical political philosophy which liberal policy must address; but in this essay I have only been concerned to reinstate an essential element in the framework for such discussions.

X

The Ethical Content of Liberal Law

1. THE LIBERAL IDEA

It is a sign of our philosophically and politically perplexed times that one can hardly discuss the ethical content of liberal law without a surprising amount of preliminary exhumation and revitalizing of the liberal idea. This may appear a perverse proposition. Is there not a sense in which 'we are all liberals now'?

I use the word 'idea' in a Coleridgean or idealist sense. The Idea of an institution, such as church, university, or law, is the legitimating vision of the purpose of that institution. And while there is a sense in which we are all liberals now, it is also true that agreement about the ethical sources of liberalism—or indeed about whether it is a doctrine that needs ethical sources at all—is eroded, fractured, and unstable. Does this matter? Does the liberal attitude to government and law require an Idea? Or is it more likely to flourish if we do not search too explicitly for its Idea?

The sense in which we are all liberals now is that 'we' live in liberal societies whose basic features of a secular State, democracy with entrenched civil freedoms, private property, and free exchange are no longer, for the moment at least, in serious dispute. They have not been so little in dispute since the heyday of classical liberalism in the nineteenth century. 'Actually existing socialism' in Eastern Europe has collapsed. That does not mean that the socialist idea is dead but for the moment it does not pose a real philosophical challenge. One may conjure up a threat from Islamic fundamentalism, which is certainly inimical to the liberal idea, in theory as well as practice. But I suspect that few people (rightly or wrongly) take it seriously as a threat, because they doubt its ability to roll back modernity while preserving prosperity and power. A more credible threat may be

Given as one of the William Galbraith Miller Centenary Lectures in Jurisprudence in the University of Glasgow on Tuesday, 29 Nov. 1994; first published in John Tasoulias (ed.), *Law, Values and Social Practices*, Aldershot: Dartmouth, 1997: 191–211. I am grateful to Karen Reeder Bell for providing helpful background about the American liberal tradition in jurisprudence and to Keith Graham for discussion of issues concerning individualism.

posed by some Asian models of authoritarian capitalism. Some hold that these will bury us—an interesting reversal of the conventional wisdom among nineteenth-century thinkers, both liberal and revolutionary, who held that 'Asiatic despotism' was a stagnant system incapable of withstanding the creative destructiveness of Europe. At any rate it is still possible to argue that as Asian countries achieve stable prosperity they will develop towards the liberal democratic model. So one might conclude that liberal civil society and its political economy is no longer likely to be overwhelmed by socialism, nor likely to be outpaced by authoritarian forms of capitalism.

This conclusion may be heartening, complacent, or depressing according to one's point of view—or just premature.[1] But if it is correct then what has triumphed is a politico-economic social formation—a combination of private ownership, free markets, and extensive civil and political freedoms. That gives no clue as to what ethical idea, in the liberal view, should be set before the legislature and guide it in its enactment of statutes, its conferment of powers on executive and judicial bodies, and not least, its sense of its own limits. In fact it has become a cliché to claim that the material success of liberal society is accompanied by an inner ethical void.

At this point those in my audience familiar with the broad developments of the last thirty years in Anglophone philosophy may well ask: have we not in fact witnessed a remarkable revival of liberal political philosophy, in which ethical questions about liberalism's foundations and stability have indeed been discussed? True. Yet although contemporary American academic political philosophy has certainly revived an interest in the concept of liberalism, one cannot help being struck by the contrast between the concept of liberalism it has developed and the liberal tradition which reached its classical formulations in the nineteenth century, before the long twentieth-century eclipse of liberal philosophy. There are considerable continuities. But the differences are also striking and they are particularly striking at the level of ethical fundamentals. Contemporary American academic liberalism has moved significantly away from the classical liberal idea.

To remind you of that classical idea let me mention four broad points in a preliminary way.

First, nineteenth-century liberals who thought about ethical foundations by and large thought teleologically, not deontologically. They did not think the right was prior to the good. This applies as much to liberals influenced by German idealism as to those influenced by British utilitari-

---

[1] Witness the debate occasioned by Francis Fukuyama's *The End of History and the Last Man* (Fukuyama 1992).

anism: thus, in Britain, to Thomas Hill Green as much as to John Stuart Mill. There was a general dismissal of natural rights and a general agreement about the emptiness of the categorical imperative. Both the natural right tradition and the Kantian deduction of 'abstract right' were in disrepute.

A certain conception of justice remained, to be sure, essential to the liberal stance—this is the second point. Liberalism rejected rights of inherited or ordained status and affirmed formal equality of rights for all citizens. The affirmation of formal civil and political equality is the essential juridical framework laid down by liberal social thought, though it took the whole century and more to be fully translated into law. Such civil and political equality under the law could be, and in the nineteenth century it often was, associated with metaphysical or religious doctrines of equal respect or worth. But these doctrines are not essential to liberalism in the way that the framework of formal equality which gives juridical substance to equal respect is essential.

The third point concerns the ethical content which, in the minds of those nineteenth-century philosophical liberals, gave significance to the liberal juridical framework. It was a vision of human good grounded in a moral psychology of human nature—a romantic and hellenic vision. It was concerned with the culture of the whole human being, of the feelings as well as of rational will. Thus while it did not reject the importance Kant attached to rational autonomy it sought to balance it by giving due scope to human powers of expressive spontaneity.

Lastly, there was a notable preoccupation among nineteenth-century liberal thinkers (and among non-liberal ones as well, of course) with the dangers of democratic mass culture—especially the danger of tyranny by a mediocre and conformist majority, which would stifle the originality on which moral and intellectual progress depends. This was associated with a political sociology according to which creative and progressive moral energies are released primarily through conflicts of social forces and collisions of ideas.

I will call the nineteenth-century outlook which encompasses these four themes and derives a liberal order from them 'classical liberalism'.[2] It is in particular romantic hellenism—the notion of human good as the balanced development of human powers of both rational will and feeling, together with a wish to give all human beings equitable access to this good, that seems to me to constitute classical liberalism's *ethical* idea. It is still in this sense that we speak of a liberal idea of education—this is an older idea

[2] A recent study of the role played by them in the thought of three important 19th-cent. liberals (Tocqueville, Mill, and Burckhardt) is Kahan (1992).

than romantic hellenism, but one which it thoroughly transformed. Without that notion of good, the framework of formal equality can easily become mere indifferentism, a mere dissolution of bonds of hierarchical loyalty. Without that notion of good, it is impossible to understand the fears classical liberals harboured about democratic equality. We shall come back to it (Section 4). But for the moment I want to contrast classical liberalism with the image of liberalism presented by both critics and proponents in contemporary American academic political philosophy.

It diverges from the classical idea in two ways. First of all it is notably preoccupied with strong theories of justice, rather than with a conception of human good. This is true of both its left variations as in Dworkin or Rawls, and its right-libertarian variation, as in Nozick. Secondly and connectedly, it puts forward a doctrine of the 'neutrality' of the State.

Both these preoccupations are by now familiar objects of comment, particularly by what are called 'communitarian' critics of liberalism. But here I am discussing them from a point of view within the liberal camp, that of classical liberalism. It is important to see them from this *liberal* point of view, because we are in danger of sliding into the very impoverishing notion that they constitute liberalism itself. They do not. On the contrary, they may augur a radical transformation of the liberal tradition; the final passing, as it may yet turn out, of its classical liberal phase. Contemporary American academic liberalism insulates classical liberal ideas of human good from the legislative, executive, and judicial activities of the State. The liberal state, in this new view, is not permitted either to endorse or to reject them. So let us consider these two contemporary preoccupations, or obsessions, with justice and with ethical neutrality, more closely.[3]

2. JUSTICE AND THE LIBERAL IDEA

The most influential presentations of 'liberalism' in recent political philosophy have actually been theories of justice. These theories of justice have been important, their influence well merited—nor is any of them incompatible with the liberal idea. But by the same token none of them

---

[3] In characterizing this new liberalism as 'American academic liberalism' I do not mean to suggest that liberal (and non-liberal) critics of its preoccupations cannot be found in American academe or that it has no roots in broader American political culture. I simply mean to highlight its specific site in the longer evolution of philosophical liberalism. For a liberal critique of 'liberal neutrality' see in particular Galston (1991). In Britain, related criticisms are made by Joseph Raz (Raz 1986).

should be presented as definitive expressions of it. To present any one of them as definitive of liberalism, rather than as simply consistent with it, would give the theory of justice an importance in the liberal idea which it does not have. As far as justice is concerned, the only principle definitive of liberalism is that a just State institutes formal equality of civil and political rights, in particular liberty rights. Obviously liberals can argue for stronger principles of justice. What justice is is one of the fundamental questions of moral and political philosophy. Liberal political philosophers, just like any others, can and should seek to answer it, or to show why it cannot be answered. But liberalism in its ethical core is about what it is to live a free and full human life. It touches on questions of justice through its ambition to establish the conditions required to give *all*, and not just a particular estate, the opportunity to live such a life.[4] What these conditions are and what we mean by an opportunity for all are extremely important questions; however about the only thing liberals have agreed on in answering them is that among the conditions required are prosperity and social and political freedom.

Consider then John Rawls's recent book *Political Liberalism*.[5] Rawls makes a distinction there between comprehensive and political liberalism. Comprehensive liberalism presents a conception of 'what is of value in human life, as well as ideals of personal virtue and character, that are to inform much of our nonpolitical conduct (in the limit our life as a whole)'.[6] Rawls cites the liberal philosophies of Kant and Mill as examples of comprehensive liberalism. Political liberalism, on the other hand, is a set of principles for the organization of the State, defended not by appeal to a comprehensive doctrine but insofar as possible by appeal to an overlapping consensus of comprehensive doctrines. These comprehensive doctrines may or may not be liberal, so long as they are 'reasonable'. Political liberalism, Rawls says, does have a conception of the good of free and equal persons but it is a political one: it is one that can be shared by all reasonable citizens and thus does not presuppose any one reasonable comprehensive doctrine in particular.[7]

The overlapping consensus that can be derived from, or at any rate accepted by, all reasonable doctrines will in Rawls's view be restricted to

---

[4] As Joseph Raz (1986: 2) rightly says 'The specific contribution of the liberal tradition to political morality has always been its insistence on the respect due to individual liberty. To the extent that liberal theories of justice present a distinctive conception of justice, this is due to the way their principles of political freedom feed into and shape their conception of justice.'

[5] Rawls (1993).   [6] Ibid. 175.

[7] Ibid. 176. For useful exposition and explanation of this and related issues in *Political Liberalism* see Freeman (1994).

principles of justice as fairness. Hence Rawls thinks the State should restrict itself to the implementation of these principles. He requires the State to be neutral as between 'comprehensive' conceptions of the good. And he continues to hold that the principles of justice as fairness are those expounded in his *Theory of Justice*—a list of liberties prioritized over the Difference Principle. The latter, it is true, has a surprisingly low profile in *Political Liberalism*. Somewhat cryptically, Rawls says that reasons for and against it 'fall under questions of basic justice and so are to be decided by the political values of public reason'. What he is saying, as I understand it, is that the Difference Principle can quite legitimately be put forward in the public arena as the platform of a political movement, and that he himself supports it, but that he is not proposing that it be constitutionally entrenched. He does nevertheless think that a somewhat weaker principle of social justice, guaranteeing a minimum of social provision to all citizens, should be so entrenched.[8]

'Political liberalism', in Rawls's sense, builds on a core of common sense. One should not put out hostages to fortune by appealing to more controversial ethical ideas to justify one's political practice than it actually needs. And yet, as Rawls works it out, its final effect is far from commonsensical. In his hands the ethical content of liberal constitutional law turns out to be driven by a very strong notion of social justice, while being entirely precluded from reflecting ethical notions other than those of justice.

This seems to me to be simultaneously too strong and too weak. I myself have no quarrel with a background distributive principle which provides, where possible, a flexible minimum of provision to all, and puts that goal ahead of the unconstrained pursuit of prosperity when a reasonable level of prosperity has been reached. I would be prepared to argue that such a principle is superior, as a distributive function from the good of individuals to the general good, to both aggregative utilitarianism and the difference principle—and superior to a Nozickean approach which treats property rights as if they were fundamental.[9] Moreover, if we combine it with liberal ideas of human well-being, it may produce a rather generous conception of what the social minimum should ideally be. But this conception must be argued for as part of a comprehensive ethical theory. It is tendentious to make it definitive of 'political liberalism'. It is also unrealistic to suggest that it could be accepted as a *constitutional essential*, on the basis of purely political arguments, by all adherents to all 'reason-

---

[8] 'A social minimum providing for the basic needs of all citizens is [a constitutional] essential, . . . the "difference principle" is more demanding and is not' (ibid. 228–9).

[9] See Essay IV.

able' comprehensive moral positions. At least it's unrealistic if one is using the word 'reasonable' in a reasonable way.[10] Whether one agrees with the principle is one thing, whether one wants it enshrined in constitutional law, or in a social chapter of a treaty is another. I would say that these very important and substantive—to a large extent practical—questions about justice should be decoupled from the idea of liberalism itself.

Consider, in contrast, libertarianism as exemplified by Robert Nozick's *Anarchy, State and Utopia*.[11] That was an important book because it gave a clear new formulation to a line of thought which has been very important to the political tradition of the West, and remains very important. Individuals have natural rights to life, liberty, and property; moreover they have natural rights of self-defence against, punishment of, and compensation from aggressors who violate these rights. The sovereign State has no authority over an individual except by the consent of that individual.[12] Individuals cannot transfer to the sovereign any right over themselves or others which they did not themselves naturally have.

Once again, such doctrine is of course an important strand in the liberal tradition. But not only is it not definitive of it, it can become positively inimical to its spirit if it becomes a dogmatism of natural rights. The dogmatic libertarian asserts the self-evident inherence of property and liberty rights in individuals, independent of any underlying ethical idea of these rights. In contrast Mill's rejection of appeals to 'abstract right' as a foundation for his principle of liberty is familiar:

I forego any advantage which could be derived to my argument from the idea of abstract right, as a thing independent of utility. I regard utility as the ultimate appeal on all ethical questions; but it must be utility in the largest sense, grounded on the permanent interests of a man as a progressive being.[13]

In rejecting 'abstract right' and appealing to the permanent interests of a man as a progressive being, Mill speaks for what I have called classical liberalism. But one may equally contrast Locke on natural law:

Law, in its true Notion, is not so much the Limitation as *the direction of a free and intelligent Agent* to his proper Interest, and prescribes no further than is for the

---

[10] The weaker the sense attached to 'reasonable', the more difficult it is to show that a constitutional claim is justifiable to (or even consistent with) all reasonable comprehensive positions. But the stronger the sense, the greater the danger that 'political liberalism' sanctions a new and subtle form of intolerance: If you don't agree with these proposals your positions can't be reasonable. On Rawls's use of 'reasonable', see Gaut (1995).

[11] Nozick (1974).

[12] But one of Nozick's main aspirations was to find a satisfactory way of amending this doctrine while keeping to the spirit of the tradition.

[13] Mill (1963–91), xviii. 224–5 (*On Liberty*, ch. 1, para. 11).

general Good of those under that *Law*. Could they be happier without it, the Law, as an useless thing would of it self vanish.[14]

In Locke's view the law of nature which confers rights on free and intelligent agents does so for a reason: to promote their proper Interest. And it prescribes no further than is for their general Good. Of course Locke, unlike Mill and like Nozick, does think that natural reason alone can tell us that individuals have property rights and he does not spell out the general good in a utilitarian way. But in recognizing that Law has a function— the proper interest of free and intelligent agents—he presents a more penetrating ethical idea than does the dogmatic or merely abstract libertarian.

But even if dogmatic libertarianism is not a particularly penetrating form of liberalism, why should I say that it's inimical to it? Because of the way in which it removes any cultural role from the State. Libertarianism would restrain the State by law from pursuing any ethical or cultural ideal. No individual has the right to make others contribute against their consent in pursuit of ethical or cultural ideals; the State only has rights which all individuals have conferred on it; so unless all individuals freely give it the right to promote such ideals it has no right to do so. Like Rawls the libertarian refuses to let any ethical idea get on to the political agenda.

So I now turn from the preoccupation with justice to the preoccupation with neutrality.

3. THE MYTH OF LIBERAL NEUTRALITY

The development in liberal understandings of morality and law since the war testifies to liberalism's loss of its Idea.

Take that well-known debate which started from Lord Devlin's commentary on the Wolfenden report.[15] Devlin asked what the connection is 'between crime and sin and to what extent, if at all, should the criminal law of England concern itself with the enforcement of morals and punish sin or immorality as such?'[16] It proved all too tempting to simplify the liberal answer into a doctrine that law should not enforce morals at all. Thus for example Ronald Dworkin cites 'John Stuart Mill's liberal theory' which, he says, lays it down 'that the only proper reason for limiting a person's liberty is that his act is likely to cause harm to others'. And he immediately

---

[14] *2nd Treatise of Government*, §57 (Locke 1988: 305).
[15] Report of the Committee on Homosexual Offences and Prostitution; Devlin (1965).
[16] Quoted from the extracts reprinted in R. M. Dworkin (ed.) (1977: 67).

glosses the doctrine thus: 'It is not sufficient, according to Mill, that the act will harm the actor, *or that it is immoral.*'[17]

The phrase appended by Dworkin has no basis in Mill's theory. In Mill's account of the matter *both* morality and law place restrictions on what the individual can do or omit to do. Mill defines a moral wrongdoing as an act for which the individual ought to be punished 'if not by law, by the opinion of his fellow-creatures; if not by opinion, by the reproaches of his own conscience'. 'It is' (he continues) 'a part of the notion of Duty in every one of its forms, that a person may rightfully be compelled to fulfil it. Duty is a thing which may be *exacted* from a person, as one exacts a debt.'[18]

Morality is concerned with that which an individual may be 'compelled', and not merely 'persuaded and exhorted', to do. It is not Mill's view that morality is a matter of individual choice from which society should stay clear. Morality and law are in his view both penal devices by which society exercises its sovereignty over individual behaviour. There are important questions about when society should exercise its sovereignty by means of moral penalty alone and when it should do so by positive legal sanction. But in the essay on Liberty Mill is not concerned with this issue—his concern is to ensure that that sovereignty is exercised within its proper limits in *either* case. His doctrine is not that there are immoralities which are harmless to others and should hence be unmolested by society. An immorality, by his own definition, is something which society has the right, and if expedient the obligation, to seek to prevent. His doctrine, rather, is that an action which breaches no duty to others is not an immorality.

Moreover this liberal doctrine of morality must be put in the context of the liberal ethical idea. It would be, Mill says, 'a great misunderstanding' of it 'to suppose that it is one of selfish indifference, which pretends that human beings have no business with each other's conduct in life, and that they should not concern themselves about the well-doing or well-being of one another, unless their own interest is involved'.[19] There are 'self-regarding virtues' as well as 'social' ones and 'It is equally the business of education to cultivate both.' Self-regarding virtues are qualities of character and activity which exercise our higher faculties and enter into the full development of human personality. I will call them ethical ideals

[17] Ibid. 9, my emphasis. I am not assuming that Dworkin would make the same claim now. I quote the passage because it succinctly illustrates how the image of liberalism has developed in this century—so that it comes to be unreflectively assumed that someone famous as a liberal must have been a neutralist about morality.

[18] Mill (1963–91), x. 246 (*Utilitarianism*, ch. 5, para. 14).

[19] Mill (1963–91), xviii. 276–7 (*On Liberty*, ch. 4, para. 4).

of character and activity, using the word 'ethical' to indicate a wider
sphere of evaluation than 'moral', which Mill defines, we have just seen,
as that with which it is blameworthy not to comply. Ethical ideals include
the moral but range beyond it to every kind of excellence in character
and activity. They cover what we find admirable, rather than just that
whose absence we blame. The liberal idea is then a specific conception of
these ideals, an idea of what is admirable in human beings. Its idea of this
will differ from that of other ethical ideals such as those of the Trappist
monk, the cool dude, the deep green drop-out, or the Islamic fundamentalist.

Is liberal society or a liberal State neutral about these ethical ideals? Not
if it is responding, as it should, to the liberal idea. What is true, if we accept
Mill's account, is that it does not enforce the ethical ideal, as against the
moral duty—either by legal or by other means of social compulsion.
'Human beings owe to each other help to distinguish the better from the
worse, and encouragement to choose the former rather than the latter.'
'But disinterested benevolence can find other instruments to persuade
people to their good than whips and scourges, either of the literal or the
metaphorical sort.'

Nothing Mill says here prohibits a liberal society from taking up legitimate instruments of persuasion, as against compulsion, to advance its
ethical idea of good as the full development of human powers. In particular nothing prevents it from using the resources of the State to do so.
Acknowledging that the State has this cultural and ethical role is not ruled
out by any basic principle of liberty or right, as it might be for the libertarian. For according to Mill human beings *owe* each other help to distinguish the better from the worse. That is, they have a moral obligation:
something which, as we have seen, society can enforce. If we owe each
other a duty of education (in the true sense of that word), then the question of whether that duty should be discharged through public or private
expenditure is a question of efficient policy; not a question touching on
principles of liberty. What certainly would be ruled out by principles of
liberty is an intervention which *prevented* any group of citizens from
advancing their own ethical and cultural ideals—so long as they do it
justly, which in this context means, in accordance with a law which
enshrines formal equality. But that is a separate issue, difficult as it may be
to disentangle it in practice.

Compare then this Millian picture with Rawls's account of the neutrality of the State. Rawls concedes that 'the term *neutrality* is highly unfortu-
nate; some of its connotations are highly misleading, others suggest
altogether impracticable principles.' But he nevertheless uses it, if 'only as

a stage piece',[20] and he takes political liberalism to be neutral in at least two ways. First it ensures 'for all citizens equal opportunity to advance any conception of the good they freely affirm'—so long as those conceptions respect the principles of justice, and 'equality of opportunity' is appropriately understood. And secondly it affirms 'that the state is not to do anything intended to favor or promote any particular comprehensive doctrine rather than another, or to give greater assistance to those who pursue it'.[21]

I will refer to these two ways as permissive and persuasive neutrality. The State is permissively neutral when it neither puts up legal obstacles to the advancement of any particular conception of the good (it being understood that that conception is not advanced in a way that infringes principles of justice) nor legally requires that individuals should adopt or even acquaint themselves with any particular notion of the good (above the age of maturity).

This is common ground between Rawls and Mill. Permissive neutrality formulates traditional liberal doctrines of liberty of action and discussion, securing the right of citizens both to pursue their conception of their own personal good in a just way and to advance their comprehensive ethical ideals through free discussion.

But what about persuasive neutrality? Must the State refrain from taking any part in the discussion or advancement of ethical ideals, whether as the proponent of some particular ideals or as the patron of some such proponents? This is a very strong doctrine of self-limitation for a liberal state to adopt. 'The liberalisms of Kant and Mill', Rawls says,

may lead to requirements designed to foster the values of autonomy and individuality as ideals to govern much if not all of life. But political liberalism has a different aim and requires far less. It will ask that children's education include such things as knowledge of their constitutional and civic rights so that, for example, they know that liberty of conscience exists in their society and that apostasy is not a legal crime, all this to insure that their continued membership when they come of age is not based simply on ignorance of their basic rights or fear of punishment for offences that do not exist. Moreover, their education should also prepare them to be fully co-operating members of society and enable them to be self-supporting; it should also encourage the political virtues so that they want to honor the fair terms of social co-operation in their relations with the rest of society.[22]

This seems to restrict the State's persuasive role to lessons in economic self-sufficiency and the civics of political liberalism. Is there nothing more

[20] Rawls (1993: 191).
[21] Ibid. Here Rawls draws on Joseph Raz's discussion of political neutrality, see Raz (1986: ch. 5).
[22] Ibid. 199.

that a liberal society can permit itself to teach or to fund by way of ethical ideas?

The ethical content of liberal law is shown not only in what it prevents individuals from doing or requires them to do, but also in what it allows the State to do. Rawls's doctrine shares classical liberalism's anti-paternalist thrust, but it also institutes a very strong constitutional limit on the State's educational and cultural role. Should we accept this limit?

4. THE ETHICS OF CLASSICAL LIBERALISM

At this point we must say a little more about the liberal idea. I have said that it involves the balance between the culture of rational will and the culture of the feelings, of sensibility. With the culture of rational will we are on what is in one way reasonably familiar ground—namely the concept of autonomy in its more or less Kantian sense: that is, the capacity to recognize and act on good reasons. Now Kant gave this idea an impossibly dominant role in his ethics. In particular he treated rational will, the capacity to recognize and act on reasons, as an aspect of the real self, the self as it is in itself, the self which inhabits the realm of freedom; while feelings are relegated to the apparent self, the self which inhabits, or appears as inhabiting, the realm of causal necessity.

Much still needs to be said about the impossible things Kant tried to do with the concept of autonomy if we are to have, clearly before us, the rooted historical understanding of the moral philosophy of liberalism which we presently very much need. But here I want to make just two points. The first is this. While it is perfectly true that the Kantian image of autonomy is of great importance to classical liberalism, its importance lies, ironically, in the fact that its kernel notion, that of rational will, survives criticism of virtually every aspect of the ethics and metaphysics in which Kant sets it. In particular, the thinkers who were to influence classical liberalism sought to reconcile autonomy with the development of the whole human being, balancing the culture of rational will with the culture of the feelings, which (as they saw it) Kant's ethics demoted at every point. If the culture of rational will is the culture of autonomy, we may call the culture of the feelings the culture of expressive spontaneity. It is this culture of expressive spontaneity which injects diversity into the liberal ideal. Reason is one but the potentialities of feeling and sensibility in human beings are many.

The nineteenth-century emphasis on expressive spontaneity partly came from a conscious reaction to Kant's autonomy-obsession and partly from a direct recovery of Greek ideas of self-development. Both influences, for example, were active in shaping Mill's ethical outlook. So the first point is that while nineteenth-century liberalism retained the concept of rational will which Kant asserted against the enlightenment, it balanced it with an ideal of expressive spontaneity for which Kant's moral philosophy had no room. The liberal idea was a romantic-hellenic idea of free self-development in every aspect of one's human powers. That brings with it a liberal idea of aesthetic education—in the broad sense which includes the liberal study of philosophy and science—and a potential role for the State in advancing that aesthetic education and enabling the self-culture of its citizens. Matthew Arnold is the most obvious English representative of this vision; his insistence that a fully developed being has 'spontaneity of consciousness' as well as 'strictness of conscience' bears directly on the issue at stake.

The second point I want to make is also about autonomy. Flint Schier, that fine Glasgow philosopher, memorably emphasized that autonomy of the Kantian kind, the ability to recognize and act on reasons, is a capacity that one could in principle have even in the Gulag.[23] External liberty is not logically a precondition of it. It is, rather, something that liberals value in its own right. To be sure, the relationship between the two is very important but it tends to be obscured in edifying haze by the very broad and loose, not to say incantatory, way in which the word 'autonomy' is used in current discussions of liberalism. Of course it's quite proper to use 'autonomy' to refer to a concept of external liberty. Autonomy, in this sense, call it external autonomy, refers to the *liberty* to make and follow one's own plan of life, within one's sovereign domain, without interference from others. Autonomy in the Kantian sense, call it internal autonomy, refers to the *power* or *capacity* to form a rational and responsible plan of life, and carry it out without being blown off course by inclination. They are logically distinct. But they are nevertheless importantly connected and the question of how they are connected is as central to the liberal ethic as the question of balancing internal autonomy with expressive spontaneity.

It is wrong to represent external autonomy as simply the liberty of doing as one likes. It is rather the freedom to do as one likes in one's sovereign domain. So it presupposes the notion of my domain, my territory or space, versus the common or public space. And it means that when a person is forcibly prevented from invading the sovereign domain of another, his or her external autonomy is not thereby restricted. It is not a pre-ethical notion then. It is an ethical notion, to which liberal ethics gives a central

[23] Schier (1993).

significance. But it is a pre-political notion, on which the political institution of liberty builds. Locke's formulation of natural law, which I quoted
earlier, illustrates these points splendidly:

Could they be happier without it, the *Law*, as an useless thing would of it self vanish; and that ill deserves the Name of Confinement which hedges us in only from
Bogs and Precipices. So that, however it may be mistaken, *the end of Law* is not
to abolish or restrain, but *to preserve and enlarge Freedom*: For in all the states of
created beings capable of Laws, *where there is no Law, there is no Freedom*. For
Liberty is to be free from restraint and violence from others which cannot be,
where there is no Law: but Freedom is not, as we are told, *A Liberty for every Man
to do what he lists*: (For who could be free, when every other Man's Humour
might domineer over him?) But a *Liberty* to dispose, and order, as he lists, his
Person, Actions, Possessions, and his whole Property, within the Allowance of
those Laws under which he is; and therein not to be subject to the arbitrary Will
of another, but freely follow his own.[24]

Here Locke is speaking of law in general, including the law of nature, and
he is also using the word 'property' generally to cover the individual's sovereign sphere. So he could agree that there is a pre-political but not pre-
ethical notion of freedom, characterized in terms of liberty to do as one
likes within one's sovereign sphere. ('*Freedom of Nature* is to be under no
other restraint but the Law of Nature' (§22).) Moreover he links this external autonomy with internal autonomy by the doctrine (§57) that nobody
can be said to be under a law which is not promulgated to him and that
only those who come under the law of nature or reason have external
autonomy. If I cannot recognize and act on the law of reason, it is not promulgated to me and in that case my external autonomy is also impaired.
Thus children who have not reached the age of reason cannot be under the
law of reason, so cannot be free, but must come under the authority of
parents.

The desire to maintain a sphere in which one is free of others' direction
is partly a basic human need for sovereign space. But beyond that it flows
in large part from a positive desire to make and enact a plan of life, to
impress one's image on things, to be objectified and embodied in a life-
history with its material and social expressions. Of this process internal
autonomy is a condition. For *self*-realization is more than a spontaneous
expression of essence—the kind of expression found in a freely developing
plant or animal. Spontaneity of this kind is valuable, but it is not yet
self-expression—it does not involve giving oneself the law. Full self-
realization—realization of the self by the self—requires both autonomy as

[24] *2nd Treatise of Government*, §57 (Locke 1988: 305–6).

a capacity and autonomy as freedom. Insofar as the impulse to it under-lies the desire for autonomy, it unifies the two dimensions of autonomy into a single end.

It is in this way that a liberal order builds on and enlarges the human end of external autonomy. It builds on it the institutions of liberty both because it recognizes it as a human end and because it recognizes it as a means of promoting those character-ideals of rational will and feeling which it holds dear.

See how indispensable it is to keep returning to the liberal idea if we are to determine the true extent of liberal freedoms. Locke's theory of parental authority already illustrates that. An even better illustration is provided by the idealist liberalism which briefly flourished in Britain at the end of the last century. It was a characteristic argument of that movement that legal coercion was to be avoided wherever possible because it produced the right action for the wrong motives—fear of positive sanction, rather than recog-nition of inherently good reason—and hence did not build the internal autonomy, or in a more common word, the responsibility of the individ-ual.[25] But T. H. Green, the leader of these idealist liberals, was also will-ing to narrow the domain of external autonomy when he felt that doing so would build internal autonomy—or as he famously referred to it, positive freedom: 'a positive power or capacity of doing or enjoying something worth doing or enjoying.'[26]

This phrase comes from a well-known lecture on 'Liberal Legislation and Freedom of Contract' in which Green defends a raft of new liberal legislation: on factory safety, tenancy, temperance, education—legislation which was seen as interventionist and opposed on the grounds that it weakened people's 'self-reliance, and thus, in unwisely seeking to do them good . . . lowers them in the scale of moral beings'.[27] Green was not object-ing to the high moral value placed on self-reliance. He was not criticizing the view that there is a scale of moral beings. His point was that it was only by means of constructive legislation that the development of self-reliance could be secured for all citizens. His disagreement with Mill was not on the value of liberty but on whether, for example, temperance legislation, which infringes Mill's principle of liberty, is nevertheless justified because it helps people to develop and retain positive freedom. Green thought it was, but he also thought that the role of the State should be limited by this enabling criterion: it should strengthen, not substitute for, self-reliance and it should never undermine 'the self-imposition of duties'.

---

[25] See Nicholson (1990, Study V).   [26] Green (1885-8: iii. 370-1).
[27] Ibid. (iii. 365).

So in this discussion among liberals the ethical idea shapes the content of liberal law and the scope of the individual's sovereign domain. All of them draw on the liberal idea in their discussion of the proper content and limits of law. Indeed we cannot restrict ourselves in such matters to an argument couched at the level of something called 'public' or 'political' discourse, which eschews any reference to comprehensive ethical positions. On the contrary, it is only by such ethical reference points, however uncertain their practical guidance, that we retain a grip on the true nature of liberal law and distinguish it from false conceptions of what liberalism is.

A timely if not perfect illustration of this point is Lord Woolf's[28] recent suggestion that some of the money spent on keeping offenders in prison should be spent on crime prevention instead. It might be spent for example on devices for immobilizing cars and then 'just as we can be fined for not protecting ourselves by wearing seat belts, so we can be fined if we do not take steps to protect our property.' That is an idea that has an ingenious managerial ring but it is fairly clear how it offends liberal notions of autonomy. One is also struck by the way in which it makes fines for not protecting one's own property ride on the back of fines for not wearing safety belts. Safety-belt legislation, after all, may not itself be an important issue, but it is hard to see how it's reconcilable with liberal and not just libertarian principles.

On the other hand another suggestion in Lord Woolf's speech, that drugs should be at least partially legalized, is directly comparable to the nineteenth-century discussion I have just referred to about drink laws, and raises similar issues which we should be discussing in a similar spirit. There is, on the one hand, the restriction of external autonomy involved in outright interdiction of drugs and on the other, there is the argument that that interdiction, by preventing some people at least from enslaving themselves to the drug habit, maintains their chance of achieving internal autonomy. Here I certainly agree with Lord Woolf:

Should we not at least be considering whether it would be preferable for drugs or at least some drugs to be lawfully available in controlled circumstances so that it would no longer be necessary for addicts to commit crimes to feed their addiction.

We certainly should. Of course I am not for a moment suggesting that reference to liberal ethical ideas alone will supply the answer to difficult questions of public policy which turn on complex questions of fact. But these ideas—of internal and external autonomy, as well as the obvious issues of

---

[28] Address to the New Assembly of Churches, reported in *The Times,* 14 Oct. 1993.

security which Bentham was so clear about—can and should provide the terms of debate.

5. THE CULTURAL ROLE OF THE STATE

These are examples of complex issues of legal policy to which the ethical ideas of liberalism are highly relevant—while in contrast controversies about distributive justice are not. Can we really say that we should scrupulously exclude such ideas from consideration, keeping only purely political issues about civil liberties or principles of justice at the forefront of our minds? This strikes me as absurd. But let me now turn more generally to the doctrine of persuasive neutrality, and the ethical and cultural role of the State.

While permissive neutrality is firmly grounded on liberties of action and speech which liberalism honours, the same does not hold for persuasive neutrality. Nothing in liberalism requires a self-restraining interdiction on state actions designed to promulgate liberal ideals and notions of the good. That of course leaves open the practical question: namely, is it on the whole a good thing, even if it is permitted in principle, for the State to involve itself in such matters? To ask that question is to put the issue on a much better footing. And having got it on that footing we should begin by noting the ways in which, in this country at least, the State already plays a cultural role which goes beyond the neutral enforcement of justice. It will be useful to list some of these.

A first way is its role in upholding free speech itself. Free speech is a right of individuals but that does not mean that the best account of the right derives it from a theory of justice. It is best regarded not as a justice-right, functioning to protect a vital interest of the individual who has the right, but as a matter of general or public good. The entrenchment of free speech reflects the high value the liberal idea places on the dissemination of truth and of rationally held belief. This can be seen both in the tendency to give speech actions a kind or degree of legal protection differing from actions in general and in the reasons given for this protection. Thus for example when Mill gives his account of 'liberty of thought and discussion' in the essay on Liberty he argues for it directly in this way; whereas his account of the general principle of liberty has to be understood in relation to his account of justice-rights and of 'individuality' as one of the most fundamental elements of well-being.[29]

[29] Mill does say that the liberty of thought and discussion is 'one branch' of his 'general thesis' concerning liberty of action. But he does not in fact treat it thus. For more on this see Skorupski (1989: ch. 10, Sects. 9–11).

It may however be disputed that upholding free speech really does go beyond enforcing principles of individual right.[30] In any case, even if we justify free-speech principles by a non-neutral appeal to ethical ideas, rather than as a right of justice, the State's protection of free speech still does not constitute direct partisanship for a particular conception of the good as against another, of the kind exhibited if the State itself enters the lists as a persuader, or funds activities which promote this or that particular ideal. But certainly the State does these things. It advances arts, sciences, and a variety of pursuits by means of various policies, educational and other, and in ways which are not justified solely on economic grounds. I mean that their justification is not restricted solely to an appeal to benefits which can be characterized quite neutrally—though for obvious reasons these benefits tend to be much emphasized. The State also, and again not solely on economic grounds, seeks to uphold the heritage, identity, and solidarity of the nation and its natural environment. Finally, in this country at least, the State still has a role in matters of faith and ritual.

In fact the British State's image of its ethical and cultural role is in part formed by religious doctrines and institutions going back to the reformation (Scottish and English) and in part by liberal ethical ideas, including ethical ideas about the limits of intervention such as those mentioned above, which go back to the Victorian era. It is a kind of settlement between Anglicanism and Presbyterianism and the hellenic-romantic ideals of nineteenth-century liberalism.

This inherited understanding of its cultural role has plenty of ingredients which the liberal may want to criticize (its wide-ranging involvement with matters of faith and ritual for example). But the British State also plays a variety of cultural roles which a liberal should not object to and indeed should be ready to defend. It does so not only by exercising direct control but also in the form of tax-relief, positive funding, State-established bodies distanced from government by the 'arm's-length principle' and so on. Consider various types of funding of arts, scientific research, scholarship, a historic building, a nature reserve, road and rail access to a remote heritage community (whose maintenance embodies an ethico-aesthetic ideal rather than a distributive principle), commemorations such as Remembrance Day—all represent ethical choices.

Should it be the State or should it be voluntary associations which take on the role of promoting those goods which cannot be adequately supplied by the free market? This, one might say, is to a large extent simply a divergence between American and Continental traditions of liberalism,

---

[30] See Scanlon (1972).

with Britain, as ever, somewhere in between. More theoretically, it's a matter of ethics and political economy, not of Rawls-type constitutional principle.[31] Voluntary associations have liberal virtues, but they also have Lady-Bountiful—or corporate—vices. Similarly, the arguments against State-involvement have to do with bureaucracy, self-perpetuation of elites, museum-driven art, and journal-driven science/scholarship etc., rather than any matter of neutralist principle.

6. THE FUTURE OF AN IDEA

In exhuming the nineteenth-century liberal idea (as I put it at the beginning) I do not want to give the impression that it's in as good shape now as it ever has been. Not that it was ever in tremendously good shape! It would certainly be a mistake to think of the nineteenth century, or even any part of it, as the 'liberal' century—if that suggests that the liberal idea had any hegemony. Its power of attraction declined sharply with distance, even at its height, and was in any case rather short-lived. One could trace this in the art and literature of the nineteenth century as well as in its philosophical ethics (particularly in Germany, whence much of its original impetus came). That would bring out the hostile climate and the internal tensions and obscurities it encountered, even before the explosion of twentieth-century modernism, which killed it for so long. This story deserves detailed and extended examination, on a large cultural canvas.

We cannot say quite what the results of such a historical revaluation, or critical regeneration and transformation, of the classic liberal idea would be. But we *can* say—it seems to me—that such historically informed ethical revaluation is the necessary starting point for fresh thinking about liberalism and that the diversion into disputes about justice or neutrality is a *cul-de-sac*. Liberalism without the liberal idea has no protein from which to keep regenerating itself. Instead it generates moral anxieties which threaten to bring down good principles with bad.[32]

---

[31] Rawls acknowledges in passing that 'statutes protecting the environment and controlling pollution; establishing national parks and preserving wilderness areas and animal and plant species; and laying aside funds for museums and the arts' are not constitutional essentials or questions of basic justice and that 'restrictions imposed by public reason may not apply to them; or if they do, not in the same way, or so strictly' (Rawls 1993: 214–15). Thus he allows that there may be such statutes, but he does not discuss how they should be squared with a principle of persuasive as well as permissive neutrality.

[32] This seems to me to be the danger of contemporary communitarian critiques of liberalism—though I would not say that it is presently more than that.

So I cannot agree that questions of right are sufficiently distinguishable, philosophically or emotionally, from questions about good to make *setting aside* ethical conceptions of the good a possible and desirable rule for political discourse and legislation. This is not to go to the other extreme; I certainly do not deny that there are a lot of important ways in which politics should give the right priority over the good. However let me end by warding off another possible misunderstanding of what I have said.

'Ethical conceptions of the good' covers both ideals (what is admirable in human character and activity) and ends (what human well-being consists in). In this lecture I have been much concerned with classical liberal ideals of excellence in character and activity. However I would not want to say that I am defending a 'perfectionist' as against a 'neutralist' idea of liberalism. This is becoming something of an orthodox dichotomy but it is a false one. The term 'perfectionism', it is true, is used variously: if it simply means that invocation of ideals and ends as well as rights is legitimate and unavoidable in political discourse then I have to count myself a 'perfectionist'. But this is a misleadingly loose use of the word. There are stricter senses which should be preferred.

In a very narrow sense perfectionism (1) characterizes excellence in human character and activity by reference to a priori arguments about what is essential to human nature and (2) distinguishes human excellence from human well-being and attaches intrinsic value only to the former. Neither thesis is endorsed in what I have said. Excellence, it seems to me, is to be characterized not by a priori arguments about human essence but by appeal to human sentiments—specifically, to what we find admirable, spontaneously and reflectively, in one way or another. I doubt that what we thus find admirable either turns on beliefs about human essence or unconsciously tracks facts about human essence. And further: what is admirable seems to me to have ethical value[33] only so far as its achievement contributes to well-being. Well-being, the well-being of all individuals, is what has intrinsic ethical value. It need not be thought of either as pleasure and the absence of pain or as desire-satisfaction. One can be a pluralist about well-being. Understanding of one's situation, rootedness in reality, recognition, autonomy (internal and external) are parts of it as well as pleasure. They are desirable as ultimate ingredients of one's well-being. They are also intertwined with ideals we spontaneously admire. But it is nevertheless confusing to call this kind of pluralism about human ends 'perfectionism'. I agree with Thomas Hurka that the defining characteris-

---

[33] Ethical value: a brilliant violin performance (say) has aesthetic value whether or not it contributes to well-being. There is reason to admire it; but only if it contributes to well-being is there reason to do it, emulate it, fund it etc.

tic of perfectionism should be that it takes human excellence to have ethical value as such, whether or not it contributes to well-being.[34]

So against perfectionism I believe that the horizon within which ideals are defended must be a horizon of human ends. Human ends must be characterized in a down-to-earth moral psychology, free of both transcendental and reductionist urges, wishful ideology or self-imposed silences. If some revitalized version of the liberal idea carries conviction, it will be because its hierarchy of human excellence is seen to advance well-being, so understood, more fully than hierarchies propounded by other ethical ideals.

In the long run the character of a civil society is set by which great ethic acquires a leading authority (I do not mean hegemony) in its culture. One of those ethics is the liberal idea, and liberal order is its expression. Hence the stability of a liberal order requires its continued vitality (though not its monopoly). One consequence of the liberal idea is that liberal law must not forbid the propounding of any ethical idea. But that does not mean that it must positively prohibit the liberal State from advancing the liberal ethic, or expunge any trace of that ethic from its own legal content.

---

[34] In his fine book, *Perfectionism* (Hurka 1993). He calls the combination of (1) and (2) 'narrow perfectionism'. Broad perfectionism drops (1), 'mixed perfectionism' attaches ethical value to things other than excellence as well as excellence.

XI

Liberty's Hollow Triumph

1. LIBERALISM AS AN ETHICAL IDEAL

The history of liberalism is the history of an ethical ideal as well as a set of political and social arrangements. In the latter sense liberalism entrenches the juridical equality of all citizens, their equal civil and political rights—including among those rights a set of liberties strong enough to restrict the authority of society over the individual in a fundamental way. How to express in institutions this politically fundamental restriction is an important matter of debate, but that debate will not concern us. For present purposes I assume I can refer to liberalism as a set of political and social arrangements without further examination. Our concern will instead be the liberal ethical ideal and its present prospects.

What is this ideal? The question is best answered historically, both because the ideal has gone through significant changes and because many people who think of themselves as liberals are now seriously unsure about what it is or should be. Or so it seems.

Undoubtedly a central element of the liberal ideal has been an ethical and not just juridical idea of equal respect. It has been of utmost political importance. For more than two centuries, one might say—that is since the French Revolution, but certainly with earlier roots in the growth of towns, trade and individualism—it has helped to generate a drive towards juridical equality in all spheres, abolition of all forms of social discrimination. Most of us would say that this has been pure gain. Yet even if the ethical conception which asserts that all human beings deserve equal respect simply as human beings has helped to bring about the juridical equality of rights which we approve, it seems in itself eminently questionable. Historically a kind of ground for it was found in Christian faith. As Alexis de Tocqueville (for example) put it, 'Christianity, which has declared all men equal in the sight of God, cannot hesitate to acknowledge all men

First published in John Haldane (ed.), *Philosophy and Public Affairs*, Cambridge: Cambridge University Press, 1999. I am grateful to Samuel Brittan, Geoff Cupit and Dudley Knowles for helpful discussion.

equal before the law.'[1] But that hardly satisfies. What is it about human beings that makes them all equal in the sight of God? More generally, what are we to make of equal respect, if we find rest neither in the faith that all are equal 'in the sight of God', nor in a transcendental doctrine of absolute autonomy, nor an empirical hope that human beings can be equally worthy of respect if only society empowers them to become so?

Historically, however, equality of respect has certainly not been the only or the main ingredient in the liberal ethic. Its most significant element in the early nineteenth century was a determinate ideal which in fact stood in some potential tension with equality of respect. Liberty was justified as the condition which permitted the full and balanced development of human powers. This vision lay at the heart of the classical liberal ideal; but historically its force within liberalism has varied. Broadly speaking it was relatively great in the nineteenth-century phases of liberalism and small in the twentieth-century phases; while equal respect, in comparison, has played a significantly larger role in twentieth-century liberalism as the substantive ideal has faded. The change is striking and seems to require explanation. It is true that in general the nineteenth century is the century of ethical reflection *par excellence*, while twentieth-century ethical thought has at least until recently been in comparison thin, marginalized, and largely inexplicit; but then this in turn seems to require explanation. At any rate after a hundred years of modernism in culture and socialism or social democracy in politics we find ourselves going back to Hegel, Mill, and Nietzsche if we want to think hard about the viability of the liberal ethical ideal and the place of equal respect within it—in other words to a type of reflection which modernism and 'scientific' socialism combined to destroy, and which recent discussions of liberalism in moral and political philosophy are only just beginning to revive.

These two elements of the liberal ethic, their relative significance and the tension between them will be our subject. I shall distinguish four phases of the liberal tradition, two in the nineteenth century (early classical and late idealist), and two in the twentieth century (early modernist and late neutralist). I shall sketch the role the liberal ethical idea played in these four phases, as a preliminary to some questions about its current state.

2. CLASSICAL LIBERALISM

To call the liberal thinkers of the first half of the nineteenth century classical liberals seems just, for it was in this period that liberalism first

---

[1] Quoted in Siedentop (1994: 49).

reached maturity. In response to political and spiritual revolutions in France and Germany it established its ideal and discovered its inner tensions and fears. Classical liberalism in this sense is represented at its earliest in Germany by Schiller, Humboldt, and then later Burkhardt, in France by Constant, Guizot, Tocqueville, in Britain above all by Mill and in a later and more disenchanted way by Matthew Arnold. Mill was also a 'classical liberal' in the more common sense, that is, a believer in free trade. But he took pains to distinguish his qualified defence of free trade from his case for the liberty principle itself.[2] He defended free trade within certain limits[3] on grounds of efficiency but, in the great third chapter of *On Liberty* which deals with 'Individuality', he grounded liberty on the ethical ideal of classical liberalism.

Classical liberalism got its vision of human good largely from a revival of hellenism and a response to Kant. It set a 'Greek ideal of self-development' (Mill's phrase) against the Kantian, or more broadly Protestant Christian, conception of human worth. For Kant the dignity of human beings and the respect owed to them rests on their capacity to give themselves the moral law. To act autonomously is to act from reason alone and not 'inclination'; only such action has 'moral worth'. But Schiller—a seminal thinker in this story—wanted to reaffirm a Hellenic conception of the culture of the whole human being, of feeling as well as of rational will: 'It will always argue a still defective education [*Bildung*] if the moral character is able to assert itself only by sacrificing the natural.' 'Wholeness of character must . . . be present in any people capable, and worthy, of exchanging a State of compulsion for a State of freedom.'[4]

The issue is deep. To affirm the 'Greek ideal of self-development' is to place human worth on a basis of contingency. Beauty of character, the developed balance of freedom, intelligence, and emotional spontaneity, are not wholly or even mostly under one's control. Admiration based on such excellence will be very unequally shared. Whereas what Kant calls autonomy is, at least according to his theory of transcendental freedom, not a merely contingent capacity of human beings. Kant thinks that autonomy, if it exists at all, exists non-empirically. Each of us is aware of it within ourselves, or at least we necessarily take ourselves to have it in deliberating how to act. Respect turns out to rest on something we must attribute to anyone we think of as a free chooser. Moreover that something, 'the causality of freedom', lies as firmly in the Beyond (to use

---

[2] Mill (1963–91), xviii. 293 (*On Liberty*, ch. 5, para. 4).

[3] For an account of them see Schwartz (1972).

[4] Schiller (1967: 19, 23). These letters were written from 1793 to 1795; a revised version appeared in 1801.

Nietzsche's telling phrase) as does the Christian appeal to our equality 'in the sight of God'.

Not that classical liberalism repudiates the importance Kant and Christianity attach to this capacity of the individual. On the contrary, personal responsibility, the capacity to govern oneself, to recognize and act on good reasons—positive freedom—is central to nineteenth-century liberalism as a whole, both early and late. Nevertheless, liberals of the earlier period trod largely in the footsteps of Schiller not Kant. The important thing was to balance and fill out self-government by allowing due scope to human powers of emotional spontaneity. They agreed with Schiller that developed spontaneity is achieved by education of feeling. Spontaneity of feeling is no more incompatible with education of feeling than spontaneity of reason is incompatible with education of reason. A determinate potential or disposition is in both cases developed by self-culture. And the ideal is balance of the two.

In this same spirit, Mill does not straightforwardly reject 'the Platonic and Christian ideal of self-government'. Rather it represents to him the one-sided vision that Kantian moral worth represented to Schiller. 'There is a Greek ideal of self-development' which this narrower ideal 'blends with, but does not supersede. It may be better to be a John Knox than an Alcibiades, but it is better to be a Pericles than either.'[5]

A similar contrast is present in Matthew Arnold's well-known pairing of 'Hellenism' and 'Hebraism':

The uppermost idea with Hellenism is to see things as they really are; the uppermost idea with Hebraism is conduct and obedience . . . The governing idea of Hellenism is *spontaneity of consciousness*; that of Hebraism, *strictness of conscience*.[6]

Arnold acknowledges the 'grandeur of earnestness and intensity' of hebraism as Schiller acknowledged the 'dignity' of acting from the moral law. But hellenism gets the fullest share of Arnold's eloquence. Hellenism has what Schiller called 'grace' and Arnold famously refers to as 'sweetness and light'. It has light because it sees 'things as they really are':

To get rid of one's ignorance, to see things as they are, and by seeing them as they are to see them in their beauty, is the simple and attractive ideal which Hellenism holds out before human nature; and from the simplicity and charm of this ideal, Hellenism, and human life in the hands of Hellenism, is invested with a kind of aerial ease, clearness, and radiancy; they are full of what we call sweetness and light.[7]

[5] Mill (1963–91), xviii. 266 (*On Liberty* ch. 3, para. 8).
[6] Arnold (1960–78: v. 165).   [7] Ibid. 167.

Yet Arnold belongs to a rather later part of this story and is not quite in the spirit of classical liberalism. He calls himself 'a Liberal tempered by experience, reflection, and renouncement'.[8] He affirms with classical liberalism that human good and worth lie in the balanced development of human powers, and that balanced development is also harmony with the world—the capacity to see things as they are and thus to see them in their beauty. But classical liberalism aspires to give all human beings equitable access to this good. It believes in the realizability of an inclusive ethical community based on it. At least in more radical moments it still has revolutionary enthusiasm about the possibility of such a fully realized human community, living in equality and truth—in liberty, equality, and fraternity. This radical optimism enables it to combine romantic hellenism with the 'desire to be in unity with one's fellow creatures' on equal terms—a 'powerful natural sentiment', as Mill says—'a powerful principle in human nature',[9] and certainly a powerful principle in Mill's nature. It is memorably expressed in the revolutionary music to which Beethoven sets the words of Schiller:

> Seid umschlungen, Millionen,
> Diesen kuss der ganzen Welt![10]

From the beginning, however there was another and no less important moment in classical liberalism, a strain of apprehension as well a strain of enthusiasm: a sense of the danger posed to the human spirit by democratic mass culture. It was associated with a political sociology developed particularly by the French liberals,[11] which held that creative and progressive moral energies are released primarily through conflict and dissent. Democracy, just because of its equality and fraternity, threatened a spiritual if not political tyranny; the imposition of mediocrity, the stifling of great individualities and dissenting voices on which moral and intellectual progress depends. I will call this *the worrying hypothesis*.

Freedom for individuals to develop in full diversity was the only prescription against this danger—hence the cardinal importance of entrenching negative liberty in democratic states. Another theme of the early

----

[8] Arnold (1960–78: v. 165), 88.

[9] Mill (1963–91), x. 231 (*Utilitarianism*, ch. 3, para. 10).

[10] O ye millions I embrace you/ Here's a kiss for all the world.
The Ode to Joy continues: Brüder! Über'm Sternenzelt/ Muss ein lieber Vater Wohnen. (Brothers, above the starry canopy/ there must dwell a loving father.) Compare Arnold's fifth 'Switzerland' poem:
Yes! in the sea of life enisled/ With echoing straits between us thrown/
Dotting the shoreless watery wild/ We mortal millions live *alone*.

[11] Siedentop (1994) gives a brief account.

nineteenth century also came to the rescue—a new faith in the historical progressiveness of human nature and society. The human spirit could yet flourish in democratic equality because there was virtually no limit to the eventual improvement of human beings in good and progressive states of society. This was the faith in which at least the radical end of classical liberalism placed its trust. It allowed long-term optimism as well as short-term pessimism. In a future good society the romantic-hellenic ideal would be reconcilable with equality of respect. Indeed even now it was possible to 'see things as they are'—without a Kantian or Christian Beyond—and yet still to recognize the potential that is present if not actualized in all human beings. One could respect the *potential*. This was a naturalized equivalent of equality 'in the sight of God'—the promise of an inclusive this-worldly community of the future rather than a heavenly city or a transcendentally conceived kingdom of ends.

3. CRITICISMS

Like any ideal substantial enough to inspire, the romantic-hellenic ideal of classical liberals can also alienate. Objections come broadly from two sides. On one side is the moralistic—the side of 'hebraism', 'Christian self-denial', Kantian moral worth. Also on this side is the collectivist spirit of living for others. On the other side is the aesthetic. It finds the classical liberal's romantic-hellenic ideal in one or another way unattractive—anachronistic, or cold and inauthentic, unactual and imparticular. Both forms of criticism already arose in the nineteenth century.

From the moralistic-collectivist side comes the Hegelian objection that the classical liberal ideal is too individualistic. It gives too much to free spontaneity and subjective conscience, and too little to the self-realization which individuals achieve in the ethical life of the community. This objection must be stated with care. Classical liberalism's Periclean ideal certainly does not deny that virtue and civic contribution are a part of the realized individual. It recognizes them as intrinsic elements in the balance of moral freedom and spontaneity. So its individualism does not lie in putting private self-culture, still less the pursuit of selfish material interest, ahead of public duty and disregarding the latter in favour of the former. That may be true of some liberalisms but not of classical liberalism. So where does its individualism lie? In Hegel's own hands the criticism is that the elements which the classical-liberal ideal seeks to balance—individual conscience and spontaneity of feeling—are *both* conceived too individualistically. He agrees with Schiller in rejecting Kant's one-sided valuation of conscience and devaluation of feeling, but thinks the antidote cannot simply consist in adding back in a revalued feeling and looking for a 'balance' between the two. For this accepts the dichotomy between them, instead of transcending it; whereas the drift of Hegel's argument is that it can be and must be transcended, in an ethical disposition which identifies itself with a social order. And this conclusion also implies the simultaneous overcoming of another dichotomy—that between individual and society. To this a classical liberal might robustly reply—in my view thoroughly plausibly—that there are untranscendable dichotomies of which these are two. But to leave it there, without exploring what dissatisfaction might lie behind the criticism, is unsatisfactory. The root of dissatisfaction (it seems to me) is that classical liberalism's developed individual is not an ideal to which most human beings can aspire—at least in actually existing societies, whatever one may hope about the Future Beyond. This ideal places too much worth in the accomplishment and satisfaction of the outstanding individual rather than in the trans-individual worth ('objective reason') embodied in the social order. In contrast an ethic which takes performance of the duties of one's social position, whatever they may be, as the condition of human worth places worth in something which all human beings can share:

The *right of individuals* to their *subjective determination to freedom* is fulfilled in so far as they belong to ethical actuality; for their *certainty* of their own freedom has its *truth* in such objectivity, and it is in the ethical realm that they *actually* possess *their own* essence and their *inner* universality.[12]

Powerful words. In a properly constituted ethical order—one which is realizable in the human beings we know—*everyone* can discharge their role in ways that merit recognition.[13] Not that classical liberalism has to deny that in any way. Still, this is not the ethical insight which it distinctively brings to the fore. Rather it acknowledges and embraces a hierarchy of excellence in human attainment; it emphatically honours supreme human achievement without pretending that any and every kind of achievement is supreme. Moreover it presents its ideal of development and excellence as a universal ideal, not just the ideal of an aristocratic class. When an ideal is generally acknowledged as appropriate only to a certain class, then failure to achieve it in one's life damages self-esteem only if one is a member of that class. But the classical liberal presents the romantic-hellenic ideal

---

[12] Hegel (1991), 196 (§153).

[13] Note that Hegel does not reject the modern principle of 'subjective freedom'; in that respect he regularly distinguishes his view of the State from Plato's, specifically rejecting the idea that social roles may be *allotted* to individuals, e.g. §185, §262.

as an ideal for humanity—while simultaneously affirming that 'the initiation of all wise or noble things' can come only from the few. 'The honour and glory of the average man is that he is capable of following that initiative; that he can respond internally to wise and noble things, and be led to them with his eyes open.'[14] This is honest—but it does not avoid the incipiently divisive character of the ideal. Were there a transcendental or divine backdrop on which the ethical equality of human beings was inscribed, and from which 'the initiation of all wise or noble things' could be held to come, then it would be that much easier to acknowledge the unequal performance of humans on the empirical stage. Failing that, it is still at least a little easier if one can believe in the approach of an equal yet fully human community in some Future Perfect. But what if we definitively recognize that the Future Perfect is a non-existent tense? Wholeness of character and excellence of achievement offer no salvation precisely to the poor in spirit.

Classical liberalism, the critic says, cannot overcome this diremption. This is the real shape of its 'individualism'. The ethics of autonomous conscience and the ideal of spontaneity cannot yield *Sittlichkeit*: objective ethical community, and the ethical disposition. Let us next turn to the equally powerful aesthetic criticisms.

The first is that the romantic hellenism of classical liberals is anachronistic—it was so in their time and is even more clearly so now. We can recapture neither the primitive unity of the polis nor the 'aerial ease, clearness, and radiancy' of the Greek vision. In late nineteenth-century classicism (for example Lord Leighton) nineteenth-century people look wistfully out of classical kit, in an elegaic nowhere-land. There is a similar nostalgia about *Culture and Anarchy*. By the time Arnold wrote it, classical liberalism's ethical ideal had already come to seem problematic, not least to Arnold. Mill one might say still belongs to the world of Beethoven and Schiller, Arnold belongs to the world of Brahms.[15]

Why should the romantic-hellenic ideal seem anachronistic? Human suffering, conflict, finitude, etc. were as present for the Greeks as for us and are objectified and acknowledged in the clearness and radiancy that comes from seeing things as they really are. Or if they aren't, then this is a perennial limitation of the Apollonian spirit and not a problem of anachronism. The problem of anachronism is rather that the ideal relegates to the realm of means what most people in modern society must spend most of their lives doing—and these are free citizens not slaves.

---

[14] Mill (1963–9), xviii. 269 (*On Liberty* ch. 3, para. 13).

[15] Brahms's personal motto, 'frei aber froh' (free *but* joyful), expresses the distance travelled from that earlier liberal world. It was itself, apparently, a response to the motto of his friend Joachim—'frei aber einsam' (free but alone).

This problem was recognized by Schiller—his answer was that full human freedom is possible only when specialization is transcended.[16] But specialization and the dynamism of constant change is the essence of modern life. Furthermore, although in modern society the realm of means is in a process of constant change (a fact which undermines the Hegelian ethical disposition as much as it challenges the romantic-hellenic ideal) it will never be transcended. Specialism and change must be embraced in our ethical life or we are alienated from modernity.

What is at stake is thus not purely aesthetic, in the sense that the aesthetic preference for the depiction of modern mass everyday life, or the affirmation of many unashamedly partial perspectives against some single fully balanced perspective which 'sees things as they are', is not *just* that. Behind the idea that the classical-liberal ideal is anachronistic we find again a rejection of its exclusiveness, or an increased pain at the sense of its exclusiveness on the part of those who continue to uphold it. This felt diremption pushes romantic hellenism into its elegaic Arnoldian or Brahmsian phase. It is not the only thing that makes the ideal seem anachronistic but it is an ingredient.

Nietzsche is the philosopher who sees most clearly the tension in classical liberalism between the hellenic ideal and the ethic of equality and fraternity. He is capable of representing this agonizing tension with great sympathy—'today there is perhaps no more decisive mark of the "*higher nature*", of the more spiritual nature, than to be divided against oneself in this sense and to remain a battleground for these oppositions.'[17] But he is of course a critic of liberalism *in toto*, and not just a critic of the classical-liberal ideal from the standpoint of equality or fraternity, or of equality and fraternity from the standpoint of the classical-liberal ideal. Familiarly, equality and fraternity are for Nietzsche residues of slave-morality. But Nietzsche equally rejects the classical-liberal ideal—not however from the standpoint of 'modern civilization', i.e. because of its inadequacy to the specialization and dynamism of modern life. Rather Nietzsche finds it too Periclean, too Apollonian, cut off from pain, frenzy, life.[18] This is criticism from an equally 'anachronistic' standpoint of authenticity; it is still informed by hellenic nostalgia, but now for Homeric society and pre-Socratic philosophy rather than Athenian democracy.

[16] see the Sixth Letter in Schiller (1967). It is of course also the problem that Marx, whose ethical ideal of the developed human being is Schiller's, took very seriously.

[17] Nietzsche (1996: 34–5). (First published 1887; Brahms's third symphony, for which 'frei aber froh' provides the motto theme, was first performed in 1883.)

[18] In *Twilight of the Idols* both Mill and Schiller appear on Nietzsche's list of 'impossibles', Mill for his 'offensive clarity' and Schiller as the 'Moral-Trumpeter of Säckingen' (Nietzsche 1990: 78).

The ethic of authenticity is far more obviously incompatible with democratic equality than is classical liberalism; clear-thinking Nietzschean modernists have seen that. In affirming the necessity of a 'pathos of distance', 'discipline', 'breeding', the exploitation of the many for the perfection of the view and so on Nietzsche is only being realistic and consistent to his ideal. In contrast, just because classical liberalism's ideal is Periclean, not Homeric, it is not evident that it is irreconcilable with the institutions of liberal democracy. On the other hand the question of its inauthenticity remains. Nietzschean affirmation of life is anti-democratic but not anti-demotic. It may be incompatible with equality but it is not so obviously incompatible with community—the people can join in the dance. Whereas the ideal of realized balance, with its far-seeing philosopher-poet-statesmen and cold marble pediments, alienates the liberal from the people and indeed from his own demotic self. Affirming authenticity again turns out to be about the overcoming of diremption.

4. MORALISTIC OR IDEALIST LIBERALISM

So in all these criticisms one can find a common strand. It is the difficulty of reconciling the liberal balance of moral freedom and spontaneity, the liberal ideal of 'seeing things as they are', in proportion and not one-sidedly—with one's authentic self, with the world of modern work, with the life of the community, with at-one-ness with the people. The conflict with Nietzschean authenticity, important as it is, must be set aside here in that it was not a conflict experienced *within* the liberal spirit. But the other conflicts were. How to overcome these diremptions? One way is through replacing the romantic-hellenic ideal with an ideal of service, and basing liberal equality of respect on that. Another is to cut off equality of respect from ethical grounding—either by grounding it instead on the denial of normative objectivity or by making it a 'political' rather than a 'philosophical' doctrine. These are respectively the communitarian, the populist, and the neutralist directions in post-classical liberalism.

In Britain the prime exemplar of the liberal-communitarian direction is T. H. Green. On the one hand (unlike Hegel) he reaffirms Protestant/Kantian notions of personal responsibility at the expense of the classical liberal's hellenic ideal of individuality; on the other he affirms the ideal of inclusion in an equal community in which selfhood is realized through pursuit of 'the common good'. This is a spirit that suddenly seems alive again. As others have pointed out, T. H. Green the New Liberal is also a spiritual forefather of New Labour. Compared to Mill and Marx, at any rate, he was the Third Way.

His object was to incorporate the working class into the moral community. He sees this project in Kantian terms, as an education into positive freedom, autonomy. Autonomy makes you a member of the kingdom of ends and is the only thing that has moral worth. For Green this has a well-known political implication. He argues that negative liberty can legitimately be limited by legislation which stabilizes and builds individuals', and in particular workers', positive freedom. Thus he thinks for example that legislation to enforce temperance can be justified because alcoholic addiction undermines autonomy. But it can be justified only to the extent that it promotes moral growth. The exercise of autonomy is the one thing that has moral worth, so in so far as legal compulsion introduces heteronomous motives into the free pursuit of one's duty it is bad.

This reassertion of Kantianism against romantic hellenism is a telling difference between Mill and Green, but it is also important to see where they agree. As already noted, Mill did not reject the idea of positive freedom—the idea that a person's capacity to act rationally, to make and stick to a rational plan of life, is what makes that person *morally* free. He thinks that negative liberty develops this capacity as well as developing individual spontaneity of feeling. Both Mill and Green are teleological liberals; both must therefore recognize that the question whether we make people freer in the positive sense by interventionist legislation, for example by criminalizing drugs, is one in which arguments can be made on both sides. And yet politically Mill is a more unqualified champion of negative liberty than Green. Why is this, given that neither of them thinks negative liberty is itself, in Mill's words, an 'abstract right'? What we see here is the strain placed on the connections between liberty, autonomy, and equal respect as working-class enfranchisement, social as well as political, approaches. Mill does not think that each of us is equally possessed of moral freedom, and by our more populist standards he is far from reluctant to spell that out—but he thinks that in a good state of society we could all be morally free, and for all his acknowledgement of historicity his view of how quickly such a state might be attained retains a blithe enlightenment naivety, relying heavily on the enlightenment's associationist psychology. Green's sense of its imminence is tempered by social reality. He puts equal respect at the more abstruse horizons of idealist metaphysics and Christian religion. Each one of us in our highest self is identical with God; but in practice Green's willingness to see in everyone a potential to cultivate their *own* positive freedom, unassisted by law, is notably less robust than Mill's. Positive freedom, the foundation of equal respect and of membership of the kingdom of ends, turns out to be something that most individuals must be helped to attain.

As well as re-emphasizing autonomy at the expense of expressive spontaneity Green takes another step against the diremptiveness of classical liberalism. Though he affirms autonomy he presents it as pursuit of the 'common good'. What belongs to common good is non-competitive—what does not belong to it is not truly good. 'The only true good is to be good' because this is 'the only good in the pursuit of which there can be no competition of interests, the only good which is really common to all who may pursue it'.[19] Freedom in the positive sense is freedom to make the best of oneself—but to make the best of oneself, it turns out, is to contribute single-mindedly to common good, and to one's own self-perfection as a harmonious part of common good. Even to have a right is only to have a claim on society 'in respect of a capacity freely . . . to contribute to its good'.[20]

This is a liberalism impoverished by moralism and collectivism. Of course it is important to have a worth while role to discharge, but service is not the only or even the highest good. Likewise, it is profoundly true that some things cannot be properly enjoyed unless shared, or if others lack them. But then other goods are enjoyed at least in part because they are competitive achievements, and others again are neither competitive nor common but quite simply private. The sense of human diversity and individuality, which Mill fully registers—with its acceptance of irreducible public-collective, social-competitive, and private domains—receives at best notional recognition from Green.

In Green's hands self-realization turns out to be self-transcendence—one of the deepest *fin-de-siècle* themes:

[S]in consists in the individual's making his own self his object, not in the possible expansion in which it becomes that true will of humanity's which is also God's, but under the limitation of momentary appetite or interest.[21]

This elevates egoism into exalted spheres in another attempt to overcome a division. In free action, Green thinks along with Hegel, the self always makes *itself* its object—not a thesis Mill would have endorsed. But the object turns out to be something very different from what one thought; it is not a particular self among others but the universal 'self', God, the general will. Self-transcendence is one of the great human ideals—but it is a strange ideal to put at the heart of liberalism.

---

[19] Green (1906: 288).   [20] Green (1885–8: ii. 463).   [21] Ibid. (iii. 73).

5. MODERNIST OR POPULIST LIBERALISM

The *fin-de-siècle* revival of idealism was part of a widespread revulsion against the nineteenth-century liberal self: a heroically finite, self-propelling, and self-cultivating item set in the actual, natural world. The culture of modernism which succeeded it contained an ideal of authenticity which undermined the liberal tradition even more powerfully than the earlier, shorter-lived ideal of self-transcendence. It is still with us (post-modernism is modernism gone populist), even though there is at the same time a revival of the ethics of character which is favourable to the classical-liberal ideal of self-culture and to which we shall return. For the classical-liberal ideal assumes a human nature of determinate if diverse and historically structured potential. I achieve individuality, or self-realization, by *discovering* the particular life which is best for me. No doubt options and choices are involved but they are limited by my historical horizon, my own determinate powers, and the objective ethical hierarchy of human ends and ideals. In the modernist ethic of authenticity each of these—history, human nature, ethical objectivity—gives way (for many reasons and by many paths). To live authentically is to live by values that one chooses in some bafflingly radical sense. I do not discover myself, I make myself—from no materials and by no plan.

There is in fact a pincer movement in modernist ethical (or anti-ethical) thought—on the one hand, social determination eliminates an independently determinate self, on the other hand, existential freedom eliminates an independently determinate self. In this climate liberalism was always going to find it difficult to survive irrespective of other great political forces working against it. It survived by emptying itself of first-order content and withdrawing to a meta-level. In place of arguing for liberty and equality under the law from determinate ethical ideals—rational autonomy, diverse affective spontaneity—it began to argue for the institutions of liberalism by what I will call a *strategy of epistemological detachment*.

The populist version of the strategy is familiar. All 'values' are subjective—matters of choice. Thus the ends, ideals, moral principles of one individual cannot be regarded as more or less admirable than those of another. Since it is their 'values' that we judge people by, it follows that we have no ground for giving greater respect to one person than another, or imposing on anyone a way of life which they do not choose. Understood as a negative argument against unequal respect this is sound reasoning from the given premisses. To make it an argument for a positive doctrine of equal respect or for liberal institutions based on such doctrine is unsound; nevertheless the unsound argument has been very influential, and inasmuch as it argues for liberalism from an epistemological thesis—in this case anti-objectivism about values—it exemplifies the strategy of epistemological detachment.

Popper is the modern liberal philosopher closest to populism. He also, it is true, inherits a large part of the legacy of classical liberalism. Thus for example, while the assault he launches on 'historicism' is quintessentially modernist, the story he tells of a transition, through the growth of critical rationality in Greece, from magical, tribal, and collectivist societies to open societies in which criticism is free but the 'strain of civilization' and the nostalgia for tribalism is acute—that is very much of a piece with the classical liberals' sociology of liberty. He sees the enlightenment as 'the greatest of all moral and spiritual revolutions in history'[22] and his admiration for Pericles equals Mill's. What he does not inherit is classical liberalism's Schillerian ethical outlook. For Popper the crucial attitude in an open society is 'critical rationalism'. It is, purportedly, an epistemological not an ethical attitude,

very similar to the scientific attitude, to the belief that in the search for truth we need co-operation, and that, with the help of argument, we can in time attain something like objectivity.[23]

Adopting it is however a 'moral decision'. Popper insists that a moral decision is not simply 'a matter of taste'; nonetheless his affirmation of the 'dualism of facts and decisions' has the moral fervour which one is used to hearing in some people's insistence that all ends and ideals are subjective. Proclaiming this dualism is, he evidently believes, an essential bulwark against authoritarianism.

Note the striking epistemological turn since Mill. Mill does argue, passingly but pregnantly, from fallibilism to liberty of discussion in the second chapter of *On Liberty*—in a manner somewhat similar to Popper's argument from critical rationalism to liberalism in general. But he treats fallibilism as a truth about finite human beings rather than a moral attitude that one 'decides' to adopt; and his argument is made only as part of a case for free speech. The main weight of his case for liberty in general lies in the classical-liberal analysis of human flourishing and the classical-liberal sociology of liberty which he propounds in chapter 3.

---

[22] Popper (1945: i. p. ix).   [23] Ibid. (ii. 213).

6. VALUE-PLURALIST AND NEUTRALIST LIBERALISM

In the 1950s and 1960s liberal philosophy continued to pursue the strategy of epistemological detachment. Like Popper, Berlin inherits important parts of the legacy of classical liberalism—in his case, the very parts with which Popper has least sympathy: the German counter-enlightenment, its appreciation of historicity, its sympathy for a variety of values, and its liberality of mind. The value-pluralism on which Berlin's liberal argument rests reflects this source. There are incompatible systems of value which cannot be put onto a single scale. Berlin does not see this as a form of subjectivism, and thus his argument is not as close to the populist argument as Popper's. Nonetheless value-pluralism, however one interprets it,[24] is apparently an *epistemological* doctrine about values, and not just a classical-liberal affirmation of the objective value of diversity. The idea that objectivism about value leads to authoritarianism in politics is present in Berlin as it is in Popper. Perhaps it was not a misguided thing to say in its time. There can be such connections in specific historical contexts and the context then was the struggle against totalitarianism. But that context has passed some time ago and the supposed connection between objectivism and authoritarianism has become a will-o'-the-wisp.

The most recent period in the discussion of liberalism, at least in academic philosophy, has been dominated by John Rawls. No doubt one main reason for this has been his success in focusing liberalism on the theory of justice—a topic which had never played such a salient role in liberalism before. That in itself is telling. But there is another side of his thought which is just as important and has become increasingly so—his neutralism. In his more recent work Rawls places a new degree of emphasis on his distinction between 'comprehensive' and 'political liberalism'. Comprehensive liberalism is one of a number of philosophical and ethical positions, liberal and non-liberal—Rawls cites Mill and Kant as developing comprehensive forms of liberalism. 'Political liberalism' refrains from endorsing any one comprehensive position, liberal or other. Thus in particular it eschews the classical-liberal ideal. As a further refinement on the epistemological detachment of Popper and Berlin, it does not even take a view on meta-ethical questions about the existence and nature of truth in ethics, since these are philosophical questions which should not be dragged into the political domain:

[24] See Essay IV.

Once we accept the fact that reasonable pluralism is a permanent condition of public culture under free institutions, the idea of the reasonable is more suitable as part of the basis of public justification for a constitutional regime than the idea of moral truth. Holding a political conception as true, and for that reason alone the one suitable basis of public reason, is *exclusive, even sectarian, and so likely to foster public division.*[25]

Political liberalism restricts itself to assessing which comprehensive positions are 'reasonable' and then arguing to constitutional proposals from an 'overlapping consensus' of such reasonable positions. Moreover Rawls, with the mainstream of recent American liberal theory, puts forward a very strong doctrine of state neutrality. The State must not favour any conception of the good, *either* (1) by prohibiting any individual from pursuing his or her conception (within just limits) *or* (2) by acting as a persuader in favour of some conception. But while (1) was also a central tenet of classical liberalism, (2) was not. The classical liberal had a definite conception of the good and was ready to accept in principle that the State had a role in fostering, as against enforcing, that ideal through educational and cultural policies such as the curriculum of State schools, the setting up of free museums, the public funding of the arts, conservation, scholarship or scientific research.[26]

7. THE HOLLOW TRIUMPH

This brings the story up to the present—admittedly at breakneck pace! What can be learnt from it? Classical liberals feared that democracy would produce a culturally or spiritually levelling conformism. It might not take the form of a political tyranny, though democracy without the institutions of liberalism might easily produce that. However even a liberal democracy with constitutionally entrenched freedoms might, they feared, still tend towards effective imposition of mediocre consensus through social rather than political means. The triumph of liberty would then be hollow, in that political emancipation of individuals would have destroyed the individual.

The combination of idealism and foreboding can be tiresome. Nevertheless it is one of the classical liberals' strengths. Their analysis of the dangers attendant on their own political programme was penetrating

---

[25] John Rawls (1993: 129) (my emphasis). Rawls has again set out his conception of 'public reason' in Rawls (1997).

[26] I argue this point with reference to Mill in Essay X, Sect. 3. Obviously there can be and was debate about how useful it is for the State to get involved in such things; my point is that it was not conducted at the level of a philosophical thesis of State-neutrality.

in both ethical and sociological terms; it gives us a well-considered measure against which to set the liberal democracies we know.

The evolution in the philosophy of liberalism which we have considered in previous sections already seems to go some way towards confirming their fears. Classical liberalism's central tension was between its ambitious hellenic ideal of human excellence and its wish to live with others in community on equal terms. This tension—contrary to classical liberalism's critics—was a strength not a flaw. It registered an ineliminable conflict in human aspiration which must come into the open whenever people escape hierarchy and mythical social charters. So a truly liberal society, committed to escaping these things, has to accept the conflict and try to find ways of coping with it—as does any individual to whom the liberal ideal means something. And yet, as it turned out, the reality of the tension was soon lost or denied within the liberal tradition itself. After a brief interlude of moralistic idealism, liberalism in this century has moved with increasing firmness towards the strategy of epistemological detachment. The most influential liberalism of the 'post-modern' period, that of Rawls, confirms this in a striking way: by its division between the political and the comprehensively ethical, its strong doctrine of State neutrality and its preoccupation with developing a 'theory' of justice—of rights as against goods—which can emerge from an overlapping consensus. I think it is fair to say that in practice the most influential liberal philosophies in this century concede ground (in more or less subtle ways) to the populist version of the ethic of equal respect. And this is at least *consistent* with the classical liberals' worrying hypothesis.

On the other hand, caution urges that even now we still have very little material to test it. For the century and a half since they wrote has turned out to be one of the great periods of conflict in Western history and simultaneously a period of immense cultural revolution and renewal. We are hardly well supplied with data to test the idea that peaceful and prosperous liberal democratic States destroy individuality. Perhaps only with the end of Cold War and then the collapse of the socialist model have we reached the right laboratory conditions, so to speak, for testing it.

Let us fix more clearly where, according to the worrying hypothesis, the problem is supposed to lie. It is not a problem of liberty or material affluence, nor quite a problem of morality or intellectual attainment. Improving the freedom and material security of individuals is always possible and important, but it does not diminish its importance to say that these are not crisis areas in modern liberal democracies. Nor is it the case, at least from any liberal point of view (including the classical), that there is a crisis of morality in the West. Any liberal must reckon the softening of the traditional ferocity of the moral, the elimination of sheer moral prejudice and irrational taboo, as a great gain for the human spirit. This can be acknowledged even by those liberals who feel a need to pull back from 'liberalism' in the current loose and unphilosophical sense of 'permissiveness'—for example, in the irresponsibility with which we now bring children into the world and shuffle onto others the complex and demanding charge of bringing them up. (Such unpermissive thoughts would not of course have seemed at all outrageous to a Mill or a Green.)

Similar remarks apply to the intellectual domain of science, philosophy, and scholarship. They are at unparalleled levels of development and support. Maybe here some worries about mediocritization and conformism begin to seep in. Still these collective activities continue solidly, and in doing so, underpin rationality steadily—which is their pre-eminent indirect social function. They expand and solidify mentality, 'objective spirit', just as technical progress expands and deepens its material base. More: we see striking reversals of strong modernist trends. Philosophy witnesses a restoration of normative objectivity, a revival of interest in the ethics of character and excellence, while history and biology gradually unravel the modernist illusion that human beings are blank canvases, on which either they themselves or atemporal 'social structures' paint.

In short there is no evident crisis of liberty or material security, nor of intellectual culture or morality. If there is a crisis, it is a crisis of ethical and aesthetic self-identity. Which takes us back to Schiller. The problem, it seems, is not the corruption of the right, or the weakening of the true, but the coarsening or diminution of the good. It is a problem of our art, our ideals, our aspirations for our own improvement as human beings, not of our cognitive inquiries or moral commitment. We lack powerful and inspiring models, whether in art or philosophy, of a life worth living. So much recent art seems to fall on a spectrum between sheer childishness or vacuous gimmickry and alienation or inner exile. Is this the 'weariness' which Nietzsche thought would afflict modern life?

If so, what is its cause? The worrying hypothesis is not the only available one. The cause could be the intellectual decline of faith and thus of serious as against wacky or folksy religious ideals. Or it could be that we are at the end of the modernist and socialist century—which just because it was one of the greatest cultural and spiritual flowerings (and traumas) of the West could understandably produce a period of spiritual weariness in its decline.

All three hypotheses could be true. However, the worrying hypothesis is the one we are considering. It says that liberal democracy has an inbuilt demotic drift which eventually cuts down all great ideals to a 'tolerant' equality of standing, removes public and objective acknowledgement of their grandeur, and instead gives public reinforcement only to those emotions strongly ('profoundly') felt by the Many. It also explains why equality of respect has flourished even as the religious and metaphysical bases for it have been removed. Older liberals sought to give the ethical doctrine of equal respect intellectual support. But it is now quite obvious that when equal respect catches the demotic tide it no longer needs such support. At that point it becomes an obfuscating anti-ideal, a golden calf around which one must dance (or if dancing is not one's *forte* supply philosophical rationalizations). Nietzsche was right to locate modern 'weariness' here.

But to agree with his diagnosis is not to accept his prognosis or prescription. We can reject the ethical doctrine of equal respect as demotic ideology without throwing out anything liberalism needs.

(1) We do not need the thesis of equal respect to affirm juridical equality, of civil and political rights and duties, for all citizens. Juridical equality in liberties, claims, and duties remains the keystone of the arch of liberal institutions. But the arch can bridge a void without support from the wooden scaffold of metaphysical or religious ideas which was needed while it was being built; the keystone ties together the structure of liberal democracy and that structure keeps the keystone in place.

(2) We retain the sentiment of our common humanity; an emotion of fellow-feeling and companionable understanding which requires no intellectual support and no belief in equality of powers.

(3) Given these two firm bases, we can and must still have civility—easy to recognize but hard to define: not treating people demeaningly, as though they and their views were of no account, or they were inferior just because of what they do, where they come from or who they are. 'The first law of good manners (*des guten Tones*) is: *Show respect for the freedom of others*; the second: *Show forth freedom in yourself.*'[27]

(4) We can still accept that the quality of moral agency, and its character as 'autonomy', that is, personal responsibility, is the basis of a certain distinctive *respect* (something separate from civility as such). Kant was right in that, and right to emphasize that moral respect can be gained irrespectively of one's place in society or one's achievements in life. Yet it is also true that people differ deeply and irremediably in the quality of their moral sensibility, their force of will, their self-restraint, their independence of mind, etc. There is no level, empirical or other, at which those differences are annulled; a liberal democracy is rightly committed to applying

---

[27] From Schiller's *Kallias* letters, quoted by the editors in Schiller (1967: 297).

the standard of moral responsibility, so far as possible, to every mature human being but in doing so it must find ways of recognizing this difficult fact.

(5) Finally we can recognize, irrespective of equality of respect, that the well-being of all must be impartially taken into account in the making of policy, that is by all of us in our role as citizens. This ethical imperative of impartial concern does not rest on any thesis of equal desert.[28]

Consider again then the 'desire to be in unity with our fellow creatures' on equal terms. Is that a desire which can be satisfied if (1)–(5) are fully realized? If so, it is concrete and finite and could be satisfied without coming into conflict with any other aspect of the good. On the other hand if it requires the ideology of equal respect then it is not in that way concrete and finite: it is abstract and infinite, it does not determine its own limits and so must ultimately become inimical to the pursuit of any great ethical ideal, in particular to the pursuit of the liberal ideal.

The desire of classical liberals to be in unity with their fellow creatures was abstract. They did not know their fellow creatures. Or rather they thought they did not know them because they believed in their unknown potential. To know the people (they would have agreed) you have to emancipate the people—that has been the work of this century not the nineteenth. But in this century knowledge of the people has been distorted by revolution, dictatorship, genocide, global and civil war, passages of crisis which reveal the depths to which people can fall and the heights to which they can rise. In the last three or four decades in the West the character of the people in conditions of stable liberal democracy has begun to emerge. No doubt it is still far too early to draw any firm conclusions, but it would just be sheer complacency to deny that what is emerging provides some confirmation of the worrying hypothesis.

The antidote is not to be found in the moralism of Green. On the contrary, moralistic liberalism, which we are in some danger of returning to, is part of the problem rather than part of the solution to spiritual weariness. Moreover moralism and populism can all too easily combine: there are worrying signs that that is happening. On the other hand, it is even less helpful to go on affirming the ethical neutrality of the State as a fundamental liberal principle, or searching for ever more ingenious and unconvincing bases on which to affirm equal respect. The best to be hoped for from that approach is a situation in which ethical and aesthetic seriousness is maintained in elite enclaves but insulated from the common culture and preserved on condition of presenting a suitable outward face. That may be

---

[28] As to what it requires see Essays V and VI.

a path along which modern liberal societies are going, and from a liberal point of view there are worse paths, but it cannot be the best path for anyone who shares the hopes of classical liberalism.

If one shares those hopes, then, on the contrary, one must do what one can to resist demotic-liberal ideology while affirming the true bases for living together in freedom, the bases given in (1)–(5): equality under the law, the sentiment of common humanity, civility, respect for moral worth, acceptance of the responsibilities of citizenship, that is, of impartial concern for the well-being of all. Beyond that, however, though philosophy and policy can do much to remove the obstacles in the way of public affirmation of great ideals, there is little they can do to give such affirmations life, attraction, influence. The classical-liberal ideal of wholeness and balance between moral freedom and spontaneity could be philosophically stated but its aesthetic substance and hence main influence on public imagination and sensibility was realizable only in creative works of art. To the limited extent that nineteenth-century art attempted to express it, it tried to do so, more often than not, through the literary and visual invocation of the hellenic world. But the aesthetic substance given to an ideal must fit its time, and nineteenth-century hellenism flowed into academicism and nostalgia: there is scant reason to think that hellenism is the aesthetic substance (as against the philosophical idea) to which classical-liberal ideals must always return.[29] Whether they can still be given authentic aesthetic substance, or what shape and historical resonance that substance requires—what strands of aesthetic modernism or contemporary multiculturalism it needs to draw on for example—depends, as ever, on how the possibilities to hand can be worked on creatively by the aesthetic inspiration of the Few.

[29] The Schillerian element in classical liberalism's ideal—spiritual freedom embodied in honest aesthetic semblance—is better expressed by, for example, those paintings in which Cézanne achieves it, or perhaps by the enigmatic classicism of Seurat, or in some high modernist architecture, than in any of the nineteenth century's exercises in hellenic nostalgia—Lord Leighton, say (for all the power with which he conveys that nostalgia).

XII

The Post-Modern Hume: Ernest Gellner's 'Enlightenment Fundamentalism'

Sceptical doubt, both with respect to reason and the senses, is a malady, which can never be radically cur'd, but must return upon us every moment, however we may chace it away, and sometimes may seem entirely free from it. 'Tis impossible upon any system to defend either our understanding or senses; and we but expose them farther when we endeavour to justify them in that manner. As the sceptical doubt arises naturally from a profound and intense reflection on those subjects, it always encreases, the farther we carry our reflections, whether in opposition or conformity to it. Carelessness and in-attention alone can afford us any remedy. For this reason I rely entirely upon them; and take it for granted, whatever may be the reader's opinion at this present moment, that an hour hence he will be persuaded there is both an external and internal world.

(David Hume, *A Treatise of Human Nature*)[1]

1. AN AUTHOR AND THREE CHARACTERS

Postmodernism, Reason and Religion[2] is one of Ernest Gellner's finest contributions to a genre of which he is this century's outstanding master, certainly in the English language. I mean a sort of essay in cultural criticism or untimely meditation. Like other masters of this art, Gellner is unblinkingly disrespectful of fashions and motives in the world of ideas, but treats it nonetheless with humanity, high understanding, and a moral purpose. Alas, the competition is sparse. There is something nineteenth-century about this genre, with its combination of shrewd low blows and high philosophy, and the directness with which it addresses an audience it

First published in I. C. Jarvie and John A. Hall (eds.), *The Social Philosophy of Ernest Gellner*, Poznan Studies in the Philosophy of the Sciences and the Humanities, 48, (Amsterdam and Atlanta, Ga., Rodopi, 1996): 467–96.

[1] Hume (1968: 218).   [2] Gellner (1992).

presumes to be untramelled by specialisms and correctitudes, but fully serious.

The same scrutiny should be turned on Gellner, of course. What are *his* assumptions? What does *he* represent? A full picture is beyond my talent or space, but *Postmodernism, Reason and Religion* gives us at least a very substantial starting point.

Here Gellner presents a cast-list of three characters in contemporary cultural and philosophical debate. With one of them he openly identifies: the one he calls—partly in jest and partly in earnest—the Enlightenment Fundamentalist. So this is the one over whom we shall cast an appraising eye. But we must take account of the other two characters, about whom Gellner has many forceful and penetrating things to say. The first is the religious fundamentalist, who is represented by the resurgence of Islamic fundamentalism. The second is the Postmodernist[3] as observed in contemporary literary and anthropological circles. Gellner does not put them on a par; they are, as he rightly says, 'grossly incommensurate in scale and importance':

Muslim fundamentalism is an enormously simple, powerful, earthy, sometimes cruel, absorbing, socially fortifying movement, which gives a sense of direction and orientation to millions of men and women, many of whom live lives of bitter poverty and are subject to harsh oppression. It enables them to adjust to a new anonymous mass society by identifying with the old, long-established High Culture of their own faith, and explaining their own deprivation and humiliation as a punishment for having strayed from the true path, rather than a consequence of never having found it; a disruption and disorientation is thus turned into a social and moral ascension, an attainment of identity and dignity.

Postmodernism, by contrast, is a tortuous, somewhat affected fad, practised by at most some academics living fairly sheltered lives: large parts of it are intelligible only and at most (and often with difficulty) to those who are fully masters of the nuances of three or four abstruse academic disciplines, and much of it is not intelligible to anyone at all. But it happens to be the currently fashionable form of relativism, and relativism as such is an important intellectual option, and one which will continue to haunt us.[4]

Gellner knows a great deal about both Islamic fundamentalism and Postmodernism, so to speak in line of duty. His claim, in juxtaposing

---

[3] 'Throughout this essay 'modernism' labels roughly the first half of this century, 'modernity' the whole period of modern European history, i.e. from the European renaissance. I also use it as shorthand for the developing cultural, ethical, and scientific traditions of that period. 'Postmodernist' refers to the cultural period which follows modernism and which we live in. 'Postmodernism', with initial capital, labels the set of ideas which currently goes under that name. One of those ideas is that modernity itself is a completed period which we have passed beyond. That view is not endorsed here.

[4] Gellner (1992: 72).

them, is that they represent the two paradigmatic reactions to the pain caused by modernity's protagonist: 'Enlightenment Secular Fundamentalism'[5] or 'Enlightenment Rationalist Fundamentalism'.[6] They are the antagonists from within and from without modernity's camp. Islamic fundamentalism is the purest assault on modernity from without since the seventeenth century. Unlike religious fundamentalist opposition to the new science (and the new ethics and political economy) in early modern Europe, however, it has to cope with modern science's stunning explanatory and technical success. 'Postmodernism' is the latest version of the romantic reaction to Enlightenment, which seeks to defuse the dangerous aspects of modernity from within, by relativizing them. And it is a fundamental theme of the essay that these three positions—religious fundamentalism, enlightenment fundamentalism, and romantic relativism are irreducible:

Three primary colours are required for mapping our condition . . . Each expresses a fundamental option of the human spirit, when facing the world as it is now.[7]

All this rather strongly suggests that the only way of being on the side of the Enlightenment is the fundamentalist way. Either you shape up and get back to Enlightenment basics, or you slide off, either into religious wishful thinking, perhaps even bigotry, or into the shifting marshlands of the Postmodernist. Can this really be right? Has philosophy done nothing since the eighteenth century to deepen and stabilize modernity's self-understanding?

2. THE PACKAGE DEAL

Gellner's view of modernity is Weberian. He takes its driving force to be the search for purely rational legitimation in all domains of action and thought. This was the fundamental characteristic of the early modern period in the West, and in due course it achieved enormous gains both in knowledge and control of nature, and in emancipating and enriching the individual. It has a darker side, however, in the form of two spiritually troubling problems which Gellner elsewhere labels 'the issue of Validation, and that of Enchantment'.[8] They are generated by the quest for rational legitimation itself. That quest produces a sceptical crisis which leaves no evident source of validation for the most basic practical and theoretical

---

[5] Ibid. 76. [6] Ibid. 80. [7] Ibid. 1.

[8] Gellner (1979: 1). 'Enchantment' comes from Schiller's phrase which Weber made famous, about 'the disenchantment of the world' (*die entzauberung der Welt*).

elements of our world-view, and it menaces the sentiment of location in, at-oneness-with the world—both the natural and social world. These are the aspects of modernity which generate pain.

I agree with Gellner in accepting this Weberian, or post-Romantic German,[9] account of the evolution of the modern West and its differentiation from other cultures, both traditional and primitive. But how far do the features differentiating modernity hang together? In Gellner's treatments of modernity they seem to come as a package deal. Let me spell that out a little more explicitly. The package-deal thesis says that it is not possible, in the long run, to have the technical mastery and material prosperity which modernity brings, without its naturalism in philosophy and its liberalism in every aspect of social organization, cultural, economic, and political. These belong to the long-run mental and material equilibrium of modernity. Equally unavoidable, in that long-run equilibrium, is a sceptical impasse in epistemology and ethics and a corresponding spiritual homelessness—the problems of validation and identity. Now this is a sociological and psychological thesis, not just a direct claim about rational connections. Its underpinning is nonetheless interpretative, i. e. it rests on an exploration from within of rationally intelligible connections between apparently diverse aspects of modernity as well as on postulation of brute facts of nature, human and physical, constraining the path of modernity's evolution.

The package-deal thesis underlies Gellner's attitude to the critics of modernity, within and without. It is a hotly contested thesis, because many people want to pick and choose from modernity's menu—typically they want the prosperity and technical mastery without partaking of this or that other dish. Some aspects of the question are currently topical in the most urgent way. Can you, for example, separate economic from political and cultural liberalism, implementing the former without the latter? Economic liberalism, it increasingly seems, is the most effective way of converting technical control into economic prosperity—and free inquiry, or cultural liberalism at least within the scientific community, the most effective way of speeding technical progress. But can you maximize the rate of technical progress and of its conversion into mass affluence without buying into every other aspect, cultural and political, of the modern package deal—including the problems of validation and estrangement? Or is every attempt to retain some vestige of a non-modern philosophical outlook bound either to put a brake on the growth of prosperity or to be

---

[9] A vivid sense of the problems of validation and enchantment and their connection with rational legitimation stems from the hangover after German Romanticism's attempt to overcome them.

broken by it? Or can one argue to the contrary, that even if cultural and political liberalism was the original precondition of take-off into scientifically driven prosperity, it is now the case that politically and culturally authoritarian societies have the advantage in maintaining its forward momentum?

The package-deal thesis emerges most strongly, to my mind, not from an economistic and neo-Marxist way of putting the questions—as though the decisive issue was what superstructural social relations and ideologies optimize the growth of productive forces—but from the Weberian point of view which takes the decisive arena to be the arena of ideas. What then underpins it is a hypothesis of this kind: that the virus of rational legitimation, once inserted at *any* point in a cultural organism, reproduces itself spontaneously and spreads without limit. There is no lasting antidote. It can be delayed or accelerated but it cannot be stopped.

We shall refine this hypothesis in a moment; but one can see how, if something like it is right, the question whether politically authoritarian but economically liberal societies might have a long-run economic advantage would not arise, since rational legitimation would inevitably spread from the economy and science of an authoritarian society to its general politics and culture and there undermine opposing hegemonies imposed by tradition, charisma, or sheer coercion rather than persuasive argument. More deeply, the same would apply to attempts to sustain philosophical alternatives to modernity's naturalism—whether religious-fundamentalist or romantic-relativist.[10]

Is this irresistible virus of rational legitimation, if that is what it is, benevolent or malignant? On the one hand it produces scientific knowledge, technical mastery, mass material affluence, and the emancipation of the individual. That these are among the effects of rational legitimation is by now pretty clear, and few people deny outright that they are benefits. It is more common to point to other, negative, effects—the distempers of scepticism and disenchantment or estrangement. Are they in fact the only two? Many of the anxieties in liberal societies which may seem to be unrelated do indeed trace back to them. For example, deep-ecological philosophies, which go beyond the simple message that external costs imposed on the environment must be fully accounted for, trace back to the original Romantic recoil from the Enlightenment's humanistic naturalism. Like

---

[10] People may want prosperity or oneness-with-the-world in preference to freedom. It may then be rational for them to choose a less emancipated politics and philosophy. But if rational legitimation is a virus without an antidote they do not have the choice. Dissatisfaction with anything other than transparently rational modes of legitimation will undermine non-liberal political, and non-naturalistic intellectual, validation.

German Idealism, deep ecology looks for a metaphysical and ethical alternative to that. On the other hand nineteenth-century liberals like Tocqueville and Mill, who were not in the backwash of German Idealism, worried more about a third distemper—the decline of aristocratic virtues and the growing tyranny of conventional opinion—the problem of Individuality, one might call it. And they worried also about the binding forces of a liberal democratic society, its sources of resilience and solidarity: the problem of Allegiance. There are links between these problems and also between them and the problem of Enchantment—a problem which they would also have recognized. On the other hand, the problem of Validation, taken as something different from the problem of Allegiance—understood rather as an epistemological and metaphysical question—that they hardly took seriously at all. They did not link the ethical and cultural problems of liberal democracy to the metaphysics of naturalism as German Idealism did. In this they seem to me to have been prescient. I will come back to that at the end. But in the main part of this essay I want to consider just one aspect of the package-deal thesis, namely, whether and why the problems of validation and enchantment are a necessary part of the deal. We shall also examine 'enlightenment fundamentalism' more closely and I shall argue that Gellner's claim that it is the only way of avoiding religious fundamentalism or romantic relativism is seriously misguided.

3. RATIONAL LEGITIMATION AND FIDEISM

What is rational legitimation? Let us start with what it is not. Any discourse or practice has its immanent rules or standards. One can try to formulate them in a systematic, comprehensive, and orderly way. Such *formal codification* is not itself legitimation, rational, or otherwise. It specifies what the rules of a discourse or practice are, without addressing the question of what justifies those rules. Nor does that question always arise. It doesn't arise, for example with truly arbitrary conventions or with rules of games. But there certainly are discourses and practices for which it does arise. Those are the ones to which the notion of legitimation applies. To legitimate those rules is to justify them by appeal to norms about reasons, by which I mean, propositions about what there is reason to believe, do, or feel.

Received norms may state that certain traditions or charismatic words give reasons to believe, do, or feel. Philosophically, however, it is always open to someone to ask why the fact that something is traditionally or charismatically laid down gives reason to accept it. One can respond simply by formally codifying the underlying norm: that when a certain specified tradition, or charismatic source, pronounces that one has reason to believe, do or feel thus and so, then one does. But must this formally codified proposition about reasons be evident to reason alone? Or can it be itself legitimated traditionally or charismatically? It can be—but then at that higher-order level the question why one should believe this proposition, just because tradition or charisma says one should, again seems permissible. It seems permissible to *reason*, because the norm one is being told to believe is a norm about *reasons*. Hence the asymmetry, in point of legitimating power, between tradition and charisma on the one hand, and reason on the other. This insight, about the autonomy, or spontaneity of reasons, is always liable to break out. Though I label it in this Kantian way, it is as old as Euthyphro's dilemma. It registers the connection between reasons and spontaneity. And once it has taken hold, the regress of legitimation stops only when a norm is spontaneously found evident by individual reasoners. In this way reason trumps other sources of legitimation. The social consequence is that traditional or charismatic authority can no longer be relied on as ultimate. It legitimates only under rational licence. All claims to authority must have credentials readable by rational, that is, spontaneous, insight alone.[11]

Recognition of the autonomy of reasons is the unstoppable virus, rather than rational legitimation as such. For rational legitimation in itself need not involve this recognition. It is never absent from any practice in any culture. There are always norms which are legitimated simply as rationally evident; and rules and standards of practice can change through rational criticism from within, in a first-order way, by unselfconscious and informal appeal to the spontaneity of certain norms.

The rise of the new science in the sixteenth and seventeenth centuries seems to have been a case in point. Its roots lay in a widening *first-order* realignment of standards of legitimation, encouraged by the Reformation and the recovery of classical texts. The Reformation in turn began as a fairly local questioning of Church practices, which only later expanded into a realigning of standards of legitimacy in the religious sphere. Church tradition, papal and conciliar decrees, were put in question; the charismatic authority of Scripture was reaffirmed. Scripture was to be interpreted by individual conscience and reason. This was not an appeal to new

---

[11] 'Even the Holy One of the gospel must first be compared to our ideal of moral perfection before we can recognize him as such . . . where do we get the concept of God as the highest good? Solely from the *Idea* of moral perfection, which reason traces *a priori*', Kant (1964: 76).

standards excogitated by self-conscious epistemological inquiry—it was a reordering of the relative priority of standards, all of which would in principle have been recognized before. The questioning of Church authority spread into a questioning of the scholastic Aristotelianism taught in the schools. And in a variety of ways, reformed religion assisted and encouraged the emergence of scientific method.

These developments were largely independent of the growing sceptical crisis at the second-order level of epistemological reflection. The reverse, however, is not true: as Popkin has argued,[12] the 'crise Pyrrhonienne' emerged from the crisis of the Reformation, as well as the dissemination of ancient sceptical writings in the late sixteenth century. Popkin points out that Pyrrhonism was both used fideistically (as by Erasmus, and the Jesuits), to bolster the standard of Christian tradition, and, on the other hand, was tamed into a 'constructive' or 'mitigated' scepticism which supported the standards of reasonable appeal to observation as against received authority or a priori construction.

Fideism can be defined, for our purposes, very generally. It is the non-rational endorsement of an ultimate legitimating norm, the acceptance of a norm about reasons without rational insight. You can be fideistic in this broad sense about any 'values' or 'commitments' of a culture, not just its religious ones. Now one can always try to bolster a fideistic stance by arguing that the ideal of rational insight, and thus of rational legitimation, is ultimately incoherent. But the obvious flaw in this sceptical strategy is that it is overpowerful. If rational insight does not legitimate, what does?

Radical scepticism insists that only rational insight could legitimate and then claims that there is no such thing as rational insight. 'Constructive' or 'mitigated' scepticism stops at the first step. It methodically insists on spontaneous rational insight. This constructive scepticism was used against scholastic apriorism and in favour of empirical scientific method by the ideologists of the new science. Since it is not easy to see what the criterion of rational insight requires, or to live up to it even if one sees it, there is room for constructive scepticism to grow into constructive epistemology—an epistemology which studies those norms about reasons which appear on stable reflection to be spontaneously compelling, and codifies them in a form designed to be a useful discipline for thinking—a method. That is the constructive side of constructive scepticism, and it is what much modern epistemology has been about. *Constructive scepticism*, rather than rational legitimation as such, is the developed form of the virus, resistant to all known antidotes.

---

[12] Popkin (1960).

Constructive scepticism differs from fideism in that it claims to appeal to something beyond culture—reflective natural agreement on what constitutes a reason: what reasoners from different cultures have in common, rather than what sets them apart. Does it produce a crisis of validation for modernity? That would be so only if constructive scepticism must turn into the unconstructive and unmitigated form—and if that radical scepticism were just as infectious as the constructive form is. For all the throwing up of fideistic dust in the seventeenth century, the development into radical scepticism about reason, at a really deeply thought-through and widely influential philosophical level, does not occur in the early modern period. It only comes with Hume.

4. HUME'S FIDEISM

In effect Hume puts together three things. The first we have already discussed—the autonomy of reasons. The second is the notion that all genuine propositions—as against mere analyses of relations of ideas—are propositions about facts. All content is factual content. I will call this very powerful philosophical idea 'unequivocal realism'. Finally, the third idea is that all propositions which have factual content are a posteriori, accountable to experience. This is epistemological empiricism. Combining the three ideas yields the conclusion that there are no normative propositions, only positive ones. For normative propositions are not mere relations of ideas. Nor are they reducible to factual propositions (if they were they would have to be accountable to experience). There can be positive laws, laid down by a real sovereign, human or divine, and there can be conventions. But by the autonomy of reasons, the normative question whether we should abide by such laws or conventions remains open. Yet the combination of unequivocal realism and empiricism leaves no scope for any objective answer to this question. This drives Hume to doubt the very intelligibility of normative utterances when they are taken at face value as expressions of judgement, with propositional content, and to adopt a revised view of them as expressions of feeling: *'belief is more properly an act of the sensitive, than of the cogitative part of our natures'*, 'Morality . . . is more properly felt than judg'd of.'[13]

Seen in one aspect Hume is a constructive sceptic who wants to clear away preconceptions standing in the path of a natural science of man. Rightly, this naturalism of his is often stressed. But he is also a radical

---

[13] Hume (1968: 183, 470).

sceptic who holds that normative propositions, propositions about reasons, are inherently indefensible—as indefensible by reason as by any other purported legitimating source. And he seems to think that the very activity of constructive epistemology leads by its own momentum into radical scepticism—crossing no philosophically defensible frontier as it does so. Sceptical doubt, the natural outcome of 'profound and intense reflection on these subjects' is intellectually unstoppable once raised. 'Carelessness and in-attention alone can afford us any remedy.' On Hume's view, there can be constructive epistemology, done in a naturalized vein—the classification of norms which we naturally and stably agree on—*but there can be no genuine rational legitimation.*

Hume presents the problem of validation in its most powerful form. Our beliefs and actions cannot be rationally legitimated; they are matters of feeling. But by no means does he think the virus of radical scepticism to be infectious. He is strikingly unworried by it. That is because he thinks nature is too strong for radical scepticism, not because he thinks there is some philosophically principled way of cutting a line between it and the constructive kind. We accept certain norms not because we have rational insight into them but because nature compels us to do so. Hume's constructive epistemology rests on a fideism about natural norms of feeling (including belief).

The enlightenment fundamentalist, as Gellner presents him and identifies with him, seems to me to be a Humean. When he defends science or ethics against various forms of irrationalism, he has to do so fideistically—so the term 'fundamentalist' is perfectly appropriate. He is a 'fundamentalist rationalist' because the object of his fideism is natural norms of reasoning, not tradition or charisma, and because his fidelity to these norms involves only a claim of natural compulsion and no claim of rational insight. Not surprisingly, this gives him a perverse affinity with the critics of enlightenment naturalism. But to think that the only way of being on the side of enlightenment reason is the Humean way, that is, by carelessness and inattention, is, I shall argue, as deep a philosophical error as there can be. First, however, we must remind ourselves of what happened after Hume.

5. WHAT HAPPENED AFTER HUME

In brief summary one observes the following lines of thought. First, there is a continuation of enlightenment naturalism and its constructive epistemology of science and ethics, a continuation which markedly rejected

Hume's radical scepticism. It had a secular left wing held by Bentham, Comte, and the Mills, and a mild—non-fundamentalist—Christian right wing held by Thomas Reid and the Scottish and French regiments of common sense. The left wing simply ignored Hume's scepticism. From their progressivist and scientific point of view, it was an unserious, attention-seeking, literary device, and a Tory device at that. Reid, on the other hand, responded to radical scepticism by claiming that it derived from an untenable psychological hypothesis, the theory of ideas. Positively, he simply appealed to a codification of the principles of common sense. This was constructive epistemology; what was remarkable about it was the multiplicity and fine detail Reid discovered in common sense, in contrast to the stark normative landscape of the philosophical radicals. Among all these naturalists however there was a methodological consensus—that fundamental norms are those which people spontaneously and stably agree on in practice and reflection. From this natural agreement there is no higher court of appeal, and radical scepticism is misguided insofar as it seems to require it.

It was left to Kant to engage with Hume's scepticism head-on. In doing so he inaugurated a second well-known direction—the various post-Kantian nineteenth-century idealisms. Kant identifies the source of Hume's scepticism in the dichotomy between propositions concerning matters of fact and propositions expressing relations of ideas, and he escapes it by rejecting naturalism itself. There are a priori principles in our science and our ethics—we are justified in accepting them because we determine the object of our thought in accordance with them. Kant thinks the very possibility of knowledge presupposes free rationality, rationality as self-legislation: knowers who give themselves the principles by which they construct their natural world cannot be said to find those principles in reality as it is in itself. This connection between knowledge and freedom as self-legislation opened the door to the extraordinary romantic-idealist attempt to rescue Reason from naturalism, an attempt whose ruin still weighs so heavily on theorists of modernity influenced by the German tradition.

These two directions are the important ones for the topic of this essay, but we should note a third direction in nineteenth- and twentieth-century discussion which opposed Kant and naturalism equally. Call it Platonistic conceptual realism, or Platonism for short. For most of the nineteenth century it was a kind of sporadic sniping from Catholic Central Europe, the outpost of resistance to both Franco-British naturalism and German idealism. But a form of it was also propounded by Frege, and then another form in the brief period of conceptual realism in Cambridge before the

Great War. Just as German idealism was an aspect of the romantic movement, and naturalism an aspect of the liberal-bourgeois revolution, so this
new Platonism of Frege and Cambridge was an aspect of early modernism, and early modernism's recoil from the nineteenth century in both
its romantic and its liberal-bourgeois sides.

From both a Kantian and a naturalistic standpoint such realism
must seem untenable, since it credits us with a knowledge of cognition-
independent non-natural facts, facts-in-themselves, without any account
of how such facts act on cognition—an account which its strong notion of
factuality indispensably requires.

But these three directions still do not bring us up to date. For the second, Viennese phase of analytic philosophy saw an attempt to end the
contests of nineteenth-century metaphysics which was not Platonistic but
'post-critical', as one might say. It was Wittgenstein's and Carnap's
attempt at a dissolution of metaphysics. Rejection of Platonism is central
to it. Instead of taking concepts and propositions as the fundamental
explanans of meaning, it takes the *explanans* to be rules of language-use,
rules stipulating when the assertion of a sentence and the derivation of a
sentence from another sentence is warranted. Alberto Coffa has neatly
described it as the 'second Copernican Revolution',[14] this time inverting
the priority between concepts and rules of language-use. Concepts are no
longer self-subsistent entities which those rules must subserve, instead,
talk about grasping a concept now becomes a reifying way of talking
about the fundamental thing, which is mastery of those rules. This post-
critical view of meaning, like Kant's transcendental idealism, promises a
decisive cut between constructive epistemology and radical scepticism.
Its affinity to Kant is that it sees the need to diagnose and deal with the
sources of radical scepticism. Radical epistemology and metaphysics in
general are now revealed as pseudo-problematic—their successor is simply logical syntax (Carnap) or logical grammar (Wittgenstein). On the
other hand post-critical philosophy also has a potential affinity to naturalism. It offers a definitive justification for the naturalist's disengage-
ment from radical scepticism, and his constructive appeal to the test of
natural agreement. One might call the resulting position post-critical naturalism.[15]

This 'second Copernican Revolution' is now rather unfashionable in
English-language circles. English-language philosophy is in a postmod-

---

[14] Coffa (1991: 263). The first Copernican revolution is Kant's: see the second-edition
preface to the *Critique of Pure Reason*, Bxvii (Kant 1968: 22).

[15] The summary sketch given in the last few paragraphs is filled out in Skorupski
(1993*b*).

ernist stage, and its way of being postmodernist, unlike continental Postmodernism, is to re-establish continuity with its premodernist naturalistic forebears. The mainstream of current analytic philosophy, one might say, renews the nineteenth-century British naturalistic axis—with important new elements, of course, centring on recognition of the hypothetical method, and the substitution of cognitive science for associationist psychology. From the standpoint of a Kantian or a Carnapian or Wittgensteinian it is pre-critical. It shows, in brief, the same adherence to naturalistic epistemology and the same naturalistic interest in philosophy of science and philosophy of mind that Reid and Mill showed.

But there is also a less widespread but rather significant return to Hume's divided stance: his peculiar combination of naturalism and radical scepticism. Significantly, the orientation of these New Sceptics or New Humeans, as Michael Williams has called them[16] tends to be humanistic rather than scientific, though like Gellner they place great stress on the internal vindication of scientific knowledge by its pragmatic success. They are naturalists but they stress the irresolvability of the problem of validation. It is to this rather small, mandarin group that Gellner belongs.

To put my own cards on the table: I adhere to another rather small group—those who still maintain the post-critical tendency. I take it that radical scepticism can and must be dissolved. If naturalism really does lead to the conclusion that we have no reason to accept naturalism, then we *have* no reason to accept naturalism. It becomes just as much a matter of faith as theistic alternatives to naturalism are. The term 'Enlightenment Fundamentalism' is justified, as in the case of Hume, precisely because the New Sceptics' position is a fideistic adherence to naturalism.

We seem then to have in current English-language philosophy a mainstream which does not take the problem of Validation seriously, and does not see it as necessary to explain why it should not be taken seriously. Then we have two much smaller groups. There are New Sceptics or Humeans who consider that sceptical doubts are unanswerable but are not serious either, because they are unnatural—powerless to destabilize our normative convictions the moment we come out of our brief epistemological moods. To this fideism they add a strong emphasis on the internal vindication of science by its actual success. On the other hand we have post-critical naturalists who think that radical scepticism can and must be dissolved. Noticeably, on all these views we find naturalism entrenched and little sense of a legitimation crisis for theoretical reason (we have not yet asked ourselves whether there is more of a crisis of practical reason).

[16] Michael Williams (1991).

But let me turn now to the problem of Enchantment, about which nothing has yet been said. This surely, unlike the problem of Validation, has a much more evident presence in our culture. Is it somehow permanently connected with naturalism and liberalism? One can make a strong case for seeing it rather as a transitional phenomenon, even though we are such a long way into modernity. The breaking up of cosy cocoons offered by traditional cultures is a very painful process. Yet each successive historic reaction against liberal-naturalist medicine seems feebler, like a fading series of stomach cramps. Is there any real reason to think that life outside the cocoon will permanently be attended by a chronic ache of estrangement?

I want now to pin down what seems to me to be the deepest such reason.

6. THE MYSTICAL AND THE THEORETICAL INTERESTS

First we must recover a conception of knowledge which naturalism rules out. A neglected but still classic starting point is Lucien Lévy-Bruhl's work on the 'primitive mentality'. Everyone knows that Lévy-Bruhl characterized it as 'pre-logical'—a term which he later regretted and withdrew as inaccurate.[17] But the phenomena on which Lévy-Bruhl based that thesis are real enough, and the conclusion he drew from them about the driving objectives or interests of primitive thought is of great interest. He questioned an assumption which had been dominant from Comte to Frazer. This held that primitive religion and magic are essentially products of the theoretical and the technical interest in nature—the objectives, respectively, of understanding the fundamental principles which regulate natural processes, and of gaining mastery over them. According to Lévy-Bruhl, however, the characteristic feature of the primitive mentality was its 'mystical orientation' towards the world. That orientation was still a cognitive orientation—a mode of understanding the world. It was not the non-cognitive 'symbolic-expressive' orientation which a later phase of modernist anthropology attributed to 'primitive ritual' (echoing the non-cognitive, expressivist view of the normative realm taken in the later Viennese phase of analytic modernism). But though it was a mode of understanding, the mystical orientation made possible a relationship of spiritual at-one-ness with the world which the theoretical interest precluded; at the same time it discouraged

---

[17] For his later thoughts on this subject see Lévy-Bruhl (1975; first published in Paris, 1949).

attitudes of detached analysis and inference which the theoretical interest required.

The idea of a 'mystical orientation' can be removed from the modernist casing in which Lévy-Bruhl enclosed it when he built on it a sharp and exclusive opposition between primitive and modern—the 'contrast/inversion' schema which Robin Horton has attributed to modernist anthropology, as against the 'continuity/evolution' schema of nineteenth-century anthropologists.[18] *All* cosmologies, 'primitive' or modern, are shaped by theoretical and technical interests. In fact a perspective which lays stress on the historical evolution of mentalities is better placed to recognize the real depth of the idea. 'Primitive' mentality in this view is primitive in the sense that it is *pensée sauvage*—thought in its wild state—as yet undomesticated by cognitive disciplines and drills which develop in literate cultures. The cognitive dispositions which one finds in it are the spontaneous dispositions which remain implanted in all of us, whatever subsequent domestication may do to enforce or diminish them.

If thought can be shaped by radically different kinds of cognitive interest, then developments which serve one of these interests may not coincide with developments which serve another, and may even be mutually incompatible. And indeed one aspect of modernity is that the theoretical interest blossoms like the upas tree and monopolizes all the soil in which an equally deeply implanted conception of what knowledge is could flourish. The impulse to understand one's world defines no single criterion of success. For any such criterion requires a conception of what understanding or knowing is, and there is more than one spontaneously tempting conception to be had.

Both the theoretical and the mystical interests are, in a certain sense, unlike the technical interest in being non-practical.[19] The defining interest in each case is that of achieving a certain kind of understanding or knowledge—or perhaps apprehension or possession—of reality. In the case of the theoretical interest, the objective is to discover the constitution of things, and to explain by what fundamental principles they act, interact and change. Its method is that of profane observation of perceptible qualities, analysis of the concepts under which the world is pre-theoretically categorized, and reasonable inference from such observation and analysis

---

[18] Robin Horton, 'Lévy-Bruhl, Durkheim and the Scientific Revolution', in Horton (1997).

[19] But both of course can be connected to the technical interest. The fusion of the mystical and the technical interest is 'magic': mimetic identification, for example, is a technique which stands to the mystical interest somewhat as enumerative induction, say, stands to the theoretical interest. See Skorupski (1976: 9).

to a refined, or even substantially novel conception of the constitution of objects, their fundamental properties, and the principles relating these properties. Enumerative induction and inference to the best explanation are the indispensable tools of the theoretical interest.

The understanding sought by the mystical interest is of an altogether different order. What it desires is not a mediated knowledge of reality, achieved through analysis of and inference from appearances, but a direct, immediate apprehension of the world as it really is. Understanding or 'true seeing', unveiling, of this kind is not to be achieved by the methods of ordinary observation, analysis, and reasonable conjecture: only by a heightening or intensification of perception, or perhaps by a kind of intuition or insight, conceived as a mode of direct perception but which transcends or bypasses the ordinary perception of the senses. Such insight or intensified perception may come unbidden. Or it may be sought through intellectual, ascetic, medical, or ecstatic techniques. It may be interpreted in the context of some stable philosophical or religious framework, but it will almost always be regarded as at best only partially statable. In this it differs from theoretical understanding. Both interests may be said to search after an understanding of the essence, unity, and order of things, and of the self as a part of that unity and order. But theoretical knowledge, precisely because of the methods by which it is achieved, is inherently communicable. In the case of mystical understanding, on the other hand, the truth is not inferred but immediately experienced and lived. Consequently the master cannot simply teach it to his pupil. He can only try to create the conditions in which the pupil can gain it for himself. There are, of course, many conceptions of knowing which mix these two ideal types. Moreover in its more philosophic guise, the mystical understanding of the world may be presented as the result of a chain of *a priori* reflections, as e.g. in Parmenides or in Hegel. But a philosophical approach route, via a priori reasoning, is not incompatible with a final mystically experienced realization of self-world identity.[20]

There corresponds to this contrast a vital difference in the emotional or spiritual significance of the two kinds of understanding. Theoretical understanding, however absorbing it may be, remains detached, objective—'theoretical'. ('Theoretical': from the Greek *thea*, spectacle.) Mystical understanding is engulfing; in its characteristic form it is an apprehension of the differentiated identity of one 'object' with another or of self and world. Such a state is experienced as a mode of *knowledge*—but

[20] For the suggestion that Parmenides 'personally experienced the *unio mystica* with true Being' see Frankel (1975: 365 ff). (I owe this reference to Stephen Makin.) On Hegel see n. 23.

knowledge of a direct, and in Lévy-Bruhl's term, 'participatory' kind. It is knowledge as identity with the world rather than knowledge as mirroring the world. When Meister Eckhart remarks that

As long as man has time and place and number and quantity and multiplicity, he is on the wrong track and God is far from him[21]

he anathematizes the primary qualities which constitute an early modern corpuscular philosopher's theoretical conception of the world, and in doing so epitomizes the opposition between the mystical and the theoretical interest. That opposition had emerged in philosophy much earlier, in the archaic Greek world, in the shape of the Eleatics' critique of the Ionians, and in particular in Parmenides' contrast of the way of seeming and the way of truth.

These accounts of the mystical and the theoretical interest are ideal types. By their very explicitness they risk presenting them, and the modes of experience which can seem to vindicate them, in an altogether too reflective and discriminated form. For the same reason, the word 'mystical' itself is not very satisfactory. Following Lévy-Bruhl I am using it broadly to refer to the underlying and pervasive interest, whether or not it is interpreted in terms of any developed philosophical or religious framework.[22]

Certainly one should not identify the mystical interest in the world with the religious attitude. That would be anachronistic in any discussion of the personalistic cosmologies, and associated rituals, of primitive religion. Primitive religion is animated by all these interests, technical, theoretical, mystical. It is we who distinguish them for the purpose of our argument. In any case religion, as it differentiates and develops into traditions and institutional forms, is shaped by many impulses—personal salvation, emotional coherence, communal solidarity, a rule of life. The mystical idea of an immediate apprehension of God can seem blasphemous to religious believers. Nor is the theoretical interest the same as a scientific outlook. A single-minded pursuit of the theoretical interest is part of what we mean by 'science'; but it makes no sense to speak of a scientific outlook where a certain background of traditions and institutions is lacking. Yet even without traditions and institutions, the theoretical interest as such can flourish.

---

[21] Eckhart (1958: 202).

[22] Lévy-Bruhl was not entirely happy with the word (Lévy-Bruhl 1975, Leenhardt's preface, xviii). But apparently he refused to substitute the word 'mythical'. In some ways it might be better to talk of the Eleatic and Ionian interest instead of the mystical and the theoretical interest, but that would particularize too closely on the Greeks.

7. NATURALISM AND THE MYSTICAL INTEREST

Naturalism is the philosophy which holds that the world of nature is the world. So the knowing subject can be nothing more than a part of nature, and perception, thought, knowledge, must be entirely natural processes. That has two epistemological implications. First, our perceptual knowledge of the world is necessarily 'perspectival': that is to say, conditioned by the sensory modes in which we perceive our environment. Creatures with different senses would perceive the world in a different way. Second, there can be no direct, immediate apprehension of the nature of things which would provide a way of short-cutting or bypassing this perspectival predicament. On a naturalistic view, any mode of cognition of natural reality must itself be a natural, causally mediated—and hence perspectival—process. An immediate apprehension of things as they absolutely are is ruled out, because it would call for nothing less than an identity of subject and object, or a magically unmediated act in which the knowing act 'is' the object simply in the very process of conceiving or speaking it.

The point is simple, yet fundamental. Naturalism undercuts the mystical impulse: the search for an immediate, participatory knowledge-as-identity. No possible mode of experience, no possible state of mind, could, on the naturalistic view, satisfy that search.

On the other hand, naturalism underwrites the theoretical interest. Since, on the naturalistic view, our direct knowledge is only of things as they appear to us, a knowledge of their real nature, if possible at all, can only be indirect and inferential. Theoretical understanding can only transcend appearances by the method of reasonable hypothetical inference to the best explanation of appearances.

The positivism of the nineteenth century pulled against its naturalism at just this point. If knowledge is only of 'phenomena' and their correlations, naturalism becomes an impermissible metaphysical view, making assertions which transgress beyond the limits of what can be known. While naturalism imprisons the mystical interest but liberates the theoretical interest, positivism imprisons both of them. This instability in the nineteenth-century combination of naturalism and positivism, as in Comte or Mill, was a weakness which thinkers in the post-Kantian tradition of idealism were not slow to seize on. They rejected naturalism and they cut positivism down to an account of scientific knowledge. The positivistic interpretation of science then undermined the ambition of theoretical inquiry to arrive at a knowledge of the absolute nature of things, while the rejection of naturalism left space for the mystical interest to flourish. In this fashion, German idealism opened up the possibility of a defence of the mystical understanding of self and world. *Vernunft* (Reason) came to stand to the mystical understanding as *Verstand* (Understanding) to the theoretical understanding.[23]

But the unstable amalgam of naturalism and positivism can also be avoided in another way—by retaining naturalism, and rejecting positivism. That, in fact, is one of the most striking philosophical sea-changes of this century. The resulting view, which is now dominant, marks something of a return to the seventeenth-century programme for science—in which scientific inquiry was envisaged as arguing from observation of secondary, or phenomenally relative, qualities to a theoretical understanding of the primary, or absolute, qualities of things.[24] But there is a major difference, for seventeenth-century scientific realism was a restricted charter for science—a revealed framework of religious doctrine was still taken for granted. A fully naturalistic attitude, according to which human beings are only a part of the natural reality they seek to know, cannot be completely harmonized with the belief that they are also souls, standing in some extra-natural relationship to the creator of that natural reality.

---

[23] From Hegel's lectures:

the meaning of the speculative is to be understood as being the same as what used in earlier times to be called 'mystical' . . . When we speak of the 'mystical' nowadays, it is taken as a rule to be synonymous with what is mysterious and incomprehensible; and, depending on the ways their culture and mentality vary in other respects, some people treat the mysterious and incomprehensible as what is authentic and genuine, whilst others regard it as belonging to the domain of superstition and deception. About this we must remark first that 'the mystical' is certainly something mysterious, but only for the understanding, and then only because abstract identity is the principle of the understanding. But when it is regarded as synonymous with the speculative, the mystical is the concrete unity of just those determinations that count as true for the understanding only in their separation and opposition . . . As we have seen, however, the abstract thinking of the understanding is so far from being something firm and ultimate that it proves itself, on the contrary, to be a constant sublating of itself and an overturning into its opposite, whereas the rational as such is rational precisely because it contains both of the opposites as ideal moments within itself. Thus, everything rational can equally be called 'mystical'; but this only amounts to saying that it transcends the understanding. It does not at all imply that what is so spoken of must be considered inaccessible to thinking and incomprehensible. Hegel (1991*b*), 133 (§82, Addition)

See also §573 (Hegel 1971: 302–13) for Hegel's rejection of pantheism and his account of the mystical apprehension of the absolute in Hinduism and Islam.

[24] 'The method of hypothesis, known since antiquity, found few proponents between 1700 and 1850. During the last century, of course, that ordering has been inverted and—despite an almost universal acknowledgement of its weaknesses—the method of hypothesis (usually under such descriptions as "hypothetic-deduction" or "conjectures and refutations") has become the orthodoxy of the twentieth century' (Laudan 1981: 1). Methodology preceded ontology. The rehabilitation of the method cleared the ground for a renewed and more coherent naturalistic advance.

Religious faith, understood as something that essentially outreaches natural theology, is anti-naturalist in its implications.

To sum up, then. Philosophical idealism, in various nineteenth-century forms, combined with a positivistic view of science to undercut the claims of the theoretical understanding, while leaving open the possibilities of a mystical understanding of the world. In contrast an unrestricted naturalism, cleared of positivist epistemology, leaves no intelligible space for the idea of a mystical understanding; but it legitimates and encourages a theoretical understanding of the world.

8. NATURALISM AND RATIONAL LEGITIMATION

But how does naturalism grow out of the quest for rational legitimation? This is the most abstract aspect of Weber's 'disenchantment of the world'.

Let us use the term 'theoretical rationality' to mean the combination of a strategic pursuit of the theoretical interest with exclusively rational legitimation of norms of inquiry. 'Strategic pursuit' means that the theoretical interest is clearly identified and isolated from other objectives, with emphasis placed on the effective use of intellectual resources and methodical disciplines to ensure their productive use. (Simplicity and economy of argument, systematic analysis of data, cooperation and sharing of tasks, surveyable presentation of results.) Modern society exhibits not only the growth of economic rationality and of rational legitimation of rules of action, but also the growth of theoretical rationality.[25] What explains the increasingly monopolistic claims of theoretical rationality? Unquestionably the success of science in providing an adequate explanatory understanding of the world is fundamental. Yet we have noted that it remains intellectually possible to neutralize epistemologically the apparent implications of this scientific success. A positivist view of science reduces its advance to a matter of enhanced predictive adequacy: 'savoir, pour prévoir'. That still allows the search after a direct, unmediated apprehension of the world.

Nevertheless the substantive success of science and the philosophic interpretation of what science is are far from independent.

Theoretical rationality and naturalism are not the same. The one is an interest, and a distinctive method of pursuing that interest, the other is a

[25] In contrast, as Lloyd (1979) stresses, theoretical rationality in the Greek world never achieved a parallel position of dominating prestige. It was always one way of trying to understand the world among others.

philosophical outlook. It is possible to have the outlook, without having the interest, or that way of pursuing the interest. It is also possible for theoretical rationality to flourish without the philosophical context of a full-blooded naturalism. Yet although there is no strict inference from the predictive success of science to the philosophical correctness of naturalism, there is a powerful psychological, or pragmatic, connection between recognition of the one and acceptance of the other. The connection is not rationally inescapable, but neither is it rationally indefensible. The continuing success of our scientific tradition is what ensures, over the long run, that naturalism comes up with increasing frequency and ubiquity as the dominant philosophical outlook.

It is by this indirect route that theoretical rationality comes to exercise exclusive rights over the impulse to understand the world. Its success in producing ever more satisfying explanatory conceptions of nature pragmatically strengthens naturalism, and naturalism rules out philosophically the possibility of any kind of knowledge of reality other than that provided by theoretical understanding. Naturalism *is* the 'disenchantment of the world'.

And yet even though the growth of naturalism cuts down the mystical interest and its understanding of what true knowledge is, it does not follow that it destroys it. If the mystical interest is indeed a spontaneous cognitive interest, as firmly rooted in natural dispositions of mind as the theoretical interest is, then however far naturalism cuts it back it will not uproot it. Since the justification of ends, of conceptions of knowing, and of rules of reasoning must all—on naturalism's own showing—be finally grounded in our natural dispositions, that also means that the mystical interest, however marginalized, will stubbornly retain a resilient and undeniable authority. We are not mere observers of it—we must acknowledge in ourselves its *prima-facie* rights.

9. THE TWO NATURALISMS

If the deepest source of disenchantment is imprisonment of the mystical impulse, if naturalism is what does that, and if the mystical impulse is naturally rooted, then some degree of disenchantment must be the permanent condition of modernity.

But I do not think the two kinds of naturalism which I earlier distinguished, the 'enlightenment fundamentalist' and the 'post-critical' kind, are estranging or disenchanting in quite the same way. The difference is rather subtle. Here is Gellner on enlightenment fundamentalism:

It is a position which, like that of the religious fundamentalists, is firmly committed to the denial of relativism. It is committed to the view that there is external, objective culture-transcending knowledge: there is indeed 'knowledge beyond culture'. All knowledge must indeed be articulated in some idiom, but there are idioms capable of formulating questions in a way such that answers are no longer dictated by the internal characteristics of the idiom or the culture carrying it but, on the contrary, by an independent reality. The ability of cognition to reach beyond the bounds of any one cultural cocoon, and attain forms of knowledge valid for *all*—and, incidentally, an understanding of nature leading to an exceedingly powerful technology—constitutes *the* central fact about our shared social condition.[26]

On these points the post-critical naturalist does not disagree. In particular, he allows no relativism at the level of fundamental norms. That follows from the connection between objectivity and ideal convergence—where there is fault-free normative divergence what we have is not relativity but indeterminacy.[27] There are not different fundamental norms; there is, as it turns out, *no* fundamental norm. Norms transcend culture just insofar as they can survive cross-cultural discussion. It is also true that the sheer explanatory fruitfulness of some epistemic norms gives them a constantly increasing advantage in that discussion. They are 'idioms capable of formulating questions in a way such that answers are no longer dictated by the internal characteristics of the idiom'. Moreover the fact that all knowledge must be 'articulated in some idiom', or put another way, that all inquiry must start with some default norms of inquiry, is consistent with an unrestricted fallibilism at the level of beliefs about the world.

Nevertheless there is a difference between the enlightenment-fundamentalist and the post-critical view. It emerges when we raise the possibility that shared norms of inquiry, taken together with any amount of data, determine no single optimal theory of the world. That kind of underdetermination cannot be ruled out—and if we could ever have positive reason to believe, of two genuinely distinct overall theories of the world, that both were optimal, then on the post-critical view it would make no sense to ask which was true. Truth could be predicated within such overall theories but not of them.

We have no positive reason to think that, and it is no trivial task to make it even plausible that we ever could have.[28] For we are talking here of underdetermination by *all* norms of inquiry, not just by the requirement of predictive adequacy. However, if the idea of such radical underdetermination can be made intelligible, however notionally, it can be used to bring

---

[26] Gellner (1992: 75).   [27] See Essay IV for a more detailed discussion.
[28] See Essay I (together with its appendix).

out the difference between the post-critical and the enlightenment-fundamentalist sense of the relation between knower and world. For the post-critical naturalist, truth could not transcend such plurally optimal cognitive traditions. But the enlightenment fundamentalist combines his naturalism with what I called in Essay I a 'correspondence conception of objectivity'. This is what *makes* him a fundamentalist, or Humean fideist about norms of inquiry. And it further commits him to holding that if there were several optimal overall theories we could ask, but could not answer, the question which was true. For this position the problem of validation is insoluble and the sense of estrangement from the world intense. The theoretical interest's diremption of subject and object and the mystical interest's blunt effort to force them into unity come to stand at diametrically hostile poles. With the rejection of the correspondence conception of objectivity the opposition between them still, it is true, remains—but it is not quite so stark. There is point, on the post-critical view, in saying that the world is our world, even though it is not an idealist point.

This is important, yet elusive. In the interpretative human sciences the contrast between the fundamentalist and the post-critical naturalist stands out more clearly. It has to do with the non-cognitivism of the former and the cognitivism of the latter about norms. For the post-critical theorist, interpretation is above all a matter of locating the norms which underlie the practice of an intelligible other: the objective, culture-transcending norms to which he and the other both respond. Only in this common grid can the difference between one culture and another be spelt out. Different human cultures may be, so to speak, different programmes for thinking, acting, and feeling, but they use the same underlying operating system. That makes them translatable, hermeneutically accessible, however many default settings in the operating system have been switched off. On the non-cognitivist view of norms, in contrast, conventionalist or emotivist, there is less reason to expect such underlying unity. Conventions are, precisely, arbitrary. Feelings and preferences, we think, can and do diverge—it is reason that converges. The Platonist explanation of the convergence, from Plato to Frege and Moore and the later Popper, is that reason tracks a transmundane realm of Ideas or Propositions and their Logical Relations. That is metaphysics as charisma; but without the mystical conception of knowledge, as identity or 'participation' of knower and known, of thought and object—which Plato had to hand but we no longer do—such 'explanation' of convergence is bankrupt.

It is extraordinarily hard to throw out the Platonic explanation of rational convergence and still maintain that the convergence is rational.

Non-cognitivism, at this point, is very tempting. If the argument of earlier essays is sound, however, it can be resisted by discarding the correspondence conception of objectivity and attending carefully to the discursive epistemology of normative propositions. Central to this epistemology, however, is the *spontaneity* of normative judgement; but even apart from the correspondence conception of objectivity we now have a difficulty about this idea, a difficulty which an eighteenth-century opponent of Hume like Thomas Reid did not have.

Reid could appeal to natural principles of *common* sense, common to all human beings, with the confidence of the Enlightenment's belief in a constant human nature. Nothing, in contrast, is more characteristic of the modernist spirit than to dismiss such confidence as misguided and naïve. Modernism downgrades nature and upgrades convention. In doing so it closes the door to a non-Platonist, naturalistic, account of the objectivity of reasons.

10. NATURE AND NORMATIVITY

I suspect that Gellner may say the post-critical naturalism I have outlined is nothing but a moderate and qualified version of an old doctrine— hermeneutic or cultural fideism, which he rightly sees as a traditional sheltering place for critics of the Enlightenment. This, he may say, justifies putting post-critical naturalism with 'Postmodernism', and maintaining the simple dichotomy between 'Postmodernist' and 'Enlightenment Fundamentalist'. At least this is the line he has taken, over the years, on Wittgenstein's late philosophy. So let me briefly consider the relation between that philosophy and what I have been saying here.

Gellner has always seen Wittgenstein as a hermeneutic relativist, or pluralistic fideist, who thinks that in any culture there are tenets which must simply be recognized as non-rationally but properly authoritative for that culture. There are good grounds for taking that interpretation—after all many of Wittgenstein's followers have taken it. Moreover Wittgenstein was by deep instinct an enemy of the Enlightenment and its values, and on not a few occasions a pretty unpleasant one at that.

Yet it is also possible, despite the familiar difficulties in interpreting late Wittgenstein, to see him as an insightful proponent of post-critical naturalism. Wittgenstein's philosophy was never monolithically unified—it was always riven by inner conflicts, to-ing and fro-ing among alternative temptations. It is less plausible to see post-critical philosophy as an antienlightenment doctrine if one takes Carnap as one's case study rather than

Wittgenstein. Carnap was generous in acknowledging his indebtedness to Wittgenstein in the philosophy of language and logic. But he 'sometimes had the impression that . . . any ideas which had the flavour of "enlightenment" were repugnant to Wittgenstein':

His intellect, working with great intensity and penetrating power, had recognized that many statements in the field of religion and metaphysics did not, strictly speaking, say anything. In his characteristic absolute honesty with himself, he did not try to shut his eyes to this insight. But this result was extremely painful for him emotionally, as if he were compelled to admit a weakness in a beloved person . . . I had the impression that his ambivalence with respect to metaphysics was only a special aspect of a more basic internal conflict in his personality from which he suffered deeply and painfully[29]

This hits it very well. Wittgenstein and Carnap both developed the anti-Platonist, rule-of-use account of meaning which post-critical naturalism requires:[30] the account itself is separable from the intense spiritual quest which gave it personal significance for Wittgenstein. For him it was, at least in part, a response to what I have called the mystical impulse. Philosophy's self-dissolution is a means of attaining oneness with the world. The impulse is detectable not only in the famous ethical propositions in the *Tractatus* but also, for example, in the foreword to the *Philosophical Remarks*.[31] Wittgenstein's disdain for scientific explanation does not stem from *fear* of science; it is the disdain of the mystical interest for the merely theoretical interest—Parmenides' disdain for the way of seeming.

But whatever diagnosis one is rash enough to make of that side of Wittgenstein's character, the post-critical standpoint developed in 1930s Vienna cannot be treated as though it was nothing more than an attempt to re-enchant the world. Philosophy and culture are not so closely

---

[29] From Carnap's Intellectual Autobiography, in Schilpp, ed. (1963: 26, 27).

[30] 'requires' is too strong. I would now argue that the 'rule-of-use account of meaning' developed in the 1930s in Vienna should be replaced by an account of concepts as patterns of norms. But this is still a post-critical standpoint, and it can be argued that Wittgenstein's later work moves towards it. On both these points see Skorupski (1997*a* and *b*).

[31] Wittgenstein writes:

This book is written for such men as are in sympathy with its spirit. This spirit is different from the one which informs the vast stream of European and American civilisation in which all of us stand. *That* spirit expresses itself in an onwards movement, in building ever larger and more complicated structures; the other in striving after clarity and perspicuity in no matter what structure. The first tries to grasp the world by way of its periphery—in its variety; the second at its centre—in its essence. And so the first adds one construction to another, moving on and up, as it were, from one stage to the next, while the other remains where it is and what it tries to grasp is always the same. (Wittgenstein 1975: 7; see also the version in Wittgenstein 1980: 6–7)

connected. Yet it is not that there is no connection with the problem of Enchantment either—I indicated a connection in Section 9. It is also true that the rule-of-use conception provides a tool which the cultural fideist can use. However, while Wittgenstein's philosophy can be, and has been, developed in that direction, 'cultural fideism' is by no means inherent in the post-critical stance.

What is crucial here is one's understanding of fundamental normative claims. Can they be assessed as valid or invalid—do we have rational insight into them? On this issue the Vienna Circle was thoroughly modernist—voluntarist or expressivist in its view of norms. In contrast Wittgenstein came increasingly to stress the importance of our nature as against convention.[32] The norms we find compelling lie under the conventional surface of language-use and belong to our nature—the 'savage mind', 'species-being'—not the conventions of this or that cultural institution evolved from it. In his later philosophy Wittgenstein has two regular targets. One is the Platonism of earlier analytic philosophy, to which the Viennese emphasis on the priority of language-rules over concepts was a reaction—the other is the conventionalism which went with that reaction.

Nineteenth-century naturalism, liberal or Marxist, historicized human nature and normative spontaneity but did not reject it. It maintained that naturally human normative dispositions provide the continuity through cultural evolution, and for that reason it could treat evolution as progress. Human beings had determinate potentialities, a species-being—the question was what form of society best realized them. But modernism removes both the historicism and the human nature, leaving a brute diversity of cultures with no thematic normative unity. The consequence is that we either maintain an allegiance to some one cultural tradition, stemming from the contingencies of our history rather than from rational insight, or we throw off those ties and face a supermarket of options among which we non-rationally 'choose'.

---

[32] In this respect Gellner seriously misreads the significance of the 'rule-following' argument in the *Philosophical Investigations* (Wittgenstein 1963). The point of the argument, I believe, is precisely to highlight the inadequacy of the Viennese dichotomy between factual statements in a language and rules constituting the language. Applying a rule to a particular case always requires a normative judgement about the right way to apply it: that judgement neither expresses some further rule nor corresponds to any fact, natural or Platonic. It is irreducibly normative: its epistemology turns on spontaneity and the convergence commitment alone. This is not a 'social theory of concepts'—not the view that '*it is social consensus which makes for conceptual compulsion, and which indeed makes concepts at all*' (Gellner 1985: 185, 170). It does not hold that the *truth conditions* for concept-constituting epistemic norms concern facts about consensus (actual or ideal).

Gellner guys the more or less undignified motives and manœuvres of cultural fideism and cultural voluntarism brilliantly. But he offers simply another kind of fideism—fideism about reason. There is an intellectual dandyism or spiritual machismo in his rejection of hermeneutic comfort blankets. This posture, however, plays into the hands of modernity's critics. Of course they are happy to believe, with Gellner and Hume, that naturalism forces radical scepticism—for that may unlock the door of the iron cage. So a new agreement emerges between the New Humeans and naturalism's new critics—a replay of the original agreement between post-Kantian idealists and Hume. A fine current example of this is Charles Taylor's *Sources of the Self*.[33] Like Gellner, Taylor has a strong sense of the interactions between enlightenment emancipation and romantic revolt. And like Gellner he emphasizes the historic importance of science's technical success. Finally, like Gellner, he takes it that naturalism must be Humean naturalism; that is, that it has no way of grounding knowledge or normativity. But whereas Gellner takes his dandified Humean stand on this conclusion, for Taylor it offers an escape route to sources of legitimation outside nature.

One could go on citing examples from among diagnosticians of modernity. The same dichotomy recurs again and again—either you transcend nature or you are bound by culture. In effect this carries forward the assessment which prevailed in the melodrama of German philosophy from the time of Kant's Copernican Revolution through to Nietzsche. But there has always been another possibility, taken for granted in the quieter non-Humean reaches of naturalism: fundamental normative claims are neither non-natural nor culture-bound nor products of superior will.

This quiet voice is not widely heard today. Non-cognitivism is one important component in the cultural normlessness which presently afflicts Western societies. It is an ingredient of 'Postmodernism' but it is a much wider phenomenon than that. In principle it has the makings of a crisis of liberalism, inasmuch as liberalism is an ethical ideal and not just a prosperity-providing device. Popular non-cognitivism about norms has a persistent tendency to diminish the ideal, which rests on objective notions of higher and lower kinds of human well-being, and to transmute liberalism into the populism which classical liberals feared.

But non-cognitivism is *not* built into the basic philosophical structure of modernity in the way that the caging of the mystical impulse *is*. It relates, rather, to the social relations of science-based liberal democracy. So as well as criticizing it philosophically we also need to consider its sociology.

---

[33] Taylor (1989).

11. LIBERAL NATURALISM AND THE TWO CULTURES

It is unoriginal but true that contemporary liberal democracies have two broad cultures; the world of science, politics, economics, law, and administration, and the world of the arts, criticism, interpretative studies. Certain subjects swim between the two worlds: notably philosophy and history. Anthropology and sociology started in the last century as fledgling members of the first culture but now seem to be on a long march towards the second.

There is no legitimation crisis in the first culture but there is presently an acute crisis in the second. Philosophy reflects the situation. Philosophers trading with the first culture debate pretty much the same epistemological and foundational issues about science and ethics as those trading with the second; but, roughly speaking, whereas the former do so without anxiety about subverting knowledge and value itself, the latter operate in a sustained atmosphere of romantic revolt and non-stop 'radical revaluation'.

From the standpoint of a New Sceptic, this may seem readily explicable. Consider this passage from the very interesting closing pages of *Postmodernism, Reason and Religion*:

The mild rationalist fundamentalism which is being recommended here does not attempt, as the Enlightenment did, to offer a rival counter-model to its religious predecessor. It is fundamentalist only in connection with the form of knowledge, and perhaps . . . the form of morality, insisting on a symmetry of treatment for all. (I hesitate at this point: in the sphere of knowledge, rational symmetry is pragmatically underwritten, so to speak enforced, by its practical success and power. This does not apply in morality.) . . . Where no good reasons are available one can go along with the contingencies of local development, the accidents of local balance of power and taste. Serious knowledge is not subject to relativism, but the trappings of our cultural life are.[34]

Here we have the New Sceptical point that scientific method is underwritten pragmatically, that is, internally, by its 'practical success and power'. The same, one may add, applies to the formal and instrumental rationality of the world of modern business and politics. That point immediately leads to a hesitation about the groundings of morality, equally characteristic of this outlook.[35] And, of course, it is not just morality but other forms of value that cannot be pragmatically vindicated by their 'practical

---

[34] Gellner (1992: 94).
[35] It is also, for example, a leading theme in Williams (1985).

success and power'. So the difference of confidence between the two cultures is readily intelligible—the first finds its rationalizing methods retroactively strengthened by their success and power, in the case of the second, nothing comparable is even in principle on offer. The inevitable effect is a downgrading of the second culture, and that is what Gellner lays out in these closing pages, though in the courteous and genial rather than the bullying and abrasive mode. Serious knowledge is not subject to relativism—the 'trappings' of our cultural life, such as morality, 'where no good reasons are available', are.

To these New-Sceptical themes Gellner adds a characteristic *motif* from another camp—that of the critics of the 'Enlightenment Project'. Secular enlightenment visions have been disastrous, he argues—enlightenment trust in reason and nature led first to French revolutionary terror and then, respectively, to communism and fascism.[36] One might add (to complete the indictment of our guilty past) that nineteenth-century cultural evolutionism—the whole broad phenomenon, not specifically social Darwinism—provided an ideological charter for colonial exploitation.

There is truth in these sociological claims just as there is truth in the epistemological claim that science is internally vindicated by its explanatory power. But they are misleading because they are only part of the truth. Internal vindication can substantially strengthen our reasons for belief if they had some strength in the first place. It cannot raise them from degree zero. Historicist notions of a developing human potential may be exploitable by imperialists, but that does not make them false or dispensable in our account of the spontaneous grounding of rational norms.

Cut away the ideas which these half-truths ignore, whether on grounds of their philosophic inadequacy or their historic toxicity, and cultural fideism or optionality is what are you left with. Taken seriously, this radical decommissioning of our liberal-naturalistic legacy *ought* to produce a global crisis of validation, as crisis-generalizers from the humanities rightly point out. The pragmatic success of science, business, and bureaucracy may make fideism about theoretical and economic rationality—that is, scientism and instrumentalism—a socially and psychologically tenable attitude but that does not save it from intellectual bankruptcy.

My disagreement with the crisis-generalizers is not on their idea that these are the consequences of decommissioning the liberal-naturalistic philosophical legacy but on the idea that it can and must be decommissioned; that some of sort of pluralism of 'cultural trappings' must now take its place. And here I seem to disagree also with Ernest Gellner, who in this respect appears to be on their side.

[36] Gellner (1992: 86 ff).

Of course I do not mean that one can simply reassert the ideas of nineteenth-century liberal naturalism. I have already suggested that its epistemological framework needs complete rethinking. Its core ideas of a developing human nature and of a diversity of humanly higher and lower goods have to be rethought just as thoroughly. Nineteenth-century philosophical liberals—Mill is a prime example—tended to a combination of utopian egalitarianism about humanity as it could be and self-confident elitism about humanity as it was. It is impossible to sustain either of these and the consequences of moving away from them must be considered.

Regenerating the liberal-naturalistic framework does nevertheless also require reassertion of some unsayable things and rejection of some still powerful modernist dogmas. To rethink nineteenth-century evolutionism and elitism is not simply to reject them in the populist manner of this century, which Postmodernism (or modernism in its state of final exhaustion) continues *à l'outrance*. For we also have to count in the collapse of modernism's critiques of actually existing liberal societies, of its romantic projects of emancipation, and of its Nietzschean pathos of voluntarism and authenticity.

Can liberal naturalism cope, however powerfully it may be regenerated in purely intellectual terms, with the problems of individuality and allegiance which nineteenth-century liberals wisely foresaw, and which Gellner engages with in his closing pages? He believes that Enlightenment rationalism

has a number of weaknesses from the viewpoint of its use as a practical faith, as the foundation either for an individual life or for a social order. It is also too thin and ethereal to sustain an individual in crisis, and it is too abstract to be intelligible to any but intellectuals with a penchant for this kind of theorising. Intellectually it is all but inaccessible, and unable to offer real succour in a crisis . . . In practice, Western intellectuals, when facing personal predicaments, have turned to emotionally richer methods, offering promises of personal recovery, such as psychoanalysis.[37]

He thinks that '[t]he valid style of inquiry generates neither stability nor normative authority.'[38] If you are an enlightenment fundamentalist, then of course *nothing*, strictly speaking, can for you generate normative authority; and your best hope of stability is in carelessness and inattention, plus the pragmatic addition of material prosperity and a lengthy *à la carte* menu of 'constitutional religions'.[39] But it would certainly be foolish to imagine that the question Gellner asks, namely, whether liberal naturalism can be the foundation for a stable and creative social order,

---

[37] Gellner (1992: 86 ff), 86.   [38] Ibid. 88.   [39] Ibid. 91 ff.

arises only on his fundamentalist version of it. The question has a philosophical dimension but it is not mainly a philosophical question. You can be an optimist or a pessimist about its answer but you would have to be a prophet to know it. One can only point to the horrors to which 'emotionally richer methods' have led in this century, and to the absence of any really solid grounds for pessimism about the liberal ethic's prospects as a focus of allegiance.

BIBLIOGRAPHY

Allais, M. (1953). 'Le Comportement de l'homme rationnel devant le risque: critique de postulats et axiomes de l'école américaine', *Econometrica*, 21: 503–46.

—— (1979). 'The so-called Allais paradox and rational decision under uncertainty', in M. Allais and O. Hagen (eds.), *Expected Utility Hypotheses and the Allais Paradox*. Dordrecht: Reidel.

Allison, Henry E. (1990). *Kant's Theory of Freedom*. Cambridge: Cambridge University Press.

Arnold, Matthew (1960–78). *The Complete Prose Works of Matthew Arnold*, ed. by R. H. Super. Ann Arbor: University of Michigan Press.

Bauman, Zygmunt (1990). 'From Pillars to Post', *Marxism Today*, Feb. 1990.

Bennett, Jonathan (1989). 'Two Departures from Consequentialism', *Ethics*, 100: 54–66.

Berlin, Isaiah (1969). *Four Essays on Liberty*. London: Oxford University Press.

Blackburn, Simon (1984). *Spreading the Word*. Oxford: Oxford University Press.

—— (1993). *Essays in Quasi-Realism*. Oxford: Oxford University Press.

Brink, David (1992). 'Mill's Deliberative Utilitarianism', *Philosophy and Public Affairs*, 21: 67–103.

—— (1997). 'Kantian Rationalism: Inescapability, Authority, and Supremacy', Garrett Cullity and Berys Gaut (eds.), *Ethics and Practical Reason*. Oxford: Oxford University Press: 255–91.

Broome, John (1991). *Weighing Goods*. Oxford: Blackwell.

—— (1995). 'Skorupski on Agent-Neutrality', *Utilitas, 7:* 315–17.

Coffa, J. Alberto (1991). *The Semantic Tradition from Kant to Carnap: To the Vienna Station*. Cambridge: Cambridge University Press.

Coleridge, Samuel Taylor (1976). 'On the Constitution of Church and State', in *Collected Works*, x, ed. J. Colmer. London: Routledge & Kegan Paul.

Crisp, Roger (1997). *Mill on Utilitarianism*. London: Routledge.

—— and Moore, Andrew (1996). 'Welfarism in Moral Theory', *Australian Journal of Philosophy*, 74: 598–613.

Devlin, Patrick (1965). *The Enforcement of Morals*. Oxford: Oxford University Press.

Dworkin, R. M. (ed.) (1977). *The Philosophy of Law*. Oxford: Oxford University Press.

Eckart, Meister (1958). *Selected Treatises and Sermons*, trans. J. M. Clark and J. V. Skinner. London: Faber.

Frankel, Herman (1975). *Early Greek Poetry and Philosophy*, trans. Moses Hadas and James Willis. Oxford: Blackwell.

Freeman, Samuel (1994). 'Political Liberalism and the Possibility of a Just Democratic Constitution', *Chicago Kent Law Review*, 69: 619–68.

Frohlich, N., Oppenheimer, J., and Eavey, C. (1987). 'Choices of Principles of Distributive Justice in Experimental Groups', *American Journal of Political Science*, 31: 606–36.

Fukuyama, Francis (1992). *The End of History and the Last Man*. Toronto: Maxwell MacMillan.

Galston, William A. (1991). *Liberal Purposes: Goods, Virtues and Diversity in the Liberal State*. Cambridge: Cambridge University Press.

Gärdenfors, Peter, and Sahlin, Nils-Eric (eds.) (1988). *Decision, Probability, and Utility*. Cambridge: Cambridge University Press.

Garforth, F. W. (1980). *Educative Democracy, John Stuart Mill on Education and Society*. London: Oxford University Press (published for the University of Hull).

Gaut, Berys (1995). 'Rawls and the Claims of Liberal Legitimacy', *Philosophical Papers*, 24: 1–22.

Gellner, Ernest (1979). *Spectacles and Predicaments*. Cambridge: Cambridge University Press.

—— (1985). *Relativism and the Social Sciences*. Cambridge: Cambridge University Press.

—— (1992). *Postmodernism, Reason and Religion*. London: Routledge.

Gibbard, Allan (1990). *Wise Choices, Apt Feelings*. Oxford: Clarendon Press.

Gray, John (1993). *Post-Liberalism, Studies in Political Thought*. London: Routledge.

—— (1995). *Isaiah Berlin*. Harper Collins.

Green, T. H. (1885–8). *Works of Thomas Hill Green*, ed. R. L. Nettleship. London: Longmans, Green.

—— (1906). *Prolegomena to Ethics*, 5th edn. Oxford: Clarendon Press.

Griffin, James. (1986). *Well-Being*. Oxford: Clarendon Press.

—— (1996). *Value Judgement*. Oxford: Clarendon Press.

Hacking, Ian (1983). *Representing and Intervening*. Cambridge: Cambridge University Press.

Hare, R. M. (1993). 'Could Kant Have Been A Utilitarian?', *Utilitas*, 5: 1–16.

Harsanyi, John (1976). *Essays on Ethics, Social Behavior and Scientific Explanation*. Dordrecht: Reidel.

Hegel, G. W. F. (1971). *Hegel's Philosophy of Mind* (*Encyclopaedia of the Philosophical Sciences*, pt. 3), trans. by William Wallace and A. V. Miller, foreword by J. N. Findlay. Oxford: Clarendon Press.

—— (1991a). *Elements of the Philosophy of Right*, ed. by Allen W. Wood, trans. by H. B. Nisbet. Cambridge: Cambridge University Press.

—— (1991b). *The Encyclopaedia Logic* (*Encyclopaedia of Philosophical Sciences with the Zusätze*, pt. I), new trans. with introduction and notes by T. F. Geraets, W. A. Suchting, and H. S. Harris. Indianapolis: Hackett Publishing Company, Inc.

Hooker, Brad (1999). 'Rule-consequentialism', in H. LaFollette (ed.), *The Blackwell Guide to Ethical Theory*. Oxford: Blackwell.

Horton, Robin (1997). *Patterns of Thought in Africa and the West*. Cambridge: Cambridge University Press.

Horwich, Paul (1990). *Truth*. Oxford: Blackwell.

Hume, David (1968). *A Treatise of Human Nature*, ed. by L. A. Selby-Bigge. Oxford: Clarendon Press.

Hurka, Thomas (1993). *Perfectionism*. Oxford: Oxford University Press.

James, William (1890). *The Principles of Psychology*. London: Macmillan.

Kahan, Alan S. (1992). *Aristocratic Liberalism, the Social and Political Thought of Jacob Burckhardt, John Stuart Mill, and Alexis de Tocqueville*. Oxford: Oxford University Press.

Kant, Immanuel (1956). *Critique of Practical Reason*, trans. by Lewis White Beck. New York: Liberal Arts Press, Inc.

—— (1964). *Groundwork of the Metaphysics of Morals*, trans. and analysed by H. J. Paton. New York: Harper & Row.

—— (1968). *Critique of Pure Reason*, trans. by Norman Kemp Smith. London: Macmillan.

—— (1987). *Critique of Judgement*, trans., with an Introduction, by Werner S. Pluhar. Indianapolis: Hackett.

—— (1991). *The Metaphysics of Morals*, Introduction, trans. and notes by Mary Gregor. Cambridge: Cambridge University Press.

Korsgaard, Christine M. (1985). 'Kant's Formula of Universal Law', *Pacific Philosophical Quarterly*, 66: 24–47.

—— (1996). *The Sources of Normativity*, with G. A. Cohen, Raymond Geuss, Thomas Nagel, Bernard Williams, ed. by Onora O'Neill. Cambridge: Cambridge University Press.

Laudan, Larry (1981). *Science and Hypothesis*. Dordrecht: Reidel.

Lévy-Bruhl, L. (1975). *The Notebooks on Primitive Mentality*, preface by Maurice Leenhardt, trans. by Peter Rivière. Oxford: Blackwell.

Lewis, David (1993). 'Attitudes *De Dicto* and *De Se*', in David Lewis, *Philosophical Papers*, i: 133–59.

Lissowski, G. (1994). 'Ustalanie Sposobu Podzialu Dóbr w Sytuacji Eksperymentalnej' [Determining a Method of Dividing a Good in an Experimental Situation], *Studia Socjologiczne*, 3/4: 173–215.

—— and Swistak, P. (1995). 'Choosing the Best Social Order: New Principles of Justice and Normative Dimensions of Choice', *American Political Science Review*, 89: 74–96.

—— Tyszka, T., and Okrasa, W. (1991). 'Principles of Distributive Justice, Experiments in Poland and America', *Journal of Conflict Resolution*, 35: 98–119.

Lloyd, G. E. R. (1979). *Magic, Reason and Experience*. Cambridge: Cambridge University Press.

Locke, John (1988). *The Second Treatise of Government*, in *Two Treatises of Government*, ed. Peter Laslett. Cambridge: Cambridge University Press.

Lyons, David (1976). 'Mill's Theory of Morality', *Nous*, 10: 101–20.

McClennen, Edward F. (1988). 'Sure-thing doubts', in Peter Gardenfors and Nils-Eric Sahlin (eds.), *Decision, Probability, and Utility*. Cambridge: Cambridge University Press.

MacIntyre, Alasdair (1981). *After Virtue*. London: Duckworth.

Mackie, J. L. (1976). 'Sidgwick's Pessimism', *Philosophical Quarterly*, 26: 317–27.

McMahan, Jeff (1995). 'Killing and Equality', *Utilitas*, 7: 1–29.

Marquand, David (1987). 'Beyond Social Democracy', *Political Quarterly*, 58: 243–53.

Mill, John Stuart (1963–91). *The Collected Works of John Stuart Mill*, ed. by John M. Robson (33 vols.). Toronto: University of Toronto Press.

McNaughton, David, and Rawling, Piers (1991). 'Agent-relativity and the Doing-Happening Distinction', *Philosophical Studies*, 63.

—— —— (1995). 'Agent-Relativity and Terminological Inexactitudes', *Utilitas*, 7: 319–25.

—— —— (1998). 'On Defending Deontology', *Ratio*, 11: 37–54.

Moore, G. E. (1903). *Principia Ethica*. Cambridge: Cambridge University Press.

Nagel, Thomas (1970). *The Possibility of Altruism*. Oxford: Oxford University Press.

—— (1986). *The View from Nowhere*. Oxford: Oxford University Press.

Nicholson, Peter P. (1990). *The Political Philosophy of the British Idealists*. Cambridge: Cambridge University Press.

Nietzsche, Friedrich (1990). *Twilight of the Idols and the Anti-Christ*. Harmondsworth: Penguin.

—— (1996). *On The Genealogy of Morals*, ed. Douglas Smith. Oxford: Oxford University Press.

Nozick, Robert (1974). *Anarchy, State and Utopia*. Oxford: Blackwell.

—— (1997). 'On Austrian Methodology', in R. Nozick, *Socratic Puzzles*. Cambridge, Mass.: Harvard University Press.

Pippin, Robert (1995). 'Hegel on the Rationality and Priority of Ethical Life', *Neue Hefte für Philosophie*, 35: 95–126.

Popkin, R. H. (1960). *The History of Scepticism from Erasmus to Descartes*. Assen: Van Gorcum.

Popper, Karl (1945). *The Open Society and its Enemies*. London: Routledge.

Raz, Joseph (1986). *The Morality of Freedom*. Oxford: Clarendon Press.

Rawls, John (1971). *A Theory of Justice*. Oxford: Oxford University Press.

—— (1993). *Political Liberalism*. New York: Columbia University Press.

—— (1997). 'The Idea of Public Reason Revisited', *University of Chicago Law Review*, 64: 765–807.

Regan, Tom (1983). *The Case for Animal Rights*. London: Routledge & Kegan Paul.

Riley, Jonathan (1988). *Liberal Utilitarianism*. Cambridge: Cambridge University Press.

—— (1993). 'On Quantities and Qualities of Pleasure', *Utilitas*, 5: 291–300.

Rosen, F. (1998). 'Individual Sacrifice and the Greatest Happiness: Bentham on Utility and Rights', *Utilitas*, 10: 129–43.

Savage, L. J. (1954). *The Foundations of Statistics*. New York: Wiley & Sons.

Scanlon, Thomas. (1972). 'A Theory of Freedom of Expression', *Philosophy and Public Affairs*, 1: 204–26.

—— (1982). 'Contractualism and Utilitarianism', in A. Sen and B. Williams (eds.), *Utilitarianism and Beyond*. Cambridge: Cambridge University Press.

Schier, Flint (1993). 'The Kantian Gulag', in Dudley Knowles and John Skorupski (eds.), *Virtue and Taste, Essays in Memory of Flint Schier*. Oxford: Blackwell.

Schiller, Friedrich (1967). *On the Aesthetic Education of Man, In a Series of Letters*, ed. and trans. by Elizabeth M. Wilkinson and L. A. Willoughby. Oxford: Clarendon Press.

Schilpp, P. A. (ed.) (1963). *The Philosophy of Rudolf Carnap*, La Salle, Ill.: Open Court.

Schneewind, J. B. (1977). *Sidgwick's Ethics and Victorian Moral Philosophy*. Oxford: Clarendon Press.

—— (1992). 'Autonomy, Obligation, and Virtue: An Overview of Kant's Moral Philosophy', in Paul Guyer (ed.), *The Cambridge Companion to Kant*. Cambridge: Cambridge University Press: 309–41.

Schorske, Carl E. (1981). *Fin-de-Siècle Vienna: Politics and Culture*. Cambridge: Cambridge University Press.

Schwartz, Pedro (1972). *The New Political Economy of J. S. Mill*. London: Weidenfeld & Nicolson.

Sen, Amartya (1979). 'Utilitarianism and Welfarism', *Journal of Philosophy*, 76: 463–89.

—— (1982). *Choice, Welfare and Measurement*. Oxford: Blackwell.

Sidgwick, Henry (1888). 'The Kantian Conception of Free Will', *Mind*, 13: 511–16.

—— (1893). *The Methods of Ethics*, 5th edn. London: Macmillan.

Siedentop, Larry (1994). *Tocqueville*. Oxford: Oxford University Press.

Skorupski, John (1976). *Symbol and Theory*. Cambridge: Cambridge University Press.

—— (1979). 'Sidgwick's Ethics', *Philosophical Quarterly*, 29: 158–69.

—— (1989). *John Stuart Mill*. London: Routledge.

—— (1990–1). 'The Legacy of Modernism', *Proceedings of the Aristotelian Society*, 91: 1–19.

Skorupski, John (1993a). 'Autonomy in its Place', in Dudley Knowles and John Skorupski (eds.), *Virtue and Taste, Essays in Memory of Flint Schier*. Oxford: Blackwell.

—— (1993b). *English-Language Philosophy, 1750–1945*. Oxford: Oxford University Press.

—— (1997a). 'Meaning, Verification, Use', in R. Hale and C. W. Wright (eds.),

The Blackwell Companion to the Philosophy of Language. Oxford: Blackwell: 29–59.

—— (1997*b*). 'Logical Grammar, Transcendentalism and Normativity', *Philosophical Topics*, 25: 189–211.

—— (1998*a*). 'Introduction: The Fortunes of Liberal Naturalism', in John Skorupski (ed.), *The Cambridge Companion to Mill*. Cambridge: Cambridge University Press.

—— (1998*b*). 'Rescuing Moral Obligation', *European Journal of Philosophy*, 6: 335–55.

—— (1999). 'Irrealist Cognitivism', *Ratio*, 12.

Taylor, Charles (1989). *Sources of the Self*. Cambridge: Cambridge University Press.

Tocqueville, Alexis de (1964). *Oeuvres, Papiers et Correspondances d'Alexis de Tocqueville*, ed. J. P. Mayer *et al*. Paris: Gallimard.

Trilling, Lionel (1972). *Sincerity and Authenticity*. London: Oxford University Press.

Walton, Kendall (1990). *Mimesis as Make-Believe*. Cambridge, Mass. and London: Harvard University Press.

Warnock, Mary (1989). *Universities: Knowing Our Minds*. London: Chatto & Windus.

Williams, Bernard (1985). *Ethics and the Limits of Philosophy*. London: Fontana Paperbacks.

—— (1993). *Shame and Necessity*. Berkeley and Los Angeles, California: University of California Press.

Williams, Michael (1991). *Unnatural Doubts*. Oxford: Blackwell.

Wittgenstein, L. (1963). *Philosophical Investigations*. Oxford: Blackwell.

—— (1975). *Philosophical Remarks*, ed. by Rush Rhees, trans. by Raymond Hargreaves and Roger White. Oxford: Blackwell.

—— (1980). *Culture and Value*. Oxford: Blackwell.

Wood, Allen W. (1990). *Hegel's Ethical Thought*. Cambridge: Cambridge University Press.

Wright, C. (1992). *Truth and Objectivity*. Cambridge, Mass. and London: Harvard University Press.

—— (1996). 'Truth in Ethics', *Ratio*, 9: 209–26.

INDEX